T0389534

Doing Authentic Inquiry to Improve Learning and Teaching

Bold Visions in
Educational Research

The titles published in this series are listed at *brill.com/bver*

Doing Authentic Inquiry to Improve Learning and Teaching

Edited by

Kenneth Tobin and Konstantinos Alexakos

BRILL

SENSE

LEIDEN | BOSTON

Cover illustration: Innisfree Garden, Millbrook, NY, photograph © Mitch Bleier

All chapters in this book have undergone peer review.

Library of Congress Cataloging-in-Publication Data

Names: Tobin, Kenneth George, 1944- editor. | Alexakos, Konstantinos, editor.
Title: Doing authentic inquiry to improve learning and teaching / edited by Kenneth Tobin and Konstantinos Alexakos.
Description: Leiden ; Boston : Brill | Sense, 2021. | Series: Bold visions in educational research, 1879-4262 ; volume 69 | Includes bibliographical references and index.
Identifiers: LCCN 2020050726 (print) | LCCN 2020050727 (ebook) | ISBN 9789004424241 (paperback) | ISBN 9789004424258 (hardback) | ISBN 9789004446885 (ebook)
Subjects: LCSH: Student-centered learning--Research--Methodology. | Inquiry-based learning--Research--Methodology. | Education, Urban--Research--Methodology.
Classification: LCC LB1027.23 .D65 2021 (print) | LCC LB1027.23 (ebook) | DDC 371.3--dc23
LC record available at https://lccn.loc.gov/2020050726
LC ebook record available at https://lccn.loc.gov/2020050727

Typeface for the Latin, Greek, and Cyrillic scripts: "Brill". See and download: brill.com/brill-typeface.

ISSN 1879-4262
ISBN 978-90-04-42424-1 (paperback)
ISBN 978-90-04-42425-8 (hardback)
ISBN 978-90-04-44688-5 (e-book)

Contents

Acknowledgments

A project such as this, which comprises 18 chapters, can only reach fruition with the help of many. In that context we offer our gratitude to the authors and co-authors, and to an enormous number of participants who consented to be involved in the research described in the chapters. We trust that the rewards for participation will be in the dissemination of wisdom contained in the chapters and associated ripple effects that result in uptake of an approach to research that seeks to learn from practice while transforming what happens for the general good. We anticipate research genres that enhance the quality of learning for better lives, characterized by harmony, well-being, and wellness. An expansive methodology that investigates potential for learning of all across our birth through death continuum, in fields extending beyond schools and colleges to include institutions such as hospitals, hospices, nursing homes, gyms, sports clubs, churches, temples, monasteries, and homes.

The editors are grateful to Mitch Bleier for allowing us to use an image from Innisfree garden (https://www.innisfreegarden.org/) that conveys the spirit of harmony, the middle way, and difference – tenets that are foundational in our ongoing social inquiry. Japanese and Chinese gardens inspired Lester Collins' design of Innisfree Garden. As conditions changed continuously, Collins created a cost-effective, environmentally sensitive garden, listening to Garden communities as he improved them.

Importantly, we offer love and gratitude to our spouses, Barbara and Dina without whose love and support our lives would have been so much less.

Finally, and certainly not least, we say thanks to our teachers and scholars who have, over the years inspired us to undertake research for the purpose of improving the quality of social life, and more specifically, our own practices. Through their efforts we have embraced several mantra, including research as a transformative art and the centrality kindness, compassion, sustainability, wellness and well-being in "knowing myself."

Figures and Tables

Figures

Tables

Notes on Contributors

Jennifer D. Adams

 is a Tier 2 Canada Research Chair of Creativity and STEM and Associate Professor at The University of Calgary where she holds a dual appointment in the Department of Chemistry and Werklund School of Education. Her research focuses on the intersection between creativity and STEM postsecondary teaching and learning contexts. She has scholarly expertise in STEM teaching and learning in informal science contexts including museums, National Parks and everyday learning. She was awarded a National Science Foundation Early Career (CAREER) award to study informal learning contexts and formal/informal collaborations for STEM teacher education. Her research portfolio also includes youth learning and identity in informal science contexts, with a focus on underrepresented youth and place/identity in transnational communities and environmental education.

Konstantinos Alexakos

 is Professor and program coordinator for Adolescence Science Education at the School of Education, Brooklyn College, CUNY as well as a professor in the PhD Program in Urban Education, at The Graduate Center, CUNY. His research focuses on teaching and learning, emotions, wellness and critical social issues such as race, gender, and sexuality with the goals of improving personal and global well-being, sustainability and education.

Arnau Amat

 is a professor at the Universitat de Vic – Universitat Central de Catalunya in Spain. His research focuses on sociocultural approaches in three different areas: involving the community in the school through science education, education for sustainability and science teaching education. Prior to that he worked as environmental educator for various private companies and education authorities and as a science teacher in high school.

Marissa Bellino

is an Associate Professor in the Department of Educational Administration and Secondary Education at The College of New Jersey (TCNJ). She is currently teaching Educational Foundations courses and Methods in Science Teaching for Secondary and Elementary pre-service teachers. She is also involved in the Environmental Sustainability Education and Urban Education programs at TCNJ. Marissa received her doctorate in Urban Education at The Graduate Center, City University of New York (CUNY). Prior to coming to TCNJ she was an adjunct faculty member at Brooklyn College, CUNY and Long Island University as well as an Instructional Technology Fellow at Hunter College, CUNY. Her teaching interests include social foundations of education, environmental sustainability and science education, qualitative research methods, and adolescent learning and development with a critical youth studies lens. Marissa's research interests include youths' experiences in urban environments, environmental education, critical pedagogy, and participatory research. Marissa taught high school in New York City for 11 years where she developed ecological and molecular ecology research curriculum as well as critical participatory research methods with environmental science students.

Mitch Bleier

is a science teacher and teacher educator. He attended New York City public schools and universities for his entire student career. As an educator, he taught K-12 science and graduate and undergraduate science education at the City College of New York for over thirty years. He was a science education consultant for schools and school districts in New York State, Nevada and California. He received his PhD in Urban Education from the Graduate Center of the City University of New York.

Corinna Brathwaite

completed her doctoral degree in the Urban Education Department of The Graduate Center, CUNY, in the Spring of 2019. She works at St HOPE Leadership Academy in New York City teaching mathematics to middle schoolers and co-leading The Natural Hair Club. She also is an adjunct at the City College of New York teaching Elementary Math Methods to pre-service and in-service teachers.

Olga Calderón

has a PhD in Science Education from the Graduate School and University Center at CUNY. She has a Master's Degree in Biology from Queens College (CUNY); and a Master of Philosophy in Urban Education from the CUNY Graduate Center. She received her Bachelors in Biology and Geology from Queens College; and an Associate's in Liberal Arts and Sciences from LaGuardia. Olga Calderón is an associate professor of biology and microbiology at LaGuardia Community College, Long Island City, NY. She conducts biological research at LaGuardia on environmental entomology, microbiology and symbiotic associations of plants, insects and microbes. Her pedagogical research focuses on the role of emotions and mindfulness in the science classroom as a transformative pedagogic tool. Among other interests is to work on increasing the participation of disadvantage students and women in STEM careers.

Katelin Corbett

is a high school physics teacher in New York City and an Adjunct professor of secondary science education at Brooklyn College. She is a graduate of the Urban Education doctoral program at the Graduate Center of CUNY where she studied emotions in teaching and learning.

Amy DeFelice

is an adjunct lecturer of STEM methods at Montclair State University. Previously she held positions as a visiting assistant professor at Long Island University, Brooklyn and adjunct lecturer at City University of New York (CUNY) Brooklyn College. Before and during her doctoral studies in Urban Education at the CUNY Graduate Center, Amy was a high school science teacher of living environment, AP biology, science research, and field studies at Brooklyn Academy of Science and the Environment (BASE) High School in Brooklyn, NY. Amy continues to consider new ways to incorporate local natural environments into teaching and learning.

Gene Fellner

is an Assistant Professor of Education at City University of New York in Staten Island where he teaches Master's Pre-service Special Education teachers. He spent 25 years as a fine artist and political activist before earning his Master's degree in English as a Second Language and his PhD in Urban Education.

Helen Kwah

is an artist and teacher-educator interested in the use of social theory, and artistic and contemplative practices to address issues of race, gender, identity, community and wellness. She received a PhD in Educational Communications and Technology from New York University, a Master's in Health Education from the University of Hawai'i, and a BA from Yale University.

Manny Lopez

is Associate Dean for Student Development at Bronx Community College of the City University of New York (CUNY). He has advanced degrees in urban affairs, philosophy and earned a PhD in urban education, learning sciences. His research primarily explores adult learners' acquisition of life skills in both formal and non-formal learning environments.

Anna Malyukova

is a PhD candidate in Urban Education at the Graduate Center, CUNY. Anna is engaged in research on mindfulness, wellness and emotions, focusing on teaching and learning of participants along the birth-death continuum. Anna began her post-secondary education in Russia in 1997, pursuing a degree in engineering. After arriving in the USA, she received an Associate Degree in Early Childhood Education from BMCC, CUNY, a Bachelor of Arts Degree from City College, CUNY, and

a Master of Arts Degree from The Graduate Center, CUNY. In addition to her research and studies, Anna teaches research courses in the early childhood program at Brooklyn College.

Kate E. O'Hara

is an associate professor in the Interdisciplinary Studies Program at New York Institute of Technology. With a background in urban education and instructional design, her research focuses on (1) the effective use of technology to empower users to become agents of social change and enact a critical pedagogy, and (2) the function of education as it relates to contexts of power, oppression, and social justice. She employs the use of arts-based methods in her social science research; in particular, the use of photography as phenomenological approach to understanding structures of experience and consciousness.

Malgorzata Powietrzynska

earned her PhD in Urban Education at the Graduate Center of the City University of New York (CUNY). As an Academic Affairs Manager, she works with faculty and students and coordinates grant writing and grant administration activities at the Brooklyn Educational Opportunity Center of the State University of New York. In addition, an Adjunct Assistant Professor, she teaches in the Secondary Teacher Education Program at Brooklyn College, CUNY as she continues to be involved in research focusing on emotions and mindfulness in education.

Wolff-Michael Roth

is Lansdowne Professor of Applied Cognitive Science at the University of Victoria (since 1997). He taught high school science, mathematics, and computer science for much of the period from 1980 to 1992 after which he began a university career teaching quantitative and qualitative research methods (Simon Fraser University). He has been investigating knowing and learning across the lifespan in formal educational, workplace, and leisure settings.

Isabel Sellas

is a professor at the Universitat de Vic – Universitat Central de Catalunya in Spain. Her research revolves around how mathematic Pedagogical Content Knowledge is constructed by preservice and in-service teachers. For ten years, she has combined the courses of didactics of mathematics at University for preservice teachers with several assessments for in-service teacher in elementary schools, in order to improve the mathematical and the mental calculation strategies.

Kenneth Tobin

is Presidential Professor Emeritus in the Urban Education program at the Graduate Center of CUNY (2003-2019). Prior to becoming a university science educator in Australia in 1974, Tobin taught high school physics, chemistry, biology, general science, and mathematics for 10 years. Then, he held university appointments at the Western Australian Institute of Technology (now Curtin University), Mount Lawley College and Graylands College (now Edith Cowan University).

In the United States he had positions as tenured full professor at Florida State University (1987 to 1997) and the University of Pennsylvania (1997 to 2003). Tobin began a program of research in 1973 that continues to the present day. His current research interests include contemplative practices, wellness and wellbeing.

Yau Yan Wong

has a bachelor of science degree in psychology from Virginia Polytechnic Institute and State University in the USA and a master of science degree in research methods in psychology from University College London in UK. She is currently a PhD student in science education studying at Kasetsart University in Thailand. Her research interests include mindfulness, wellbeing, human adaptation, sustainable development and science education as a lived experience. Prior to her study,

she has been an elementary school teacher for over 13 years. Besides her administrative role as the sub-committee member of science department, she has been leading the mindfulness research projects and providing mindfulness training to her fellow teachers, students and parents in an international program of a Thai public school since 10 years ago. She is also the leader of a professional learning community that aims to promote mindfulness, wellbeing and wellness of students and teachers. She has developed a mindfulness-based social emotional learning program that integrates Buddhism and contemporary psychology for kindergartens up to grade 6 based on her research findings. She plans to expand the program to other age groups across the lifespan.

CHAPTER 1

Improving Learning and Teaching through Authentic Inquiry: An Overview

Kenneth Tobin and Konstantinos Alexakos

Abstract

In this introductory chapter we set the stage for what is to come in a brief review of the following 17 chapters that provide clear descriptions of methodologies and methods used in studies that explore critical issues of our time. Each chapter in the book is explicit about the theoretical frames employed and provides readers with rich examples that portray contexts that afford emergent and contingent designs and associated, dynamic multilogical framework.

Keywords

multilogical research – authentic inquiry – event-oriented inquiry – autoethnography – emergence and contingence – mindfulness – race

1 Authentic Inquiry

What is educational research and how do we do it? These may be primary questions to consider when we first encounter educational research. Certainly, they were ours. Based on each of our experiences with physics, neither of us could envision how research could be done in a dynamic, chaotic, and messy discipline such as social science. This was to change when we each began our careers in teacher education where we each were required to teach prospective and practicing teachers about teaching and learning.

In Chapter 2, we begin to lay out a historical foundation for how I (Ken) approached research since he began his first study in the early 1970s. The journey presented in the chapter continues to the present day with the two of us (Ken and Konstantinos).

Briefly, we describe how we, and in particular Ken, employed interpretive research in an endeavor to improve the credibility of our research through the

use of methodologies that could address current issues considered as significant by practitioners. The approach we used was flexible, in the sense that the
design was radically contingent on what was happening and what we wanted to
learn next. We emphasize here that what we do in our research is continuously
evolving, reflecting what we learn through experience and from one another
and as our research squads change membership over time. Furthermore, we
consistently search for ways to improve, and when we identify something we
feel is promising, we adapt it to fit what we are doing already, the nature and
purposes of our research, our understandings of what the innovation means
and involves, and how it could be adapted to benefit our research quality.

In the instance of authentic inquiry, the work of Egon Guba and Yvonna
Lincoln was central to our gradual evolution from interpretive research
(Erickson, 1986) to fourth-generation evaluation (Guba & Lincoln, 1989). We
emphasize here that new approaches were adapted and used in conjunction
with our ongoing practices if and as desirable. Frameworks regarded as no
longer viable or appropriate were set aside. The process of adding, adapting
and deleting was continuous. Rather than being bound by the artificial dichot-
omy of either "qualitative" or "quantitative," methodologies used depended on
the appropriateness for that research and that time. The design we began a
study with was considered from the outset to be changeable — emergent and
contingent. We have fully embraced hermeneutic-phenomenology and seek
to build understandings around the lived experiences of participants. In contrast to mainstream hegemonic crypto-positivistic research, we endeavor to
include participants' voices and have adopted the stance of multiple truths
and multiple interpretation. What any person may regards as true represents
that person's lived experience and interests, historically constituted and radically shaped by social categories such as social class, race, age, sexual identity, and gender. We view such participants' interpretations as just as "valid,"
just as real and just as valuable as those of the researchers. Accordingly, we
regard experiences as polysemic and endeavor to incorporate this standpoint
into our research. When we make claims we are careful to do so with nuance
and to be inclusive. Participants are not viewed as "subjects" to be studied but
rather as fellow coresearchers whose voice and interpretations are not only
welcomed but expected and sought after. Thus, much of our published work is
coauthored with these participant | coresearchers.

Reflecting our dialectical, dynamic, multidimensional, emergent and contingent approach to doing research, our framing theories too changed to meet
contextual exigencies — such as, studying teaching and learning in inner-city
high schools in Philadelphia and New York City, where participants differed
greatly from our research squad and often from their teachers and fellow

students. Our methodologies needed to be appropriate for studying fields characterized by the different sounds of a multitude of cultures, often resistant or in conflict to one another, and being produced at much the same time. Importantly, we sought to understand how different students produced and adapted culture to afford individual and collective successes.

Authentic inquiry to us is a methodology that is fluid and pays attention to all participants learning from their involvement in the research, understanding and respecting everyone's constructions of what is happening and why it is happening, and ensuring that what is learned from the research is used to benefit all participants equitably.

2 The Spike in the Curve

The spike in the curve discussed in Chapter 3, is a complement to authentic inquiry and the supplementary methodologies we describe in the second chapter. Spike in the curve is a metaphor for difference and contradiction. We have come to refer to the methodology associated with it as event-oriented inquiry and it relates to researching and learning from difference.

As is Ken's custom, he provides an autobiographical context for the journey that includes event-oriented inquiry. There is common ground in Chapters 2 and 3. However, in Chapter 3, Ken examines a methodology that has the purpose of understanding the potential of a contradiction to enhance social life for all participants as well as at a collective level (i.e., institutional). Since contradictions are not usually anticipated, it is important that the design of a study has a flexible, emergent character and multiple perspectives are consulted in the process of identifying contradictions that are potentially ripe for deep analysis. What is so important in event-oriented inquiry is to always identify patterns having thin coherence, together with associated contradictions. Then, in understanding contradictions as spikes in the curve, it becomes necessary to thoroughly examine the context before, during, and after the spike occurs. Selection of the appropriate context is an important aspect of the art of doing event-oriented research. It can take a while to puzzle over how to see, and then how to seek solutions that accompany what you see.

In Chapter 3 I (Ken) begins a narrative with such an event. This event is identified from finger-pulse oximeter data that shows relatively high pulse rate and quite low blood oxygenation for a short time while the teacher addressed her class. Within the selected video vignette, the contradiction concerned certain utterances (in this case syllables) having, as what many in the classroom described, as an annoying twang to them. Some students referred to these utterances as shrill. As we undertook prosodic analyses together with video, frame-by-frame analyses, we realized that sporadic bursts of speech occurred either side of a pause in which a short, shallow breath was taken in and out through the mouth. We were completely stumped and had to systematically search through many sources before we eventually had a breakthrough in discovering an impressive body of research involving nitric oxide in animals, including humans, and problems associated with mouth breathing (McKeown, 2016). Insights from this ongoing research in medicine and physiology energized our analyses that examined physiological changes in the context of polyvagal theory and functioning of the autonomic nervous system (Porges, 2011). This event-oriented study opened doors for important curriculum modifications in teacher education programs, ongoing research on teaching and learning, and self-help regarding wellness (Tobin, King, Henderson, Bellocchi, & Ritchie, 2016).

3   Research as Methodological Journey

In Chapter 4, Wolff-Michael Roth adopts an autobiographical approach that examines his research frameworks through lenses that provide insights into quality and credibility of his research. His narrative illustrates the ever-changing nature of what he studied and how he enacted research.

Michael begins by situating his research in the reflexology sociology of Pierre Bourdieu (1992). He also distances himself from the constructivist turn of the 1980s and 1990s (Tobin, 1993). In so doing, he introduces passivity, foreshadowing its importance in his own research in a variety of intellectual fields, and in the work of others (Roth, 2008). Noting that he sees considerable distance between what he did as a beginning researcher and what he is doing now, the journey begins with Roth's early innovative work situated in schools. This work involved practices such as coteaching and cogenerative dialogue, and ways in which theoretical tenets framed his ongoing research, including dialectical relationships, practice theory, and cultural historical activity theory. He points out that moving the context for his studies from schools to research in the everyday world afforded an expansion in the methods he employed, changes being attributed to continuously evolving types of research questions.

The storied nature of Michael's chapter allows readers to consider some of his thinking in regard to what he researched and how he researched it. The narrative moves from video to studies of language in everyday life. Once again, Roth shows how his studies grew over the past three decades and in so doing he provides critique of what others were doing in the mainstream (e.g., conceptual change studies). Among the gems addressed in the chapter are discourse analysis, conversation analysis, and uses of a metaphor of apprenticeship as a research method. Just as Roth's research and associated frameworks evolved in an emergent and contingent manner, so too does each section of this chapter, as the context moves across situations, from schools, to fish hatcheries, and to the cockpit of a plane — just to mention a few.

The approach that Roth adopts is to historically situate each of the major sections, thereby providing a cycle that often spans decades. In so doing, Michael uncovers key aspects of his research within changing contexts that include phenomenology, ethnomethodology, and interaction analyses. His concluding section takes us back to the beginning of the chapter as Roth returns to some of the issues he addressed to begin with, notably rigor and reflexivity.

We positioned Wolff-Michael Roth's chapter at the beginning of this book to provide readers with perspectives that are often quite different than those described in Chapters 2 and 3. It seemed important to us that readers become acquainted with different perspectives with them on their journey through the chapters of this book. After all, we are not peddling "a truth." Instead are laying out our own landscape of a bricolage of methodologies and methods in a journey, like Roth's, that spans more than five decades. While our own participation in research and its associated privileges may be drawing to a close, it is important to note that the river that serves as a metaphorical representation of ongoing research, will continue to flow as individual scholars join and leave academia. In producing this book, we try to lay out a sense of continuity. We joined an ongoing living process that continues with and without any one of us. We feel it is important to contribute to this process in ways that expand what we know from research and improve the quality of social life as it may be construed in local through global contexts.

4   Emotional Conversations about Race

The initial chapters highlight uses of narrative in research with the authors discussing what has been learned and accomplished from authentic inquiry. Katelin Corbett begins her chapter (Chapter 5) in narrative mode. This chapter was part of a dissertation she successfully defended in 2018 and is based on events that took place the previous summer. Her narrative is very timely today as, through mostly a highly emotionally valanced, inner conversation with herself, she addresses an issue that is very emotional, intimate, vulnerable and challenging both at the personal level as well as at the societal level, that presently has galvanized action in the United States and sent tidal waves crashing onto the shores of many countries around the world. Police violence. Black Lives Matter. Civil rights. Racial injustice. Such calls associated with discussions on race, are all highly inflammatory in the United States, a country that was founded on and profited from the slavery of countless millions of people of African descent and the dispossession and genocide of Native Americans. In the summer of 2020, as we write this chapter, the United States is embroiled in racial protests sparked by the murder of African American George Floyd by a white police officer who maintained deadly pressure with his knee placed on Floyd's neck for nearly eight minutes. The publicity and protests that followed his murder, lay bare even more killings and brutality inflicted by the police on black, brown and Native populations across the country.

The need for change is evident, not just in legislation, but in especially educating a citizenry that has been divided on issues of race, slavery, and social justice since the colonization of the Americas.

The context for Katelin's chapter is the fatal shooting death of Alton Sterling, in 2016. Sterling was African-American. His death followed a struggle as Sterling, who had been selling homemade CDs, fled from the police and was shot in the back three times. Corbett sets the scene in a college science education class for teachers she is present in as a teacher |researcher and which Konstantinos Alexakos (KA) was teaching. Her narrative is explicit in showing that the Sterling shooting was not an isolated event, but a common historically constituted occurrence. KA asks "how are these things happening? I want answers."

At that point, as readers ponder what the answers might be, Corbett switches to a description of the methodology employed in the chapter. As Katelin explains as her chapter unfolds, her use of a methodological approach is theoretically saturated. In our work we recognize a dialectical relationship between methodology and method, and are explicit on this point as the use of methods is inextricably linked to a multilogical foundation. Just as we are explicit about this point, so too is Corbett in her chapter. Corbett describes the theoretical foundation for her work as stories and impressionistic tales (Van Maanen, 1988), a bricolage that includes hidden curriculum, event-oriented inquiry, agency and power, reflexivity, and hermeneutic phenomenology.

Katelin returns to her story, revealing that KA, the teacher of the class, has two African-American sons. Her impressionistic tale draws readers into the story through a powerful description of her own *inner* emotions that include shock, sadness, empathy, and compassion. We are saved somewhat from too much trauma as Corbett again switches to weave insights into hidden curriculum and what is involved in discussing this highly relevant, controversial, emotion-laden topic at the beginning of a physics class. As well as weaving the important issue of what constitutes a curriculum into an impressionistic tail, Katelin draws us to consider issues of citizen education, necessity for teachers to be aware of and responsive to the emotions that students bring with them as they enter a classroom door and, in a broader sense, what should be the goal for teacher education and what really matters. Following further explication of event-oriented inquiry, Corbett expands her impressionistic tale by the inclusion of gender, religion, and use of cogenerative dialogue in conversations characterized by emotional differences.

The power of an impressionistic tale is palpable as one event (i.e., spike in the curve) is addressed after another. Among the issues addressed in the story are emotions, empathy for a teacher, physical and social safety and danger in classroom climates, and physiological expression of emotions and associated potential wellness concerns. Corbett concludes with a discussion of implications for teacher education and research. In so doing, she places her research in a larger context of how she incorporates authentic inquiry and considers curricula as emergent. In broadening her discussion from teacher education to high school teaching and learning, she highlights safe spaces as a critical focus for inquiry, especially in a context of race, gender, religion, and excess emotions. Importantly, Katelin emphasizes the role of reflexivity, becoming aware, as part of the mission to know one self.

The mantra, "know myself" is recurrent throughout this volume, and is central in the next chapter as well as this one.

5   Autobiography of an Educator's Journey in Awakening, Healing and Liberation

We are struck by Yau Yan Wong's commitment to learning through total immersion into knowledge systems — in particular, intensive engagement with different mindfulness traditions that have emerged since the life of Siddhartha Gautama. Using narrative, in Chapter 6, Yau Yan provides insights into her experiences with three Buddhist mindfulness traditions: Vietnamese Mahayana, Burmese Mahasi Sayadair Vipassana, and Thai Forest Vipassana. Yau Yan's intense engagement provides an insider perspective of the effort needed to practice these traditions, the nature of the activities, and her accomplishments. Interestingly, we also see how subsequently she applies what she has learned to education and ongoing research. Wong plans interventions based on what she learns and folds them into her teaching and the research she undertakes with elementary level students to ascertain what her students learn and whether what they learn is useful in their lifeworlds.

Wong's autoethnographic approach embraces narratives built around hermeneutic phenomenology, authentic inquiry, and event-oriented inquiry. An evident strength of her scholarship is a commitment to knowing herself as a gateway into learning from the three contemplative traditions she explores in the chapter. Mindfulness, as enacted in these Buddhist traditions, has commonalities and striking differences. These are portrayed with thick descriptions, in a journey that is spiritual, emotional, and rewarding.

Yau Yan's present (i.e., now) is radically multilogical in that she is informed by the breadth and depth of what she has learned along the path from Catholicism to Buddhism. Furthermore, it is clear in the chapter that even within the Thai Forest Tradition of Buddhism, there are lineages that can be depicted as different, but interconnected, streams or pathways. She focuses on an enlightened lineage of monks that includes Luangpor Pramote and emphasizes a path to self-enlightenment that involves practices in everyday life.

Wong weaves a bricolage of methodologies into a historically constituted narrative that involves continuous research on mindfulness and contemplative inquiry. Her chapter shows how impressionistic tales can be used in conjunction with interpretive approaches that embrace hermeneutic phenomenology, authentic inquiry, event-oriented inquiry, and an overarching umbrella of emergence and contingence.

6   Facial Expression of Emotions

In Chapter 7, Olga Calderón presents her ongoing research on emotion expression as it relates to teaching and learning college level science and science education. A starting premise is that teachers need to be more reflective about their emotions while teaching, that is, increase awareness about emotional expression during classroom interactions. Olga further makes the argument that teachers need to heighten their awareness about emotions that make students uncomfortable and plan interventions to create and sustain appropriate emotional climates.

Olga uses Paul Ekman's coding system for analyzing facial expression of emotions (Ekman & Friesen, 1971). As part of ongoing research, that we refer to as the Brooklyn College Study (Alexakos, 2015), Calderón's study is multilogical, emergent, and contingent and incorporates authentic and event-oriented inquiry. Calderón's underlying foundation is hermeneutic phenomenology. Data resources for the study include video and audio analysis, fieldnotes, students' responses to heuristics, and cogenerative dialogues involving teachers, students, and researchers. Students also assessed emotional climate of the classroom at regular intervals throughout each class, using clickers that connected via Bluetooth to a computer, which recorded the data. Olga's chapter uses narratives, vignettes that include thick description of an event that involved intense facial expression of emotions, and subsequent emotional contagion. Calderón framed some of her interpretations using Randall Collins' (1984) theories of emotion and building solidarity in communities.

7 Physiological Expression of Emotion

Corinna Brathwaite uses event-oriented inquiry and autoethnography in Chapter 8 to examine synchrony and heartrate between her as a student | researcher and her professor (in this case Konstantinos Alexakos). Her research incorporates video and audio analyses synchronized with heart rate data obtained from finger pulse oximeters. Corinna uses narrative to draw the reader into classroom interactions and associated emotions and physiological responses.

Race is addressed explicitly, and Brathwaite describes it as a tricky matter for her; one that extends far beyond skin-color. To us, her chapter powerfully speaks to race as polysemic. Corinna reminds us that we, as researchers and educators, writ large, need to tread carefully when discussing race and, ensure that nuances are discerned as they arise, and maintain high levels of awareness. Importantly, with an eye to educative authenticity, it is important to understand others' understandings, as well as your own.

Corinna highlights issues of synchrony that can arise without either awareness or control of participants. Examples of resonance involving heart rates of a teacher and student were apparent in a context of teaching about thorny issues. Brathwaite concludes her chapter with unanswered questions about the ethics of discussing difficult questions, especially around race, even in spaces regarded as safe. When permission is given to remain silent, thorny issues are still thorny, and may catalyze physiological expressions that manifest in trauma and wellness projects.

8 Visual Arts-Based Research Methods for Self-Care and Transformation

In Chapter 9, Helen Kwah creates a first-person ethnography to show her involvement in, and the development of, arts-based methodologies. In so doing, she uses her artistic practices to provide rich insights into the way that emotions associated with doing research on racial oppression, gender disadvantage, and ways in which highly motivated, but oppressed persons from marginalized social categories (e.g., social class, LBTQ+) deal with failure to succeed, or to be recognized as successful.

Gene Fellner, a co-author of the chapter, provides voiceover for the narrative. Kwah and Fellner employ metalogues to review what has been laid out in the autobiography and explore potential horizons of opportunity that accompany arts-based research.

As is the case with most chapters in this volume, racial inequities and injustices are front and central. We are intrigued by similarities in forms of suffering experienced as Helen grew up in the United States as an Asian American and those of Alysha, an African-American student, who is represented in vignettes that intertwine with Kwah's biography and her art.

This chapter connects directly with the earlier chapters by Yau Yan Wong, that addresses Vipassana meditation, and Katelin Corbett, that examines difficulties in participating in dialogues about thorny issues. Similarly, Helen and Gene provide fertile ground for several chapters to follow.

9 Leaving Home

Anna Malyukova uses arts-based research, hermeneutic phenomenology, use of images as a heuristic and narrative in her work in Chapter 10 that explores her emotional responses to her son leaving home for college. Thus autoethography becomes an important constituent of a multilogical approach that she adopts in her study. Malyukova addresses how a photograph of her children, receding into the distance, evokes emotions like those she experienced when her son left home to go to college.

Anna illustrates how her participation in a craft project ameliorated the strength and stickiness of her sadness – she stitched fabric on which her children's images were printed, onto a blanket her mother had given her following the birth of her son. The act of stitching the fabric onto a blanket that carries strong emotional attachment to Anna's past was therapeutic and healing for her.

Features of Malyukova's chapter include uses of stories from her childhood and early adulthood to give added meaning to emotional attachment and loss than many parents feel as they children transition to separate lives.

10 A Reflexive Approach to the Study of Emotions

Arnau Amat and Isabel Sellas collaborate in a study of emotion and learning to teach science and mathematics. Their research (Chapter 11) adopts a frame that is both interpretive and socio-critical. They embrace complexity of social environments that characterize science and teaching and learning and seek to understand contextual factors that are ever in-play.

Becoming aware of expressed emotion and building an understanding of emotions and their spread through a social environment is an important contribution of the research presented in this chapter. Their approach is expansive and, as is the case in most chapters of this volume, they use a number of methodologies in ways that reflect emergence and contingence in a bricolage that includes authentic, event-oriented, and multi-level inquiry. Hermeneutic phenomenology permeates a collaborative effort, which explicitly highlights dialectical relationships and attentive listening to many voices and learning from difference.

Arnau and Isabel acknowledge a research tradition grounded in conceptual change and big ideas such as pedagogical content knowledge. They accept that preservice teachers come to teacher education programs with an enormous reservoir of knowledge from being in classrooms in their pre-k-12 years of schooling and recognize that what is learned in a teacher education program should build on what is in this reservoir of knowledge. A reflexive approach is adopted so that preservice teachers become more aware of what they know and its salience to teaching and learning.

11 Researching Place-Based Environmental Education in an Urban Park

In Chapter 12 Amy DeFelice adopts a hermeneutic phenomenological approach to her study of place-based environmental education. Amy's research incorporates photovoice, a form of action research, embracing a dialectical relationship between researcher | teacher. A primary goal of her study was to improve science curricula while students learn science.

In her study, Amy's classroom was an urban park, proximate to the school in which she taught science so to allow students to undertake field work in environmental science studies. Amy's students planned and enacted field observation projects and then presented what they learned at their science fair. Students shared a camera with a peer and were invited to photograph anything they thought was interesting, inspirational, or germane to science. The photographs were then pooled, organized, and used as foci for dialogue in cogenerative dialogues. These photographs were viewed by DeFelice as a way to represent the voices of her students, capture whatever caught their attention and serve as sites for reflection on what happened and what might be improved. In cogenerative dialogues, selected photographs became foci for expansive dialogues that facilitated attainment of emergent goals such as science identity transformations, and aesthetics of doing science, and an expanded sense of place—as it related to a local urban park.

12   Using Images Heuristically to Heighten Awareness and Reflexivity

In the study discussed in Chapter 13, Marissa Bellino shows how mental mapping can be used with urban youth from an inner-city high school as a participatory methodology in the context of teaching and learning environmental science. The methods used by Bellino parallel those previously outlined by Amy DeFelice above, Helen Kwah and Gene Fellner (Chapter 9), and those employed in Chapter 14 by Kate O'Hara. Collectively, these researchers use photographs, sketches, and magazine cut-outs as ways to expand youths' voices, and in so doing, explore differences within the standpoints of young people as well as patterns of coherence.

Students experienced positive features of mental mapping, including knowledge and feelings about the neighborhood and its environment. Collaborating with student researchers also illustrated that even though salient issues were uncovered by mental mapping, there was discomfort in participating on difficult issues – similar to those that Konstantinos Alexakos and colleagues (2016) referred to as thorny issues, where students felt inhibited from participating and even noted feelings of guilt. These revelations have similarities to issues addressed by Katelin Corbett (Chapter 5) and Corinna Brathwaite (Chapter 8).

Marissa addresses a number of issues that science educators and urban educators will find interesting. From a methodological | methods point of view, uses of storytelling and reflection, while using photographs, sketches and magazine cut-outs heuristically, afford transformative possibilities associated with heightened awareness about local places/spaces and associated environmental issues and the social relations that emerge along with increased awareness.

Bellino's attention to youths' identities and the potential for educating about local lifeworlds, outside of formally designated spaces such as schools and museums raises important considerations for researchers, policymakers, teachers and learners. In a broader sense questions arise about boundaries that constrain thinking when it comes to priorities for what should be included in a school curriculum. Just as biologists might be exhorted to emphasize "knowing oneself," geography and social studies educators might consider the importance of youths knowing their own local communities and associated environments as well as those that spiral out from the local to the global.

13   Photographs for Meaning Making

Similarly, Kate O'Hara in Chapter 14 uses first-person narrative to illustrate her uses of photographs and photography in a service learning context to heighten participants' awareness of issues that are central to teaching and learning in an urban elementary school setting. Kate explains how her work embraces critical reflection and employs a bricolage of frameworks that serve as a foundation and credibility filter for her story-based approach to disseminating what she has learned from research. The uses of photographs heuristically heighten participants' awareness about their ontologies and axiologies while giving voice to their stories, what they value, notice about teaching and learning, remember, and choose to tell.

14   Benefits of Action Research

In Chapter 15, Marissa Bellino and Jennifer Adams undertake research on new teachers' experiences as they engage in action research and teacher-participant action research. Bellino and Adams build on Lawrence Stenhouse's (1975) development of action research as a vehicle for creating and adapting school curricula. They also employ critical perspectives that build on the work of scholars such as Paulo Freire and Joe Kincheloe. Marissa and Jennifer argue that teachers should engage in action research in their own classrooms and adapt enacted curricula continuously, while embracing critical and emancipatory frameworks to guide an emergent and contingent process.

Bellino and Adams maintain that teachers have little time to study, reflect-on, and learn from their own teaching and learning practices. Accordingly, they educate new teachers in their programs to plan and enact critical action research that seeks to identify and transform unjust school structures, derived from research on high-stakes test achievement. Marissa and Jennifer note that recommended reforms emanating from this process are mainly focused on teacher change, as distinct from changing ways in which students engage.

Given the power of this form of self-inquiry they advocate that action research ought to be a required constituent of teacher education programs. Of course, there are policy issues that also would need to be resolved so that action research methods learned in the certification process could be enacted in school classrooms after graduation. For this to happen, action research would have to be considered legitimate, necessary, and a central constituent of professional development. Present regulations about doing research in classrooms inhibit action research. This ought to be an imperative for change. After all, how can teachers be effective unless they undertake self-study to better know themselves, and how best to enact curricula from which all students learn what they need to know to enhance their lifeworlds?

15   Ethics of Research in Education

Mitch Bleier (Chapter 16) addresses issues associated with research ethics and gaining the approval of peer committees established by universities, Department of Education, and other institutions such as museums and hospitals, that engage in educational research. Mitch provides historical context for the necessity of regulation to afford the highest possible level of ethical conduct, while also encouraging ongoing research. He provides a case study of his own experiences with the Institutional Review Board of a University (IRB), in a study of a young woman's experiences and practices as she learned about cheese and eventually became an internationally renowned cheesemonger.

Bleier describes the design of his research as emergent and contingent, embracing hermeneutical phenomenology, and including authentic and event-oriented inquiry. Importantly, he addresses issues of purposively selecting participants in research and associated issues of generalizability. Mitch's specific examples of the IRB's critical comments of his proposal, and his letter of response, will be useful for students and researchers going through a similar process.

The question that arises in this chapter is what constitutes a "peer" when one's human subject protocols are being reviewed? Institutions need to take care that review panels are appropriately qualified to do their job. Importantly, for each research proposal that is submitted, review needs to involve those who are sufficiently educated in the areas involved to see ethical concerns that may present themselves. In the examples provided by Mitch, it seems as if at least one of his IRB reviewers was distracted by contradictions which likely had their genesis in ontological and axiological differences that underpin a conviction about what constitutes research. Failure to understand the emergent and contingent designs proposed by Bleier and to value his non-positivistic approach, set the stage for critiques of the design and assumed assumptions that were far from the mark. The result was initial denial of permission to undertake the research, even though the review was supposed to have focused on ethical issues. Accordingly, Bleier was "encouraged" to change the design of his study to align with the values and ontologies of one or more reviewers. The lengthy back-and-forth that ensued is a sign of a need for change in selecting and assigning peer-reviewers. Although the outcome was positive, it seems possible that many researchers would have changed their proposals under such pressure—even though this was neither their preference nor their intention. In such circumstances, the Review Board is not performing as intended i.e., protecting research participants from harm but instead are policing what methodologies are considered real research based on their own biases.

16   Institutional Review Board: A Metalogue

In their metalogue (Chapter 17), Mitch Bleier, Manny Lopez and Malgorzata Powietrzynska discuss the essential nature of the IRB, and its overreach, and possible ways in which to improve functioning of the IRB. These coauthors were doctoral students in the same program at The City University of New York. At the time of writing, all three were newly minted PhDs. They co-authored Chapter 17 as a metalogue. Each co-author presents their research and associated stories to depict difficulties encountered with the IRB. The metalogue expands on the points Mitch introduced in the previous chapter, while providing concrete examples of these researchers' encounters with the IRB.

17   Research for Transformation and the Greater Good

We begin Chapter 18 with a review of where our research began, and an evolution of an overarching framework which is intuitive, emergent, and oriented toward transforming practice in ways that empower learners. We address the salience of our incorporation of a multilogical methodology, including authentic inquiry, event-oriented inquiry and a mantra that transformation, and the conduct of research, should serve the greater good. Importantly, benefits of our research are expected to catalyze ripple effects, changes in the lives of all those who participate in our research and those with whom they interact.

References

Alexakos, K. (2015). *Being a teacher | researcher: A primer on doing authentic inquiry research on teaching and learning.* Sense Publishers.

Alexakos, K., Pride, L. D., Amat, A., Tsetsakos, P., Lee, K. J., Paylor-Smith, C., Zapata, C., Wright, S., & Smith, T. (2016). Mindfulness and discussing "thorny" issues in the classroom. *Cultural Studies of Science Education, 11,* 741–769. doi:10.1007/s11422-015-9718-0

Bourdieu, P. (1992). The practice of reflexive sociology (The Paris workshop). In P. Bourdieu & L. J. D. Wacquant (Eds.), *An invitation to reflexive sociology* (pp. 216–260). The University of Chicago Press.

Collins, R. (1984). *The role of emotion in social structure: emotion as a micro basis for macro-sociology: Approaches to emotions.* Lawrence Erlbaum Associates Inc.

Ekman, P., & Friesen, W. V. (1971). Constants across cultures in the face and emotion. *Journal of Personality and Social Psychology, 17*(2), 124–129.

Erickson, F. (1986). Qualitative research on teaching. In M. C. Wittrock (Ed.), *Handbook of research on teaching* (3rd ed., pp. 119–161). Macmillan.

Guba, E. G. & Lincoln, Y. (1989). *Fourth generation evaluation.* Sage Publications.

McKeown, P. (2016). *The oxygen advantage: Simple, scientifically proven breathing techniques to help you become healthier, slimmer, faster, and fitter.* William Morrow Paperbacks (an imprint of HarperCollins).

Porges, S. W. (2011). *The polyvagal theory: Neurophysiological foundations of emotions, attachment, communication and self-regulation.* W.W. Norton & Company.

Roth, W.-M. (2008). Agency and passivity: Prolegomenon to scientific literacy as ethico-moral praxis. In A. Rodriguez (Ed.), *Multiple faces of agency: Innovative strategies for effecting change in urban school contexts* (pp. 103–119). Sense Publishers.

Stenhouse, L. (1975). *An introduction to curriculum research and development.* Heineman.

Tobin, K. (Ed.). (1993). *The practice of constructivism in science education.* Erlbaum.

Tobin, K., King, D., Henderson, S., Bellocchi, A., & Ritchie, S. M. (2016). Expression of emotions and physiological changes during teaching. *Cultural Studies of Science Education, 11*, 669–692. doi:10.1007/s11422-016-9778-9

Van Maanen, J. (1988). *Tales of the field on writing ethnography.* University of Chicago Press.

CHAPTER 2

Doing Authentic Inquiry

Kenneth Tobin and Konstantinos Alexakos

Abstract

We adopt a historical and autobiographical approach to the development and evolution of authentic inquiry and its applications as methodology. We address post positivistic perspectives and approaches to research, including learning from difference and applying nuance, while eschewing essentialism and reductionism. We regard the value of authentic inquiry holistically, beneficence being associated with learning from research, learning from others' different perspectives, transforming social fields based on what is learned from research, and improving the quality of social life for all participants, not just for those who are socially placed to take advantage of what is learned. Central to authentic inquiry is emergence and contingence. We seek to answer what is happening in social contexts, why it is happening from perspectives of participants, and what more can be learned when disharmonies occur in social settings. Above all, authentic inquiry acknowledges that more is known than can be expressed, more can be learned from additional research, and there is more to be known than can be learned from research.

Keywords

authentic inquiry – methodology – catalyzing change – teaching – learning – learning to teach – heuristics – hermeneutic phenomenology

1 Research That Makes a Difference

In this chapter we present our emerging appropriation of a research methodology we refer to as authentic inquiry. We situate our work historically in Egon Guba and Yvonna Lincoln's *Fourth Generation Evaluation* (1989) and William

Sewell Jr.'s theory of culture (1999). Substantive transformation of authentic inquiry also reflected our ongoing research for 25 years and inclusion of powerful theoretical frameworks – leading to changes in how we viewed and valued the world and our regard for research as a collaborative endeavor bridging the theory-practice divide. Important ideas concerning difference, bricolage, polysemia, and an awkward relationship between research and crises of representation unfold in a steady evolution of authentic inquiry.

Quite central to our research is reflexivity, which we regard as essential to the high value we place on the necessity for research to catalyze positive changes for individuals and collectives, while ensuring that these changes provide equity in regard to beneficence for all. As an illustration of how we use what we have learned from our research to catalyze change, we include heuristics for coteaching and cogenerative dialogue, which we developed from our research. Our dynamic, reflexive, fluid, emergent and contingent, participant centered approach highlights the educative, transformative and catalytic nature of authentic inquiry.

2   Getting Started

I (Ken) first encountered authentic inquiry in *Fourth Generation Evaluation*, authored by Guba and Lincoln (1989). The primary tenets of Guba and Lincoln's book were subversive in many ways, especially in the overt manner in which the authors challenged legitimacy of positivism and eschewed what Joe Kincheloe and I described as crypto positivism (Kincheloe & Tobin, 2009). When I first became aware of *Fourth Generation Evaluation*, I was embroiled in arguments about radical constructivism and its potential as a framework for understanding teaching and learning and for expanding methodologies for research in social sciences (Tobin, 1993). Accordingly, I paid close attention to Guba and Lincoln's rejection of objectivism in favor of social realism. There are many gems in *Fourth Generation Evaluation*, and some of the most salient took time to fully appreciate. One of these was the idea that adherence to the authenticity criteria alone was sufficient to maximize the quality of research. Also, of interest were what Guba and Lincoln referred to as parallel criteria, a list of methods (e.g., member checking, progressive subjectivity) that might be followed to maximize legitimacy of what many referred to as qualitative research. (N.B.: I never accepted that it made any sense to refer to a methodology by a label for the data resources used – so I much preferred the label of interpretive research for the methodology we employed at that time.)

3   Transforming Methodologies and Interpretive Frameworks

In the 1980s, I seemed to be on an endless quest to improve the quality of our ongoing research by changing and improving methodologies and also using new interpretive frameworks that pertained to teaching and learning in K-12 schools (usually science and mathematics). Also, I valued a stance that I learned from Russell Yeany Jr., to always study and learn from my own teaching. Accordingly, I sought to apply appropriate methodologies and interpretive frameworks to the problems that emerged from my lived experiences as a teacher, teacher educator, and researcher. Changes were essential since, from my point of view, I did not value the methodologies and interpretive frameworks I used as a graduate student, and it was evident that mainstream debates in science and mathematics education, and more generally in educational research, were limiting as far as addressing major problems we experienced in our research.

3.1   *Adapting Fourth Generation Evaluation*

I have written elsewhere about some of the details associated with changes to which I allude in the previous paragraph (e.g., Tobin, 2006). To avoid needless repetition, I focus here on those changes associated with adaptations of *Fourth Generation Evaluation* and to subsequent perturbations that catalyzed transformations and distinguished our work from others. Initially we employed the parallel criteria and also emphasized each of the four authenticity criteria. However, as we viewed our research through the lenses of bricolage (Kincheloe & Berry, 2004), we were much more content to allow design features to emerge as we sought to address three broad questions that reflected phenomenology (Schutz, 1962), hermeneutics (Ricoeur, 1991), and ethnomethodology (Garfinkel, 1967) – i.e., what is happening? why is it happening? and what more is there? The third of the questions is subversive, a reminder that there always will be more to what we can learn from research (Varela, 1997), that culture reveals itself in unsettled times (Swidler, 1986), and what we learn from research must be nuanced, incorporating patterns that have thin coherence together with contradictions (Sewell Jr., 1999).

In hindsight, use of Guba and Lincoln's parallel criteria for several years allowed us to build deeper understandings of the authenticity criteria and, eventually, recognize the parallel list as one of many legitimate ways to represent and enact authentic inquiry. Importantly, the list was not regarded in an essentialist way, since components of the list were constituents of a whole, linked to contingence and emergence. An eventual departure from working through the list of parallel criteria allowed us to pursue answers to the three broad questions (presented above), and ensure that authenticity was forefront. Once answers are obtained for what is happening? and why is it happening? It is essential to search for salient nuance to reflect the value of difference as a resource for learning from research. Importantly, all participants might review what we have learned to a certain point in a study and address the question of what more is there?

3.2   *Authenticity Criteria*

We realized that Guba and Lincoln's four authenticity criteria were interdependent and we began to consider them as dialectically related constituents of a whole. Because of our values concerning collaborative research, we felt that all authenticity criteria should be symmetrical in regards to researchers and all other participants (e.g., teachers, students, researchers). Accordingly, we broadened the first of the criteria, ontological authenticity, to include a goal of all participants in a study changing their ontologies as a result of their participation in the research.

Similarly, educative authenticity also applies to others involved in the research being aware of their own perspectives and their meanings, as well as those that differed from them. The intention was to heighten awareness of different ontologies and associated practices, respect and understand differences, and seek to find the value of diverse schemas and practices in a learning community (and in a research community). We do not adhere to a principle of expecting and anticipating thick coherence within communities of practice. Instead, we value difference as a resource and embrace the necessity to understand and respect diverse perspectives (Derrida, 1998). We do not expect culture (i.e., practices and schemas) to be changed merely to conform to the mainstream. If individuals consider their cultural practices to be viable, and do not cause harm to others, then our expectation is to seek to understand and highlight strengths of diversity.

Catalytic authenticity assumes that as changes occur in participants' practices and schemas, the nature and quality of interactions with others in the research field, and potentially in all fields of an individual's lifeworld, will be enhanced. That is, changes in one field ripple outward, providing resources for altered practices in all fields in which research participants live their lives. Similarly, as those with whom research participants interact change their practices and schemas (i.e., produce new culture), there is a groundswell of increased potential for change. In this way (i.e., ripple effects), without having to plan for it to happen, cultural changes emanating in a school, can spread, with and without conscious awareness, to change communities at large.

A second way to consider catalytic authenticity is that what we learned from our research can be used to produce improvements in the quality of enacted curricula and the quality of social life in the institutions involved in the research. These changes can be designed, emergently and contingently, to benefit individuals and collectives involved in the research. In our own work, we have used cogenerative dialogues and heuristics as tools for planning and enacting changes 'from now on.' We consider it an ethical imperative for all participants to have the opportunity to benefit from participation in research as soon as possible.

We consider the fourth authenticity criterion, tactical authenticity, to best be considered as social justice. For many years and studies, we adopted a mantra: to help those who are not able to help themselves – due to their positions in social space. We were concerned that researchers embracing authentic inquiry would invest to assist those to succeed who are ill-served by the institutions we were studying. For example, in our research at City High, in Philadelphia, school practices locked out students who were late arrivals at school (Tobin, Seiler, & Walls, 1999). Often times, their late arrival to class was due to transit system problems, lengthy lines at the sole entrance to the school, and subsequent passage through two metal detectors. Rather than just recognizing this issue and reporting it in our publications, we accepted responsibility to find out who was disadvantaged, why, and how the disadvantage could be addressed by changed policies and practices.

When it comes to enhancing the quality of learning in urban education, we did not want to see changes being implemented if those interventions increase the gap between the best and the rest. Instead, we valued research and its emergent qualities to reduce and even eliminate gaps, and provide resources to support those who experience difficulties in helping themselves to succeed equitably in the current resource environment. Accordingly, in this chapter, we chose the labels social justice to draw attention to the nub of the problem – social issues militate against particular students being able to appropriate resources to enhance their success. To meet this criterion, plans and research practices need to zoom in on underlying equity issues that sustain disadvantage.

Underpinning the authenticity criteria are theoretical frames to which we adhere – notably polyphonia, polysemia, and radical listening (see Alexakos, 2015; Alexakos & Pierwola, 2013). Polyphonia is central to cogenerative dialogue (hereafter cogen), which we often use as methodology | method in our research. Each participant in cogen is entitled to speak as long and as often as any other. Similarly, in our research, we seek many voices to inform our research and also invite those who wish to speak – to speak out. In our enactment of research, it behooves us to find ways for participants to express themselves in ways that allow them to show what they know and can do. Hence, we are not only committed to oral expression in providing opportunities for participants to have voice in our research. We have shown in this book, a variety of ways in which participants have spoken, and we have preserved and learned from their voices (see Kwah & Fellner, Chapter 9, this volume).

The essence of polysemia, as we appropriate it for use in our research, is that the truth underlying what is happening, and why it is happening, depends on a participant's position in social space. We expect to learn about different meaning systems when we seek the assistance of multiple participants to answer questions such as what is happening, why is it happening, and what more is there to understanding the event? In other words, we expect to obtain and learn from multiple ontologies as we interact with the participants in our research.

To attain authenticity criteria, it is essential that we adopt radical listening (Tobin, 2009a). Willingness to listen and understand what others are saying before judging whether or not it needs to be modified. Suspend judgment and try to ascertain the affordances of another's speech. If listeners are aware of and value the importance of difference as a learning resource, then it can make sense for them to work hard to find the viability of a different perspective or practice. What is radical about the process is willingness to defer judgment until a full assessment has been made of particular enacted culture.

In our reports of what we learn from research we describe patterns of coherence for which we have evidence (i.e., assertions) as well as contradictions for those patterns. We do not explain contradictions away as if they are errors. Instead, we highlight and seek to learn from contradictions. Following Sewell (2005), we regard contradictions as seeds for transformation, events from which we can learn, all the while recognizing that we never can know it all – there always will be more (Greene, 1994). We address event-oriented inquiry in detail in the following chapter.

Our acceptance of the methodologies suggested by Guba and Lincoln initially involved adaptations of interpretive research (Erickson, 1986). The primary changes concerned ontology, in that we embraced von Glasersfeld's (1993) ideas about viability, which acknowledged social realism rather than absolute truths. Hence, the goals of social research were to identify social realities, recognizing that different persons would experience social life in unique ways and that their accounts of what happened and why it happened would share family resemblances, while being immersed in unique contexts. That is, we gradually accepted polysemia (i.e., many meaning systems, Bakhtin, 1981) and ensured that our approach to research included polyphonia (i.e., many voices, Bakhtin, 1981). Since the purpose of polyphonia was to learn more about what happened and why it happened, an integral part of research was to document how meaning systems relating to what is happening changed over time and differed from person-to-person.

We acknowledge that individuals experience social life uniquely – even though each individual is dialectically related to the collectives in which they coparticipate. That is, unique is understood also in terms of a dialectical relationship of same | different. Accordingly, as researchers, what we learn about social life depends on who we select as participants in our research. Descriptions of what is happening and why it is happening are nuanced because people who are placed differently in social space have different experiences of social life. In selecting participants to be involved in our research we exercise contingency, taking account of the desirability to learn from differences. When culture is enacted (i.e., produced), patterns of coherence together with contradictions are the norm. Furthermore, all acts of production are both reproductive (as evident in patterns) and transformative (characterized by contradictions). Hence, in our research we take care to identify differences in renderings of what, why, and what more is there to all of this. All claims we make are nuanced by counterclaims and we emphasize that what we have learned is inclusive of assertions and associated contradictions. In a nutshell, authentic research focuses on the importance of learning from research in the sense that researchers do not design studies to verify their hunches, or to prove assertions that align with their value systems. As a result of participating in authentic inquiry, all participants learn new things about what is happening and why it is happening. That is, they change their ontologies. I emphasize here that all participants will change ontologies due to their participation in the research and associated learning. This idea expands Guba and Lincoln's ontological authenticity to include all stakeholder groups, not just designated researchers. Accordingly, ontological changes for all stakeholder groups can provide focus for research that incorporates authentic inquiry.

Changes we observe as we enact research (i.e., in ways participants enact culture) are incremental and frequently occur without participants being consciously aware that changes have occurred. Awareness of change usually is post-hoc, occurring when participants, individually and collectively, make efforts to become aware of the unaware.

Central to the most significant changes in methodology and interpretive frameworks was gradual theorizing of learning as cultural production and dramatic changes in our theorizing of culture. These issues are addressed in the next section.

4   Re-Viewing Culture

Having moved from Florida State University to the University of Pennsylvania, I commenced a study of teaching and learning science at City High, an inner-city school in Philadelphia. In a context of teaching, learning, and learning to teach, much of what we accepted as canonical knowledge in science education was being challenged by almost everybody associated with our activities at City High (i.e., as researchers, teacher educators, and coteachers; Tobin, Seiler, & Smith, 1999). With Wolff-Michael Roth (hereafter Michael) and a relatively large research squad, we were dramatically transforming our practices as teachers, teacher educators, and researchers. On a personal level, what I knew and could do, was constantly challenged and transformed by my experiences as teacher, teacher educator, and researcher at City High. In particular, teaching in an inner-city context, which was new for me, drew attention to the aware | not aware relationship concerning cultural enactment. In order for me to enact teaching fluently I had to anticipate what was happening and enact appropriate teaching practices in a timely manner. I experienced my inability to teach fluently as frustration. I had to think clearly and deliberately as my habitus seemed to be in constant breakdown. As Michael pointed out to me – habitus reveals itself in its breakdown. As frustrating as this experience was, it also was a salient, continuous, learning experience. Usually habitus is enacted fluently, without awareness. However, as I stumbled in my teaching, I became acutely aware of what was not working, and what I was seeking to do unsuccessfully. That is, my teaching produced learning moments in which I could interrogate myself about what I was doing, its appropriateness, and reasons for its apparent failure (Tobin, Seiler, & Walls, 1999).

Of course, it was not just me who failed to enact culture appropriately, in a timely and anticipatory manner. Students also were in strange territory, having to interact with a teacher with whom they were relatively unfamiliar. Accordingly, they too experienced frustration as they had to develop new culture to afford success. No doubt, escalating levels of frustration catalyzed increasingly dysfunctional learning environments and paved the way for emotions such as anger and fear to mediate what was happening, not only in school, but also more generally in social life.

In our collaborative work at City High, Michael and I were researching and developing programs that incorporated coteaching and cogenerative dialogue. We employed frameworks from cultural sociology, especially those associated with Francesco Varela (1997), Pierre Bourdieu (1992), and Yrjö Engeström (2001). Increasingly, I had concerns that our approach to research and its associated theoretical frameworks were somewhat ad hoc and decided to enroll in doctoral level courses in African-American psychology and cultural sociology. This decision was fortuitous in that participation in these courses strengthened my sociological underpinnings and, especially, introduced me to the work of Elijah Anderson (1999) and William Sewell Jr. (1992, 1999). The emergence of potential new frameworks afforded new ways of researching difference and making sense of cultural change.

4.1   *Changing Views of Culture*

Central to Frederick Erickson's interpretive research (Erickson, 1986), was Clifford Geertz's theory of culture (Geertz, 1973), that conceptualized culture as occurring in patterns of practices experienced as thick coherences – which reflected schemas about which participants might be aware or unaware. All exceptions to these observed/experienced cultural enactments had to be explained in terms of patterns of coherence – regarded as social truths. To accept an assertion about what was happening, there needed to be a strong preponderance of evidence, and all assertions had to be explained in terms of the assertion. Usually, there was an interplay between assertions and contradictions as assertions were nuanced to accommodate contradictions. Accordingly, interpretive research was both intensive and extensive. Patterns in enacted culture were understood from the perspectives of both insiders and outsiders, and all contradictions to the patterns needed to be understood before researchers settled on what they had learned from a given study.

When Sewell Jr. (1999) critiqued Geertz's theory of culture, he proposed that when culture was enacted, it was experienced as patterns that had thin coherence. This perspective opened the door to search for patterns that were supported by some evidence and at the same time to search for contradictions, that might also be experienced as patterns with thin coherence. As we began to adopt a view that contradictions were part of all cultural enactment, and would likely be experienced as threads of coherence, we realized the salience of difference and its centrality to a theory of culture. Thus, in our renderings of culture we would take care to nuance all claims, highlighting patterns and contradictions as ever-present, providing incomplete glimpses into what was happening, why it was happening, and emphasizing that what more is there would be a driver for further (never-ending) research; that, at best could provide incomplete portraits of social life. The transcendent nature of what we learn from research (Varela, 1997) and the crisis of representation (Greene, 1994) did not instill fear or initiate a sense of learned helplessness. We maintained that incomplete portraits provide insights and heuristics to guide potential transformation, leading to higher-quality social life. The one caveat to emphasize is that ongoing research activities, such as in education, are essential; but what is learned, never will be essentialistic. What is learned from research always will be contingent, its utility reflecting dynamic contexts of the fields in which participants choose to adapt what is learned from research to their own ongoing, historically constituted lifeworlds.

4.2   *Learning as Cultural Production/Enactment*

As culture is enacted in a field, all participants have the possibility of experiencing enacted practices and associated schemas. That is, by being-in a field, with others, there is a potential to experience and be transformed by what is happening. Quite possibly, this chance to learn can be enhanced if a person is receptive to learning from others, by being in-with-them. Emmanuel Lévinas (1999) referred to this process as passivity – i.e., receptivity: prostrating oneself to learn from others. We regard passivity as a dialectical partner to agency (i.e., agency | passivity). Agency involves intentionality to appropriate structures (i.e., resources, including opportunities) to learn in a given field. Since agency and passivity are ever-present, it behooves researchers to seek to understand how each participant learns (i.e., produces culture), not only from agency, but also from passivity. Our theoretical view of cultural production, is that each act of production is both transformative and reproductive. This can be represented dialectically as transformation | reproduction. In essence, what this means, is that whereas every action is unique, all actions are historically constituted and are grounded in what has happened before – here represented as reproduction. This can be thought of as enactment producing family resemblances that are similar to, but not identical with, what has been done historically.

4.3   *Catalyzing Change Equitably*

Transformations were evident in both the frameworks used to make sense of what was happening, and how we studied what was happening. We employed dialectical reasoning, whereby related social constructs each presupposed one another, that is, they coexisted and were co-related. For example, we regarded the authenticity criteria to be dialectically related – that is, all four tenets coexisted and each presupposed the existence of the others.

We need to do more than design research to investigate a-priori hypotheses and associated assertions that reflect what we know already and value. The design of our research needs to be radically contingent on what we are learning, what we expect to learn next, and the high-value we assign to differences and nuance. We expect all participants in our studies to benefit from participating in the research. The nature of beneficence needs to extend beyond what individuals might express as their interests. Additionally, all participants should learn about what we are learning from a study, how other participants are benefiting, and the importance of equity and social justice for all – especially the responsibility of participants in a learning community to act in ways that help others who are not well-placed to help themselves.

In addition to our research practices being ethically solid, i.e., fair, honest, caring, and compassionate, we realized that four authenticity criteria – ontological, educative, catalytic, and social justice provided necessary and sufficient rationale for assessing the quality of research and evaluation projects. Accordingly, we began to use ethical conduct and the authenticity criteria as tenets for the quality of our work – replacing more traditional criteria such as validity and reliability. In contrast to many traditional methodologies, the quality of authentic inquiry is monitored continuously in terms of participants' changing ontologies, participants learning about and valuing of others' perspectives and practices, changes that are catalyzed by what is learned from the study, and equitable distribution among participants of the benefits produced in the fields of study. Similarly, the generalizability of our research was reconceptualized in terms of what is often referred to as verisimilitude – although we do not use this term, because we prefer use of theoretical generalizability (Eisenhart, 2009) and ripple effects (Tobin, 2009b). To the extent possible, ripple effects are documented as participants benefit from research and also their practices in fields additional to those directly involved in the research. That is, we document how beneficence attributed to a study is enacted in other fields to increase success levels of participants in those fields.

Authentic inquiry is radically transformative in the sense that research is dynamically designed to identify and understand salient differences and adapt and appropriate what is learned in a study to maximize success for all. Changes are planned and enacted continuously, and changes in cultural enactment are studied intensively, heightening awareness and fostering tenets of compassion for self and other, together with communal responsibility to act to afford others' beneficence.

4.4   *Intervening to Benefit Participants*

Each of the authenticity criteria involves participants' beneficence as a result of being involved in the research. Accordingly, the design of a study should address the four criteria in ways that acknowledge their dialectical relationships with one another, that is, they are constituents of a whole, whereby changing one criterion will change all. Also, changes will occur with and without awareness. In the spirit of all participants learning from research, a study design will seek to heighten awareness about those changes that are salient to the purposes of the study and that are valued by participants. We have addressed the goal of beneficence for all by designing interventions based on what we have learned from ongoing research. In the sections that follow we address some of the interventions we have designed in studies that have employed authentic inquiry. The foci for these interventions are coteaching, cogenerative dialogue, and mindfully interacting.

5 Coteaching Heuristic

In our teacher education program at the University of Pennsylvania, coteaching emerged because of difficulties experienced by most teachers in effectively managing urban youth at City High school – an inner-city school that was racially segregated, with a student population that was about 100% African-Americans. In the remainder of this chapter we use the term resident teacher to refer to a certified teacher who is employed by the school district. The term new teacher is reserved for a teacher who is enrolled at the university for the purposes of obtaining teacher certification. New teachers are assigned to City High for at least a full semester to learn to teach inner city youth.

The school principal suggested that two of the new teachers enrolled in a master's degree be afforded the chance to coteach science classes as their required field experience. His plan was intended to solve a problem whereby resident teachers at City High did not have the confidence to allow new teachers to teach their classes solo. His plan called for the new teachers to be granted temporary certification by the school district, allowing them to coteach without the oversight of a resident teacher. Since the two new teachers each had a science degree, they were able and willing to follow this path. The plan was successfully enacted as the two new teachers assumed responsibility for the science classes in a designated small learning community (i.e., a school within a school) and developed teaching skills by teaching together and teaching solo.

Based on this successful application of coteaching, we subsequently assigned all new teachers in pairs or threes to a resident teacher with the expectation that coteaching would be employed as an activity to enhance learning to teach. The expectation was that all coteachers would learn from one another – through agency and passivity. During a period of about five years, we learned a great deal about learning to teach through the use of numerous permutations of new teachers coteaching together, resident teachers coteaching with new teachers, and resident teachers coteaching together. Most frequently, the size of coteaching groups was 2—3 teachers.

- I listen attentively to my coteaching partner.
- My coteaching partner listens attentively to me.
- I am aware when my coteaching partner wants to contribute.
- My coteaching partner is aware when I want to contribute.
- I am in synchrony with my coteaching partner.
- My coteaching partner is in synchrony with me.
- Overall, I collaborative well with others.
- Overall, others collaborate well with me.
- I coparticipate with my coteaching partner.
- My coteaching partner coparticipates with me.
- When I am teaching my coteaching partner supports me.
- During coteaching I support my coteaching partner.
- When difficulties arise I can count on my coteaching partner to try to collaboratively resolve them.
- When difficulties arise my coteaching partner can count on me to try to collaboratively resolve them.
- During coteaching, I can anticipate what my coteaching partner is about to do.
- During coteaching, my coteaching partner can anticipate what I am about to do.
- I am aware of the ways in which I am 'becoming like' my coteaching partner.
- I am aware of the ways in which my coteaching partner is 'becoming like' me.
- I am open to making changes based on suggestions made by my coteaching partner.
- My coteaching partner is open to making changes suggested by me.
- I value differences between my coteaching partner and me.
- My coteaching partner values differences between us.
- I regard planning with my coteaching partner as successful.
- My coteaching partner regards planning with me as successful.
- My teaching practices are fluent when coteaching
- My coteaching partner's teaching practices are fluent when she/he is coteaching.
- I enjoy coteaching.
- My coteaching partner enjoys coteaching.
- My coteaching partner helps me alleviate my negative emotions.
- I help my coteaching partner alleviate her/his negative emotions.
- During coteaching I act in ways to allow my coteaching partner to contribute.
- During coteaching my coteaching partner acts in ways to allow me to contribute.
- I pay attention to my coteaching partner as we coteach (e.g., physiology, prosody, body language).

- My coteaching partner pays attention to me as we coteach (e.g., physiology, prosody, body language).
- I show compassion to my coteaching partner.
- My coteaching partner shows me compassion.
- When things go wrong when my coteaching partner is teaching I step forward to maintain effective coteaching.
- When things go wrong when I am teaching my coteaching partner steps forward to maintain effective coteaching.
- When things go wrong my coteaching partner helps me recover emotionally.
- When things go wrong I help my coteaching partner to recover emotionally.
- I help my coteaching partner stay focused.
- My coteaching partner helps me stay focused.
- I help my coteaching partner to stay positive.
- My coteaching partner helps me to stay positive.
- My coteaching partner knows if something is bothering me.
- I know if something is bothering my coteaching partner.
- When we are coplanning a lesson I strive to make sense of what my coteacher wants.
- When we are coplanning a lesson my coteaching partner strives to make sense of what I want.
- I trust my coteaching partner.
- My coteaching partner trusts me.
- I feel safe when coteaching with my partner.
- My coteaching partner feels safe when coteaching with me.
- My coteaching partner is aware of my emotions as expressed in my voice, face, positioning, and body movements.
- I am aware of my coteaching partner's emotions as expressed in her/his voice, face, positioning, and body movements.
- My coteaching partner can tell when something is bothering me.
- I can tell when something is bothering my coteaching partner.
- I show compassion to my coteaching partner when she/he is unsuccessful.
- My coteaching partner shows compassion when I am unsuccessful.
- I am aware of the emotional climate.
- My coteaching partner is aware of the emotional climate.
- I am aware of how I may affect the emotional climate.
- My coteaching partner is aware of how they may affect the emotional climate.
- When coteaching I am aware of the audience.
- When coteaching my coteaching partners are aware of the audience.

FIGURE 2.1   Characteristics associated with coteaching

Not surprisingly, students from the class also were frequently called upon to coteach with one another and with new and resident teachers. Accordingly, within a relatively short time span we experienced a variety of coteaching configurations and our vision for potential applications of coteaching expanded to include learning to teach, learning subject matter (e.g., science, mathematics, history), doing research, and evaluating teaching and learning.

During my 16 years at the Graduate Center in New York City, I have collaborated with Konstantinos Alexakos as well as numerous doctoral students to further develop coteaching. In the process, we have incorporated coteaching among students in almost all the classes we teach. Typically, two or three students sign on to coteach segments of two or three classes in a 15-week semester. Almost all classes contain significant amounts of coteaching. Not surprisingly, there have been ripple effects because doctoral students taught teacher education classes as adjuncts in colleges in New York City, and opted to follow our modeling of coteaching. Also, teachers who were completing graduate degrees often chose to study coteaching, situated in middle and high school classes, for dissertation and thesis research.

Initially, Michael and I were reluctant to provide coteachers with a list of criteria on which to base coteaching. We realized that such a list would be context dependent, and we wanted coteachers to develop strategies in an organic and dynamic way. This approach was not really successful and we designed a coteaching heuristic, which we conceptualized as a fluid shape shifter, for the characteristics of coteaching, provided in the heuristic. We considered the heuristic to be radically dynamic – depending on context (e.g., nature of the class being taught, values and skills of coteachers).

Following years of experience with coteaching, Konstantinos and I created a lengthy heuristic for coteaching (Figure 2.1). This heuristic has been adapted based on ongoing research and used in many K-College contexts. Several of the chapters in this book have used heuristics like this one, and provide further insights into the potential for heuristics to be used to transform teaching and learning through coteaching.

6   Cogenerative Dialogue

Cogen was developed as an activity associated with coteaching. Since cogens were developed in parallel with coteaching, we also created a heuristic to foster heightened awareness about salient characteristics and potential change. Before providing a list of salient characteristics from the heuristic we present a brief history of the emergence of cogen and its various applications in our practices.

6.1   Learning from Voices of Youth

When we began our research in inner-city schools in Philadelphia, we were asked to collaborate with researchers involved in an existing project in which each classroom taught by a new teacher recruited two high school youth as experts, who would coach new teachers to 'better teach kids like me.' I loved the idea of giving urban youth voice about how they were being taught and how to enhance learning environments. In fact, we expanded the project to routinely include youth as student researchers in our own ongoing research. We selected youth who were different from one another to provide diverse insights on how to improve the quality of learning environments.

A problem we quickly recognized was that students frequently had 'bad' ideas, grounded in gaining and maintaining an authoritarian-style learning environment. Their advice was saturated with schemas associated with rewards and punishments being used to obtain particular forms of engagement that valued learning and recalling facts – often in drill and practice activities. A related, significant problem was that students were regarded as experts and there was no provision for dialogue about what was happening, how to improve what was happening, and the rationale for the given advice. With the wisdom of hindsight, how could it be different? Students would speak about improvement from a context that was bounded by their lived experiences and their levels of awareness about what was happening and why it was happening. In the absence of alternatives to consider, their imaginations and values for improvement would be constrained by their lived experiences.

6.2   Cogen as a Transformative Activity

Based on what we learned from our ongoing research, and associated values, Michael and I created cogen as an activity that would involve selected participants from a particular lesson. We insisted that those involved would have been coparticipants in a lesson – a shared experience. We purposively selected participants to ensure that diverse perspectives (especially ontologies and axiologies) would be represented in the cogen.

In our initial framing of cogen the purpose was to obtain consensus in an activity in which all participants were respectful of one another, all were regarded as having equal status and power, all would have equal turns of talk and equal time spent talking. Nobody would interrupt a speaker, dialogue on a topic would continue until a resolution on a given issue was obtained, and at the end of cogen a summary list would be drawn up – containing recommendations for the next class; including, but not limited to, what should change, and what should remain the same.

6.3   *Difference as a Resource for Transformation and Cultural Production*

After the first few years of cogen, we noticed how much participants learned from being involved. Not only did students' grades increase, but they often stepped forward to assist their teacher – as coteachers. Changes like these encouraged us to capitalize further on the differences we built into cogen membership. We changed focus on the outcomes of cogen through the use of metaphors such as, 'cogen as seedbed for learning' and 'cogen as seedbed for growth of new culture.' Rather than insisting on cogen participants negotiating consensus during cogen, we focused on the potential of understanding and respecting others' different perspectives on important issues that arose in dialogues about shared lesson experiences. It was clear to us that consensus could be an outcome, but only one of many; and surely not essential as an indicator of success. Instead, we wanted to assign high value to successfully dialogue with others who were different from one another in many salient ways. That is, a primary goal of cogen was to learn from and about others, to build respect for difference, and to heighten self-awareness and self-respect.

6.4   *Selected Characteristics and Rules*

Collaboration with Konstantinos catalyzed many changes in the characteristics of cogen and its applications (Alexakos, 2015). He was a researcher | teacher in his college science education classes at Brooklyn College and also with doctoral students at the Graduate Center. In addition, the two of us have served as advisor for 26 doctoral dissertations at the Graduate Center, which have incorporated cogen into their research. A cogen heuristic is provided in Figure 2.2 as one version of a set of characteristics that can be selected and shaped for specific uses in and out of schools.

7   Mindfully Interacting

Effective social communication is central to a productive learning environment. Also, understanding what is involved in effective social communication is complex, dynamic, and context dependent. Over the past decade of our research we have gradually created, multifaceted understandings of effective social interaction, situated and framed by our authenticity criteria. To facilitate

- I strive to make sense of what others are saying.
- I try to get others to contribute to what is being discussed.
- Others try to get me to contribute during discussions.
- There is a place for me to speak. Therefore, I speak as much as others in my group.
- Others in my group have the opportunity to speak as often as I do.
- Every member of the group has equal opportunity to talk as I do.
- My talk is respectful.
- When I talk others listen to what I have to say.
- When I talk I build on what others have to say.
- I try to learn from others' talk.
- I try to understand different perspectives.
- I feel as if I belong with this group
- The members of the group have a sense of solidarity.
- I maintain focus during dialogue.
- Dialogue in the group is timely.
- Dialogue in the group is appropriate.
- Dialogue in the group is anticipatory.
- My oral contributions are thoughtful.
- As I listen to others, I attempt to put aside my own perspectives and understand theirs.
- I test the potential of others' ideas.
- During group discussions there is a least one review of what was accomplished.
- Different perspectives from members of the group have contributed to my own learning.

FIGURE 2.2   Characteristics developed for use in a cogenerative dialogue heuristic

others' applications of what we learn, we have created a heuristic that can be used reflexively. In this section, we provide insights into the key tenets of what we have learned about mindful interaction from our ongoing research.

7.1   *Speaking and Listening Mindfully*

Most of us take speaking for granted. When we feel safe enough to speak, we speak. As a person speaks, they should be mindful of the extent to which listeners benefit from what is being said. Efforts can be made to ensure that speech is comprehensible to listeners, taking into account the pace of delivery, pausing between phrases so that listeners can process what is being said, using vocabulary that is appropriate for all listeners, and being cautious to avoid inflicting social violence through what and how it is said. Speech and associated actions should not be harmful to others. As well as being aware of speech utterances, it is important for speakers to monitor others' faces in an endeavor to gauge their emotional states, making adjustments to speech in an effort to initiate and sustain a positive emotional climate. It is imperative that loudness, frequency distributions of words and their constituent syllables, and intonation of utterances are appropriate in the sense that coparticipants remain attentive, and appropriately engaged. Speakers should not speak for too long i.e., individuals should not monopolize talk time.

While speaking, nonverbal interaction can enhance or inhibit high levels of engagement among coparticipants. With the goal of creating and sustaining high levels of positive emotion, speakers can be aware of the appropriateness of their facial expressions, body orientation and movement, and gestures involving arm, hand, and finger orientation. As necessary, speakers can query coparticipants about the appropriateness of their interactions while speaking, and when they are listening. Active listening also needs to orientate toward the interests of the collective, being aware that listeners' actions should encourage high quality speech and should not discourage the speaker from speaking.

If and when a speaker is intentionally or unintentionally harming others, it is appropriate for anyone in the collective to act in ways that prevent further harm from being done. That is, compassion and care are characteristics of mindful interaction.

When a person speaks, it is important that they maintain the focus of dialogue until a particular topic or issue has been resolved to the satisfaction of the collective. For example, the focus of a person's talk should be in synchrony with what was previously said – unless the group has decided to move on to a new focus issue.

The quality of interaction should reflect respect for others and values such as: not interrupting them, and sharing the amount talk and the number of speaking turns. Importantly, the speaker should not be a turn shark – i.e., begin to speak when it is someone else's turn to talk. To the extent possible, participants should enact culture fluently, without stopping and starting. Factors that can influence fluency are loudness, frequency, timbre, and intonation. In addition, the speaker needs to ensure that speech is relevant, appropriate, and timely i.e., the right speech at the right time – delivered in a viable manner. Talking and commenting while another is speaking may be appropriate in some situations while disrespectful in others. A number of factors can breach the flow of speech. For example, asynchronous speech, such as speaking over or speaking under the previous speaker can be discordant. Similarly, while speaking it makes a difference if the speaker holds eye contact with coparticipants, and so too does the presence and nature of gestures, head nods, smiles, and head orientation (Roth & Tobin, 2010). In much the same way, facial expressions make a significant difference to the quality of interactions (Ekman, 2004).

As we have noted previously, synchrony is an important characteristic of every turn of talk – that is, whether or not a given utterance forms an effective bridge with what comes before and provides a bridge to what will follow. Questions that arise in relation to synchrony go beyond physical characteristics of the sound and include perceived benefit of what is said to others, whether it was the speaker's turn to talk, if the speaker has been talking too often or perhaps not enough, and the extent to which others listen to, and value, what the speaker is saying.

7.2   *Being Aware of Emotional Styles*

The extant emotions of self and others ameliorate learning and participation. Richard Davidson and Sharon Begley (2012), described five emotional styles that characterize people's emotional state in interactions with others. Resilience refers to the extent to which a person can recover, or bounce back, from adversity. Outlook concerns the length of time a person can sustain positive emotions. Social intuition involves the capacity to detect social signals concerning others' emotional states. Self-awareness requires awareness of self-emotions that occur in the moment and enacting changes if and as necessary. Sensitivity occurs when a participant regulates emotions and associated actions in relation to their appropriateness in a particular context. Finally, attention is the extent to which a participant is sharp and clear in the focus of their actions and interactions.

Heightening awareness about emotional styles affords reflection in practice, whereby participants can identify characteristics of one or more emotional styles, and invite dialogue about whether changes are desirable. Similarly, recognizing characteristics of specific emotional styles in others can lead to changes in the moment in an endeavor to act in ways that are appropriate for a participant's concerns about the use of appropriate practices, given a context of particular emotional styles.

7.3   *Emotion and Physiology*

Expressed emotions are closely related to the body's physiology, including factors such as pulse rate, blood oxygen levels, blood pressure, body temperature, breathing patterns, breathing force, and the mode of entry of the breath in and out of the body i.e., nasal or oral. The body's physiology effects expressed emotions and vice versa. Also, actions, including speech, effect emotions and also the body's physiology.

Pierre Philippot, Gaëtane Chapelle, and Sylvie Blairy (2002) described how breathing patterns produced characteristic emotions and vice versa. For example, happiness was produced when the breath was slow, deep, regular, and through the nose. Similarly, anger occurred when the breath was fast, deep, irregular and nasal. Sadness was evident when nasal breathing was characterized as having average amplitude and frequency. In an extension of this work my colleagues and I related pulse rate and the concentration of oxygen in the blood to expressed emotions and the speaker's prosody (Tobin, King, Henderson, Bellocchi, & Ritchie, 2016). Through the lenses of polyvagal theory (Porges, 2011), we illustrated that the quality of spoken words was higher when the speaker had normal levels of blood oxygen (especially not too low) and average pulse rate (especially not too high). In contrast, when pulse rate was high and/or blood oxygenation was low, the timbre of the voice was consistent with fight-flight (i.e., sympathetic) functioning and expressed emotions of anger and fear. In a later study, we concluded that parasympathetic functioning and expressed positive emotions were more likely when nasal inhalation and nasal exhalation occurred (Tobin, 2018).

- I listen with the purpose of understanding what is said
- I show interest by connecting nonverbally with speakers
- I seek deeper understanding of what has been said before I offer alternatives
- I am aware of others' emotions
- I provide time to allow speakers to complete their talking turn
- I am aware of my breathing as I speak
- I use belly breathing
- I breathe in and out through my nose
- I do not monopolize talking time
- I am aware of whose turn it is to talk next
- I use my breath to control my emotions
- I use my breath to control the harmony in my body (e.g., pulse, blood oxygenation, body temperature)
- I monitor the loudness of my voice
- I am aware if my voice is shrill
- I maintain interest by varying the intonation of my voice
- I monitor my gestures and body orientation
- I take appropriate action when social violence occurs

FIGURE 2.3   Characteristics developed for mindfully interacting

Based on what we learned from numerous ongoing studies we developed a heuristic to serve as a potential agent for change/improvement of interacting with others, in classes of various persuasions and more generally in social life. A sample of characteristics that we used in the heuristic are presented below. Even based on the partial review above it is quite apparent that additional characteristics could be included in the heuristic or to replace one or more of those that are included in Figure 2.3.

8   Abdominal Breathing to Ameliorate Unwanted Emotions

Our initial foray into meditation was grounded in an intention to ameliorate intense and unwanted emotions if and when they arose. Most commonly, such emotions were on the anger spectrum. The rationale for using the breath as an intervention was based on my experience of meditating to calm the mind. Although our intended use was secular, my experience was associated with Buddhist meditation, primarily informed by an American Tibetan approach that emphasized constructs such as compassion, empathy, and lovingkindness (Tobin, 2016a). Breathing was regarded as a reliable way of calming a 'monkey mind,' where scattered thoughts skipped from issue to issue, often driven by high levels of stress in the body. In many instances, the stress was associated with a commute to College in a huge bustling city – usually following a full day of work. We recognize that learning environments would be improved by less stress and calmer mind states.

After years of studying physiological expression of emotion, we were aware of research that connected breathing patterns with emotions (e.g., Philippot, Chapelle, & Blairy, 2002), and we felt an ethical obligation to ensure that high intensity emotions did not catalyze serious health projects, such as stroke, heart ailments, and myriads of lifestyle issues associated with stress (Tobin, 2016b). When one of our teacher | researcher colleagues announced 'teaching makes me sick,' following heart surgery, we knew it was time for us to proactively intervene in our research to ameliorate excess emotions, if and when necessary (Tobin & Llena, 2011).

In the Brooklyn College study (Alexakos, 2015), we fully committed to authentic inquiry and the necessity to enact emergent and contingent research that seriously addressed authenticity criteria. Accordingly, we incorporated practices such as coteaching, cogenerative dialogue, polysemia, polyphonia, and radical listening into our practices as we proceeded to study emotions, physiological expression of emotions, and amelioration of unwanted emotions.

When we consider the use of breathing meditation in this collaborative study, it took some time to reach consensus on how best to do this in a secular way. Finally, consensus was reached, to the effect that we would use two former students to teach the class how to use belly breathing in a 3–5 minute meditation. Since the class was scheduled for three hours, we planned to do two meditations – one at the beginning of class and the second mid-way through the scheduled time. Students who did not wish to participate could opt out of the activity. A few students opted out, but nearly all of the class participated in breathing meditation activities.

We were struck by the success of breathing meditation in meeting our primary goals of settling the class down and thereby affording focus and high-quality participation. Quickly, ripple effects occurred as those of us who were teaching other classes began to use breathing meditation and undertake authentic inquiry on what was happening, why was it happening and what more was there. In this way breathing meditation was used in middle, high school, and teacher education classes.

9 Emergence of Free Writing as a Contemplative Activity

In my doctoral level classes at the Graduate Center, we began each class with five minutes of breathing meditation, and students from the class cotaught during each scheduled session, usually in pairs or in threes. A pattern began to emerge following breathing meditation sessions. After five minutes of quiet, there was a tendency for participants to erupt into talk and even humor, which caused the entire class to laugh. In other words, the intended calm was ruptured by undesirable practices that unsettled the just-established, calm state of the learning environment. We decided that the breathing meditation activity should be followed by a freestyle writing activity of 5–10 minutes duration. Initially we were concerned that a total of 15 minutes contemplative activity would be too much time in a scheduled 2-hour class. However, we finally settled on 10 minutes for the free write, because the results of the activity were considered to be highly favorable (Tobin, 2016a). Most students wrote fluently, on a topic of their own choice, for the entire time. Given the necessity for doctoral students to complete a dissertation, and the frequency with which students reported writing blocks, the freestyle writing activity appealed as a way to overcome what is colloquially called writers' block.

In some cases, the name of the activity was truncated to free writing or free write. The best label depended upon the context in which the writing assignment was grounded. For example, in some classes the teacher preferred that students write freely about the topics to be discussed in the class today, or the readings that had been assigned for today. In other classes teachers regarded the activity as a way to give voice to the authors, allowing them to write about anything they so desired. This was my preference, since I was gradually seeing the free write as a contemplative activity. In fact, in my own mind I thought of it as mindfully writing. Writing fluently would be the focus object for the activity, but there would be no effort to force the mind to write on any particular topic.

As the mind wanders, so too can the writing stream. In this case, it is important to notice the wandering, but not to control it. The potential of thinking about the free write in this way, is that dissertations and other writing activities, such as preparing chapters for books, could be formulated as a mindful activity, to be edited at some later time.

The principal advantages of the free write were, from our perspective, that they allowed students to write with a calm mind, without forcing the mind to focus. Rather than control the mind to write about a particular topic, it was as if the activity gave free rein to the mind to write what was on an individual's mind at that particular moment in time. As was the case with breathing meditation, the free write activity was incorporated into classes taught by Konstantinos as well as those taught by our students. Some of them too undertook research on the use of meditation followed by free writing as a transformative practice.

10   Toward a Holistic Methodology

Although the authenticity criteria have been developed as a set of four, it is important to emphasize that we regard them as constituents of a whole – that is, the four criteria coexist, and together they are more than the sum of the parts. There is a dialectical relationship between the four authenticity criteria, an indicator that there is not a necessary linear alignment that begins with ontological authenticity and ends with tactical authenticity. On the contrary, all four authenticity criteria coexist, and changes in any one, perturb and thereby transform all others. In addition, we emphasize that there is no temporal isolation that militates against ongoing changes, that we refer to as ripple effects, in all of the authenticity criteria. Authentic inquiry is undertaken in a context of an ethic of care. We hasten to include compassion and remind readers that care and compassion apply to all, not only to all others, but also to self.

The implications of the constituents of authentic inquiry being dialectically interrelated include a caution against exercising criteria as an ordered set that begins with ontological authenticity and concludes with tactical authenticity. All criteria coexist and presuppose existence of the other. We regard our dialectical perspective of authentic inquiry as a hedge against reductionism.

When we first appropriated authentic inquiry, we adapted Guba and Lincoln's fourth generation evaluation for use as research methodology. Over the years, we appreciated the value of the methodology in evaluation contexts – that is, the methodology could be a foundation for evaluating any activities. For example, cogens were used extensively as both research methodology and as a constituent of learning environments. It was clear that using the label of cogen was no guarantee of a high-quality learning environment or that teachers and students were enacting cogen authentically. Our use of authentic inquiry as an evaluative framework served as an opportunity to examine what was happening and why it was happening from diverse perspectives, and also to transform what was happening to improve quality and ensure that beneficence was equitably distributed during activities that participants considered to be cogenerative. Similarly, authentic inquiry was an ideal framework for evaluating the quality of activities such as coteaching, meditation, mindfulness, and radical listening.

11 Ripple Effects

As we illustrate in the following examples, authentic inquiry acknowledges and assumes that cultural production, that is unbounded, propels ripples across time and space; seamlessly interpenetrating lifeworlds. Accordingly, cultural production that occurs in a study, becomes a resource for further production, that is, reproduction and transformation, in an unbounded sense.

The idea of ripple effects is that participants in authentic inquiry learn from doing authentic inquiry and from being with others as authentic inquiry is practiced. Furthermore, as participants enact activities throughout their lifeworlds, they enact aspects of authentic inquiry with and without awareness, if and when it is appropriate to do so. Through the use of the tenets of authentic inquiry throughout lifeworlds, an increasing number of participants experience, and can appropriate authentic inquiry to improve the quality of their lives.

Ripple effects can spread benefits from a study to permeate participants' lifeworlds. For example, a study that was situated in a public high school produces culture (i.e., schemas and practices) that is enacted within the school and then, as and if desirable, in other fields in which participants engage. In so doing, other people in those fields interact and also produce new culture.

That is, learning occurs throughout social life, reminding us that fields are unbounded and that a change in any social space can catalyze changes elsewhere/everywhere. This stunning realization drew our attention to the salience of studying teaching and learning for participants along a birth through death continuum, everywhere and anywhere. Just as learning in schools can spread benefits throughout lifeworlds, it follows that learning in any social space can benefit school learning, and more generally in enhancing learning/practices throughout the social spheres in which humans participate.

11   *Glancing Back While Looking Ahead*

In the time since we first adapted and adopted *Fourth Generation Evaluation*, we have evolved a powerful methodology that has given equal weight to each of the authenticity criteria. The purposes of research are grounded in the four authenticity criteria, and research and project designs are focused on those criteria. Authentic Inquiry, the label we adopted, is a powerful framework that acknowledges a dialectical relationship of theory (ontological and educative authenticity) and practices (catalytic and tactical authenticity). As a theoretical framework, we began to envision possibilities that expanded our research projects in terms of focus. Notably, we undertook research in every class we taught – for the purpose of improving teaching and learning in graduate level programs. The equal weighting given to learning from research to improve institutions and equitable learning for all, encouraged us to design and enact inquiry along a birth through death continuum, and to learn about teaching and learning in any context in which learning might occur e.g., home, hospital, prison, senior citizen centers. Also, we moved on from studying science education, mathematics education, and urban education to embrace wellness, meditation, mindfulness, and specific health projects including diabetes, high blood pressure, effects of Pranayama Yoga, and educating for death and dying. Common to these changes was authentic inquiry and its value for emergent and contingent designs. For us authentic inquiry became an evaluation methodology to not only research and investigate but also to assess the quality of coteaching activities and cogenerative dialogue, for example.

Authentic inquiry is an affordance that provides a structure for bricolage, embracing theories and methodologies that include polysemia, polyphonia, event-oriented inquiry, narrative, theoretical generalizability, and ripple effects of beneficence. In the next chapter, I, Ken, address other central parts of our methodological bricolage – characteristics that have enhanced the relevance of our research and have continued to expand the nature of research, especially collaborative efforts that include all stakeholders as co-researchers in studies designed to expand what we know, produce new ways to view learning and teaching, and regard research as an indispensable ingredient of improving quality of practice and benefiting all in socially just ways.

References

Alexakos, K. (2015). *Being a teacher | researcher: A primer on doing authentic inquiry research on teaching and learning.* Sense Publishers.

Alexakos, K., & Pierwola, A. (2013). Learning at the 'boundaries': Radical listening, creationism, and learning from the 'other.' *Cultural Studies of Science Education, 8,* 39–49. doi:10.1007/s11422-012-9470-7

Anderson, E. (1999). *Code of the street: Decency, violence, and the moral life of the inner city.* W.W. Norton.

Bakhtin, M. M. (1981). *The dialogic imagination.* University of Texas Press.

Bourdieu, P. (1992). The practice of reflexive sociology (The Paris workshop). In P. Bourdieu & L. J. D. Wacquant (Eds.), *An invitation to reflexive sociology* (pp. 216–260). The University of Chicago Press.

Davidson, R. J., & Begley, S. (2012). *The emotional life of your brain: How its unique patterns affect the way you think, feel, and live-and how you can change them.* Hudson Street Press.

Derrida, J. (1998). *Monolingualism of the other; Or, The prosthesis of origin.* Stanford University Press.

Eisenhart, M. (2009). Generalization from qualitative inquiry. In K. Ercikan & W-M. Roth (Eds.), *Generalizing from educational research* (pp. 51–66). Routledge.

Ekman, P. (2004). *Emotions revealed. Understanding faces and feelings.* Phoenix.

Engeström, Y. (2001). Expansive learning at work: Toward an activity theoretical reconceptualization. *Journal of Education and Work, 14,* 133–156.

Erickson, F. (1986). Qualitative research on teaching. In M. C. Wittrock (Ed.), *Handbook of research on teaching* (3rd ed., pp. 119–161). Macmillan.

Garfinkel, H. (1967). *Studies in ethnomethodology.* Prentice Hall.

Geertz, C. (1973). *The interpretation of cultures.* Basic Books.

Greene, M. (1994). Postmodernism and the crisis of representation. *English Education, 26,* 206–219.

Guba, E. G., & Lincoln, Y. (1989). *Fourth generation evaluation.* Sage Publications.

Kincheloe, J., & Berry, K. (2004). *Rigour and complexity in qualitative research: Conceptualizing the bricolage.* Open University Press.

Kincheloe, J. L., & Tobin, K. (2009). The much exaggerated death of positivism. *Cultural Studies of Science Education, 4,* 513–528. doi:10.1007/s11422-009-9178-5

Lévinas, E. (1999). *Alterity & transcendence* (M. B. Smith, Trans.). Columbia University Press.

Philippot, P., Chapelle, G., & Blairy, S. (2002). Respiratory feedback in the generation of emotion. *Cognition & Emotion, 16*, 605–627.

Porges, S. (2011). *The polyvagal theory: Neurophysiological foundations of emotions, attachment, communication and self-regulation*. W.W. Norton & Company.

Ricœur, P. (1991). *From text to action: Essays in hermeneutics, II*. Northwestern University Press.

Roth, W.-M., & Tobin, K. (2010). Solidarity and conflict: Prosody as a transactional resource in intra- and intercultural communication involving power differences. *Cultural Studies of Science Education, 5*, 807–847.

Schutz, A. (1962). Common sense and scientific interpretation of human action. In M. Natanson (Ed.), *Collected papers I—The problem of social reality* (pp. 3–96). Martinus Nijhoff.

Sewell, Jr., W. H. (1992). A theory of structure: Duality, agency and transformation. *American Journal of Sociology, 98*, 1–29.

Sewell, Jr., W. H. (1999). The concept(s) of culture. In V. E. Bonell & L. Hunt (Eds.), *Beyond the cultural turn* (pp. 35–61). University of California Press.

Sewell, Jr., W. H. (2005). *Logics of history: Social theory and social transformation*. University of Chicago Press.

Swidler, A. (1986). Culture in action: Symbols and strategies. *American Sociological Review, 51*, 273–286.

Tobin, K. (Ed.). (1993). *The practice of constructivism in science education*. Lawrence Erlbaum & Associates.

Tobin, K. (2006). The changing faces of research in science education: A personal journey. In K. Tobin & W.-M. Roth (Eds.), *The culture of science education: Its history in person* (pp. 47–58). Sense Publishers.

Tobin, K. (2009a). Tuning into others' voices: Radical listening, learning from difference, and escaping oppression. *Cultural Studies of Science Education, 4*, 505–511. https://doi.org/10.1007/s11422-009-9218-1

Tobin, K. (2009b). Repetition, difference and rising up with research in education. In K. Ercikan & W.-M. Roth (Eds.), *Generalizing from educational research* (pp. 149–172). Routledge.

Tobin, K. (2016a). Mindfulness as a way of life: Maintaining wellness through healthy living. In M. Powietrzynska & K. Tobin (Eds.), *Mindfulness and educating citizens for everyday life* (pp. 1–24). Sense Publishers.

Tobin, K. (2016b). Connecting science education to a world in crisis. *Asia-Pacific Science Education, 1*. doi:10.1186/s41029-015-0003-z

Tobin, K. (2018). Methodological bricolage. In S. M. Ritchie & K. Tobin (Eds.), *Eventful learning: Learner emotions* (pp. 31–55). Brill | Sense.

Tobin, K., King, D., Henderson, S., Bellocchi, A., & Ritchie, S. M. (2016). Expression of emotions and physiological changes during teaching. *Cultural Studies of Science Education, 11*, 669–692. doi:10.1007/s11422-016-9778-9

Tobin, K., & Llena, R. (2011). Producing and maintaining culturally adaptive teaching and learning of science in urban schools. In C. Murphy & K. Scantlebury (Eds.), *Coteaching in international contexts: Research and practice* (pp. 79–104). Springer.

Tobin, K., Seiler, G., & Smith, M. W. (1999). Educating science teachers for the sociocultural diversity of urban schools. *Research in Science Education, 29*, 68–88.

Tobin, K., Seiler, G., & Walls, E. (1999). Reproduction of social class in the teaching and learning of science in Urban high schools. *Research in Science Education, 29*, 171–187.

Varela, F. (1997). The naturalization of phenomenology as the transcendence of nature. *Alter, 5*, 355–381.

von Glasersfeld, E. (1993). Questions and answers about radical constructivism. In K. Tobin (Ed.), *The practice of constructivism in science education* (pp. 23–38). Lawrence Erlbaum & Associates.

CHAPTER 3

The Spike in the Curve

Kenneth Tobin

Abstract

I begin with autobiography to show my roots in educational research, including initial denial that research in the social sciences is a viable activity. I describe a beginning that employs testing of hypotheses in quasi-experiments that adopt statistical tests of hypotheses. Then, I describe an evolution that begins with interpretive research, and adopts authenticity criteria proposed by Egon Guba and Yvonna Lincoln.

Theories of William Sewell Jr. advanced the emergence of methodologies that were appropriate for video analysis and embraced multilevel explorations of prosody and proxemics. Furthermore, Sewell's ideas about thin coherence and contradictions heralded the emergence of event-oriented inquiry, which became a staple in our research.

I use an example of research we undertook in Australia, to illustrate applications of event-oriented methodology in a bricolage that embraces multiple social theories. In so doing, I illustrate how ongoing research that is emergent and contingent, can expand to include critical studies of health and well-being. The specific endpoint of this chapter addresses the relative importance for all humans of nasal and oral breathing, and the role of nitric oxide in maintaining life and parasympathetic functioning, emphasizing implications for social communication and emergence and expression of emotion.

Keywords

event-oriented inquiry – multilogicality – oximetry – polyvagal theory – prosody – nasal breathing – mouth breathing – nitric oxide – autonomic nervous system

1   Doing Educational Research – From Never to Here's How

It does not seem so long ago that I did not believe that research in the social sciences was even a possibility. As a physics teacher at Applecross Senior High

School, in Perth, Western Australia, I remember being asked to participate in a PhD study that involved administering a questionnaire to my senior physics class. Soon after, as I discussed the questionnaire with a colleague, I remember saying that I did not believe social science could be researched in a viable way. As a student in a master's degree in physics, the only research I knew was in a science lab. At the time, I saw myself as becoming a researcher in nuclear astrophysics. That was in 1973. However, within a few years I was doing research in science education to complete my physics degree, not using questionnaires, but closely examining the quality of verbal interaction, silent pauses between utterances, and achievement in science. Perhaps the catalyst for the change was a shift in my professional goals. In 1974 I became a science teacher educator, in a Teachers College (now Edith Cowan University). By 1975, I held a strong belief that research, well done, could provide a solid framework for teaching and learning science.

Thinking back to my initial study in science education, which focused on teaching and learning science to middle school youth, from suburban schools (proximate to Perth), the transition was eased by our research in physics which included uses of statistics. In my initial studies in physics education, we were concerned with validity and reliability of measures, and employed statistical models based on the general linear model – including analysis of variance, linear multiple regression analysis, and analysis of covariance. To an increasing extent, theory was important in our research, especially as it applied to the constructs that were the foci for research e.g., types of verbal utterances, inquiry, pausing, learning and science achievement (Tobin, 1980).

Importantly, the analyses examined the significance of statistical models in terms of measured variables and interactions between them. As I progress with my research, I was able to expand to include multivariate analysis of variance, path analysis, and latent trait analysis, that we referred to as Rasch analysis (Boone, Staver, & Yale, 2014). The latter approach was salient in its concern not only for data that conformed to hypothesized models, but also to outliers. The outliers were analyzed separately from data that fitted the model being tested.

2 Adopting and Adapting Interpretive Research

Sometime in 1984, I realized that the kind of research in which I was involved was highly reductive, convergent, and highly unlikely to provide insights into teaching and learning that would persuade policymakers, or even teachers like I had been in the 1960s and early 1970s. One of my mentors, Mary Budd Rowe (1974), suggested that we needed to adopt and adapt research methods to study macro factors that seemingly overwhelmed teachers, students, school administrators, and systems of schools. As an example, she mentioned high-stakes testing. Today, as we struggle to refocus education in times of the Covid-19 pandemic, social distancing, and group size are clear examples of macro forces associated with fear of dying from a viral infection.

In my evolution as a researcher, I was dissatisfied with the prevalence of behaviorism and positivism in all aspects of research in science education. As I searched for deeper understanding of learning in terms of radical constructivism, I had growing concerns about the theories that were underpinnings for research methods – theories of method – known as methodology. For example, in my wait-time research (Tobin, 1987), I was puzzled that I spent ages pushing the boundaries on teaching and learning away from behaviorism toward neo-Piagetian theories and beyond. At the same time, there was practically no appetite to adapt analysis techniques to obtain and employ tools that would gain insights into teaching and learning in the myriad contexts that applied along a spectrum that ranged from micro to macro. There was work to be done and, in 1984, I was stunned into action by a question asked by Walter Doyle during a presentation I gave at the University of Texas at Austin. In relation to my ongoing research on wait time – which by then spanned more than a decade – Doyle focused on my efforts to design studies that controlled as much as possible, except for the variables to be manipulated. In particular, he queried my decision to provide teachers with lesson plans that enabled them to enact higher levels of inquiry-oriented teaching and learning. As I recall his point, it was: "I am more interested in what teachers and students do when they enact curricula they have designed."

Basically, Doyle's concern catalyzed changes in the way I thought about my work. By the time I visited Fred Erickson, a few days later in East Lansing, Michigan, I was well and truly ready to read and promptly apply his prepublication version of interpretive research (Erickson, 1986). Unusual for researchers at the time, Erickson focused not only on data that conformed but also on data that did not conform with emergent assertions. My change from studies that basically involved multiple regression analysis to those that embraced interpretive research felt like a tsunami had swept through what I did and why I did what I did.

First, I consider what did not change much. After I defended my master's degree, Barry McGaw, who was an external examiner of my written thesis, and a participant in an oral defense of my research, strongly advised me to become a participant observer in my research sites, so that I could capture the context in which teaching and learning occurred. Accordingly, this became a feature of my research in classrooms. I saw the value of knowing the context for my research, and classroom visits were scheduled as central and essential components. My adoption of interpretive research moved the writing of field notes into a central position as far as being "in the field" was concerned.

For many years, interpretive research was a label I applied to the methodology I employed in my ongoing research. Even though we increasingly intertwined Fourth Generation Evaluation (Guba & Lincoln, 1989) into our approach, we adopted the key tenets of interpretive research. The methodology was sociocultural, largely appropriated from cultural anthropology and Clifford Geertz's theories of culture (Geertz, 1973). We organized data that supported a pattern, that we described as an assertion. Importantly, the assertion was to have thick coherence (i.e., lots of supporting evidence) and contradictions were to be noted and explained in terms of an assertion that was regarded as an outcome of research. That is, assertions were to have thick coherence and contradictions were seen as exceptions that could be explained – while accepting the viability of the assertion.

The adoption of Egon Guba and Yvonna Lincoln's contingent, serial, and dialectical selection of participants for research pushed what we were doing out of the comfort zone for continuing with interpretive research. Also, participants were selected purposefully, never randomly. We rejected the idea of sampling and generalizing to a population from which sampling had occurred (Tobin, 2009). By selecting students and teachers who were as different from one another as possible, we were challenged to substantively address how to create assertions when differences were central to the design. Accordingly, difference became a high bar that we had to clear.

3   William Sewell's Views of Culture

Our work in urban high schools was a wake-up call in many respects. When I taught in an inner-city high school in Philadelphia, I seemed unable to appropriate science education research to even come close to achieving what was published in the literature (Tobin, Seiler, & Walls, 1999). The situation was an inconvenient truth, not only for researchers, but also for science teacher educators, professional developers, and also funding agencies. Furthermore, I had qualms about most of the educational research I had read. The *Code of the Street* (Anderson, 1999) provided me with revealing insights, just in time. Elijah Anderson was in the same university as me (University of Pennsylvania), and I realized I needed a strong background in social theory – especially cultural sociology. Accordingly, I decided I would "go back to school." I formally registered for doctoral courses in theoretical sociology. My rationale for doing this was my observation that I seemed to regard theoretical frameworks more or less like a smorgasbord. I knew what I liked, and selected accordingly. Occasionally, something new would catch my attention and I would test its efficacy. *Code of the Street* and Pierre Bourdieu's reflexive sociology (Bourdieu, 1992) are two examples of me striking gold in selecting highly appropriate resources that I chose from what was available and what I considered viable.

Several doctoral students from our program followed my selection of courses to study, and it was useful to be able to share what seemed like most promising avenues for our ongoing work. Probably, the most memorable moment to illustrate the benefits of collaborating in this way with current doctoral students occurred when a doctoral student asked me in the hallway, "did you see the article by Sewell (1992)? I think you'd like it." I hadn't read the article, even though it was listed among the readings for the class we were just about to attend. Unfortunately, the readings for any given class seemed to be impossibly vast, and I was forced to "cherry pick."

William Sewell's paper addressed structure and agency and was highly applicable to our ongoing research. In fact, it was central to the work we were doing at City High, where I was struggling as a teacher researcher (Tobin, Seiler, & Walls, 1999). My then collaborator Michael Roth and I regarded this paper as so central to our ongoing research on high school teaching and learning, and teacher education, that we referred to it as $F = ma$ – as important to us as Newton's second law was to physics.

Fortunately for us, Sewell had also authored later papers that addressed culture more directly (e.g., Sewell, 1999a, 1999b). Most salient to us was his critique of Clifford Geertz's theory that culture was characterized by patterns that had thick coherence. On the contrary, Sewell argued just the opposite – that culture was enacted and experienced as having thin coherence and ever-present contradictions. This revelation had massive implications for how we planned and enacted our ongoing research. From then on, the way we regarded contradictions was to view them as just as important as coherence others. To say it differently, the outcomes of a study would not highlight primarily the coherences with the nuance of contradictions. Instead, contradictions might be regarded as co-stars as far as what we learned was concerned. In addition, Sewell's theory made it evident that contradictions were seeds for change. At a microlevel contradictions, as they were enacted, became resources for agency of all participants or a resource for participants to construct new culture, without awareness that this was happening. This realization led us to accept agency and passivity as dialectically related, i.e., agency | passivity (Roth, 2007).

Sewell's treatment of contradictions as seeds for change drew attention to their importance in better understanding changes in classroom environments or any other educational context. At a micro level it might be expected that a contradiction would perturb the social environment in creating an unanticipated thread/stream of interactions. At a higher social level, for example at a meso level, we might notice contradictions that are significant in that they are discernibly different than what was happening and what was expected. Metaphorically we regard this as a spike in the curve. Understanding spikes in the curve in terms of the context in which they occur, can be an important step in focusing the kind of research we do. That is, identifying and probing deeper understandings about spikes in the curve could lead to deep insights into broad questions such as those we use in authentic inquiry (see Tobin, Chapter 2, this volume): what is happening, why it is happening, and what more is there?

Following Sewell's theoretical treatment of culture, we adopted and adapted his idea of a salient contradiction being an event, a methodology we described as event-oriented inquiry (Tobin, 2018). Our uses of event-oriented inquiry became part of a bricolage of theoretical frames that included methodologies like the following: emergence, contingence and purposeful selection of participants; authentic inquiry; multi-level inquiry; narratology; and many more – depending on features of the research we engaged (Tobin & Ritchie, 2011). We were on the lookout for new frames to inform our research practices.

4   Noticing and Selecting Promising Spikes

For many years, I had an adjunct position at Queensland University of Technology (QUT). In an era in which Steve Ritchie was the leading science education researcher at QUT, the research we undertook in New York City was expanded at QUT (i.e., 2009–2015). In fact, during that time our ongoing research was funded on three occasions by the Australian Research Council. With this financial support we undertook collaborative studies on emotion, using multilogical methodologies that included event-oriented inquiry.

4.1   *Rapid Pulse Rate Prior to Teaching*
Particularly noteworthy is one of our published papers on the use of event-oriented inquiry, a study of heart rate, oxygenation of the blood, and expressed emotions (Tobin, King, Henderson, Bellocchi, & Ritchie, 2016). This study was the first in which we incorporated the polyvagal theory into the framing of the research (Porges, 2009). Data from a finger pulse oximeter identified five spikes in the curve that were associated with high heart rate (before teaching); low blood oxygenation (before and while teaching) and high blood oxygenation (while teaching). Subsequent multilogical analyses included uses of

narrative, prosodic analysis, and hermeneutic-phenomenological methods to probe the nature of expressed emotions in each of the five events.

To ascertain whether or not the spikes we identified were of practical significance, we referenced the teacher's (i.e., Donna) resting heart rate (i.e., mean, 63 bpm; standard deviation, 2 bpm) and blood oxygenation (i.e. mean, 98.2%; standard deviation, 0.4%). Indicative of a high level of stress, Donna's heart rate spiked to 118 bpm – prior to start of the lesson. We re-viewed the video, either side of the spike, and selected a segment of 42 s. The average pulse rate in this segment was 107 bpm with a standard deviation of approximately 4 bpm. Accordingly, the spike was roughly 2 standard deviations above the mean for the segment, and almost 14 standard deviations above Donna's resting heartbeat. This spike seemed very high indeed and served as an indication of a need for further inquiry. In proceeding we paid close attention to Stephen Ritchie and Jennifer Newland's caution that:

> Even the most mundane aspects of an interaction may be important for the narrative and should not be simply ignored or glossed over to create a more coherent story. Events have both temporal and contingent qualities that do not always allow for a seamless narrative. Thus, when viewing video and audio data and selecting events for further analysis, it is important to keep track of the narrative in its totality. (Ritchie & Newlands, 2016)

4.2   *Low Oxygenation, Prior to Teaching*

The second event involved a drop in blood oxygenation. While we had not yet published what we learned from our uses of oximeters in schools and colleges in New York City, we knew that blood oxygenation could fall rapidly when teachers and/or students were anxious. Perhaps oxygenation levels are sensitive to intensity of expressed emotions. Even though this is speculative, there is research that suggests its efficacy (Philippot, Chapelle, & Blairy, 2002). It is an important assertion that warrants further exploration. In the study I am describing, approximately 18 min after the first event, the oxygenation of the blood dropped to 92%, remained constant for roughly 10 s, then rose to 93% before falling back to 92%. The duration of this event was 37 s, sufficiently long to underline the importance of additional research on characteristics of teaching and learning when blood oxygenation levels fall as dramatically as they did in this event. Donna's resting oxygenation level was 98% with a standard deviation of 0.4%. During the low oxygenation event, the average for the 37 s was 92% with a standard deviation of 0.3%. The drop in oxygenation was 20 standard deviations, certainly a downturn in the curve that catches our attention. What happened to cause the blood oxygenation to plummet in this manner?

4.3 Relatively High Pulse Rate While Teaching

The third event occurred at about 22 min into the lesson. During this event Donna's heart rate averaged 111 bpm and blood oxygen was a little over 97%. As was the case in reporting what we learned from all events, we did not rely only on an interpretation of the quantitative data. Importantly, we spoke to Donna, selected students, and authors of the paper to capture not only their perspectives on the two-minute event, but also in the case of the teacher and students, the lived experiences of participants – who were unaware of the reason for identifying/selecting this event. Excerpts from the dialogues with participants and co-researchers were used throughout the section dealing with this event. Also, the authors undertook analyses of prosody, which employs microanalysis of segments of speech, involving utterances of less than 10 s duration. We used PRAAT (Boersma & Weenink, 2020) to analyze prosodic features that captured our attention (i.e., spikes in the curve). For example, when Donna described youth from year 8, the word 8 was heard as a shrill sound. Accordingly, using PRAAT we examined the power of the wave in the air when 8 was uttered and compared the value to the average of surrounding utterances. Most of the energy was not associated with the fundamental frequency, but with the second formant (i.e., 1,737 Hz). We undertook analyses with an additional 6 spikes and 5 of them produced similar results. Importantly, these analyses were undertaken because one of the students from the class described Donna's teaching in this segment as shrill. As we examined the results through the lenses of polyvagal theory, we noted that average heartbeat was notably higher than the resting pulse rate and oxygenation was lower. Changes in prosody and physiological data pointed to Donna switching from parasympathetic functioning of the autonomic nervous system to sympathetic functioning (Porges, 2011). Donna likely was teaching in a fight/flight mode.

Also, we used descriptive statistics to show that the pace of speaking in this event was 3.8 syllables per second and the average number of high-intensity peaks was 2.6 per second. We felt that these data would provide a baseline for follow-up studies.

Interplay between students' analyses of the event and analyses of prosody also were revealing in that Donna increased the duration of particular words she wanted to emphasize (e.g., the word elaboration took 2.5 s to utter and 5 distinct syllables were heard), thus allowing particular syllables within words to be emphasized. Using PRAAT, we were able to illustrate how the prosody of syllables within a word, such as elaboration, varied in energy, intensity, and frequency distribution. Donna's tendency was to put more energy into the first syllable (e-lab-or-ay-tion) and to trail off in subsequent syllables. In the two-minute event, the researchers identified 10 words with similar distributions of energy, intensity, and frequency. Some students had described this pattern of emphasis to be annoying and often loud.

4.4   *Teaching with Relatively Low Blood Oxygen Levels*

The fourth event was only 38 s, short, characterized by relatively low oxygen. Once again, the researchers began with Donna's voice; a description of what happened in the event. At that stage, she did not know why the event had been selected. The average blood oxygenation was low compared to her resting blood oxygenation (i.e., 92% compared to 98%). The heart beat rate was well above the resting average, and the blood oxygenation level was well below the resting value. What was striking about the fourth event was the magnitude of the drop in oxygenation levels.

In this relatively short period of time, Donna's voice is heard as 10 distinct utterances. Each utterance, considered a burst of speech, is separated by a short interval of time. Two bursts are separated by less than one tenth of a second and the other 7 have pauses of between 0.4 s and 1.3 s. Careful re-view of the video suggests thoracic breathing and a possibility that fear and/or sadness are generated.

Each pause separating an utterance was examined as a possible site for a breath. Given the short duration of the pauses, the breaths, if they happened at all, would be short and shallow. This pattern, and its associated possibilities, were picked up in ongoing research and are described in the next section. An important issue we would study intensively in a follow-up paper was beginning to emerge as an event that would have major significance. For the first time in our research we were noticing oral inhale and exhale during speech (Tobin, 2019).

The analyses undertaken by Kenneth Tobin, Donna King, Senka Henderson, Alberto Bellocchi, and Stephen Ritchie involved video analyses in the form of a frame-by-frame micro-analysis. In addition, the researchers employed prosodic analysis, facial expression analysis, and oximetry. Of course, the research incorporated student narratives, that were blind to reasons for selecting the video vignette. Only when students had exhausted what they had to say about the vignette did we suggest they consider breathing as a potential factor. One student remarked that the vignette was an example of horrible breathing habits. Another student made note of Donna's use of high pitch in several places.

Finally, when one student was made aware of breathing, she noted that Donna took few breaths and at one stage appeared to run out of oxygen. She examined Donna's chest, frame-by-frame and queried – "is she breathing? I don't know!"

4.5 High Blood Oxygenation Affords Social Communication While Teaching

Finally, there was an event in which blood oxygenation was 100%, substantially higher than the resting average of 98%. The selected vignette is just over 3 min long. The researchers describe what happens in the event in a nuanced way that involves emotional effervescence, on this occasion spontaneous laughter. The focus is on proxemics initially – bodily movement and proximity to students. Note is made of Randall Collins' criteria for building solidarity – mutual focus, entrainment, and shared positive mood (Collins, 2004). Donna uses humor to create a buzz in the class and engages them in different ways.

There is consensus among the participants who were involve in the research, including Donna. The mood was relaxed and verbal interaction reflected a laid-back environment that illustrated the criteria associated with parasympathetic functioning of the autonomic nervous system. Donna and students employed the full array of tools needed for effective social communication. Students described the fifth vignette as one that showed the most engagement. Donna's prosody was described as smoother, lower energy, and quite different than in the other vignettes. Prosodic analyses aligned with the students' and Donna's narratives.

4.6 Breathing in and out through the Mouth and/or Nose

The 38 s vignette, which was based on Donna's relatively high heartbeat and relatively low blood oxygenation catalyzed ongoing inquiry (Tobin, 2019). As I mentioned earlier, the initial microanalyses were focused on where, when, and how Donna breathed and spoke during the vignette. After closely examining the visual frames and the audio track to see what evidence there was for in-breaths, we realized that we could examine the face to see what happened immediately after the last oral sound occurred. This moment in time could be ascertained quite accurately using PRAAT and hence we could then go to the same moment in time on the video recording and examine what was happening on Donna's face. To say this differently, as the pause between bursts commenced, we could examine whether there were patterns in facial expressions (i.e., we would examine facial expressions during the pauses between bursts).

Analyses revealed six shallow in-breaths involving inspiration through the mouth. Accordingly, I was curious to see whether there were similarities and differences in vignette five where oxygenation levels reached 100%. Donna also was breathing in and out through her mouth in these contexts. Was this good or bad? Speaking for myself, until this study I had never asked the question about whether I should breathe in and out through the nose, in through the nose and out through the mouth, or some other permutation. Simply put, it never crossed my mind to ask such a question.

The probe to find out whether or not it made a difference whether breathing was oral, nasal, or a mixture of both, led to a surprising revelation (Lundberg & Weitzberg, 1999). Nasal breathing affords nitric oxide entering the airways, which facilitates expansion of blood cells, increases blood flow, increases oxygen in the blood cells, and protects organs from damage (Douillard, 1994). There is a voluminous literature on problems associated with mouth breathing. For example, in dentistry it has been shown that there are numerous mouth and dental issues associated with predominantly mouth breathing, including tooth decay, smelly breath, cavities, and gingival tissue problems (Taner & Saglam-Aydinatay, 2013).

In 1998, the Nobel Prize for medicine was awarded to Robert Furchgott, Louis Ignarro and Ferid Murad for their discoveries concerning "nitric oxide as a signaling molecule in the cardiovascular system." This award and its associated research catalyzed further studies and approaches across a broad spectrum that included the development of Viagra and similar drugs that stimulate blood flow to different parts of the body and, uses of nitric oxide to improve athletic performance. The research encourages athletic coaches to train athletes to breathe in and out of the nose. Trends such as these raise the question of whether research on nitric oxide should only focus on enhancing sexual performance and on-the-field performances of athletes? Should we be focusing on educating the citizenry more broadly? Emphatically, my response to these questions are – yes, and we should start with teachers and parents. Furthermore, we should educate the elderly to utilize breathing as a hedge against health problems in old age and afford self-help in institutions such as nursing homes and hospice facilities.

Interestingly, ongoing research provides deeper insight into ways in which the amount of nitric oxide in the airways, and thereafter the circulatory system, could be maximized. For example, light steady breathing permitted higher concentrations of nitric oxide to enter the airways from the paranasal sinuses, which are the main production sites for nitric oxide, which has a relatively short half-life. What this means in effect, is that in order for nitric oxide to have maximal impact, it should enter the airways quickly, and circulate through the entire body in a short amount of time. Hence, the finding that humming while exhaling can increase the volume of nitric oxide in the airways by a factor of 10–15 is highly salient. Humming can cause exhaled air to vibrate and foster an exchange of air and nitric oxide in the sinuses and nasal cavities. Patrick

McKeown, who focused his recent work on coaching athletes, advocates everybody to train the body to sleep with the mouth shut, and thereby to maximize benefits of nitric oxide.

Since approximately 90% of the nitric oxide in the body is produced in the nose, when teachers like Donna breathe in and out through the mouth, they deprive the body of nitric oxide and its associated benefits. If oral breathing is primary, there can be lower activity in the brainstem, cerebellum, and hippocampus (Park & Kang, 2017). Chan-A Park and Chang-Ki Kang noted that lower levels of nitric oxide can negatively impact memory, attention, and academic performance. Also, as Erol Selimoglu (2005) noted, benefits of nitric oxide in the body include defense reactions against bacteria, viruses, fungi, and environmental toxins. Interestingly, increases in nitric oxide production occur when the body enters a disease state, such as when the heart is deprived of oxygen. From an educative point of view, it seems like a no-brainer to teach the citizenry about the benefits of inhalation and exhalation through the nose, breathing lightly, and humming while exhaling.

5 ... and in Conclusion

Bricolage, or multilogicality, is not a mechanistic blueprint for undertaking research. Indeed, it is quite the contrary. As a research group we had a number of methodologies that have served us well for several decades, and these are continuously refined, modified, and sometimes dramatically expanded or truncated. These included video analyses that involved frame-by-frame microanalysis of proxemics and gestures. For the same time segment in which video microanalysis occurred, we routinely undertook prosodic analysis, facial expression analysis, and studies of physiological changes based on oximeter data (e.g., heart rate, blood oxygenation). All methodologies and their collective uses are reviewed by our research squad at regular meetings in which co-researchers seek to understand what is being done at a given point in time, why it is done, and whether alternative approaches and frameworks might yield outcomes with the potential to improve the quality of social life. What methodologies are employed and when they are employed and how they are employed depend entirely on the manner in which a study unfolds and possibilities to adapt to learn things that were originally not contemplated. Certainly, we do not have a blueprint that is followed lock-step and without creative application. Indeed, the approach we adopt is artistic, requiring ingenuity; and empathy and compassion for all participants in a study. Research designs unfold throughout a study and what is done depends on what we have learned already and what we have the possibility to study and learn in the moment.

Acknowledgment

The authors acknowledge financial support from the Australian Research Council, grant number DP1210369.

References

Anderson, E. (1999). *Code of the street: Decency, violence, and the moral life of the inner city*. W.W. Norton.

Boersma, P., & Weenink, D. (2020). *PRAAT: Doing phonetics by computer* [Computer program]. Version 6.1.16. Retrieved June 9, 2020, from http://www.praat.org/

Boone, W. J., Staver, J. R., & Yale, M. S. (2014). *Rasch analysis in the human sciences*. Springer. https://doi.org/10.1007/978-94-007-6857-4

Bourdieu, P. (1992). The practice of reflexive sociology (The Paris workshop). In P. Bourdieu & L. J. D. Wacquant (Eds.), *An invitation to reflexive sociology* (pp. 216–260). The University of Chicago Press.

Collins, R. (2004). *Interaction ritual chains*. Princeton University Press.

Douillard, J. (1994). *Body, mind and sport*. Three Rivers Press.

Erickson, F. (1986). Qualitative research on teaching. In M. C. Wittrock (Ed.), *Handbook of research on teaching* (3rd ed., pp. 119–161). Macmillan.

Geertz, C. (1973). *The interpretation of cultures*. Basic Books.

Guba, E. G., & Lincoln, Y. (1989). *Fourth generation evaluation*. Sage Publications.

Lundberg, J. O. N., & Weitzberg, E. (1999). Nasal nitric oxide in man. *Thorax, 54*, 947–952. doi:10.1136/thx.54.10.947

McKeown, P. (2016). *The oxygen advantage: Simple, scientifically proven breathing techniques to help you become healthier, slimmer, faster, and fitter*. William Morrow Paperbacks (an imprint of HarperCollins).

Park, C. A., & Kang, C.-K. (2017). Sensing the effects of mouth breathing by using 3-Tesla MRI. *Journal of the Korean Physical Society, 70*, 1070–1076. doi:10.3938/jkps.70.1070

Philippot, P., Chapelle, G., & Blairy, S. (2002). Respiratory feedback in the generation of emotion. *Cognition & Emotion, 16*, 605–627.

Porges, S. W. (2009). The polyvagal theory: New insights into adaptive reactions of the autonomic nervous system. *Cleveland Clinic Journal of Medicine, 76*(Suppl 2), S86–S90.

Porges, S. W. (2011). *The polyvagal theory: Neurophysiological foundations of emotions, attachment, communication and self-regulation*. W.W. Norton & Company.

Ritchie, S. M., & Newlands, J. (2016). Emotional events in learning science. In A. Bellocchi, C. Quigley, & K. Otrel-Cass (Eds.), *Exploring emotions, aesthetics and well-being in science education research* (pp. 107–120). Springer.

Roth, W.-M. (2007). Theorizing passivity. *Cultural Studies of Science Education, 2*, 1–8. https://doi.org/10.1007/s11422-006-9045-6

Rowe, M. B. (1974). Reflections on wait-time: Some methodological questions. *Journal of Research in Science Teaching, 11*, 263–279. https://doi.org/10.1002/tea.3660110309

Selimoglu, E. (2005). Nitric oxide in health and disease from the point of view of the otorhinolaryngologist. *Current Pharmaceutical Design, 11*, 3051–3060. https://doi.org/10.2174/1381612054865037

Sewell Jr., W. H. (1992). A theory of structure: Duality, agency and transformation. *American Journal of Sociology, 98*, 1–29.

Sewell Jr., W. H. (1999a). The concept(s) of culture. In V. E. Bonell & L. Hunt (Eds.), *Beyond the cultural turn* (pp. 35–61). University of California Press.

Sewell Jr., W. H. (1999b). Geertz, cultural systems, and history: From synchrony to transformation. In S. B. Ortner (Ed.), *The fate of culture: Geertz and beyond* (pp. 35–55). University of California Press. https://doi.org/10.2307/2928814

Taner, T., & Saglam-Aydinatay, B. (2013). Physiologic and dentofacial effects of mouth breathing compared to nasal breathing. In T. M. Önerci (Ed.), *Nasal physiology and pathophysiology of nasal disorders* (pp. 567–588). Springer-Verlag. doi:10.1007/978-3-642-37250-6_38

Tobin, K. (1980). The effect of an extended wait-time on science achievement. *Journal of Research in Science Teaching, 17*, 469–475. https://doi.org/10.1002/tea.3660170514

Tobin, K. (1987). The role of wait time in higher cognitive level learning. *Review of Educational Research, 57*, 69–95. https://doi.org/10.3102/00346543057001069

Tobin, K. (2009). Repetition, difference and rising up with research in education. In K. Ercikan & W.-M. Roth (Eds.), *Generalizing from educational research* (pp. 149–172). Routledge.

Tobin, K. (2018). Methodological bricolage. In S. M. Ritchie & K. Tobin (Eds.), *Eventful learning: Learner emotions* (pp. 31–55). Brill | Sense.

Tobin, K. (Ed.). (2019). *Mindfulness in education*. Routledge.

Tobin, K., King, D., Henderson, S., Bellocchi, A., & Ritchie, S. M. (2016). Expression of emotions and physiological changes during teaching. *Cultural Studies of Science Education, 11*, 669–692. doi:10.1007/s11422-016-9778-9

Tobin, K., & Ritchie, S. M. (2012). Multi-method, multi-theoretical, multi-level research in the learning sciences. *The Asia-Pacific Education Researcher, 20*(3), 117–129.

Tobin, K., Seiler, G., & Smith, M. W. (1999). Educating science teachers for the sociocultural diversity of Urban schools. *Research in Science Education, 29*, 68–88.

Tobin, K., Seiler, G., & Walls, E. (1999). Reproduction of social class in the teaching and learning of science in Urban high schools. *Research in Science Education, 29*, 171–187.

CHAPTER 4

A Career in Research as Methodological Journey

Wolff-Michael Roth

Abstract

Many researchers begin their investigations with a statement of the method to be used, which leads them to research questions that the method can answer. This appears to be a strange way of going about research. In my career, research questions were primary and driving the method to be used – which often meant that I had to learn new ways of doing research (methods). In this chapter, I present sketches of a few of the methods that have emerged in my work in the pursuit of salient research questions over the course of my research career. For each method describe, I provide a brief description of the context in which my research question and methods have emerged; and I articulate some of the affordances that the method provides. Overarching themes in my methodological journey were reflexivity and rigor.

Keywords

authentic inquiry – video-based research – discourse analysis – applied conversation analysis – apprenticeship as method – phenomenological inquiry – interaction analysis – ethnomethodology – rigor

1 Toward a Panoply of Methods

> [S]ocial research is something much too serious and too difficult for us to allow ourselves to mistake scientific *rigidity*, which is the nemesis of intelligence and invention, for scientific *rigor*, and thus to deprive ourselves of this or that resource available in the full panoply of intellectual traditions of our discipline and of the sister disciplines of anthropology, economics, history, etc. (Bourdieu, 1992, p. 227)

Many or most scholars I have met during my professional career learned a particular research method, often during their graduate studies, and then used this method for much or all of their professional careers. There are those who specialize in designing, gathering data with, and analyzing questionnaires; there are others with a bent for discourse analysis, who collect written or verbal data and then make sense of patterns that evolve from their readings; and there are colleagues who have acquired a penchant for working according to the principles of grounded theory, collecting observational data in a particular field or interviewing research participants to identify structures (theory) that completely describe the data. I was able to witness that when research is driven by a chosen empirical method, then the world described takes features that are artifacts of the method. Personally, I have always found a fixedness of method to be a shortcoming. From early on in my scholarly career, I was marked by the proverb "If all you have is a hammer, everything looks like a nail."

I was well into my second decade as a researcher when I read a chapter on the practice of reflexive sociology (Bourdieu, 1992), which came to shape my approach to research method. Bourdieu is very critical of schools and research traditions because they lead us to take as self-evident the *evidence* – the data we collect – "because we trust a *cultural routine*, most often imposed and inculcated through schooling (the famous 'methodology' courses taught in American universities)" (p. 225). He then lists, next to a number of statistical and mathematical methods, a number of examples typical of qualitative researchers, including ethnomethodology, conversation analysis, discourse analysis, participant observation, in-depth interviewing, ethnographic observation, and event-history analysis. Bourdieu does not mean to say that working by the precepts of these methods is useless and instead critiques all "mono-maniacs" of method.

The research questions I had been posing during my four-decade-long career in research were requiring me to learn new ways of looking at and analyzing data. In this way, my professional career also became a journey across the terrains of different methods. I always was in pursuit of attempting not merely to make sense of everyday life situations (in school, at work, in leisure) but, importantly, to do research that actually identified patterned ways in which we are simultaneously making, undergoing, and understanding the world in which we are all caught up together. By the time Bourdieu's text was published, I had already been employing a variety of ways (methods) of making sense of situations in which participants were learning science or mathematics – including some of the examples from Bourdieu's list.

The most important aspect of research is the identification and refinement of the research object. It requires "constant attention to the details of the research procedure" (Bourdieu, 1992, p. 228). This attention "should have the effect to putting you on notice against the fetishism of concepts, and of 'theory,' born of the propensity to consider 'theoretical' instruments" (p. 228). Bourdieu's text struck a cord and it marked my entire subsequent professional career. It certainly constituted an important background to my continuing questioning of commonly used concepts and theories in the intellectual fields to which I contributed. For example, those identifying as constructivists will say that we construct knowledge. But I personally never felt that I was constructing what I would know some time (minutes, hours, days, weeks, or years) hence. Instead, I tended to find myself seeing, knowing, or being-able-to-do something that before I had not seen, known, or was-able-to-do. This introduces an essential, radically passive feature into our everyday lives. It is this passive aspect of our lives, which we undergo as much as contribute to making, that theories and methods have tended to miss or neglect (e.g., Roth, 2011). Researching those aspects and mounting a fundamental and existential critique of the assumptions of constructivist theory also required methods – e.g., the phenomenological forms of inquiry described below.

In his invitation to write this chapter, Ken Tobin suggested writing an autobiographical journey through method. (I differentiate *method*, the patterned ways of doing research, from *methodology*, the science and study of [different] methods.) As I was thinking about how to construct this chapter, it became apparent to me that a strictly historical approach would make little sense, for I was often doing multiple studies in parallel and focusing on very different issues. In the process, I was drawing on different methods simultaneously, some of which I was using for a first time and that I would draw on with greater competence and self-assurance only much later. It makes sense, therefore, to articulate some of the ways in which I was doing research, when and how these ways came about, and under which conditions they provide a powerful means of describing and theorizing the world.

2   Methodological Fundamentals

Two overarching themes characterize my work generally. First, there always has been a search for authenticity, that is, a search for a match between what research results describe and explain and everyday human experience, including my own. Second, my research always included large amounts of video recordings.

2.1   *Authentic Inquiry*

The focus of this book volume is on *authentic* inquiry. It was my reading "Doing Authentic Inquiry" (Tobin & Alexakos, Chapter 2, this volume) that encouraged me to pull *Fourth Generation Evaluation* (Guba & Lincoln, 1989) off the shelves and re-read the section on authenticity criteria. In reading, I realized how much of an intellectual journey (adventure) I have done and undergone because of the strangeness of the constructivist discourse. The authenticity criteria focus on the politics, ethics, and pragmatics to overcome individual views and social positions toward a version of evaluation reports that not only reflect multiple views, but also allow agents to be empowered and bring about change. My own work instead had turned to understanding what we have in common that allows us to do anything of the ilk that Guba and Lincoln describe. Thus, for example, my research has increasingly taken an ethnomethodological bent toward describing and theorizing how people in social situations themselves make visible, perceive, and undergo the patterns of a social world that they contribute to producing. That is, this particular way of conducting research is designed to identify how real people actually make their social worlds and make visible relevant aspects of the world and these different forms of making.

Today, I recognize a considerable distance between my current ways of doing research and what I had done early in my career, though the authenticity criteria were important in my early research. Thus, already in 1991–1992 school year, my students were reading, commenting on, and bringing about changes in pertinent research reports (Roth, 1994). I wanted my research results concerning "student views of concept mapping" to accurately reflect what they were telling me in the interviews. This also meant that I had to make some changes after I received feedback from about 25% of the students. During that same school year, one high school student – Todd Alexander, who today is professor of pediatric nephrology and physiology – asked me to be a co-researcher and co-author in a study on physics students' discourse about epistemology, ontology, and science (Roth & Alexander, 1997). He participated in conducting and recording interviews. We talked about what we were observing in the data sources. Finally, we wrote up a study that may have been a first in science education taking a discourse psychological perspective and employing discourse analysis.

Later, in research conducted together with Ken Tobin in Philadelphia high schools, we developed cogenerative dialoguing as a way of understanding the different points of view and positions. More so than in other work, in the resulting article we did not flatten all the different voices into a single authorial voice but constructed research articles containing original email exchanges, personal notes by different participants, records of the changing positions individuals were taking in the course of inquiry, and so on (e.g., Roth et al., 2002). The article thus reflected the artifacts we collected, the voices of the people

in the various meetings we had held, and the differential learning that participants had been undergoing. given the extensive changes between all participants – including new (preservice) teachers, resident teachers, researchers,
teacher educators, and student (representatives) – our research not only contributed to the literature but also, and foremost, became an occasion of change
that the ensemble of participants brought about together.

At the time, we – initially the researchers and soon thereafter the practitioners as well – were conceptualizing the practice in terms of cogenerative dialogue, a notion that we had come to know from participatory action
research in business and industry. We thought of cogenerative dialogue as a
practice in a dialectical relationship with coteaching, which involved the same
stakeholders (e.g., Roth et al., 2000). We recognized that there is a difference
between doing something (e.g., teaching), oriented to the goals of that activity,
and talking about something, which takes episodes of the actual practice for
the purpose of analyzing what has happened. We knew from our readings in a
number of fields, including practice theory and cultural-historical activity theory that the two activities are related to different objects and outcomes, and,
thus, involve different forms of knowing-what and knowing-how (i.e., they
come with different forms of cognition and consciousness).

At that time, I was struck by the fact that we (including Ken Tobin, I, teachers, students) were pulling off these cogenerative meetings in subsequently
recognizable ways although none of us had any prior idea about them. The
meetings emerged on the fly, certainly based on the experiences that everyone
had with other types of meetings, but also because we provided each other
with every (verbal, gestural, non-verbal) sign required to allow the meetings to
succeed. My subsequent research, much of which was conducted in non-ed-
ucational settings, was focused on how we human beings make our everyday
social world. The conditions under which I conducted research in the everyday world of work required me to develop an expanding repertoire of ways of
doing research (i.e., methods) appropriate to the ever-evolving types of question I was asking.

2.2   A Preference for Video

It certainly is part because of my biographical experiences that I developed a
preference for working with video. First, ever since I almost lost my hearing
due to a painless middle ear infection (when I was 10 years old), I have been
hard of hearing. This has made it difficult for me to deal with any form of verbal
presentation (e.g., lecture). I do not remember much of what people have been
telling me. When I first learned about qualitative research – attending many of
the presentations that researchers like Ken Tobin and his colleagues gave on

their work – I felt unable to produce the type of copious notes they produced after a day in the field. Moreover, I had little trust in being able to provide accurate and indisputable accounts of the many situations I observed. Also, when I did start doing research in my own classrooms (after having obtained my PhD), I realized that setting up a video camera recording one group of students while I was attending to all student groups would provide me with a view that I would not normally get. My early experiences showed that the transcriptions of the tapes provided me with incorruptible material about the precise nature of the words that have been articulated. It provided me with a view of the classroom that my mere presence, even as a researcher, could not have given me. In subsequent research, I had numerous experiences of practitioners who, when seeing themselves, expressed having been unaware of what they actually had said or done. Half a dozen years ago, for example, I had a discussion with a very senior pilot and manager of training in the company about what he had done in flight. Our two versions differed. When I showed him the videotape of the situation, he admitted to remembering the situation very differently. I came to experience video as an ideal medium for doing *interaction analysis* (see below), a method of analyzing data in which participants hold each other accountable based on what can be seen and heard rather than what is imputed to participants.

As a classroom teacher, I worked with just one camera: in part because the costs and cumbersome use of the VHS cameras, in part because I found out that it is difficult to manage cameras and do a good job at teaching. Later, as a university-based researcher, I moved to using two or three cameras. In whole-class sessions, one camera was oriented toward the teacher from the back of the classroom and a second one focused on students. In this way, my team and I worked to assure that we would get an appropriate sound recording. When the students broke into groups, the cameras followed individual groups. Over the period of a term, one camera might follow one group, whereas a second camera switched groups after each project or type of activity. When there was a third camera available, its operator would switch groups to yield more breadth to our data set. Or the third camera might follow around the teacher or one of several teachers present. In later research, for example, on debriefing in the airline industry, we used three cameras to observe the same three individuals (captain, first officer, examiner). Because many of these sessions also used video, and the walls of the rooms held a chalkboard, posters, and other pertinent information, the cameras were placed such that as a whole, they also recorded anything that happened in front of the wall-mounted materials. In an extreme case, I participated in a study where 10 cameras were used recording all day for an 18-day period (e.g., Roth & Jornet, 2018). Some cameras were placed on desktops, others were mounted near the ceiling, and a mobile one was moved about by participants to relevant locations of the setting (e.g., for meetings in a meeting room). In addition, all computer monitors were recorded using a screen-recording tool.

In my research team, I always insisted on "smart cameras," cameras that followed the participants and focused on detail important to the ongoing research. I experienced a counter-example early in my research career in a project with Ken Tobin. Here, the graduate student had set up the camera in the back of a lecture room and left. But, after a part of the lecture, the professor and students also left to go to a different room. When Ken Tobin and I were analyzing the videotapes, we were left with video that featured a still image (reminiscent of Andy Warhol's movie "Empire State Building"). This was only the first of numerous instances where I had observed other researchers with the same kind of video tapes. In my research, when it was impossible to be present and operate cameras – such as in the debriefing meetings between pilots and examiners – we set up enough cameras to capture the entire scene.

I generally insisted on rapid transcriptions. Already while doing research as a teacher, I was transcribing videotapes within 48 hours of having recorded them. In research that I conducted together with G. Michael Bowen, this allowed us to generate and test hypotheses in a subsequent class meeting. For example, while transcribing a tape featuring students dealing with data sets, I felt like the more data pairs they had collected, the more likely the eighth-grade students were employing mathematical means, such as statistics or graphing (e.g., Roth, 1996). I designed three different versions of the same word problem differing only by the number of data From WMR pairs; Michael arranged for having students do the task during his next lessons in the different classes he was teaching. Based on the results, the hypothesis had to be rejected. After we had finished our investigation, we learned a journal article was published in which this method was described and called *design experiment* (Brown, 1992). In this way of doing classroom research, observation is followed by classical experiments, and the results of both lead to change in the classroom. This then begins another cycle of observation and experimentation. Although we had rejected our hypothesis, Michael Bowen repeated the task with preservice science teachers. We found that a lower percentage of them were using mathematical approaches than we had seen among the eighth-grade students.

The information made available to the researcher increases with the number of cameras; and so do the constraints on the possible stories about the unfolding. I tended to encourage my graduate students to collect as much information as possible. The more information available, the more constraints there are for possible narratives covering an event. I often used an example from best-fitting graphs to make my point. When one has three data points, there are many curves of lower order best-fit curves that include all three points. But when you have 10,000 data points, the number of interesting best-fit curves (narratives) is greatly reduced. Because of the large number of cameras in the case of the software startup study, we were able to reconstruct the emergence, development, and fixation of designs even though (a) the pertinent conversations had taken place in four different locations in the premises over the course of the day right to the final report to the entire developer group and (b) the cameras were fixed.

3 Analyses of Language in Mundane Situations

During my dissertation, I had used the method of *think-aloud protocol*, which requires research participants to think aloud, articulating in words what they see, attend to, cogitate, and so on (e.g., Roth, 1991). I realized that my transcriptions did not present complete, grammatical sentences of the type that I could see appearing in the books of cognitive science that I was reading. These utterances were unlike the sentences analyzed in the books on semiotics that I was beginning to read after spending an evening with Umberto Eco and some educators interested in semiotics. When I began to videotape students in my physics classrooms doing open-inquiry or collaborative concept mapping, I could see again little that could be analyzed by drawing on functional grammar (e.g., Lemke, 1990). Students often only produced individual words, and sometimes talked about non-science things in the very articulation that was to contribute to the current task, such as in this exchange that occurred in my physics classroom near the end of a concept mapping session:

> 537 R: it rang already; here=s energy; this is the energy of a photon,
> 538 K: it says has the energy of;
> 539 M: ha:s-
> 540 K: and then=ll just-
> 541 M: equals-

Whereas the exchange may make little sense for a reader – e.g., "because of missing context" – these three participants did not appear to have trouble continuing in bringing their task to a close. They did so even when one student noted that the lesson-ending bell has rung. That is, they were conducting the activity such that they were always on the same page. This requires participants not only to act but also to make visible aspects of their social work in the making. Indeed, in those days I did not carry over non-science talk from the hand-written transcriptions I had made into the typed transcriptions that I was subsequently using for analysis – other than marking that there had been "side talk." Almost by accident, I returned two decades later to the hand-written transcriptions and videotapes for a conference talk countering conceptual change research. By then I had evolved enough to recognize the importance of this talk and subsequently devoted to the phenomenon several chapters in a book featuring dialogical (Bakhtinian) perspectives on classroom talk (Roth, 2009a). While working on this project, I was wondering how much of student talk had not been analyzed in other science education studies because it had been "off topic" from the teacher and researcher perspectives.

My experiences in the classroom also encouraged me to think about the claims made in the research literature concerning the conceptions and conceptual frameworks that students construct and hold in their minds. I observed, for example, that students participated in talking about issues they had never considered before (e.g., Roth, 2008). It therefore made no sense to me to hold on to the belief that we carry around conceptions and conceptual frameworks that we apply to the situation at hand. Language and their everyday life experiences appeared to provide the students with the means to produce explanations. Such experiences arising from trying to understand what was happening in the classroom, as captured by my video recordings encouraged me to look for new ways of analyzing the transcriptions I made almost on a daily basis. Two ways of dealing with transcriptions arose from my readings of books on the topics of discourse analysis and conversation analysis.

3.1   Discourse Analysis

I got into discourse analysis during the time when I was still teaching high school physics. One of the studies I conducted concerned students' epistemology, ontology, and understanding of science. The study lasted 18 months and I had collected materials that after transcription yielded over 3,500 pages of text. Some of the text resulted from student essays, others from transcribed interviews, and still others from transcriptions of discussions we periodically held concerning epistemology and ontology. An intermediate report was published from a more traditional perspective, focusing on student views and conceptions. However, while collecting and transcribing, I already was realizing that students might take very different stances – e.g., scientific knowledge is truth versus scientific knowledge is constructed – but they were doing so using the same patterns of talk. When religion was featured together with the talk about science, my high school student and I thought that all the talk could be classified in four fundamental repertoires: science is true or constructed and religion is true or constructed (Roth & Alexander, 1997). When there was conflict in the talk about science and religion, three types of discursive strategies provided students with the resources to get around it. One strategy, for example, was the "truth-will-out" device, whereby a speaker could both claim that science is social constructed (thus fallible) and that science produces (is striving toward) truth.

The same approach worked for us when, after having taken a university position, I analyzed the entire data source together with a colleague. For example, we found that students might draw on what we called an authoritative repertoire, when students referred to or quoted one or another scientific authority in support of a claim about scientific knowledge (e.g., Roth & Lucas, 1997). We realized that whereas the students differed with respect to the contents of their claims, they accepted the underlying rationales, such as the voice of authority, the role of common sense, or religious inclinations. My work at the time was inspired by discursive approaches in science studies (Gilbert & Mulkay, 1984) and the emergent discipline of discursive psychology (Edwards & Potter, 1992). These approaches seem to me more useful and closer to the reality of the research participants than the highly technical, semiotic, and structuralist approaches that others developed.

An important aspect of discourse analysis is that the object of analysis is changing. Discourse is not a property of an individual; it is not like an individual conception. Instead, the term refers to forms of talking common to a particular group of people. In one particular study we had to make this point explicit to reviewers, editors, and ultimately readers of our target research community (Hsu & Roth, 2009). In a number of occasions, Pei-Ling Hsu had recorded a biology and career education teacher introducing various careers that students would find if they were doing an internship in a range of different workplace settings. When we were critiqued that we had only one participant (i.e., $n = 1$), we pointed out that whatever had been said was for the ears of the student recipients. It was not to be foreign talk, but talk understandable by all 28 students present. Pei-Ling and I argued: "because a teacher speaks to and *for the benefit of N students*, any teacher discourse has to be understood as a phenomenon characteristic of at least $N + 1$ individuals" (p. 558). In this, as in other studies we conducted, we were more interested in the underlying common *repertoires* of talk rather than in the particular statements and claims that could be made in the domain.

The analysis of discourse patterns is so important because the patterned ways of talking have important functions, among others, in the telling of stories and memories (e.g., Halbwachs, 1950). For example, I conducted a study that analyzed what science students, teachers, and facilitators participating in an experimental curriculum on environmental issues said one year later (Roth, 2017b). The research participants remembered because of the particular ways in which narratives are constructed, including actors and heroes, successes and defeats, typical events and the outcomes thereof. Remembering, thus, is not something individual but is interactively achieved in situation and based on patterned ways of talking. The same is the case for a phenomenon that science educators have investigated under the banner of misconceptions. My sense had been that those so-called misconceptions are, from the perspective of the individual, reasonable, plausible, and often fruitful ways of talking about phenomena in our surrounding natural and social worlds (e.g., Roth, 2008). These ways of talking are common to the social world that comprehends us, and which we comprehend precisely because of this inclusion in the world. These misconceptions are so intelligible that even ardent misconception researchers recognize them all the while failing to understand that is precisely for this same reason that such talk cannot simply be eradicated. Conceptions, opinions, feelings, and other phenomena we talk about exist because of the available forms of discourse (thus also cultural-linguistic differences with respect to these).

3.2   *Applied Conversation Analysis*

Over time, my interest in everyday talk increased, and my repertoire of references started to include the works of a number of Russian scholars, including M. M. Bakhtin, V. N. Vološinov, and F. T. Mikhailov. I also was strongly influenced by the work of the later L. Wittgenstein. In the works of these scholars, language is something living, forever changing, and always to be evaluated in terms of its function in the situation at hand rather than in terms of the structural relations between words that others advocated (e.g., Lemke, 1990). A paradigm case is a little story found in the diary of the Russian novelist F. Dostoevsky, a story that both L. S. Vygotsky (1987) and Vološinov (1930) analyzed. In it, six drunken workmen had a "conversation," which consisted of six repetitions of the same swear word. Both scholars point out that the function of the word was not the same, nor was the context in which an articulation appeared, because each appeared against a background of the original and the subsequent repetitions. I always had found those analyses interesting. As it turned out, years after I had left teaching high school, I found an instant in which a similar "conversation" occurred consisting of 10 iterations of the word "penis" in my original physics classroom recordings (Roth, 2015a). A thematic diagram à la Lemke would not have led me (or Vygotsky and Vološinov) very far – including because I would have to drop some of the talk, such as "it rang already" in the previously featured excerpt. Instead, it made more sense to understand Dostoevsky's and my situation in terms of a language game – language and the activity to which it belongs – and the game included as an important component its intonation. By the time I did this work, I already had had a lot of experience with conversation analysis (e.g., Sacks, 1992), especially in its applied rather than purely linguistic form as a method for investigating language in use for the constitution of social reality.

Conversation analysis does not simply mean analysis of conversation, as some non-initiates tend to think. Instead, it is a disciplined way (method) of investigating particular routines in talking turns at talk. Many educators are familiar with the term *IRE*, an acronym referring to a patterned exchange in which one person *i*nitiates a sequence, a second person *r*esponds, and the first person then *e*valuates the reply. In school situations, teachers tend to take the first and third turn in this pattern and students take the middle turn. Applied conversation analysis is less interested in linguistic patterns and more in the social phenomena that are brought about not only by talking but also by the ways in which people gesture, move about and position their bodies, intonate, and so on. This method was an important aspect of our work in Philadelphia high schools, where we showed, for example, how in their intonations, participants in an event produced and exhibited solidarity and conflict (Roth & Tobin, 2010). Solidarity was found to be expressed in coincident rhythmic patterns (e.g., in head, hand, or leg movements and intonations) even when the speaker was not seen. Conflict, on the other hand, expressed itself in steadily rising pitch and speaking volumes.

In my work, forms of working with data sources that can be categorized as applied conversation analysis have played an increasing role in the kinds of research questions I was pursuing. I described and exemplified the power of this particular method in the (book-length) analysis of a five-minute episode from an Australian classroom and interview materials pertaining to it (Roth, 2013). Thus, for example, I showed how something subsequently described as "change of plans" in a student's independent research project emerged from the teacher-student relation, which itself unfolded over the course of the classroom episode. The teacher and student together were doing the (joint) work of changing plans. In this, they also produced a particular classroom episode endogenously, on the spot, and by taking into account (and being subject to) the specifics of the ongoing situation. Among other important issues, I showed that knowledge and power are not things that participants *have* or own in unequal ways but instead are (abstracted) parts of a relation. Who knows and can do what is an outcome of a relation, which itself is under development. The development of the episode could therefore not be attributed to this or that student or teacher characteristic. Because this way of approaching language-in-use focuses on how any one turn at talk or listening arises *in* and *out of* another, it allows me to work out an actor's point of view of the situation. Any communicative act is conditioned by a preceding act; and it is conditioned by the fact that it is oriented toward the recipient. No single turn of a *conversation* therefore belongs to the speaker (alone), for it is grounded in the talk of another, to whom the talk then returns. (Even when a person writes a diary, the language is not her own but has come from the other and, in reading, returns to the other, which sometimes is the person other than itself – at the point of writing.) It is for this very reason – i.e., the production of what is happening on the shop floor of social reality – that this particular way of analyzing data sources has become so important in my work. Undeniably, speakers may have private thoughts that are unavailable to the analyst. But these thoughts also are unavailable to other participants in the situation. They therefore do not contribute to its evolution. This evolution of the social situation is the main object of applied conversation analysis as method.

4   Toward a View from the Shop Floor of Everyday Life

Trained as a natural scientist, it came natural to me to seek descriptions and explanations of everyday life – in school and beyond – that distanced themselves from the "biased" viewpoint of the individual social actor. Scientists take a third-person perspective on the world, as phenomena are taken to be existing in themselves so that there cannot exist different perspectives (Gilbert & Mulkay, 1984). At the same time, I was taught by experience that the third-person perspective of science has little to teach me when it came to the particulars of a social situation viewed from the perspective of those who have been living and living through the situation (e.g., the science lesson). Over time, I thus became increasingly interested in the viewpoint of the participants in my research projects. This, I thought, ought to be of special interest to (science and mathematics) educators, for how are they to help students to really understand science if what the latter perceive and describe often radically differs with what scientists see and say. How do we get from our mundane experiences in the world, also characterized by the language that goes with them – i.e., our *lifeworld* experiences – to the formal sciences especially when that step requires repudiating or relativizing the former? In fact, our lifeworld experiences are the conditions of understanding science even though the latter eventually overturn the earlier common sense that allowed them to emerge (e.g., Husserl, 1939). The question of the viewpoint of the social actor therefore required methods that would allow me to see the world through the eyes of my research participants – including fish culturists, pilots, and learners of school mathematics and science. I am not referring to what participants later say about what they have experienced and why they have acted in a particular way. Instead, I am interested in the way that perceiving, acting, talking, and so on arise in the situation itself. Here I sketch three of the ways of doing research that have been helpful over the years: apprenticeship as research method, phenomenological inquiry, and interaction analysis/ethnomethodology.

4.1   *Apprenticeship as Research Method*

Craft apprenticeship has been an important concept and metaphor for organizing my ways of being in the world (Roth, 2012a). I used it from the very beginning of the work on coteaching, when I was teaching science with elementary and middle school teachers in different Canadian communities (Roth, 2002), and later in the work with Ken Tobin in Philadelphia high schools (Roth & Tobin, 2002). Apprenticeship was also the organizing metaphor for working with graduate students, a notion that probably came quite easy because of my training in physics, where graduate students learn the trade by participating in the research of their supervisors. I thought about my work as a supervisor of master and PhD theses and postdoctoral fellows in the same terms. This way of thinking has been rather foreign to my faculty colleagues, who, coming through schools of education, are more accustomed to graduate students "doing their own thing."

Apprenticeship also has been an important research method, especially when my interests in knowing and learning moved away from school science and mathematics and to all sorts of workplace and leisure settings. The fundamental idea is that we do not know some field just by watching and listening to practitioners. Instead, we have to actually learn the practice, its various ways of knowing-how to do and talk, to appreciate what people are saying, doing, orienting to, projecting, and so on. Thus, in our research on field ecologists and laboratory (experimental) biologists, I became part of a research team, at times serving as an assistant in the capture of animals, at times (a five-year period nevertheless) being an integral member of a team conducting and publishing research on fish vision (e.g., Roth, 2014). Over a five-year period, I also studied science and mathematics in fish hatcheries. Integral to that study was to participate in doing what the fish culturists were doing – e.g., feeding fish by throwing scoops of pellets as long as the fish were not satiated, learning to stop when there were signs that the food would drop to the bottom. I participated in the capture of wild salmon for the purpose of collecting eggs and milt for the purpose of hatching young salmon that would contribute to the survival of the species in a particular river. Two of my graduate students (Stuart H. Lee and

Leanna Boyer) interested in science in the everyday pursuits became members of (different) local environmentalist groups, eventually becoming sufficiently knowledgeable to take leadership roles in those organizations. Ruggero Racca, a trained scientist, put himself through a four-year apprenticeship as an electrician, documenting knowing and learning as part of his Master of Arts in education. Finally, when I did the research in the airline industry (Roth, 2017a), I took opportunities for flying small aircraft, flying in simulators of larger aircraft, and sitting on the third (jump) seat in the cockpit during commercial flights.

Through my experience, I have learned how important apprenticeship is to appreciate what people actually do. For example, I still remember how initially I might listen to two pilots during a commercial flight or in the flight simulator and everything appeared to unfold in an unremarkable way. There were no signs of any issue, and it almost appeared as if the aircraft was flying itself. I was then surprised to hear after the fact that there had been high-workload and high-stress situations. It was only over time that I could feel some of what was transpiring to the pilots without being explicitly told about it after the fact. For example, while analyzing the debriefing session including a pilot who had failed the examination in the flight simulator, I was actually flying that very same task – getting even more lost than the pilot. Similarly, when I began that research with the airlines, I was listening to (and obviously video recording) pilots working in pairs (think-aloud protocol) evaluating the pilots in videotaped scenarios. Although the evaluating pilots were speaking English, and although there were few if any unknown words, I did not know initially what they were actually talking about. Over the course of my apprenticeship in the field, I came to the point where I could participate in their evaluation talk without experiencing issues.

Apprenticeship as research method has two ways of entry to learning about a previously unknown or unfamiliar practice. First, in the course of the apprenticeship, the researcher comes to know what those in the field know. They come to see the field through participants' lenses; and they come to talk and act in appropriate ways. That is, apprenticeship as method opens up a window to seeing the field as practitioners themselves see it. A second point of entry to knowing and learning exists in the fact that as a researcher, I can document my own learning. I will thus find out about the challenges of acquiring a new practice and, thus, about how individuals become practitioners in the field more generally.

4.2   Phenomenological Inquiry

After obtaining my PhD degree, I returned to the classroom. Here I found out that what I had been researching – quantitative studies correlating short-term memory with complexity of tasks in mathematics and science – was not help-ing me to understand learning and learning problems in the everyday world of the classroom. As a teacher, I had already noticed that students often did not see – in physics demonstrations, experiments, or word problems – what was relevant from a scientific perspective. The key experience that encouraged me to investigate learning science from the viewpoint of the learner was a six-week study of an Australian physics classroom. We had videotaped all lessons using three video cameras, conducted six recorded interviews each with 12 of the 24 students in class, and many interviews with the teacher. As I was observ-ing students, I evolved the sense that not only were they seeing different things in experiments and demonstrations, but also these differences did not come to be talked about. The teacher agreed to a psychological experiment: students would be asked prior to a teacher demonstration what they would see, then, after seeing the demonstration, would record what they had seen, and, finally, would explain what they had observed (Roth et al., 1997). It turned out that 5 of the 24 students were seeing no motion – as intended by the teacher and as pre-dicted by the relevant theory – and by and large used explanations compatible with the scientific canon. But the remaining 18 students did see motion, and created theories that would explain the observed motion. After that study I was convinced that we could not design appropriate science curriculum unless we considered the fact that students often do not see what they need to see so that the theories instructors present are consistent with the observation.

A few years after that study, I was a research fellow in the area of cognition at an institute in northern Germany. My colleagues were investigating learn-ing in the context of a curriculum on static electricity. While observing stu-dents obviously struggling to make sense, some of the colleagues made quite depreciative remarks about students who do not get it and who do not want to learn physics. I borrowed the curricular materials and conducted the inves-tigations myself, keeping extensive records of what I was doing and thinking (Roth, 2006). It turned out that I was doing and seeing many of the same things that the students were doing – and this even though I had obtained a MSc in physics. I became convinced that through careful study of my own perceptual and learning processes, I could come to results that would generalize not only to the tenth-grade students in that study but also to learners more generally.

During that fellowship, I also designed an experiment in which I would take the same bicycle trip for 20 days, on each day noting before taking off what I remembered from before. Upon returning, I would note what I remembered having seen that I had not seen before. It turned out, for example, that it was only during the fifth trip that I became aware of a white post next to the road, then there was another, and yet another. The posts appeared to be at regular intervals, and, using my watch to find out my travel time, I found that if ten inter-post spaces would be equal to 1 kilometer it would yield the approximate speed I was going. I was asking myself, "Why did I not see these posts before?" Then I realized that this very question presupposed that the posts existed there before, that a teacher would have supposed since the first lesson (trip) that I had seen the posts. In a test, I would have been unable to do the calculations that I did after I was seeing the posts and then noting that they are regularly spaced. I also realized that teachers forget that there were times in their lives when they were seeing the world differently or when they did not see (get) a particular phenomenon described by someone else. It appeared to me that teachers act in a lifeworld that is quite different from that of their students. They do not realize that there is a difference but they also act as if the students were perceiving the world in the same ways that they do.

Over the years, I engaged in similar investigations and analyses. But I was also pushing my investigations further, no longer with a perspective of how they might serve science and mathematics teaching. Instead, I became interested in investigating the underlying fundamental processes. These processes, like those observed in the learning experiments, are not particular to me. Studying my own learning and perception reveals fundamental processes common to human beings generally. But this study requires rigorous first-person methods (Roth, 2012b). Although there is only one participant ($n = 1$), observations are generalizable to large populations. The trick is to tease out from the data that which is common and general and to dismiss what is particular (Roth, 2009b). The following is a simple example of how this can be done in the context of perception. When gazing at the Maltese cross (Figure 4.1a) or Necker cube (Figure 4.1b), many see one of two simple configurations (few see still others). In

a.

b.

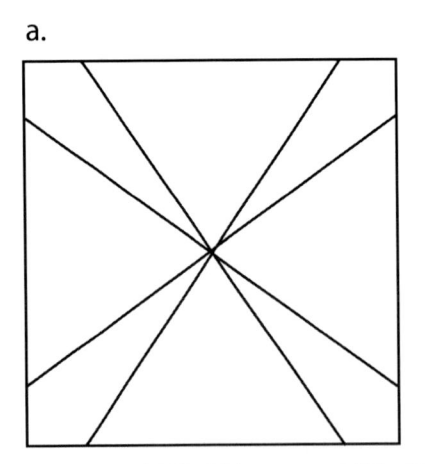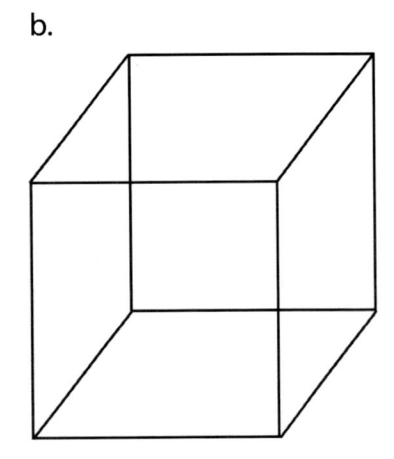

FIGURE 4.1   (a) The Maltese cross. (b) The Necker cube

the first instance, what stands out is either a cross along the diagonals with narrow blades or a cross along the horizontal and vertical axes with wide blades. In the second instance, people tend to see either a cube from below and extending to the left and back, or a cube from above and extending to the right and back. Just as in the case of individuals' views on science, epistemology, ontology, feelings, or other issues, the different perceptions may be interesting to some researchers, who then describe and report these. The method referred to as *phenomenography* is intended to achieve this – and I am only slightly interested in the collection of specimens (e.g., student views). Generally, I am not interested in just one person's views and experiences (including my own), the investigation of which often leads to woe-is-me studies that are offered up under the banner of phenomenology. My interests go further, and my method evolved from reading the works of phenomenological philosophers.

In my investigations, I ask: Under what conditions do I perceive or experience one or the other phenomenon? This requires variation and the study of the conditions under which one perception or experience occurs and those that bring about the other. Take the example of the Maltese cross. Once you are able to see one or the other cross, do this: Seeing one cross, close your eyes, intend to see the other cross, and open your eyes. As you achieve going from one perception to another, go faster and faster. Then ask: What have your eyes been doing without being told explicitly? You likely will have noticed that the focus is shifting between some point closer to the center of the bars of the cross that stands out. Similar shifts of the focus from the side face of the cube seen from below to the side face of the cube seen from above will make a quick switch between the two perceptions. It is thus the movement and the focus that allow a specific perception to emerge. What would happen if you looked at the figures without moving the eyes? This exercise is extremely difficult and takes a lot of practice but can easily be achieved with an image-fixing apparatus that psychologists have designed. Once the image is fixed, within seconds the perceptual field becomes grey. We can conclude that it is eye movement that brings about the image, and the focal point determines the particulars of the perception.

The perceptual example here is provided as an illustration of the method. Elsewhere, I show how the method can be used when the research questions pertain to aspects of mundane experience, such as memory, becoming significant, being and presence, crises and suffering, thinking and speaking, and problem solving (Roth, 2012). The method appears to be particularly apt for answering research questions that are raised in other chapters of this book, questions pertaining to emotions, contemplation, memories, and so on. Phenomenology does not mean that we just describe a phenomenon from a first-person perspective but that we describe the conditions under which a particular phenomenon comes about. In this way, we and our research community will not be drowned in a multitude of particulars but will focus on the conditions and processes that bring about all these different particulars.

4.3   *Interaction Analysis and Ethnomethodology*

Over time, I became increasingly convinced that human beings are not machine-like entities enacting plans, the origins of which are social or individual – the assumptions underlying both the constructivist and more behaviorist paradigms investigated by quantitative means., For example, I came to understand that a science or mathematics lesson is what it is because participants work together to make what it is. Thus, even the most experienced and successful teachers will be part of unsuccessful lessons. Even the most successful and empathetic teacher may contribute in essential ways to the joint work of producing disability – i.e., "losers" in schooling (e.g., Roth, 2016). This is so because teachers are not the cause of good or bad lessons (effect). They only do their part in allowing the curriculum event to emerge as it does, working together with the students. All participants are subject and subjected to what is emerging collectively, without ever knowing what will have happened once they can look back (e.g., at the hour that just passed). How do groups of people do this?

Specific social situations come about not just because people are acting ("constructing the situation"). Instead, they also contribute to making relevant issues visible to each other and by providing glosses (descriptions) of their actions. This then is how social situations can be endogenously produced without any prior plan for that specific occasion (Garfinkel, 2002). Researchers flying an ethnomethodological banner presume that such an endogenous production of structured society is possible precisely because everything required to produce an ordered world is made visible and available in the situation. To learn from and theorize a social situation, researchers need to be competent in the same cultural practices as those whom they observe. They can then see the same features that the participants in the situation make visible and available to each other. Such research is reflexive in the sense that it does not describe some hidden social or psychological patterns that are said to cause people to do what they do. Instead, this kind of research identifies what is (made) available to and is thus recognizable by the participants. The "findings" no longer concern hidden patterns that the researchers "construct," which also requires that they describe the method for doing so. Ethnomethodological research, on the other hand, seeks to identify the methods people themselves use to create and make visible any relevant aspect of the unfolding event. Interaction analysis in the way described allows us to investigate the many different ways in which human beings in everyday life not only make the social situations of which they are part but also make the situations visible in particular ways. It is a true study of the different methods of the people (Gr. *ethnos*), and thus a methodology: an ethnomethodology.

Interaction analysis is the name of an analytic practice that has evolved from the concerns of researchers to document and theorize the endogenous production of the social world (Jordan & Henderson, 1995). The practice fundamentally involves groups of researchers – in which only one of them might actually be working on the data – analyzing together some videotaped materials. The term *interaction* refers to events on two levels. On the one hand, those featured in the videotape interact producing what can be seen to be a specific recognizable social situation – e.g., most people will generally be able to identify a scene as schooling even in the absence of any introduction or commentary. Those participating in the analytic session also interact for the purpose of producing descriptions of what is happening (Figure 4.2). The single most important rule for the analysis is that participants in the data session are not allowed to *speculate* what people in the video might be thinking, intending, etc. Instead, every contribution to the analytic discussion has to be grounded in the video-based materials at hand. This means that to understand what is going on, the analysts have to hear what is said in the way that the participants themselves hear each other. The participants themselves therefore should be able to recognize what the researchers say about the situation. There no longer is a gap between practice and theory, because the methodological competencies (the *knowing-how*) required for understanding what is happening are the

FIGURE 4.2   A typical interaction analysis setting with a team of researchers investigating knowing and learning in a start-up. Multiple monitors allow the concurrent presentation of video, transcription, and any other pertinent information.

same that are required for pulling off the situation in the patterned ways in which it presents itself. It is therefore not surprising that books and journal articles featuring studies from ethnomethodological perspectives do not have to describe methods in a special section. Instead, the methods described are those of the research participants as much as those of the researchers and their readers. The description of the relevant methods is the purpose of the text, and thus does not have to be provided in a separate methods section.

We – e.g., my former postdoctoral fellow Alfredo Jornet and I – used inter-action analysis sessions in traditional university-based methods courses and, importantly for the professional development of graduate students, as a con-text for learning by participating in research (e.g., Roth, 2020). We generally video record tape such sessions. The recordings are particularly helpful for graduate students and other new researchers because they can subsequently review what has been said and done, which they could then use in their own preparation of research articles and dissertations.

When I teach research methods – e.g., the topics of interaction analysis, applied conversation analysis, or rigor in qualitative research – I model and then invite students into a kind of game (cf. Roth, 2015b). I ask one student to transcribe a small part of a video featuring a social situation of their interest and to bring the transcription to the class meeting. The students are asked not to use any identifying information, such as "teacher" or "journalist" or names, unless these are provided in the transcribed exchanges themselves. The aim of the game is to say as much as possible about who the actors are, what kind of situation they are part of, and so on. At the end of the analysis session, the stu-dent who brought the transcription will provide the judgment about whether the earlier analyses have been right or wrong. Because of the lack of identifying materials other than what the participants in the transcription make available to themselves, the participants in the analysis session are forced to focus on what they actually do and say with their words. I have not experienced a sin-gle situation where we have been wrong. Personally, I even have been able to detect when graduate students were building traps, for example, by using the same letter for marking a speaker even though there were three different indi-viduals or situations (e.g., a journalist interviewing a principal, the same jour-nalist presenting his report on television, and the news anchor).

5   Coda: Rigor and Reflexivity

Throughout my career, and perhaps because I trained as a natural scientist and as a statistician, I aimed for rigor in qualitative research. I could never buy into the argument that research produced just interpretations. I held it with the statement that the interpretation of data "has nothing to do with the sort of relativistic epistemological *laissez faire* which seems to be so much in vogue in some quarters" (Bourdieu, 1992, p. 227). A laissez faire attitude leads to anything goes. I never wanted to do research in which anything goes, as in, "Just make it up." I wanted my research to be rigorous, and also reflect aspects of human experience that are relevant to human beings more generally. Throughout my career, I also have been concerned with the distance between theory and practice, the patterns researchers claim to be underlying the social world and the social world that people make and recognize throughout their everyday lives. That is, I wanted my research to be reflexive. I therefore questioned the value of both quantitative and qualitative studies that do not consider what is happening, perceived, and done *on the shop floor* where the social world is made.

A second important aspect characterizing my approach to research is the fact that I could not ever buy into research that ended up telling the story of this or that person without attempting to show what we can learn about the human condition more generally in this one example. In this, I never sidestepped the challenge "*systematically* to interrogate the particular case by constituting it as a 'particular instance of the possible' ... in order to extract general or invariant properties that can be uncovered only by such interrogation" (Bourdieu, 1992, p. 233). I often challenged my graduate students by asking them, "Why would I be interested in reading the story if it pertains only to one person?" But if this one story is pertinent and of interest to someone else, one has already overcome solipsism and made at least a first step to identifying ways of describing and theorizing phenomena relevant to more than one person. But if a story can be told and is intelligible then there are also aspects that generalize across situations and people. Making these stand out is perhaps the most important aspect of all of research.

References

Bourdieu, P. (1992). The practice of reflexive sociology (The Paris workshop). In P. Bourdieu & L. J. D. Wacquant (Eds.), *An invitation to reflexive sociology* (pp. 216–260). University of Chicago Press.

Brown, A. L. (1992). Design experiments: Theoretical and methodological challenges in creating complex interventions in classroom settings. *Journal of the Learning Sciences, 2*, 141–178.

Edwards, D., & Potter, J. (1992). *Discursive psychology*. Sage.

Garfinkel, H. (2002). *Ethnomethodology's program: Working out Durkheim's aphorism.* Rowman & Littlefield.

Gilbert, G. N., & Mulkay, M. (1984). *Opening Pandora's box: A sociological analysis of scientists' discourse.* Cambridge University Press.

Guba, E., & Lincoln, Y. (1989). *Fourth generation evaluation.* Sage.

Halbwachs, M. (1950). *La mémoire collective* [*Collective memory*]. Presses Universitaires de France.

Husserl, E. (1939). Die Frage nach dem Ursprung der Geometrie als intentional-historisches Problem [The question concerning the origin of geometry as intentional-historical problem]. *Revue Internationale de Philosophie, 1,* 203–225.

Hsu, P.-L., & Roth, W.-M. (2009). An analysis of teacher discourse that introduces real science activities to high school students. *Research in Science Education, 39,* 553–574.

Jordan, B., & Henderson, A. (1995). Interaction analysis: Foundations and practice. *Journal of the Learning Sciences, 4,* 39–103.

Lemke, J. L. (1990). *Talking science: Language, learning and values.* Ablex.

Roth, W.-M. (1991). The development of reasoning on the balance beam. *Journal of Research in Science Teaching, 28,* 631–645.

Roth, W.-M. (1994). Student views of collaborative concept mapping: An emancipatory research project. *Science Education, 78,* 1–34.

Roth, W.-M. (1996). Where is the context in contextual word problems? Mathematical practices and products in Grade 8 students' answers to story problems. *Cognition and Instruction, 14,* 487–527.

Roth, W.-M. (2002). *Being and becoming in the classroom.* Ablex/Greenwood.

Roth, W.-M. (2006). *Learning science: A singular plural perspective.* Sense Publishers.

Roth, W.-M. (2008). The nature of scientific conceptions: A discursive psychological perspective. *Educational Research Review, 3,* 30–50.

Roth, W.-M. (2009a). *Dialogism: A Bakhtinian perspective on science and learning.* Sense Publishers.

Roth, W.-M. (2009b). Phenomenological and dialectical perspectives on the relation between the general and the particular. In K. Ercikan & W.-M. Roth (Eds.), *Generalization in educational research* (pp. 235–260). Routledge.

Roth, W.-M. (2011). *Passibility: At the limits of the constructivist metaphor.* Springer.

Roth, W.-M. (2012a). Apprenticeship: Toward a reflexive method for researching "education in 'non-formal' settings." In S. Delamont (Ed.), *Handbook of qualitative research in education* (pp. 195–208). Edward Elgar.

Roth, W.-M. (2012b). *First-person methods: Towards an empirical phenomenology of experience.* Sense Publishers.

Roth, W.-M. (2013). *What more? In/for science education: An ethnomethodological perspective.* Sense Publishers.

Roth, W.-M. (2014). *Graphing and uncertainty in the discovery sciences: With implications for STEM education.* Springer.

Roth, W.-M. (2015a). Meaning and the real life of language: Learning from "pathological" cases in science classrooms. *Linguistics and Education, 30,* 42–55.

Roth, W.-M. (2015b). *Rigorous data analysis: Beyond anything goes.* Sense Publishers.

Roth, W.-M. (2016). The collective work of engineering losers. *Learning, Culture and Social Interaction, 9,* 105–114.

Roth, W.-M. (2017a). *Cognition, assessment, and debriefing in aviation.* CRC Press.

Roth, W.-M. (2017b). Individual remembering as interactive achievement: Reminiscing in collective interviewing/remembering. In Å. Mäkitalo, P. Linell, & R. Säljö (Eds.), *Memory practices and learning: Interactional, institutional, and sociocultural perspectives* (pp. 327–354). Information Age Publishing.

Roth, W.-M. (2020). Apprenticeship as method in the teaching of research methods. In J. Richards & W.-M. Roth (Eds.), *Empowering students as self-directed learners of qualitative research methods: Transformational practices for instructors and students* (pp. 173–189). Brill | Sense.

Roth, W.-M., & Alexander, T. (1997). The interaction of students' scientific and religious discourses: Two case studies. *International Journal of Science Education, 19,* 125–146.

Roth, W.-M., & Jornet, A. (2018). From object-oriented to fluid ontology: A case study of the materiality of design work in agile software development. *Computer Supported Cooperative Work, 27,* 37–75.

Roth, W.-M., Lawless, D., & Tobin, K. (2000). {Coteaching | cogenerative dialoguing} as praxis of dialectic method. *Forum Qualitative Sozialforschung/Forum Qualitative Social Research, 1*(3). http://dx.doi.org/10.17169/fqs-1.3.1054

Roth, W.-M., & Lucas, K. B. (1997). From "truth" to "invented reality": A discourse analysis of high school physics students' talk about scientific knowledge. *Journal of Research in Science Teaching, 34,* 145–179.

Roth, W.-M., McRobbie, C., Lucas, K. B., & Boutonné, S. (1997). Why do students fail to learn from demonstrations? A social practice perspective on learning in physics. *Journal of Research in Science Teaching, 34,* 509–533.

Roth, W.-M., & Tobin, K. (2002). *At the elbow of another: Learning to teach by coteaching.* Peter Lang.

Roth, W.-M., & Tobin, K. (2010). Solidarity and conflict: Aligned and misaligned prosody as a transactional resource in intra- and intercultural communication involving power differences. *Cultural Studies of Science Education, 5,* 805–847.

Roth, W.-M., Tobin, K., Zimmermann, A., Bryant, N., & Davis, C. (2002). Lessons on/from the dihybrid cross: An activity theoretical study of learning in coteaching. *Journal of Research in Science Teaching, 39,* 253–282.

Sacks, H. (1992). *Lectures on conversation 1964–1972* (Vols. I & II). Blackwell.

Vološinov, V. N. (1930). *Marksizm i folosofija jazyka* [*Marxism and the philosophy of language*]. Priboj.

Vygotsky, L. S. (1987). *The collected works of L. S. Vygotsky: Problems of general psychology* (Vol. 1). Springer.

CHAPTER 5

Emotional Conversations about Race: Tales from the Classroom

Katelin Corbett

Abstract

Content in teaching and learning is only one component of the knowledge produced and/or reproduced as part of a classroom experience. The many interactions and emotions within a classroom are inevitable and essential aspects of formal education but are often overlooked because they are difficult to simply reduce to data or quantify. The research presented in this tale explores the use of personal narrative as a methodology. The narrator is a participant in the class as well as a researcher, student and a coteacher in the course. The reconstruction of events helps to highlight the emotions that emerged during a discussion, in a physics class for graduate inservice and preservice teachers, of the Alton Sterling shooting in Baton Rouge, Louisiana in the summer of 2016.

Keywords

narrative methods – event-oriented Inquiry – science education – impressionistic tales – emotions

> Katelin: The relationship between teaching and learning is evident in every interaction. Within a formal classroom space, the teacher is often viewed as the holder of knowledge, the transmitter of information, the "sage on the stage," while students are viewed as inactive observers or consumers. Because we are constantly learning within any social interaction, we are also always sharing in the experience of teaching those around us. This inevitable dialectic is an essential aspect of formal education but is often overlooked because it is difficult to simply imagine and interpret. The content that is taught and learned is only a small part of the knowledge produced within a classroom experience.

1 Welcome to College Physics for Teachers

The professor stands at the front of the room as his students fill in the empty seats. He leans against the front table as if to support the weight of himself and his words. Shoulders high in the air almost touching his ears. He interrupts their chatter.

"We should have a discussion about the recent events that have transpired, before we get into the physics today."

From the last desk in the back left of the room I observe sympathetic eyes and nodding heads of emotional support. Though most heads begin to shake as if to express disappointment to a small child, some sit motionless attached to curious fingers that attack keyboards, searching for answers. There is a synchronized sadness amongst those who felt the magnitude of the professor's words. It took me a second to realize I was shaking along with them, with heavy sadness weighing down my heart.

Dan's head turns to me. My seat is directly behind his, and although unassigned, the same seat in which I sat each and every day. At this point in the course we all have assumed our seats as part of our classroom identity. Rachael, always sitting next to Peter and Zara, next to Ittra. Dan's eyes ask me for reassurance and I hold myself back from reaching out to him.

The tone of the room matches its bleak décor. Off white walls reflecting incandescent light and varying shades of cheap grey and black furniture. Large lab tables sit on sloped, poorly installed tiles. These tiles thinly cover the cement below, only exposed in some areas that have been chipped away, as a result of shifting large metal cabinets filled with heavy dust.

Silence
Hand raised

"I'm in the dark, I'm sorry, what happened?" Dan's voice asks for forgiveness. I want to speak for everyone. "*We forgive you for not knowing,*" I say to Dan, but only in my head.

My heartbeat starts to pick up the pace. I wonder if my heart rate matches Konstantinos Alexakos' (KA) or Dan's or if their heart rates have increased steadily since walking into the classroom.

BumBum ...   BumBum ...   BumBum ... BumBum ... BumBum

"My son shared a video with me last night. Does everyone know what I'm talking about?" KA asks as he digs his arm out from behind his back and stretches it straight out to the twenty-four adults sitting in front of him.

Of course some of them don't know. Dan just said he didn't know what happened. Why are you asking them? It's not fair to ask who knows, who pays attention to the news, who has to care about social injustices and who gets to be ignorant to it.

BumBum ... BumBum ... BumBum ... BumBum ... BumBum ... BumBum

I take in a deep breath trying to fill my belly with all of the oxygen in the room.

Exhale ... 1 ... 2 ... 3.

No hands. Every pair of eyes diverges from contact with the lonely professor standing at the front of the room.

Does he want me to answer? The gate that holds back my tears is not strong enough for me to speak. There is no way that I could communicate what had happened clearly. There is no way that I could express myself, express the truths of what had happened in a way that was comprehensible, at least not through my own sympathetic barriers. With every emotion I beg him not to call on me, not to ask me to speak.

"You mean the Alton video?" Kevin breaks the silence.

Thank you, Kevin. I am relieved. I am off the hook.

KA smiles but only with his mouth. I can feel how forced the smile is but appreciate it all the same. I count exactly zero other smiles.

"My son showed me a video of a man viscously tackled to the ground ...

Shot.

And *Killed* by police.

A black man."

Kevin, still sitting directly in front of KA, legs spread wide apart, is bent over such that each elbow meets each knee.

He lifts himself up. Or maybe KA did it with his earlier request. And puts his hand in the air.

KA, refusing to *call on* him, gestures for him to contribute.

"I just feel for my students. You know, what they go through. What did they feel like when they found out? How do they deal with it? But also, the way they have to be careful and take care of themselves and their friends ... I mean we go to sleep thinking about Alton and wake up to Phil, it's tough."

July 5th, 2016 12.35 a.m. Alton Sterling is shot and killed in Baton Rouge, Louisiana.
July 6th 2016 9:37 p.m. Philando Castile is shot and killed in Falcon Heights, Minnesota.

The *New York Times* reports:

> The Justice Department opened a civil rights investigation on Wednesday into the fatal shooting of a black man by the Baton Rouge, LA., police after a searing video of the encounter aired on television and social media, reignited contentious issues surrounding police killings of African-Americans. (Fausset, Perez-Pena, & Robertson, 2016, p. A1)

Loud silence

"I mean how are these things happening?" KA asks looking around at the rest of the class for reactions, not answers.

I want answers.

2   Story Telling: Impressionistic Tales

> Katelin: The work that I do, my research, is not "objective" because it can't be. It is emotionally charged and laden with my own values. In reconstructing an experience, I can only share what I observed, felt and thought. I can only share what I understand from speaking with others about how they felt, what they observed and what they thought. Research that strives for objectivity attempts to separate actions and ideas from the actor and the knower. I argue that this is impossible. The emotions and experience of the researcher are an integral part of why the research is being done, who is involved in the work and what methods are used. Regardless of the researcher's acknowledgement of this fact, their own experiences are fundamental to their interpretations. The researcher has the power to choose what information to share, how it is shared and with whom it is shared. I do not take this responsibility lightly. My research is my story.

2.1   *The Role of Stories*

Stories and storytelling have been a major component of teaching and learning for different groups of people since before the advent of formal language (Egan, 1989). Whether it be drawings on cave walls, oral traditions as a way to pass on the history of a particular group of people or fables told as a way to teach morals and lessons, stories are and have always been part of teaching, learning and culture. Here, I have provided the reader with a short, contextualized snap-shot of my own experience in a college physics class taught to teachers and future teachers of all age groups and all subject areas. Although I was not the assigned instructor for the course, because of my experience as a high school physics teacher, I often took on that role by helping students work through activities and answering questions related to content. My roles as a coteacher, researcher and doctoral student were fluid and undefined throughout the course which provided me with a variety of perspectives and helped me to truly become a member of the classroom.

The focus of this story is around our difficult discussion and emotional beginning to class following the shootings of Alton Sterling and Philando Castile. Although institutional racism and the Black Lives Matter movement were not part of the explicit course content, it was an important moment in the class as it stood out as a contradiction to the way in which class was conducted previously. Kenneth Tobin and Stephen Ritchie (2012) theorize such moments as events due to the resulting transformations. This event-oriented approach to interpretive research was developed by Tobin and Ritchie (2012) from William Sewell's (2005) theory that culture consists of contradictions to collaboratively constructed and permeable patterns in social life. It is within these instances, that we can explore and learn. The research may begin with a point of inquiry, but as Alexakos (2015) describes, feedback from participants and re-evaluation of the intended focus results in a shift and so the research emerges as new knowledge is created.

In teaching and research, decisions are made that are telling of the values and views of the teacher and researcher respectively. By illuminating particular events and actions within my narrative, I have cast a metaphorical shadow on others. The ability to make these decisions consciously is an exercise of my agency. This agency resulting from a position of power as a researcher is mirrored within the instructor's decision to engage in an emotional conversation about race with his students. The axiological and epistemological stance of the teacher and/or the researcher is not only present, but essential to the way in which both teaching and research progress. As part of my own theoretical framework for teaching and conducting research I value reflexivity and transparency. If our values inevitably mediate our teaching and research decisions, it seems only right to make them clear and known. In addition, being reflexive, becoming aware of the unaware (Bourdieu & Wacquant, 1992), affords me the opportunity to transform my own practice.

2.2 *Impressionistic Tales*

Just like impressionistic paintings, a written impressionistic recreation of the events that transpired attempts to capture the atmosphere and emerging emotional climate of the moment as mediated by the author's or artist's own emotions and memory (Van Mannen, 1988). In this case, I have captured my own memory and feelings from that day. In between my personal observations of the events in the classroom that day, I present my own internal voice, representing what I felt during this event and in subsequent reflections since. Many of the sections begin with an internal dialogue which I have labeled with my name and placed within a grey background. The process of writing the story and re-living the tale is just as much a part of the research as being in the room during the discussion and participating in the shifting emotional climate. The experiences I share through the construction of a narrative were not and could not be objective and consequently should be transparent and integral to the work. My role in the room included researcher, fellow physics teacher and student. I entered the classroom as an invited guest and fellow physics teacher. I was also participating in the experience as a doctoral student, doing research for my dissertation. My role now, in sharing this tale, is interpretive and descriptive storyteller, being clear that this is my own interpretation of the events, not as some "objective" reporting but a "truth" as I experienced it and as I recollect it, while simultaneously inviting the reader to be part of the process. As John Van Mannen (1988) suggests, an impressionistic tale brings together "the knower and the known," which is critical to the interpretation of the experience. Making meaning through a hermeneutic phenomenological approach, supports and is supported by this research method, as the reconstruction of what was happening required me, as the writer, to think, question and rethink the experience (Gadamer, 2004). The questions that emerged in reconstructing the conversations, actions and thoughts highlight my inevitable shifts in understanding, what Hans-Georg Gadamer (2004) refers to as the hermeneutic process. All of our constructed understandings are based on our lived experiences and because of this new understanding, is the inevitable result of reliving the experience. The reader also has the opportunity to make sense of what is written based on their own experience and what resonates with them.

The process of learning through reconstructing an experience is hermeneutic in nature due to the recursive cycle of interpretation. In addition, looking at data holistically, through multiple lenses and seeking interpretations from others all contribute to the way in which we come to understand. Just as in having a conversation, there should not be an expected outcome when doing research. Gadamer (2004) refers to this idea as conducting a conversation. In doing so, the expectation is that the outcome is predetermined and the individuals participating are not allowing the view of the other to mediate their own thinking. The same is true for hermeneutic research. Before the research experience you cannot anticipate what you will learn and thus the meaning generated is emergent. The production of a narrative is a consistent dialogue with oneself, the reader and those included in the narrative production. As such, interpretation is essential to understanding.

2.3   *Multilogical: Whose Perspective Is Valued*

> For me, the first person present is the most immediate experience one can have with a text. It allows the reader to walk in the shoes of the 'subject' being (re)presented, which is the phenomenological project in a nutshell. (Waldman, 2015, p. 333)

The participant perspective is essential to understanding the shared experience and all those involved have something valuable to contribute. Making meaning in this collaborative sense does not mean searching for a truth within the research but instead attempting to understand, through interpretive inquiry and multiple perspectives, what was happening and why it was happening (Tobin, 2014). Including participant voices further enhances the description by gaining an opportunity to look at difference. In addition, discussions of the events provide opportunity for reflection and interpretation which could potentially result in ontological shifts for the participants, making the research align with the authenticity criteria outlined by Guba and Lincoln (1989).

Because all perspectives are valued and are essential to the research, the reader is also part of the hermeneutic process and that is why this research method | methodology is so valuable. By writing a literary tale of the experience, the reader, although through the lens of the writer, is invited to make his or her own interpretations. This emotional aspect of the tale is why Van Mannen (1988) argues that the impressionistic writer is obligated to write in such a way that the audience is emotionally stimulated. Peter Waldman (2015) describes it metaphorically as "walk(ing) in the shoes of the subject," becoming part of the experience. Yes, there are limitations to what is learned through the reading of the tale, but there are far more benefits from bringing in each perspective and interpretation, including that of the reader.

2.4   *My Own Sons*

Looking down at the chipped tile I can feel KA's heart, his tears and his emphatic smile melting away.

"I just think about my own sons." KA's voice shakes the room.

He continues. "This is why I tell my sons that you don't run from the cops."

With his hands in the air, making eye-contact with seemingly the entire room and with the deepest voice he can muster up to hide the tears that are easily visible in his eyes he says.

"You put your hands up!"

2.5 *"Silence Is Violence"*

From my own personal reflections after class that day I became very aware of myself, and my role in the silence. In my notes to myself I wrote, "I don't think that I could have done that." I don't think that I could have started that conversation. I don't think I could have given students space to speak or given students space to not speak.

In speaking with KA after the summer physics course had ended I asked him to share his memories of the emotional conversation following the shootings of Alton Sterling and Philando Castile and why he felt compelled to say something to the class that hot summer morning. He said that he could have this conversation with his class because he felt comfortable with who he is. He said that when he sees something, he can react and when it seems important he feels that he must speak up about it because "silence is violence."

3   Understanding Ourselves and the Hidden Curriculum

> Katelin: Teaching extends far beyond the scope of the explicit curriculum and pedagogy. Our personal philosophies with respect to what should be discussed in the classroom and what is left out are essential aspects of that which is taught. Traditional teacher education programs focus heavily on lesson planning, standards and pedagogical best practices, but what if we asked teachers to consider the lessons not explicitly written in the plan? What if we taught teachers how to be reflective about their decisions and aware of the role that their personal values play in the classroom? What if we told teachers that how they felt and what they thought were an important part of their students' experience because within every interaction they share a little bit of themselves with their students? I believe that we could all use some support in learning to teach our best selves.

When entering a classroom to observe a teacher, principals are instructed to write "low inference notes." This allows the principal to look back on their notes to discuss the lesson later with the teacher. While I believe the goal of this is to reduce bias, without context, perspective and rationale it is difficult to construct a clear picture and a clearer understanding of the experience. There are many moments during a lesson when teachers reveal themselves, their values and their experiences to their students, which goes unstated. It is not necessarily what is said but what is *done* that I would consider demonstrates teachers sharing themselves with their students. This is perhaps an unintentional curriculum, an emergent curriculum. In reflecting on the ways in which I share who I am with my own students, I consider my actions and choices, not my words. Alexakos (2015) referred to the significance of the teacher's own lived experiences with respect to their classroom decisions as the organic link. The concept of the organic link is significant to my work, but more significant to my understanding of his perspective of the role of the teacher within the classroom experience. It is clear from KA's classroom actions that he is aware that his decisions are critical to the experience of his students, how they learn physics, and how they learn about teaching.

3.1   *The Many Curricula within a Classroom*

The notion of teaching beyond the explicit standards has been researched at the macro level and is sometimes referred to as the hidden curriculum, the learning that occurs due to the very structure and nature of schools. Much of the hidden curriculum is implied through established routines and education policy. Longstreet and Shane (1993) refer to the hidden curriculum as the learning derived from the structures, organization and design of schools and the attitudes, values and actions of teachers and students. The learning that occurred in KA's physics class taught us about his personal values and brought to light a very critical aspect of teaching, the teacher. In a standards-based schooling system, teachers are often viewed as and treated as robotic disseminators of information, but their influence goes well beyond their ability to clearly explain concepts. This responsibility is both a benefit and a challenge for teachers.

What is not discussed in classrooms is just as much a part of what is learned as that which is discussed. Eisner (1994) writes about this idea as the "null curriculum," which is all of the things that are taught in schools because they are not part of the official curriculum. He suggests that what we don't talk to students about is just as integral to the lessons learned and values shared and it is important for educators and school systems to recognize. KA's decision to walk into his physics class that day and begin a discussion around social justice was part of the emergent curriculum and it was so even before he said something. In a personal essay on the kinds of school that we need, Eisner (1998) suggests that when humans engage in a shared objective they will always learn beyond the scope of the objective and therefore any teaching that is not tied to standards often allows students and teachers to learn beyond the scope of the original task. All of our interactions with students as we learn together are constantly reinforcing our own axiology and epistemology whether explicitly or through our decisions and actions. All of the subjects and experiences excluded from schools represent a clear message about what is valued and what is considered learning. And while it is easy to make the objectives and standards of a curriculum explicit, it is in the execution that variation is inevitable. Jean Anyon (1980), who studied social class and the hidden curriculum found that the variation in teaching approaches, expectations for student performances, and the experiences created for and with students, come with great variation and result in varied outcomes. And while no single educator can recreate the same lesson with a different set of students, because every experience is a new experience, the expectations that a teacher has for their students is just one example of what is learned.

3.2 What Else Informs the Curriculum?

In Dewey's description of curriculum (1902), he too discusses the idea of reproduction and reconstruction. For Dewey, ideally this reconstruction would originate from the child's own experience and be driven outward from there. What actually happens often in schools is that these experiences are organized into sets of studies that are predetermined and value laden. School then becomes a space where students reproduce societal norms and take on the values of those who decide what is taught, what is discussed, and what is left out (Dewey, 1990). Ignoring the dialogic nature of learning from and with the other and ignoring the significance of what is going on in students' lives and the world outside of the classroom can be detrimental.

Erickson (1986) argues that within a classroom, choices and actions of all members are part of the curriculum that is enacted in the classroom, meaning the teachers and students together make decisions based on acquired and shared understandings that are learned from and with the other. As a result, it is only by being part of the classroom experience that the researcher can discover these experiences. This was an important part of my own experience taking on roles of teacher, student and researcher simultaneously in a college physics class for teachers.

4 Event-Oriented Emotional Inquiry

> Katelin: The greatest shift I have encountered in my own thinking is in the understanding that we can learn the most by examining difference.

> An action that occurs outside of the regular pattern of experience or an alternative perspective on a single act provides the greatest opportunity for growth. If we constantly seek confirmation and validation of what we already know how will we ever move forward?

4.1   Event Oriented Inquiry

Event-oriented inquiry is a key part of my own framework and informs my methods and therefore my research. Tobin and Ritchie (2012) explain event-oriented social research as selecting a moment that is outside of the patterns of the everyday experience. For research that is based on a specific set of research questions, this would mean an ever-changing set of research questions that lead to even more questions to consider. Instead, inquiry based on studying specific contradictions is focused around learning from difference, looking for moments of interest and trying to understand it from multiple perspectives. Sewell (2005) discusses macro level events with respect to historical shifts and cultural change. Looking at the macro level structures that mediate a shared experience and then looking more closely at the events that are happening within an experience help to expand my understanding as well. This multilayered approach adds further to a fuller understanding of the whole picture.

4.2   Delayed Reactions: Moved to Speak

Sometimes it is difficult to tell when a class is over. Students file out of the room, while some stay seated. I walk to the front of the room to gain a different perspective of the space. Wanting to be supportive but not overwhelming, I approach a group of students still finishing the lab activity.

"Do you have any questions?" I ask.

I get irritated with myself for asking them. Of course they have questions, what I really want to know is how I can be of assistance. When I ask this same thing of my high school students, I get a similar response. Silence. In eight years of teaching I have yet to elicit a question from this request. Each time I ask, I cringe; yet I ask it, consistently.

On the other side of the room another group, Zara, Ittra and Arta, positioned as if afternoon tea were to be served momentarily, smile and laugh in synchrony.

KA, seated on a stool, hovered over their table. He calls me over. "Come here Katelin." I smile to communicate, "I hear you, one moment." The teacher within me is too apprehensive to leave students unattended. I remain positioned in front of the other students completing the lab activity as they finish.

As the students I was working with complete the lab activity and exit the room, wishing me a good afternoon, I walk over to the table to which I was summoned. As I arrive Arta exclaims,

"You know, Terrorism has no religion."

I sit down.

4.3 Cogenerative Dialogue

In reflecting on why she decided to stay in the classroom after class was over following our emotional discussion, Ittra writes:

> I felt like we all have something in life that affects us emotionally and mentally. The incident that happened the day before, with a shooting of Alton Sterling, caused us to have a discussion on how hard it is to live as minorities in a country that is supposed to be free of racism. As a Muslim girl living in the United States, I always feel a fear of going outside alone because of events that can cause people to look at me differently. These things do not bother us all the time, however, the emotional pain stays with us. (Ittra, reflection, November 13, 2016)

All three, Zara, Ittra and Arta are of Muslim backgrounds. Ittra, a graduate student and aspiring chemistry teacher, wears a hijab. She has been wearing the hijab since 10th grade for privacy and modesty. The pride in her voice as she shares her reasoning for wearing a hijab is profoundly beautiful. She explained that although "the Paris attack, caused many Muslim girls to take off their hijabs," she wrote in her reflection that she did not even consider it.

Although she remained silent during the full class discussion, Ittra's decision to stay after class was a salient moment. The discussion that emerged resembled a cogenerative dialogue (cogen) in many ways. Gillian Bayne (2007) describes cogen as both a research and pedagogical tool, which is important to my understanding of the unstated curriculum within KA's class and from the perspective of KA's student, coteacher and coresearcher. In a cogen, students, teachers and researchers come together with a shared goal of collective understanding and knowledge production through dialogue (Bayne, 2007). Although the formation of the cogen seemed to stem from the desire to continue the earlier discussion with respect to race and religion, the norms of cogen had been discussed in other courses that these students had taken.

At the end of class I started to video record the conversation with Zara, Ittra, Arta, KA and me. I did this so that I would have an opportunity to revisit the discussion as both a way to remember the details and as a way to reflect on my experience as a member of the dialogue. As KA (2015) discusses, in his book about being a teacher and a researcher, cogen serves as both a method and a methodology. This is telling of his personal perspectives on the value of student voice in research. Through my role as KA's doctoral student and as a researcher I can see clearly that in teaching me how to be a researcher, I have learned a lot about what he values as well as the importance of what I value. My view of the roles of teacher, researcher and student as completely separate entities has changed throughout this experience. If to be a student is to learn, then I feel that I am a student in all aspects of my social life, especially when I am teaching.

4.4   *You Look Very Emotional*

Arta's voice suddenly increases in pitch and pace.

"Anybody that does the act of terrorism has no religion, that is my comment."

KA stops her and says: "Let me ask you a question, when you talk, you speak very emotionally, I don't know if you notice that." His voice is calm.

Did he ask her because he thought she didn't notice? Maybe he asked because he is trying to help her become aware of changes in her own emotional state. Did her breathing change?

KA turns to Zara and Ittra seated across from Arta. "You notice that?"

"Yeah you're looking very emotional" Zara says laughing and looking at KA, then making eye contact with Arta and finally turning to Ittra looking for reassurances.

"Very intense." Ittra confirms and joins in the laughter.

Yet again, all three in complete synchrony, each laughing along with the other.

Arta, looking up to KA who is still seated on a stool perched over the table continues.

"It's just that in the morning you talked about it, and I couldn't speak about it. I guess it's from there."

"What was it that you wanted to say?" KA invites her comment.

"It was what you said about children. It made me very emotional."

Zara puts her hand up at chin height and stretches her neck high in the air. Her posture immediately improves.

"So many people are getting targeted."

"Black Lives Matter. Muslim Lives Matter. LGBTQ Lives Matter. It's so emotional."

Now moving her hand toward her heart and raising her shoulders above her collarbones forming a concerned shrug, Zara turns toward KA and asks.

"Who is safe?"

5 "Safe": Unexposed to Danger or Risk

> Katelin: We communicate not only through our words, but also through our tone, posture and the way we move our bodies. Regardless of sharing a common language, our words and the way in which they are delivered are ultimately left to the interpretation of those with whom we converse. Because there is no way to predict with certainty how our words will be received, we have no way to guarantee the safety of the interpreter. No conversation or experience is free of risk. I cannot guarantee that my words will never hurt you, but I can promise that I will listen to and learn from yours.

Although I believe that all conversations are worth having, I also think that there are far more risks associated with discussion around topics such as race, gender and sexuality. What I have learned from KA's discussion about the shooting of Alton Sterling and the fear that young men and women of color live with in the US, is that the decision to have the conversation sends a message to students. It is a choice that lets students know that their voices are important and that, as teachers, we care about their whole selves. Zara, Ittra, and Arta, the women who decided to continue the conversation about race and religion after class, as well as those who left; most likely left the room with a changed understanding of the values of their professor.

My tales and subsequent interpretations have illuminated my own emotional experience and highlighted the experience of three students from the class. What the discussion has failed to address is the experience of the students who did not stay behind. Students that decided not to continue the discussion, may have left at the end of class that day for a variety of reasons. It is important to consider that one of these reasons could have been the desire not to engage in this dialogue. What message did they receive from this interaction with their professor? How did they feel? Because I did not engage with students who walked out at the end of class, their feelings and emotions are not part of this narrative analysis and I will never know their perspectives of KA's decision to engage the class in this emotional discussion.

5.1 Expressions of Emotions: Proceed with Caution

Conversations involving sensitive topics can heighten an individual's emotional experience. Tobin and his research colleagues (2016) have extensively considered the physiological expression of emotions and the connections to wellness. Through micro level analysis of heart rate and blood oxygen concentration, and the use of Polyvagal theory, Tobin et al. (2016) point out the danger of intense emotions. If an individual perceived the classroom environment to be unsafe they may enter "fight or flight" mode. When this happens the emotions of anger and fear can result in physical harm due to sudden changes in heart rate and blood oxygen concentration. The implications of their work should be seriously considered when engaging students in emotional conversations.

This becomes challenging when one considers that the decision to engage students in emotional conversations comes from a position of power. As a teacher, who often holds this position of power with respect to what is discussed in a classroom, it is essential to be aware of the potential positive and negative implications. It is important to consider what options students have when they wish not to engage in conversations about race, gender or social issues and what can be done to mitigate the potential violence associated with engaging in emotional discussions. I believe that these concerns are important and need to be explored and studied further. For me, the intentional regulation of my own breathing upon realizing that my heart rate was increasing is one example of an intervention that is in support of wellness.

5.2   *What Is the Broader Context*

In order to have a multilogical interpretation of the conversation, I consider a critical race perspective to contextualize the classroom conversations and interactions within the social and political world. From the standpoint that racism is systemically engrained in our social reality, not acknowledging horrendous acts of violence that insight fear and anxiety for people of color can be perceived as not seeing the significance (Ladson-Billings & Tate, 1995). As emphasized in Critical Race Theory (CRT), all stories reflect the perspective of the storyteller and that is why I find it important to include participant voice to gain a more robust understanding. I am also aware of, and acknowledge, the privileges associated with my perspective as a white woman as well as the resulting implications. I benefit from the unequal distribution of social political and economic benefits due to systemic inequities. Critical race theorists (Ladson-Billings & Tate, 1995) emphasize story telling from the perspective of groups of people who are often marginalized and encourage members of the dominant culture to examine their constructed reality through a lens of privilege.

6   What I Have Learned

Teachers are often expected to have all of the answers. When faced with difficult questions related to course objectives, at times, teachers need to take a moment to think and research, to attempt to find an answer or craft a solution. One of the many challenges of teaching is that the questions asked don't always have easy answers. "Why are young black men dying?" "Who is safe?" What does "safe" mean? What does it imply?

The social and political world in which we live are not separate from our classroom experiences. In the class following the shootings of Alton Sterling and Philando Castile, the instructor made a choice to provide students with the opportunity to discuss what had happened. In a room full of teachers and future teachers, this opportunity acknowledged their emotions and allowed them to grapple with the realities of racism and prejudice that are part of social interactions, including teaching and learning. Some of KA's students spoke up in the moment about the empathy they felt for their students, questioning how their own students reacted to the news, while others sat silently and listened. The instructor shared his own emotions and experiences, modeling one way to have an emotional conversation with students.

6.1   *Implications for Teacher Education*

Prior to my research and teaching experiences at Brooklyn College, my understanding and experience with teacher "training" programs was focused around writing lesson plans, teaching skills and delivering content. Though these are important aspects of teaching and learning, they are not the only lessons learned. When a teacher enters a classroom for the first time they are often underprepared for the moments when teaching goes beyond assignments and assessments; the moments when students need space to question what is happening in their lives, their communities and their world. It is at this time that a teacher reveals themselves and their values to their students.

Though there are teacher education programs that emphasize social emotional learning, educators afforded the opportunity to engage in emotional conversations can learn a great deal from the experience. In addition, when a professor enters their own classroom they are modeling the ways in which they share their own values with their students, which isn't always easy. Teachers and students live out their daily lives entrenched in the social and political world around them. As they walk into school they bring with them all of the experiences and events that occur locally and globally each and every day. Whether or not we choose to engage in the conversations or provide space for students to discuss with their peers, the conversation enters the room in the minds, hearts, words and actions of all those present. The conversation following the emotional discussion in class that day, between the professor, Arta, Ittra, Zara, and me; about their own classroom experiences as Muslim women, revealed a critical need for such spaces.

I must again acknowledge the many risks a teacher takes when having conversations on challenging topics like race, gender sexuality and religion. Alexakos (2015) and his research squad described discussions that focused around sensitive and vulnerable topics associated with identity and referred to them as "thorny issues," drawing on the imagery of a thorn. These "thorny issues" are often avoided in classrooms all together because they can result in sadness, anger and discomfort (Alexakos et al., 2016). But not having these conversations can yield similar results. By promoting learning from one another and learning from difference through open dialogue we are sharing ourselves and our values with our students. These conversations should be explored with mutual respect, compassion and understanding of the potential transformations that result from learning (Alexakos et al., 2016). Deciding to value these conversations can help students to see that their experiences are important, that their values are respected, their stories are meaningful, and we have much to learn from and with each other.

7   Authentic Criteria and the Emergent Curriculum

> Katelin: Every interaction provides an opportunity for growth and knowledge production. In my research, I strive to find ways to make the most of this change. It is evident to me that the ontological shifts that I have made as a result of learning from and with participants have transformed who I am.

According to Tobin's (2013) adaptation of Guba and Lincoln's (1989) authenticity criteria, authentic research should benefit not only the researcher but also the participants. Research should contribute to similar shifts in the larger systems and structures. For me this is why we do research. As we learn and explore we cannot help but be transformed. These changes should improve the individuals and structures by addressing issues and creating positive change. Because every individual is part of multiple fields that have no boundaries, as Sewell (2005) describes, those involved in the research, take the benefits of the work with them to their next lived experiences. Not only have I become more aware of the ways in which my actions provide a window into my values and beliefs, but I am also able to see ways in which I can be more explicit and transparent with my students at both the High school and University levels. This is the way in which the work can become catalyzed. By being transparent when working with teachers; both telling them and showing them why and how our actions are expressions of who we are, can help them to be more aware when working with students in their own classrooms.

When enrolled in a teacher education program, teachers are taught strategies to address a variety of learning styles as well as methods to engage students of different abilities. But often, teachers are not prepared for the many interactions they will have each day. Whether we are aware of it or not, teachers and students consistently construct the emergent curriculum together, collaboratively transforming the classroom experience.

I cannot help but be reflexive about my own practice and think about what I would have done if I walked into my own college class, or my own high school class, the day following these shootings. While keeping in mind the risks and potential discomfort, I believe that it is important to engage students in conversations around these issues. The culture of teaching produces knowledge as we engage in discourse with others (Sewell, 2005). By having conversations about race, gender and religion with students, we contribute to the producing and reproducing a culture where students see that their lives and the ways in which they experience the world are important. I do not propose that all educators discuss issues of race, gender and religion in their own classrooms as I have described.

I do not claim that KA's way of presenting this to the class is the best or even right way to address such challenging issues. Instead, the narrative I present here is meant to be part of what I believe is a necessary conversation on the difficulties in having these emotional and thorny discussions in a classroom. I do suggest that educators become aware of the implications of having *and* not having these conversations and consider the potential significance as well as the challenges. Who we are as educators, our axiology and epistemology are not just important to what we do, they are important to why we do it and how we do it. I encourage educators and teacher educators to be reflexive about their own practice and how their values mediate their teaching.

References

Alexakos, K. (2005). *The science teacher as the organic link in science learning: Identity, motives, and capital transfer* (Unpublished doctoral dissertation). Columbia University, New York.

Alexakos, K. (2015). *Being a teacher | researcher: A primer on doing authentic inquiry research on teaching and learning.* Sense Publishers.

Alexakos, K., Pride, L. D., Amat, A., Tsetsakos, P., Lee, K. J., Paylor-Smith, C., Zapata, C., Wright, S., & Smith, T. (2016). Mindfulness and discussing "thorny" issues in the classroom. *Cultural Studies of Science Education, 11*, 741–769.

Anyon, J. (1980). Social class and the hidden curriculum of work. *Journal of Education, 162*, 67–92.

Bayne, G. (2007). *Identity, culture and shared experiences: The power of cogenerative dialogues in urban science education* (Doctoral dissertation). The Graduate School and University Center, City University of New York, New York.

Bourdieu, P., & Wacquant, L. J. (1992). *An invitation to reflexive sociology.* The University of Chicago Press.

Dewey, J. (1897). My pedagogic creed. *The School Journal, 59*(3), 77–80.

Dewey, J. (1902). *The child and the curriculum.* University of Chicago Press.

Dewey, J. (1990). *The School and society and the child and the curriculum.* The University of Chicago Press.

Egan, K. (1989). *Teaching as story telling.* University of Chicago Press.

Eisner, E. W. (1994). *The educational imagination: On design and evaluation of school programs* (3rd ed.). Macmillan.

Eisner, E. W. (1998). *The kind of schools we need: Personal essays.* Heinemann.

Erickson, F. (1986). Qualitative methods in research on teaching. In M. Wittrock (Ed.), *Handbook of research on teaching* (3rd ed.). Macmillan.

Fausset R., Perez-Pena R., & Robertson, C. (2016, July 6). Alton Sterling shooting in Baton Rouge prompts justice department investigation. *The New York Times*, p. A1. https://www.nytimes.com/2016/07/06/us/alton-sterling-baton-rouge-shooting.html

Gadamer, H.-G. (2004). *Truth and method* (J. Weinsheimer & D. G. Marshall, Trans.) (2nd ed.). Continuum.

Guba, E. G., & Lincoln, Y. S. (1989). *Fourth generation evaluation.* Sage Publications.

Ladson-Billings, G. J., & Tate, W. F. (1995). Toward a theory of critical race theory in education. *Teachers College Record, 97*, 47–68.

Longstreet, W. S., & Shane, H. G. (1993). *Curriculum for a new millennium.* Allyn and Bacon.

Sewell Jr., W. H. (2005). *Logics of history: social theory and social transformation.* University of Chicago Press.

Tobin, K. (2014). Using collaborative inquiry to better understand teaching and learning. In J. L. Bencze & S. Alsop (Eds.), *Activist science & technology education* (pp. 127–147). Springer. https://doi.org/10.1007/978-94-007-4360-1_8

Tobin, K., King, D., Henderson, S., Bellocchi, A., & Ritchie, S. M. (2016). Expression of emotions and physiological changes during teaching. *Cultural Studies of Science Education, 11*(3), 669–692. https://doi.org/10.1007/s11422-016-9778-9

Tobin, K., & Ritchie, S. M. (2012). Multi-method, multi-theoretical, multi-level research in the learning sciences. *The Asia-Pacific Education Researcher, 20*(3), 117–129.

Van Maanen, J. (1988). *Tales of the field on writing ethnography.* University of Chicago Press.

Waldman, P. (2015). Educating desire: Autobiographical impressions of addiction in alcoholics anonymous. In K. Tobin & S. R. Steinburg (Eds.), *Doing educational research* (2nd ed., pp. 321–337). Sense Publishers.

CHAPTER 6

An Autobiographical Study of an Educator's Journey in Awakening, Healing and Liberation through Mindfulness Practices

Yau Yan Wong

Abstract

This is an autobiographical study about how my lived experiences in practicing mindfulness and conducting authentic inquiry has been transforming my ontology, epistemology and axiology, and influencing my wellbeing, relationships with myself and others, and teaching practices. Highlights of my own autobiography, describing my experiences in practicing, teaching and researching about mindfulness are woven together with narratives from my mentors and colleagues. Through the use of interview transcriptions, journals and findings from my previous research projects, I provide thick descriptions of my lived experiences within several knowledge systems of mindfulness practice (e.g., Vietnamese Mahayana Buddhism, Burmese Mahasi Sayadaw Vipassana, and Thai forest Vipassana). Through this study, educators can learn how to bridge the gap between theory and practice through authentic inquiry and become powerful change agents that can catalyze positive changes in the community.

Keywords

mindfulness practice – education – wellbeing – teaching – learning

1 Autobiography as a Research Methodology

In the past, social scientists have been emulating the natural scientists in applying purely a quantitative approach to studying human phenomena in order to make social sciences more "mature" or "rigorous" (Guba & Lincoln, 1994). Statistical tests are useful for getting an overall picture and pattern of a phenomenon, but they do not help researchers understand how subjects make sense of their world and what they have experienced. Kenneth Tobin (2015) argues that positivist research often produces oversimplified and distorted knowledge that fails to illuminate social reality or contribute to any meaningful transformation. One of the common criticisms about positivist research is the attempt to achieve objectivity by separating the researcher and the researched. Wolff-Michael Roth (2000) argues that the observer and the observed are inseparable because they co-determine each other. Moreover, how an individual perceives the environment and interprets his or her experiences depend on his or her history. Hence, Edmund Husserl established phenomenology as a philosophy to challenge the Cartesian dualistic philosophy of reality (reality is separated from the observer) that positivist research is based on (Sloan & Bowe, 2014).

Phenomenological methodologies that aim to provide a rich textured description of lived experiences is a more fruitful way to understand subjects' perceptions of the world in which they live and what it means to them (Kafle, 2011). Phenomenology is the study of essential meanings of a phenomenon through penetrating deep into human experience (van Manen, 1997). There are many forms of phenomenology, such as Husserl's transcendental phenomenology, Søren Aabye Kierkegaard's existential phenomenology, and Paul Ricoeur's hermeneutic phenomenology (Kafle, 2011). Paul Ricoeur's hermeneutic phenomenology rejects transparency of self and reduction of reality, the premises that underpins transcendental phenomenology (Petrovici, 2012). Instead, Ricoeur argues that the self can be the subject matter of knowledge, creation and value acts (Petrovici, 2012). This study adopts hermeneutic phenomenology to understand mindfulness practices in various Buddhist traditions and its contributions to wellbeing and education through describing and interpreting my life story.

The core of this study is based on first-person narrative accounts from a longer version of my hermeneutic phenomenological historically constituted autobiography. Autobiography, an account of one's own life story, is a kind of phenomenological work that can be used as a critical tool for educators to evaluate and improve knowing and learning (Roth, 2000). It may help overcoming the epistemological difficulties raised by the problem of separating the observer and the observed by taking a first-person perspective (Roth, 2000). However, the study of personal experiences requires a radical suspension of judgments and a systematic method that deals with one's preexisting judgments and beliefs, so that the study does not lead to ideology, delusion and conceptual blindness (Roth, 2000). Hence, Joe Kincholoe and Kenneth Tobin (2009) recommend that scholars employ reflexive methods to identify the epistemologies, ontologies and axiologies that are salient in their scholarship. Ontology refers to the study of being and how people perceive reality (Kafle,

2011). Epistemology refers to how people know what they know. Axiology refers to people's ethics and values; and to the involvement of researchers' values in the process of knowledge generation. Our ontology, epistemology and axiology form the foundations of our way of learning and navigating the world. Hence, identifying these three aspects of knowing help scholars become aware of the influence of their preexisting beliefs.

This autobiographical study serves two purposes. First, it aims for critical reflection on the significance of the most salient events in my mindfulness practice journey and learning, teaching and researching. It is based on rich data that I have accumulated over the past 10 years from my reflective journals, students' journals, transcriptions of interviews, field notes of lesson observations, and video recordings of my lessons. Second, I intend to show other educators how authentic inquiry can be conducted to enhance their teaching practices and wellbeing. Authentic inquiry is a research methodology developed by Tobin and his colleagues that is collaborative and involves all participants as co-researchers (Tobin, 2015). It is a multilogical methodology that embraces differences while seeking to understand a social phenomenon and facilitate positive individual and collective changes. Multilogicality is based on the premise that theory and practice have a dialectical relationship and all participants should benefit from the research process. A concluding section of my chapter includes the highlights of the key features of authentic inquiry in this study and its implications in education.

1.1 *My Ancestors*

My interest in the helping profession was inherited from my grandparents and my mother. My grandparents from my mother's side used to be entrepreneurs in mainland China but escaped to Hong Kong during World War II. When Japanese invaded Hong Kong, my grandparents lost all their wealth. Despite their hardship, they continued to support their community. My grandfather, as a politician and a dentist, provided affordable dental care to the local people. My grandmother recused many young women who had been abused by the soldiers and attempted to commit suicide. My grandparents lived a very simple life and kept donating money to the poor until they passed away. Their strong will to help others came from their faith in a Buddhist Bodhisattva called Guan Yin, the Goddess of Mercy. My grandparents' lived experiences through the war inspired their children and grandchildren to live a life with compassion and generosity.

When my mother was young, she received a scholarship from a Catholic priest to study abroad. Therefore, she became a Catholic Christian after baptism. My mother worked as an English teacher and a school counselor in a public high school. She chose to work in a slum area in Hong Kong, where she felt she could contribute the most. Following the footsteps of her parents, she provided support to many disadvantaged students who had depression or suicidal attempts. However, as my mother had witnessed a lot of social injustice happening amongst her students' community, she became quite burnt out and angry. I learned from my mother's experiences that helping professionals also need support to understand their own suffering and take care of their own wellbeing.

1.2 *Being a Student*

Because of my family history, I have had a deep yearning to learn about the nature of mind and to help people out of suffering since I was young. I studied psychology for my bachelor's degree at Virginia Polytechnic Institute and State University and for my master's degree at University College London. The part of my undergraduate study from which I have learned the most was my experiences as a crisis hotline counselor at the New River Valley Community Centre, Blacksburg, Virginia. I had been an intern there for about a year and a half. My main responsibility was to take phone calls from college students and the citizens in Blacksburg who had suicidal attempts and to trace the origin of the phone calls for the police. I received training in developing skills to actively listen to patients, diagnose psychopathology, assess degree of threats, and negotiating with patients during crisis. Through listening to many stories from the phone calls, I learned from the lived experiences of the others and learned about the causes of suffering. However, towards the end of the internship, I was quite burnt out. As I did not know how to transform my own suffering, I did not know how to help the others to get unstuck from their negative emotions. I got so discouraged that I decided to give up my aspiration to be a counselor after graduation.

1.3 *Being a Teacher*

I returned to Hong Kong after graduation and worked as an elementary school teacher for three years. I learned that stress and anxiety caused by the fast-paced lifestyle in Hong Kong had a detrimental effect on wellbeing of students and teachers. The school curriculum was packed with many contents, activities and assignments but did not leave any room for students to play, to reflect and to be self-aware. All teachers and students were like hamsters running on wheels all the time, and we were exhausted.

Such a lifestyle was not sustainable in the long term. If our children are feeling that their lives are not sustainable "now," how are we going to have a sustainable future? Teaching and learning should be enjoyable, meaningful and nourishing. This discontent about the current education system motivates me to search for the way to free myself, my colleagues and my students from the imprisonment of unsustainable ways of living. Therefore, Buddha's teachings that aim at liberating us from suffering resonate with the conviction in my heart. In the following sections, I briefly explain some specific terminologies in Buddhism. Then I describe my journey in mindfulness practice and learning, teaching and researching across various Buddhist knowledge systems.

1.4 *Buddhism in a Nutshell*

Buddhism was founded by Siddhārtha Gautama (563–483 BCE), who was born in the small Shakya (Sakka in Pali) Republic, a part of the Kosala realm of ancient India and now in modern-day Nepal (Harvey, 2012). In order to search for a way to liberate all human beings from their suffering, Gautama renounced the royal life and lived as a hermit for some time studying under various teachers, before attaining enlightenment (Nibbāna in Pali). After the attainment of enlightenment, Siddhārtha Gautama was known as Buddha, the fully enlightened one and the one with full wisdom.

Buddha discovered the Middle Way and taught insight (Vipassanā in Pali) meditation to his followers so that they could attain Nibbana. The Middle Way refers to moderation, or not to indulge in sensual pleasures and not to torture oneself. Nibbana literally means 'extinguishing the flame' and refers to the state of enlightenment, the end of suffering, complete eradication of all defilements, and an equanimous mind. Equanimity (Upekkhā in Pali) refers to the capacity to see people and situations in the right proportions, and with impartiality (Koster, 2015). Buddha's teachings (Dhamma in Pali) were passed on through Dhamma talks and chanting. Dhamma also has other meanings, including natural phenomenon, mental object, truth, reality, and wisdom.

Appropriate mindfulness refers to a wholesome mental state that knows a phenomenon as it is. It is one of the eight factors of Eightfold Path that leads to the cessation of suffering (Koster, 2015). Mindfulness helps us understand the three universal characteristics of the body and mind, that they are impermanent (Anicca in Pali), uncontrollable or non-self (Anatta in Pali) and unsatisfactory or insubstantial (Dukkha in Pali), and gain wisdom to transcend the mundane world. Wisdom refers to liberating insight (Koster, 2015) or knowledge from seeing the truth of how things really are through direct experience (V. Pamojjo, 2015). When we know that all phenomena never persist and that they are conditioned to rise and fall, we gain the wisdom of impermanence. We understand non-self when we know that there is no separate self in any of the five aggregates (Khandha in Pali), including the body (Rupa), feelings (Vedana), perception (Sanna), volitional activities (Sankhara), and consciousness (Vinnana). Suffering in a Buddhist sense means burden and the body and mind of ours are the suffering proper (V. Pamojjo, 2016). Buddhist mindfulness aims at eradicating our attachment to the suffering proper.

As we accumulate wisdom through insight meditation, we gradually wash away defilements from the mind. Defilement (Kilesa in Pali) refers to the impurity that taints the consciousness (Koster, 2015). There are three main categories of defilements, including desire and attachment (Lobha in Pali), hatred or aversion (Dosa in Pali), and ignorance or delusion (Moha in Pali). Defilements in the mind enslave living beings in the vicious cycle of birth and death (Saṃsāra in Pali). Therefore, insight meditation aims to liberate sentient beings from Samara. An Arahant (fully enlightened being) is the Buddha's disciple who is free from Samara because of the right understanding of the Four Noble Truths, that are, the noticing of suffering, the cause of suffering, the possibility of ending suffering, and the path to the cessation of suffering.

1.5   *Morality Training*

I was baptized to become a Catholic Christian when I was five years old. But my heart never resonated with the Bible teachings. After marrying my Thai husband, who is a Theravada Buddhist, I became a frivolous student, searching for many encyclopedias and documentaries on Buddhism so that I could understand him better. I discovered that Buddhism is very similar to psychology because it is a study about the body and mind.

In 2010, I was invited by my husband's colleague, Dr. Morrakot, to join A Day of Mindfulness at the Thai Plum Village International Meditation Centre in Pak Chong, Khaoyai. Plum Village is a sect that belongs to Mahayana Buddhism, which puts emphasis on spreading Dhamma to the general public and attaining Bodhisattvahood through cultivating a moral lifestyle. I had a chance to meet the founder of the Plum Village, Thay (Teacher) Thich Nhat Hanh. Thay has become one of the most influential spiritual leaders in the 21st century because of his relentless work of advocating for nonviolence and justice. During the Dhamma talk, he talked about his experience in the Vietnam War and how he helped Vietnamese refugees to settle in France. His determination in uniting people from all religions and achieving world peace deeply touched me. During the seminar, I met people from different religious backgrounds, including Islamic, Christian, Catholic, Hindus, etc. I was glad to discover so many open-minded people and felt like at home.

Thay defined mindfulness as an energy that recognizes what is going on in the present moment (Hanh, 2011). Thay (2011) wrote that we can do the same things we always do – walking, sitting, working, eating, and talking – except we do them with awareness of what we are doing. He founded Engaged Buddhism based on his belief that mindfulness practice should be very close to our daily life. For the cultivation of morality, compassion and mindfulness in schools, he advocated applied ethics in education. His monastery has been actively participating in educational reform through providing mindfulness training for educators, such as Wake Up Schools, Applied Ethics Retreats and A Day of Mindfulness.

I became a regular participant in A Day of Mindfulness, held on the third Sunday of every alternate month in Bangkok. The purpose of the event is to allow practitioners to get away from their urban living and provide a blueprint for them to integrate mindfulness in their daily life. The monastics from Thai Plum Village led the activities in the event. We practiced food contemplation, sitting meditation, walking meditation, deep relaxation, group sharing and listened to Dhamma talks. All monastics and lay practitioners of Plum Village received the Five Mindfulness Training, the cultivation of true happiness, true love, deep listening and loving speech, mindful consumption, and reverence for life (Hanh, 2009). The principle that underpins the Five Mindfulness Training is to live our life in the Middle Way, that is, not to indulge in sensual pleasures or to cause any harm to ourselves and other living things.

After following the practices of Plum Village for a few months, I experienced some subtle transformation. For example, I started to see more details in my thoughts and became more aware of my speech. My understanding and compassion towards the others grew stronger because I could see the similarities between myself and others. As I experienced more moments of mindfulness throughout a school day, my mind was able to wake up from the thinking mode and spend more time in the being mode. I became more sensitive to the needs of my body and mind, which allowed me to know my limits better and remember to take care of myself whenever I felt stressed. I also became more aware of my students' needs and inserted more moments of silence within a lesson so that they could connect with their body and mind more often. As the collective mindfulness energy in the classroom grew, teaching and learning became the mindfulness practice for me and my students.

1.6   *Teaching Mindfulness to Children*

After practicing mindfulness for about a year, I began to wonder if I could introduce some simple mindfulness exercises to my students. I believed that it was the duty of a teacher to help students cultivate a strong mind. First of all, what is more important than knowing ourselves? Moreover, we spend more than eight hours together almost every day and teachers occupy a big part of our students' lives. Hence, we should make sure our time together is nurturing for each other. Thay's book entitled *Planting Seeds – Cultivating Mindfulness in*

Children (Hanh, 2011) had become a teaching guide for my first mindfulness lessons.

At first, I taught one lesson per week and tested the students' response. At that time, I was the only teacher in my school to bring mindfulness to the classroom. I picked a few core practices, like belly breathing, walking meditation, food contemplation and deep relaxation. As time went by, I became more confident in my teaching skills and practiced more with the children throughout the week. The children loved novelty and became very curious about the practice. They talked about this with the family and introduced the practice to their families.

1.7 *Mindfulness Practice and Emotional Intelligence*

I was fortunate to meet some scholars with a similar vision from Thammasat University, who would like to see how mindfulness practice could enhance children's potential in learning. So, we set up a 6-session-mindfulness course in a month based on the lesson plans of Planting Seeds. Then we launched it in a Grade 5 class in my school from 2012 to 2013. Our training course focuses on how to bring mindfulness into students' daily life. Each session includes 3 to 5 minutes of sitting meditation and activity about the understanding of our nature. We gave students a self-report emotional intelligence (EI) assessment before and after the mindfulness training course. It contains 9 components, including self-control, sympathy, responsibility, motivation, problem-solving, relationship, self-respect, sufficiency, and mindfulness. The results indicated that most students felt a general improvement in 8 out of 9 components of EI after 6 sessions of mindfulness training. We presented the findings at BAI International Conference 2012, Hokkaido, Japan (Chongpaisai, Raveewan, & Wong, 2012). The success of this research project motivated me to deepen my understanding in mindfulness practice and broaden my knowledge in other Buddhist lineages.

1.8 *Mental Training*

In 2012, I met a lecturer from Bangkok University in a Thai cultural course. She recommended me to join a Vipassana retreat in Burmese Mahasi Sayadaw tradition, which was famous for its well-structured and intensive curriculum. Hence, I joined my first mindfulness retreat with her, in Wat (Temple) Phrathachomthong Worawihan, a temple founded by Venerable Thong Sirimangolo, or more commonly known as Ajahn Thong. During the five-day-retreat, I stayed in the foreigner's section and learned insight meditation under the guidance of Ajarn Tanat. This meditation school focuses on the four foundations of mindfulness by using mental noting. Ajahn Thong defined mindfulness as to see what is arising in this body or mind (V. Sirimangolo, 2012). The Four Foundations of Mindfulness are the four things that we should observe during meditation (Table 6.1). They are body, feelings, the mind and mind-objects.

TABLE 6.1 Four foundations of mindfulness (adapted from V. Sirimangolo, 2012, pp. 34–35)

Foundations	How to observe
Body	The acknowledgement of bodily movements, including major movements (e.g., walking, sitting, lying) and minor movements (e.g., breathing).
Feelings	The acknowledgement of feelings, such as happiness or suffering, comfort or discomfort.
The mind	The acknowledgement of the rising and falling of thoughts, which usually revolves around the past and the future.
Mind-objects	The acknowledgement of five hindrances, which are pleasure, displeasure, distractions, drowsiness, and doubt.

Vipassana meditation retreats in the Mahasi Sayadaw tradition aim to cultivate Samadhi (mental stability) to lead mindfulness. Retreats in this tradition are famous for their solitude, intensity and precision. Every morning, practitioners wake up at 5 am to submit their assignments to their mentor. Then they practice sitting and walking meditations continuously, except for eating or going to the restroom, until 10 pm. The readiness of practitioners to progress to the next stage depends on the wisdom that they have attained, which is assessed by their mentor every morning. Towards the completion of a foundation course, practitioners are expected to attainthe sixteen knowledges of insight, that encompass the discerning of mentality-materiality, the knowledge of three characteristics of existence (impermanence, non-self, suffering), the desire to be free from suffering, and considering the body and mind with equanimity (V. Sirimangolo, 2012).

1.9 Mindfulness and Learning Atmosphere

After the first retreat, I was introduced to Phra Ajahn Suksan, a senior Thai monk at Wat Chomthong. He is a well-known Vipassana teacher who had students from all over the world. He had been my mentor, guiding my meditation practice for about a year. I completed eight hours of sitting and walking meditation weekly and reported my progress to him through Skype. Joy Wu, a Taiwanese nun, worked as a translator for us. During my distance training with

Ajahn Suksan, I was handling a bullying case in my classroom. Ajahn Suksan shared his valuable insights from his years of teaching experiences with me, regarding how to cultivate wisdom, compassion and awareness amongst children. Below are his teachings on compassion:

> The victim may be doing something that hurts her relationship with the others. You may want to find out why other students do not like her and help her to stop these behaviors. You also need to spend more time with the bullies, cultivate their empathy and let them know the consequences of their behaviors. Anyone who bullies will get bullied later. You can talk to them like this, 'I know that every student loves the teachers and the teachers also treat the students like their own children. But if the students hate each other, the teachers will be very sad. It is my fault as a teacher that I did not teach you well. I am sorry that I did not do a good job to let you know what is right and what is wrong. I beg you all not to hate each other and stop bullying each other.' If you use the no-blame approach, children's compassion towards the victim will arise easily.

Ajahn Suksan also shared his insights about how people can transform deep-seeded hatred:

> You need to plead to your students to be compassionate and forgiving. You can tell them that you love them as much as the victim. To teach them forgiveness, you may organize a Forgiveness Day. We (monastics) do that every week in Wat Chomthong. The students and teachers gather together and ask for forgiveness from each other. This can clear up the bad feelings accumulated.

I followed the teachings of Ajahn Suksan and implemented his recommendations in my classroom. It took some time for other students and parents to change their attitude towards the victim. Most students stopped their hurtful behaviors. The learning atmosphere in our classroom improved after that. There was more laughter in the classroom and I felt that students could focus better. The positive changes in our classroom had a ripple effect in our school community. Because of this bullying case, a committee member of the school administration and I formed an anti-bullying task force to tackle the bullying problems in school and offered support to the victims and their family members. A few co-workers became interested in mindfulness practice and explored the possibility of using it as a pedagogical tool to improve classroom learning atmosphere.

1.10   *Understanding Impermanence, Non-Self and Unsatisfactoriness*

In February 2013, I returned to Wat Chomthong to complete my foundation course. I stayed there for 9 days. In the last three days, I needed to complete the three-day determination exam. The goal of this examination was to see the truths (impermanence, non-self and insubstantiality) of the body and mind. Below is the vignette that describes my first experience in understanding the truth of impermanence:

> I realized most of these thoughts were imaginations or opinions. The minds associated with these opinions kept appearing and falling. They kept changing too. Sometimes I had faith in my teachers, but sometimes I doubted them. Sometimes I like my friends, but sometimes I didn't. It was as if I had multiple personality disease. The mind appeared and disappeared so fast, including the mind that acknowledged or knew things. All these minds are impermanent. (Transcript of hand-written journal entry, February 7th, 2013)

Impermanence and non-self are two sides of the same coin. When I understood the impermanence of the mind, I began to understand non-self principle as well. I describe this process of knowing the non-self principle in the vignette below:

> All desires kept coming and going so fast that I did not know what to do. Sometimes I walked into the restroom. Then I suddenly changed my mind and sat down. I felt these desires pushed me to do different things .... I sat down on my bed, shivering with fear. All opinions and beliefs that I had before are not real. They kept changing. That means, I don't have any belief or opinion whatsoever. All these beliefs and judgments are all delusions. I don't have a permanent self. (Transcript of hand-written journal entry, February 7th, 2013)

When I first experienced the insight of non-self, it was a shocking experience for me. However, after practicing for a while, the insights began to sink into my heart and I gradually let go of my desire to control the body and mind. I learned from the first day that this exam was about letting go the desire to control. The bodily functions, feelings, memories, defilements, or mindfulness are all conditioned and uncontrollable. When I practiced, no matter how hard I worked, the outcome was not predictable. I could not make progress just because I wanted to. Hence, expecting anything to be changed or happen is greed.

On the second day of my exam, my practices became less intentional and easier. I felt more confident to pass the exam. As the mind accumulates more energy, I saw more refined details in the mind and gained deeper understanding of the impermanent nature through seeing the birth and death of the mind. The following vignette describes the phenomena that I experienced in the last few hours of the second day:

> I saw a chain of sparkles blinking, like Christmas lights, whenever I practiced sitting meditation. Sometimes the sparkles popped up and hurt my head. I did not know what happened until I observed one of my outbreaths accidentally. I realized the knower of the mind that acknowledged the breath appeared and disappeared rapidly. Even the consciousness that observed just one breath was not continuous. The chain of sparkles is the birth and rebirth of the minds. When a feeling is acknowledged by the knower, it vanishes immediately without forming into judgments. (Transcript of hand-written journal entry, February 8th, 2013)

The last day of my examination focused on cultivating loving-kindness towards self and others. My mind was constantly filled with compassion and mercy on that day. All cruel judgments or criticisms that I had about the others were based on the belief that everyone can control the mind. When I realized I could not even control my mind, I had more compassion for the others. When people suffer because of greed, anger or ignorance, we will hurt them more by judging them. Without mindfulness, we keep hurting each other and perpetuate the vicious cycle. When we forgive, and let go, the only thing that is left in a relationship is true love.

In the last few hours of my examination, I experienced the separation of body and mind. This experience came from the penetration of non-self nature of phenomena. Below is an excerpt about my experience:

> At about 11:30 pm, I was exhausted after hours of walking and sitting meditations. I let go all my intention and desire to succeed ... After a while, the mind acknowledged the breathing and the touching points automatically without any effort. The body became very far away from the mind. All the pain and fatigue were gone. I was not asleep because I could still hear the little noises around me. Suddenly, I did not feel the body anymore. Everywhere became bright, peaceful, silent and empty. There was no birth or death of thoughts in the mind. I acknowledged the joy. The mind entered in and out of the state several times. When I finished the

sitting meditation, the fatigue and pain were completely gone ... That happiness and satisfaction were so great that could not be described with words. (Transcript of hand-written journal entry, February 9th, 2013)

1.11   The Value of Mindfulness in Facing Difficulties

My experience in Wat Chomthong was life changing. In the past, I was daydreaming most of the time without being truly present. My mind was constantly fluctuated between happiness and sadness, or comfort and discomfort. It always tries to escape from suffering and hold on to happiness. However, through mindfulness, I realized there is a healthier way of relating to feelings. It is possible for us to live above thoughts and emotions. Mindfulness, just like other things, will not stay forever. But having a taste of it helps me realize how to come back to myself when I face difficulty.

1.12   Mindful Way of Teaching

My experiences in Wat Chomthong provoked me to re-examine the goals of education. Most of the time I focused mainly on covering the formal curriculum and maintaining the daily routines in the classroom. This is the case for most schools in our modern education system as well, focusing mainly on accumulating knowledge and developing cognitive skills. However, education is not just about survival or accumulating materials. It is also about knowing ourselves, connecting with others and nature, and finding our place in this cosmos.

My deepened understanding of suffering helped me cultivate more compassion towards my students. A lot of times I felt that many students are quite helpless. They make mistakes because they do not know what they are doing. Life is difficult enough without added suffering from teachers. If teachers can stay calm and correct students' mistakes without judging them, students will respect that.

1.13   The Importance of Early Intervention

I used what I have learned from Wat Chomthong and integrated it with Plum Village practices in the mindfulness training program for my students. I conducted the second research project on mindfulness and emotional intelligence with researchers from Thammasart University and Bangkok University. The mindfulness training was conducted in my homeroom, the grade 4 classroom in 2013. We extended the mindfulness training course to one year. A lecturer from Bangkok University joined the research team and taught the same course to a group of undergraduate students. The findings indicated that many participants from both groups reported some positive changes in their emotional intelligence after the training. However, grade 4 students indicated higher overall improvement in their post-intervention self-report survey than the college students. We proposed that mindfulness practice may be more effective when it is introduced since childhood. We presented the findings at IACSIT International Conference 2013, Paris, France (Jarutawai, Lowsuwansiri, Taechamaneesathid, Tangsangob, Wong, Vasuratna, & Chongphaisal, 2014).

1.14 Wisdom Training

Vipassana meditation in the Mahasi Sayadaw tradition is great for beginners to build a good level of mental stability through mental noting. However, after completing the foundation course, I realized that mental noting made the mind busy with thoughts because it happens after a mental phenomenon and the mind had to find a word to interpret that experience. Moreover, the effects of my meditation practice did not transfer to my daily life.

My husband then introduced Luangpor Pramote's podcasts to me and said his teachings are well-structured and more suitable for modern life. Luangpor explained that most temples in Theravada Buddhism teach practitioners to practice Samatha (using concentration to lead mindfulness). However, in this digital age, most people have a busy and scattered mind. Hence, Luangpor recommended urban people to cultivate wisdom through daily life self-observation that leads to the accumulation of momentary concentration. Luangpor said the key to make progress in mindfulness practice is to become aware of the body and mind in daily life activities.

1.15 Defining Wellbeing

In the past five years, I listened to the English version of Luangpor Pramote's Dhamma talks occasionally. I attended his live Dhamma talks every month at his temple, Wat Suansantidham or in Bangkok. In Bangkok, Luangpor's assistant teachers organized a one-day mini retreat every month for followers. Occasionally, I reported my meditation progress to his teaching assistants, and they gave me some guidance on how to develop further. I gradually engaged with the community more and understood how they see the world. For Theravadans, understanding suffering is the key to happiness and progress toward enlightenment. They believe that this world is a manifestation of defilements, and we were born to this world because of our craving for sensual pleasures. However, they believe that happiness from sensual pleasures is insubstantial. They are seeking the highest level of happiness from complete freedom from Samsara. Luangpor said practicing mindfulness is the only path to see the true nature of the body and mind. Jess Koffman (i.e., Ajahn Jess), Luangpor's long-time student and my mentor, gave further explanation about the purpose of mindfulness practice in a cogenerative dialogue:

> I would say that the mindfulness in the west that's being applied is a Samatha practice. It's a practice of sustaining attention, whether it'll be adding an emotion, or trying to make it go away, or embodied to feel peaceful, and that cannot fully be reliable. But when you are good at sustaining attention, of course you won't be good at it all the time, because sometimes you are too stressed, too busy, it's not something that is completely reliable ... The mindfulness that Buddha taught, that gives us the wisdom, the mind does not get upset or waver for negative results. So, it won't be about the world having good results all the time. (Transcript of audio-recording, January 5th, 2020)

According to Koffman, the value of mindfulness is about how we can face difficulties with equanimity in an imperfect world. For Theravadans, equanimity is a wholesome state that is beneficial to our physical and mental wellbeing.

1.16   *Authenticity*

Equanimity is the outcome of practicing in the Middle Way, that means, not to indulge or to control. Understanding the Middle Way is the main objective of Luangpor's teachings. In the past, Ajahn Prasan, Luangpor's teaching assistant, mentioned a few times that I had been too controlling or intentional in my practice. However, I did not know how to practice without controlling. Until one day in the international retreat in Sri Ratcha, I had a conversation with Ajahn Prasan. It helped me become aware of my habit:

Prasan: Do you know why you want to practice Vipassana?
Wong: Because I enjoy the practice.
Prasan: No, not at all. It is because you want to be a good person.
Wong: (surprised) But ... I thought I enjoyed it.
Prasan: You have been forcing yourself to practice and that's why you experience headache. I feel sympathy for you. (Then I recalled many times in the past that I felt bored or even tortured to practice. I felt so shocked that I could not speak for a while.)
Prasan: We cannot be moral or perfect all the time. You don't need to beat yourself up when you have immoral thoughts.
Wong: Sometimes I feel that I am a hypocrite because I have so many mean thoughts.

Prasan: At least you know that. That's good enough.

          (Transcript from hand-written journal, December 15th, 2018)

On the day after talking to Ajahn Prasan, I began to understand the non-self nature of the mind in a deeper level. I walked around the courtyard in front of the temple before Lunagpor's Dhamma talk. I contemplated Ajahn Prasan's words for a while and began to feel sorry for my mind. All these years I have been imprisoning the mind and forcing it to be moral and peaceful. I did not allow it to feel bad and so it became stagnant. I felt compassionate towards the mind and began to cry. I wished the mind to be free one day.

1.17   *Impermanence of Happiness*

On December 1st, 2019, I invited Ajahn Jess to give a Dhamma talk to my colleagues and friends at Kasetsart University. Part of his talk that jumpstarted my mindfulness practice was about the impermanent nature of happiness. He said most of us are missing the main way to be happy, and instead are relying on an unreliable kind of happiness. For example, we try to get a state of happiness through earning a certain amount of money, having a family and people we love in our life, and maybe having some fun and exciting things to do, and we just want to stay like that forever. We hope that life is going to be good and happy. However, what we end up is having an unreliable kind of happiness, or sensual desire happiness. This is a kind of happiness on stilts. As one of the stilts got pulled away, life tragedy happens or sickness happens, the happiness is gone in just a few moments. He said there is a much easier and more reliable kind of happiness, which is from seeing the truth, not through concepts, thoughts, beliefs or faiths. When we see the body and mind as what they are, which does not have a self, there is no problem.

After listening to Ajahn Jess' talk, I became aware of the constant craving for happiness lurking in the background of all my thoughts and actions. Below is a vignette of our conversation about my experience:

Wong: I have been observing the fabrication of the mind. It keeps *fabricating* and then I saw that behind that ... there is this craving. And I thought that I was a really happy person. But then I think lately I've seen that and ... oh ... actually the mind fabricates things because I was not that happy or secure inside. So that's why the mind needs to fabricate some ... some happy things to entertain myself ...

Jess: To entertain yourself. That's right. We aren't the mind. The mind is something ... it's an entity of some kind that isn't us. But it believes that it's a self, because it hasn't become wise yet. That's why we work on seeing it isn't a self. But it doesn't want you ... in a sense ... it's like it doesn't want you to see it, so it keeps you entertained. It keeps you busy, thinking about this, thinking about that so that you don't ... as it happens what it does. So that it uses this body and it uses all our faculties to stay entertained.

(Transcript of audio-recording, January 5th, 2020)

After reporting my progress, both Ajahn Jess and Ajahn Prasan suggested that I should observe the rising and falling of all phenomena with a nonjudgmental attitude. Impermanence is the common characteristic of both wholesome and unwholesome states, and thus all phenomena should be given equal value in our practice. Although I knew this in theory, in practice I could not see defilements as impermanent and non-self. I suffered a lot because I could see cravings more clearly and frequently throughout a day and could not shake them off.

1.18   *Experiencing Equanimity*

On May 20th, 2020, I had a cogen with Ajahn Malee, Luangpor Pramote's teaching assistant. Despite her busy work life as the owner of five companies and a mother of three children, she spends two to three hours on formal practice every day. Her life story motivated me to practice harder. Her recommendations for my practice were similar to those from Ajahn Jess and Ajahn Prasan. She said I did not have enough mental stability and suggested that I should spend more time on formal practice. Towards the end of the meeting, she said, "Rhoda, just be yourself."

In early morning on May 23rd, I decided to follow the example of Ajahn Malee, got up and practiced walking meditation. I pondered Ajahn Malee's suggestion, "just be yourself." I wondered if there is no self, then how can I be myself? What made up a self? I witnessed the defilements rise and fall. Then a defilement is not a self. If it is a constant self, it will not disappear. Suddenly, the mind woke up. I have been deceived by defilements. I have hated them because I fear that they are me. I saw how frequently defilements arise and they whispered, "See how bad you are. You are constantly craving. And you cannot do anything about us." But then I realized they really are not who I am, instead they have been covering the pure mind, the untainted mind. I experienced a great feeling of relief. A big burden was thus lifted from the mind. The mind became joyful, light and nimble, just rise and fall without any weight. A big smile appeared naturally on my face without any effort and I couldn't help smiling. All these years I have been carrying the burden of wanting to help myself out of suffering and wanting the others to be out of suffering. But this approach was wrong. Happiness is already here now. There is no need to help the self out of suffering. I am non-self, the Dhamma, and the rising and falling of physicality and mentality.

I must have been walking for 30 mins when I realized the alarm clock had stopped. So, I walked to the cushion with a feeling of awareness and lightness. As I began to sit, the heart suddenly pumped very heavily, the whole space around me shook for a few moments, and I felt a puff of cold wind behind my neck. I felt something inside the heart was cooling down. I did not know what happened. Something has changed in me. I felt a sense of equanimity inside and around me. Then I became completely aware of every little bodily movement, like the eye twinkled, the fingertips moved slightly and the breaths were light and slow. I couldn't move because the mind saw the desire to move rise and then immediately disappear. I sat there with a feeling that this body was not mine for another 20 mins. The mind was blissful and peaceful. until I fell asleep.

After I woke up, I saw myself in the mirror. The person in the mirror was not me, not a person. It was emptiness. The body was distant. Defilements, like desire, or irritation, are still there, but did not bother me at all. Now I understood why Buddhists value equanimity more than the happiness from satisfying sensual pleasures. Equanimity heals our existential lack, the constant craving for more.

1.19   *Ripple Effects of Mindfulness Practice*

Since 2019, I have been a full-time PhD student in science education and continue to conduct research on mindfulness, wellbeing, literate citizenship and sustainability. This year there is novel corona virus pandemic. Many citizens in the world have been suffering from stress and anxiety and there is an increasing amount of social unrest in many countries. Hence, I have been conducting a weekly online forum called *Facing Crises with Equanimity* as part of the intervention of my thesis research study. The forum aims to introduce mindfulness practice to my former colleagues and other educators in the world so that they can overcome this challenge. I believe that education and mindfulness practice should not stop just because our school was closed. In fact, our job as educators is more important than ever right now because we are the change agents in society, who shape culture through our sharing of knowledge and wisdom.

The participants in the forum include educators and scientists from various countries, including Thailand, Hong Kong, Singapore, the United States, and Nepal. Since March 29th, 2020, we have had 13 cogens, covering topics such as stress management, self-compassion, mindful communication, dealing with uncertainty, handling racism, cultivating equanimity and observing aversion.

I hope through providing a platform for educators to discuss salient social issues, to share insights and to cultivate collective mindfulness, we can find the appropriate solutions to heal the world.

1.20   *Lessons Learned from Three Buddhist Knowledge Systems*

Conducting this autobiographical study has been a rewarding experience for me because I have recalled many critical incidents that I experienced in my mindfulness practice in the past and critically reflected on how these experiences had shaped the way I learn about myself, my worldview and my values. I have attempted to show to other educators how an autobiography can be a useful tool for understanding their ontology, epistemology and ontology, which shape their being, their teaching and learning practices, and ultimately their wellbeing.

My journey in mindfulness practice follows the framework of Threefold training. It includes morality, mental stability and wisdom. Although the principles sound similar across different Buddhist lineages, the foci of their practices vary and are suitable for different temperaments. For example, the Five Mindfulness Training of Plum Village focuses on ethics and morality development; Vipassana meditation in the Mahasi Sayadaw tradition is based on Four Foundations of Mindfulness, focusing on the cultivation of mental stability. Vipassana meditation from Luangpor Pramote's lineage in Thai Forest Tradition focuses on the development of wisdom that penetrates the three perspectives of existence (i.e., impermanence, non-self and insubstantiality). As I explored each knowledge system, I became aware of my preexisting ideologies and suspended my judgments so that I could fully embed myself in the community. At the same time, I was aware of how the interaction amongst the ontology, axiology, and epistemology underpinning each knowledge system may influence the way its followers define the 'truth.' Even within a Buddhist sect, the worldviews and beliefs of practitioners vary, for example, some practitioners may have more polysemic views than others. Through interpreting my life stories systematically, I draw insights from my past experiences and connect them with my present experiences. I realize every knowledge system that I have embedded in has contributed to my awakening, healing and liberation.

The Five Mindfulness Training and Gathas of Plum Village have given me a blueprint to live my daily life with morality. Thich Nhat Hanh sets a higher standard for each of the original five precepts taught by Lord Buddha and guides his followers on how to consume, love, listen, speak, and act in the middle way. Thay is a great role model and inspiration for many teachers and all global citizens because of his work in advocating world peace, social justice, environmental conservation and applied ethics in education. Thay's work has ignited many people's interests in Buddhism. Slowing down, being present, and adopting a nonjudgmental worldview has allowed me to gradually heal myself by being present in the process of teaching, learning, playing and living.

The mindfulness practice in the Mahasi Sayadaw tradition is a systematic way to cultivate mental stability, through meticulously acknowledging each physical or mental phenomenon that happens in real time. The Four Foundations of Mindfulness is a good starting point that guides me concerning which phenomenon I should focus on in my practice. Engaging in this kind of practice helps me set a strong foundation for wisdom cultivation in the future. I learned from Ajahn Suksan about the importance of cultivating awareness, compassion and wisdom in a school community. My experiences in the three-day determination exam allowed me to have a glimpse of the impermanent, non-self and unsatisfactory nature of the body and mind. The shift in consciousness was so profound that my worldview had completely changed, in terms of my relationships with thoughts, emotions, consciousness, with others, and with the cosmos. Through understanding that transient nature and similarities of all living things, I have learned to take life less personally, to empathize with others, and to live with compassion.

Morality and concentration are the foundations of mindfulness and are vital for cultivating a moral and quality life. However, for Theravada Buddhists, this is not the highest human potential. Vipassana in the Thai forest tradition is for the attainment of enlightenment. Theravadans believe that the way to end suffering once and for all is through wisdom cultivation. Because of the loving kindness of Luangpor Pramote and his assistant teachers, I learned how to live with authenticity. I learned to see defilements as they truly are and embrace them with an equanimous attitude, which is vital for reducing suffering. Experiencing the happiness from equanimity briefly has awakened me from the delusion of sensual desire happiness and allowed me to see a higher level of wellbeing.

This autobiographical study is a single translation of earlier events in my life and by no means is the only truth. My interpretation of events is based on my existing perceptions and beliefs. However, it allows other educators to understand where I came from, what I have been doing and how I have arrived at this present state of being. I intended to invite readers to experience my journey from a first-person perspective and take away what may be useful for their journeys.

1.21   *Looking Back: A Multilogical Study*
Before I began my PhD study, I did not know anything about authentic inquiry. I am a teacher, who has deep concerns about the wellbeing of myself, students,

and colleagues. After healing myself gradually through mindfulness practice, I decided that it is an important skill that everyone should learn. I applied what I have learned in my daily life and teaching practices, and then shared my knowledge with others. As a psychology graduate, I am fully aware that reality cannot be separated from the mind, that is, the observer and the observed co-determine each other. Because of such 'knowing in the conditions of knowing', I always have 'radical doubt' towards my beliefs as well as the beliefs of others. Bourdieu and Wacquant (1992) defined radical doubt as a radical questioning and suspension of beliefs. It is my compassion and radical doubt that drive all of my research projects on mindfulness education and also my exploration of multiple knowledge systems. I believe that it is important to undertake research, to constantly test my beliefs, to evaluate my practices, and to improve my mindfulness curriculum. Because of the above ontological and epistemological beliefs, I have been adopting authentic inquiry as my teaching practice and lifestyle without knowing. I believe that there are probably many other teachers like me, who have been conducting authentic inquiry all along without knowing the theory behind this research methodology. Therefore, I intend to show other teachers the theory as well as the practice of authentic inquiry based on my lived experiences.

My previous classroom research projects as well as this study have several key features of authentic inquiry. For example, the overarching framework of this study is emergent and contingent because it is an ongoing project that unfolds and responds to the salient events in the school community. It is also event-oriented as the selected narratives are the 'spikes in the curve', that is, the most critical incidents that have triggered transformations.

This study incorporates a multilogical approach because I have been living and learning in various knowledge systems which challenged my preexisting equilibrium and worldviews. The disequilibrium resulting from the challenge allows me to become aware of what I was previously unaware of and catalyzed individual as well as collective transformations.

I use an autobiographical approach in this study and, as a consequence, the research involves reflexive hermeneutic phenomenology with an historical perspective. The study incorporates mindfulness practice as reflexive intervention that enhances self-awareness and awakening. Such an approach aligns with authentic inquiry because it facilitates the process of learning about myself, others, and associated institutions like my school community and co-researchers from other universities who are involved in the research.

I employ two dialectical relationships, teaching | researching and teaching | learning. For the teaching | researching relationship, I incorporate what I am learning from ongoing research in my teaching while providing a context for additional research. Each research project is built on what is known from the previous studies and moves towards the direction of increasing synergy of what I have learned. For the teaching | learning relationship, through teaching others my understanding of mindfulness practice deepens and as my learning deepens. I can empathize with others better and improve my teaching practices.

The main goals of this study are to achieve ontological, educational, catalytic and tactical authenticity (Tobin, 2015). Through unveiling the ontologies of various knowledge systems, I intend to display the beauty of diversity and many paths that serve the same purpose, that is, freedom from suffering. This research seeks to educate all co-researchers through becoming aware of our mindless ways of living and adopt a more mindful and healthier lifestyle. This study also shows that teachers can close the gap between theory and practice through various forms of self-study (e.g., mindfulness practice, autobiography, hermeneutic phenomenology). My autobiography demonstrates ripple effects because it describes my journey from individual awakening, changes in teaching and learning experiences to real world application of my knowledge and transforming collective experiences of a wider community in society. In my current research project, I synthesize the knowledge and practices I learned from different knowledge systems and create tools that are practical for teachers, parents and every global citizen to practice every day and everywhere for cultivating a healthy and sustainable lifestyle. I believe that every teacher is a powerful change agent who can catalyze positive changes in the school community and society, if they are willing to share their knowledge, experiences, wisdom, and compassion with others.

Acknowledgement

I acknowledge support of advisory committee members of my PhD thesis, including Assoc. Prof. Chatree Faikhamta from Kasetsart University, Thailand. This chapter will be included in my dissertation.

References

Bourdieu, P., & Wacquant, L. J. D. (1992). *An invitation to reflexive sociology.* The University of Chicago Press.

Chongpaisai, P., Raveewan, M., & Wong, Y. Y. (2012). *Development of emotional intelligence with meditation-based curriculum in a primary school in Thailand.* Paper presented at BAI International Conference 2012, Hokkaido, Japan.

Guba, E. G., & Lincoln, Y. S. (1994). Competing paradigms in qualitative research. In N. K. Denzin & Y. S. Lincoln (Eds.), *Handbook of qualitative research* (pp. 105–117). Sage.

Hanh, T. N. (2009). *Happiness – Essential mindfulness practices.* Parallax Press.

Hanh, T. N., & The Plum Village Community. (2011). *Planting seeds – Practicing mindfulness with children.* Parallax Press.

Harvey, P. (2012). *An introduction to Buddhism, teachings, history and practices* (3rd ed.). Cambridge University Press.

Jarutawai, N., Lowsuwansiri, A., Taechamaneesathid, P., Tangsangob, N., Chongphaisal, P., & Wong, Y. Y. (2014). Mindfulness training at schools in Thailand: An experimental approach. *International Journal of Information and Education Technology, 4,* 123–126.

Kafle, N. P. (2011). Hermeneutic phenomenological research simplified. *Bodhi: An Interdisciplinary Journal, 5.*

Kincheloe, J. L., & Tobin, K. (2009). The much exaggerated death of positivism. *Cultural Studies of Science Education, 4,* 513–528. doi:10.1007/s11422-009-9178-5

Koster, F. (2015). *The web of Buddhist wisdom – An introduction to the psychology of the Abbhidhamma.* Silkworm Books.

Petrovicci, I. (2012). Philosophy as hermeneutics: The world of text concept in Paul Ricoeur's hermeneutics. *Procedia – Social and Behavioral Sciences, 71,* 21–27.

Roth, W. M. (2000). Autobiography and science education: An introduction. *Research in Science Education, 30,* 1–12.

Sloan, A., & Bowe, B. (2014). Phenomenology and hermeneutic phenomenology: The philosophy, the methodologies, and using hermeneutic phenomenology to investigate lecturers' experiences of curriculum design. *Quality & Quantity, 48,* 1291–1303. doi:10.1007/s11135-013-9835-3

Tobin, K. (2015). Connecting science education to a world in crisis. *Asia-Pacific Science Education, 1,* 2. doi:10.1186/s41029-015-0003-z

V. Pamojjo, P. (2013). *A meditator's guide.* Asia Books Company Limited.

V. Pamojjo, P. (2015). *To see the truth.* Prima Publishing Company Limited.

V. Pamojjo, P. (2016). *The Buddhist way to peace of mind* (2nd ed.). Luangpor Pramote Pamojjo's Teaching Media Fund.

V. Sirimangolo, T. (2012). *Path to nibbana* (Abridged ed.). Watphrathatsichomthong Worawihan.

van Manen, M. (1997). *Researching lived experience: Human science for an action sensitive pedagogy* (2nd ed.). The Althouse Press.

CHAPTER 7

Expression of Emotions through the Lens of Facial Analysis Using a Human Facial Recognition Program

Olga Calderón

Abstract

In this chapter I present a perspective on detection of micro-expressions or subtle emotions of preservice teachers in a science education class. As emotions are embedded in every aspect of teaching and learning, I wanted to analyze a vignette containing diverse facial expressions experienced by student teachers in the moment. The Facial Action Coding System program (FACS) by Paul Ekman was used as a tool to facilitate my analysis. Ethnographic narratives, sociocultural and socio-phenomenological perspectives were adopted as constructs to draw insight from observations of facial expression examination. Performing the analysis and characterizations of facial emotional expressions, took hours of on-line training on programs specialized on facial expression recognition. Such training can provide both researchers and participants with insights, skills and awareness of facial cues as part of a multilogical understanding of emotions and their physiological expressions in teaching and learning.

Keywords

facial expression – emotional climate – emotional awareness – Facial Action Coding System – emotional contagion

1 Emotions Research in Science Education

Research on emotions in science education suggests that teachers' effective emotional skills may contribute to their good relationship with students, supporting their adjustment to the learning environment, motivation, and good performance (Prosen et al., 2011). In addition, pleasant emotions in student-teacher interactions may contribute to a pleasant atmosphere in the classroom, supporting students' competency and autonomy (Meyer & Turner, 2007).

A new wave of research on emotions is grounded in theories and principles of sociocultural and socio-phenomenological perspectives that facilitate the understanding of the authenticity criteria approach during the science classroom experience (Davis & Bellocchi, 2018). Whether we refer to positive or negative, emotional experiences, these may be memorable and significant in students' minds (Tomas & Rigano, 2018). Conversely, there may be instances where teachers experience intense emotions when moderating their classes. Feelings of frustration, anger and disappointment as a result of students' poor performance are not uncommon, while high intensity positive emotions have been found to relate with students' success when teaching inquiry tasks (Ritchie et al., 2013).

Although research is increasing in this field, some teachers may not always be aware of their emotions or the role emotions play in their science classroom. This is particularly significant when the topics of discussion are controversial such as eugenics, evolution, genetics, or lessons on sexual reproduction that often trigger feelings of embarrassment for class participants (Tomas & Rigano, 2018). It is essential then, for educators to reflect on how embedded emotions are in their classes. Teachers could learn how to become aware of their own uneasy feelings experienced when teaching, identify uncomfortable emotions students experience, and have intervention plans when needed.

2 Brooklyn College Study

This reflexive social inquiry study is part of the multi-method and multi-theoretical research project at Brooklyn College of the City University of New York, that explores the intersection of emotions and mindfulness in the science classroom. Facial analyses of student-teacher interactions are recorded and analyzed using Paul Ekman's facial action coding system (FACS) (Ekman, 2002). that facilitates the study of emergent and dynamic emotions in a history and philosophy of science education class.

BASC is grounded in the *affect program theory* developed by Izard (1977) and Ekman (1994). The *affect program theory* indicates that some emotions are pan-cultural suites of coordinated responses, where anger, fear, disgust, surprise, happiness, sadness and other discrete emotions are biologically based and culturally adapted as coordinated responses; such may have evolved to deal with fundamental life tasks in ancestral environments (Scarantino, 2009). Earlier work by Tomkins (1995) suggests that *affects* are primarily facial behaviors, and secondarily outer skeletal and inner visceral behavior, making these characteristics the best when analyzing discrete emotion by facial expression (Tomkins, 1995). Facial recognition tools such as the ones offered by Paul Ekman's Group can be viewed as a form of analysis across micro through macro levels especially when salient events are identified (Poole, 2016).

In this chapter, I present how student participants have opportunities to execute their agency, foster reflexivity, and emotional awareness. In addition, participants express their perspectives and react to others' points of view as controversial themes in science are discussed each week. I also document how emotions are expressed and how they may influence teaching and learning as we deviate from the traditional ways of teaching and learning in science. Expressive facial and vocal practices are a way to look at emotion specificity (Scarantino, 2009). I think that facial expression can be used as a medium to analyze emotions in the classroom, based on the premise that facial expression of emotions can provide valuable information about the state of mind of people. I explore this concept and its implications in the teaching and learning environment in a master's-level class at a public college in New York City. My hope is that the benefits for the participants extend further to their field of work in their own classroom.

Although our research squad was primarily set to focus on investigating mindfulness, breathing meditation, emotional climate, coteaching and cogenerative dialogue i.e., cogen (Tobin, 2006), we adopted an emergent and contingent approach in our research. This emphasis emerged over a program that has extended more than a decade. The research was led by co-principal investigators, Konstantinos Alexakos and Kenneth Tobin, who are graduate faculty and advisors at Brooklyn College and The Graduate School and University Center of the City University of New York respectively. Alexakos was also the class professor. The other members of the research team were six doctoral students: Dorota, Malgorzata, Glauco, Reynaldo, Andre and me (Olga); 3 master students, Parvathy, Natasha, and Sandra; and Victor, a former high school student of Alexakos (Alexakos, 2015).

We developed and adapted salient themes that would make the study inclusive of many relevant factors to our transformative pedagogy and that would fill-in the gaps that arose throughout the entire research process. This focus permitted us to include patterns of coherence as well as nuances that make our reflexive social inquiry study a valuable resource for those interested in conducting qualitative research in science education. The goal in the design of this science education course is for students to have first-hand experience teaching the curriculum. Student coteachers' responsibilities are augmented by allowing them to assume the roles of mediators of the class. Each week one or two groups of students are assigned to present an overview of topics in: history, philosophy, trends and sociocultural aspects of science. The professor's goal in the class is to encourage students to execute their agency as participants in a democratic fashion. Konstantinos Alexakos writes in this course's syllabus:

> I view the course as one in which each of us, including myself, will collaborate to produce productive and quality learning environments in which we learn from one another. All classes in this course are to be cotaught and each teacher must also be ready to be a learner. Through the use of coteaching and cogenerative dialogue, we will work together to develop sessions that further our understandings of the main topics of the course in a respectful and thoughtful manner, and actively listening to what others are saying and contributing and encouraging everyone in developing their ideas (critical listening). (Alexakos, 2012, p. 1)

In this way, all participants in the class had the same opportunity to express their voice and contribute their perspectives, creating stimulating and in-depth discussions. The larger themes in the curriculum extended to current issues in science, as well as topics that have been traditionally controversial like evolution, sex and gender in science, eugenics, and ethics with respect to science. The debated topics often threw emotions off balance for the participants. To counteract some of the feelings of anxiety and frustration that were aroused during class discussions, we introduced concepts of mindfulness and breathing meditation to coteachers and the participant audience.

All fourteen-class sessions were video recorded from different angles of the classroom with the purpose of capturing details of events that could have been missed while taking field notes. Also, we wanted to have good facial close ups of the participants and be able to do analysis of facial expression of emotion. A thorough reviewing of our field notes provided us with information of specific events that we wanted to review further and analyze. In addition to collecting data during class, we also gathered data through informal cogen meetings before and after each class. Our aim was for everyone participating in the class, students, the professor, and researchers to attain certain levels of emotional awareness that would transcend the stereotypical science class dynamics. In other words, we wanted to deviate from the traditional college science class where there is little room for subjectivity, because the present education structure follows the Cartesian-Newtonian-Baconian ideological tradition where Cartesian (objective) science is not only the best way to understand the world, but the only way (Kincheloe, 2003). The only norm for interaction in this class, was to let go of intellectual expression inhibitions and consider the class a safe place to execute one's agency and allowing emotional arousal without hindering one's passion, a factor often absent in the science classroom.

The research approach was contingent upon emergent situations that arose from dialogue and class discussions. In this event-oriented research, subtle emotions served as the window to issues that have affected and continue to affect the life of the individuals in ways that extend in magnitude to the collective. The tenets of participatory action research were followed, where every partaker in the project provides his/her own perspective on what is being researched; also, where participants experience a sense of solidarity towards one another, and they feel that they are in a sensible place because everyone's contribution is equally important. By using this strategy, we could enrich the science learning experience for everyone involved. Also, we could attempt to tailor and transform learning and teaching science to the needs of the collective, and where students can make connections to the science in their lives.

The squad prepared the room ahead of class for data collection by setting up video cameras to record events during the entire class period; set up computers, microphones, and the pairing of the clickers program and oximeters used by students with computers gathering the data. Field notes were taken, and some in the group contributed with feedback in the development of intervention instruments of mindfulness and cogen, in addition to participating in class discussions. Every day before class, the squad met in the classroom to debrief about the plan to follow, contingent upon the developments of the previous class. In these debriefing meetings we discussed whether the data collection plan had been effective or whether we needed to change the approach. After each class, we participated in cogens, which were recorded. Student-researchers enrolled in the class were invited to stay to participate and contribute to the cogen discussions.

Several hours of video that contained interesting conversations were collected; however, we only selected incidents that were salient to us where we could apply our methods and at the same time we could correlate them to our theoretical framework and that was the foundation for our inquiry-based research (Sewell, 2005). In this chapter, I document a vignette-featuring a student participant, Louise, during her assigned coteaching class on "Philosophy of Science." Together with her coteacher, Louise's goal was to introduce the concepts of *normal science* and the *scientific method* to the class for which they planned several group activities in which students were supposed to discuss the role of science in their lives. During this class, many students expressed their disagreement on the way science is presently taught in schools, and they voiced their view on the institutionalized philosophy of science and the evolution of the field in terms of scientific progress. Class participants also articulated their concerns about how science is taught in schools, rarely considering certain relevant topics like indigenous knowledge as part of the curriculum. At that point, Louise mentioned how her Grandma was able to give her the right medicine without being a "formal scientist." We think that this particular event is where Louise's emotions combined with the anxiety of being one of the coteachers that day started fusing and building up momentum.

After the class ended that night, we had a cogen as we did every night after class. Louise stayed and took part in the dialogue and contributed her perspectives on what had transpired during class. It was then, that she talked about her grandmother in more detail. We knew at that moment that we wanted to analyze that conversation. Louise's emotions were intense at times and she seemed to have been making a strong effort to hide what she was feeling. We videotaped the session and that provided valuable data to start our analysis.

Louise is a science teacher assistant in a New York City public school. For our analysis, we chose a two-minute and five-second event where there is clear *emotive communication* that informs our social inquiry theoretical framework. *Emotive communication*, as expressed through spontaneous, physical reactions, is non-volitional and results from the need to adapt physiologically to strong emotions (Arndt & Janney, 1991). I wanted to learn how to identify subtle emotions, so I enrolled in the METT Original and METT Advanced computer training programs on facial analysis offered by Paul Ekman (PaulEkmanGroup, 2012). In addition, I became familiar with Ekman's FACS coding system, associated muscles and designated units. I started the analysis of a vignette by building an emotional landscape of micro-expressions or subtle emotions using what I have learned in Ekman's FACS program. The first step was to build a grid of the different subtle emotions displayed by Louise during the two minutes and five seconds of the vignette (Table 7.1). We obtained the recordings from a digital video camera and developed a clip reflecting Louise's face at 30 frames per second in order for emotions to be easily recognized during the analysis.

2.1   *Is Louise Just Having a "Bad" Day?*

As we did the first part of the analysis we could see that Louise's emotional arousal was a mixture of happiness and sadness (pain). At the 34-s mark in the video clip, Louise reminisces about her childhood. She goes on to narrate about how back home; they cut, wash and boil herbs from the backyard to treat injuries. During this time, she smiles and even laughs in the video, an action that is re-enacted and brings back emotions of happiness while she watches. At 40 seconds, Louise becomes thoughtful about the questions being asked, so the expression on her face changes from happiness to sadness. She continues

TABLE 7.1   Louise's video time chart

Time stamp	Emotion displayed	Muscle involved	Action unit	Keywords
:21	Neutral	Insufficient muscle action to predict an AU		
:31	Happy (smile)	*Orbicularis oris, Risorius, Zygomaticus, Levator angulii oris, Depressor angulii oris, Mentalis Buccinator, Depressor Labii inferioris, Levator Labii superioris*	6+12+25ii	Grandmother-Indigenous science
:45	Neutral	Insufficient muscle action to predict an AU		
:55	Concern, thoughtful	*Procerus, Frontalis, Corrugator supercilli*		
1:04:00	Sadness	*Corrugator supercilli* (under *Frontalis*)	16+25	Reflective-social condition
1:10:00	Happy (smile)	*Orbicularis oris, Risorius, Zygomaticus, Levator angulii oris, Depressor angulii oris, Mentalis Buccinator, Depressor Labii inferioris, Levator Labii superioris*	6+12+25ii	
1:11:00	Sadness, contempt	*Corrugator supercilli* (under *Frontalis*)	1+2+4ii	Cuts/bruises-hurt-pain
1:21:00	Neutral	Insufficient muscle action to predict an AU		
1:23:00	Sadness	*Depressor labii inferioris, Orbicularis oris, Mentalis*	16+25	Grandma treating their wounds with the available resources
1:43:00	Happy (smile)	*Orbicularis oris, Risorius, Zygomaticus, Levator angulii oris, Depressor angulii oris, Mentalis Buccinator, Depressor Labii inferioris, Levator Labii superioris*	6+12+25ii	Reflective–nurturing environment

(cont.)

TABLE 7.1   Louise's video clip time chart (*cont.*)

Time stamp	Emotion displayed	Muscle involved	Action unit	Keywords
1:48:00	Sadness	*Corrugator supercilli* (under *Frontalis*)	1+2+4ii	Reflective– grandmother– childhood
1:49:00	Sadness	*Corrugator supercilli* (under *Frontalis*)	1+2+4ii	Reflective– grandmother– childhood
2:04:00	Neutral	Insufficient muscle action to predict an AU		

to try and keep a neutral expression in her face. However at 1:12 seconds, when she says:

> *Louise:* In my backyard, it was really rocks so we, it wasn't cement, so we used to fall a lot.

Even with all the restraining she is trying to do, there is a moment of deep insight, as though she was anxious listening to herself and reliving an experience that causes her sadness. She composes her posture, because the very action of referring to her grandmother brings back strong sad emotions that overcome her. She speaks about how her experience of seeing her grandmother prepare all these home remedies to cure her injuries impacted her in a way that she wanted to pursue a career in science. She thought of that simple remedy as being "so cool," even though she didn't know why the solution could cure her bruises (Figure 7.1 depicts a breakdown of emotions with keywords). Her grandmother always wanted to be a nurse and partly Louise's decision to study science had to do with wanting to accomplish her grandmother's dream in some way. The professor for the class, Konstantinos, a cogen participant, asked Louise whether she saw herself as an extension of her grandmother. Louise responded in a very soft low tone of voice: "yes" as an expression of sorrow invaded her face.

We proceeded to analyze Louis's expressions by assigning FACS action units (AUs) to different still photographs taken from the vignette. After careful analysis of each expression, we concluded that during Louise's neutral pose (Figure 7.1a) there were no muscle action movements to predict any AUs. During the

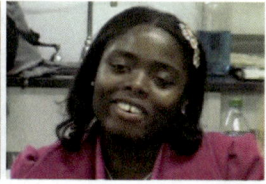

FIGURE 7.1 Louise facial expression of emotions using FACS: (a) neutral, (b) sadness, (c) happiness (stills from video)

second photograph (Figure 7.1b) AUs 16 + 25 are involved producing a facial expression of sadness. There is an obvious muscle contraction of the *Corrugator supercilli* muscle located under the *Frontalis* muscle. In the third photograph (Figure 7.1c) there is a combination of action units; AU 6+AU 12+AU 25 depicting contraction of the following muscles: *Orbicularis oris, Risorius, Zygomaticus, Levator angulii oris, Depressor angulii oris, Mentalis, Buccinator, Depressor Labii inferioris* and *Levator Labii superioris*.

2.2 *Louise's Déjà Vu*

To increase the dependability of our findings, I decided to have Louise watch herself in the video while I videotaped her again. At this point I had done the facial expression analysis of her using FACS, but I did not share the results of my analysis with Louise until she had a chance to watch herself in the video and until after I had a chance to interview her, and she could give me feedback on what her feelings were at the moment she spoke about her childhood and her grandmother.

I positioned Louise in front of the video camera, so that I could catch a full-frontal face shot and I could identify subtle facial expressions as they happened; also, I was hoping that I would not need to edit in a neutral face in post-processing.

I used a neutral pose (0.06 sec) (Figure 7.2 neutral) as the video started streaming. Louise was trying to contain laughing and seemed a bit embarrassed while looking at the video. She pressed her lips to avoid laughing, and took long thoughtful breaths as she watched herself talking in the video. It was almost as if her breath was taken away by the reminiscence of those childhood memories. It was clearly a bit uncomfortable for her to see that she was laughing in the video. Louise seemed to be trying really hard to conceal what appeared to be strong emotions.

2.3 *Emotions Reaffirmed*

When looking at Louise watching the first video, I noticed that she had a smirk – subtle smile on her face and there was a point when she felt as if someone was staring at her, so she turned to her left as if she was going to take some notes,

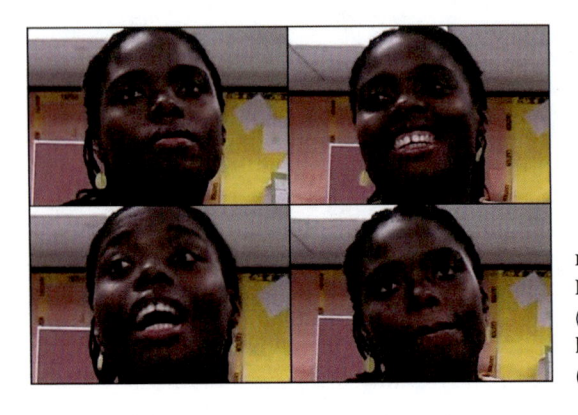

FIGURE 7.2
Facial expressions in the moment
(clockwise from top left: neutral,
happiness, sadness, and surprise)
(stills from video)

but she did not. It was clearly rough for her to see that she was expressing certain emotions in the video. She then, placed a hand on her cheek, held her earlobe and started playing with it, while she continued watching the video. At 0.34 seconds, Louise narrated and laughed about how her grandmother used to cut, wash and boil herbs from the backyard to treat injuries. During this time, she smiled and even laughed in the video, as she observed actions that were re-enacted and brought back emotions of happiness and pride as she watched herself narrate her childhood story (Louise smiles Figure 7.2 happiness). At 40 seconds, Louise became thoughtful about the questions being asked, so the expression on her face changed from happiness to a more thoughtful expression. She continued to try and keep a neutral expression in her face because, according to her, she was trying to restrain her emotions. However, at 1:12 seconds, when she said:

> *Louise:* My backyard was not cemented, so there were rocks all over and we, me and my sister, used to fall a lot.

She continued her story while I continued to record her remarks:

> *Louise:* We always had bruises and small cuts all over our feet and arms. I was always amazed to see how fast my grandmother's home remedies heal our injuries.

Even with all the restraining Louise tried to do, there were moments of deep sighs; almost as if she was anxious to listen to herself re-live the experience that caused her to feel sad (Figure 7.2 sadness expression). As she continued to watch the video and she mentioned her grandmother, Louise composed her posture, because the very act of referring to her grandmother brought back strong emotions that overcame her. She spoke about how her experience of seeing her grandmother prepare all these home remedies to cure her injuries impacted her in a way that she wanted to pursue a career in science. She thought of that simple remedy as being so cool, even though she didn't know why the solution could cure her bruises.

That day, I interviewed Louise and I discussed my analysis with her and related my results with her view on what had transpired. I realized that powerful things were happening as I conversed with Louise about her emotional awareness. I had gained her trust and she was able to open up to me about her restrained feelings, which were mostly due to the norms of her culture and her grandmother's legacy of having to be strong in order to survive and raise five children of her own. Louise explained that she often tried to inhibit overwhelming emotions she was experiencing in the moment by distracting herself with something she had at hand; in this case playing with her left earring, or by redirecting her emotional awareness to another part of her face. She tried to restrict her facial emotional expression from others, because her cultural background deemed the expression of certain expressions as a sign of weakness.

Ekman has coined this expression regulation sustained by Louise as *display rules* (Ekman, 1971), which are characteristic practices of cultures and are usually learned early in life. Display rules are meant to regulate our automatic impulses during emotional arousal in social environments. According to Ekman and Friesen, there are ways that people can regulate facial expressions. (1) Emotions can be expressed as they are; (2) emotions can be amplified, in other words they can show more than what is actually felt; (3) they can be neutralized to show nothing; (4) can be qualified by combining and showing with other emotions; (5) can be masked or concealed, so that the emotions expressed are different to the ones actually felt; (6) emotions may be simulated or shown when they are not felt at all (Ekman, 1971). According to Louise's accounts, she was encouraged to be strong and not to demonstrate any sign of vulnerability to others when she has overwhelming emotions. Louise speaks about the social forces that limit her emotional expression, but also she speaks about how she is now aware of such limitations, where these shortcomings originate and how they mediate her interaction with others. Louise reflected on how she represses her emotions in every social circle to maintain the status quo. She opened up to me about her inhibited emotions, which it is not always the case with student-teacher interactions in the science classroom.

Different cultures may prohibit the open expression of emotions in certain social contexts, while others may mask or qualify the original emotion to keep certain social appearances. Studies conducted by Ekman on how cultural norms for expressions differ among Western (Americans) and Eastern cultures

(Japanese and Chinese from Hong Kong), show that while Americans believe that expressions should be amplified, the Eastern cultures believe certain emotions should be masked. In other instances, this regulation of emotion applies to class. Emotional expressions such as anger, disgust and contempt need be regulated when with a higher status person.

Facial expression of emotions may be identified using other methods of analysis. My colleague Andre Poole used a computer interface program (EmoVision; Poole, 2016) to analyze the same video-clip I analyzed featuring Louise's facial expression of emotions. We had kept each of the results of the analysis to ourselves and did not share our findings with Louise until she had a chance to watch herself in the video and could give us feedback on what her feelings were at the moment she spoke about her childhood and her grandmother. After all the data were collected and analyzed, we decided to look at each individual analysis and correlate what we learned with Louise's accounts of her feelings while watching the video. Not only did we want to corroborate our individual findings and how close we were in the identification of emotions using each method of analysis, but we wanted to confirm that emotions are resonant structures that when we experience re-enactment of past situations, we are very likely to experience the same emotions experienced when we first lived that experience.

There are multi-methods of analysis to detect different aspects of emotions. In this analysis I use two methods; Ekman's FACS and ethnographic narratives through an interview. I learned that the analysis of Louise's facial expression of emotions recorded during cogenerative dialogue after class is consistent with her accounts during the interview of the recollection of emotions she felt during that event that night. The data also correlate with post-interviews conducted with Louise after the analysis. I also observed when I interviewed Louise, that there was emotional resonance of sadness during the time she watched herself on video while telling her story and during the interview. The data and observations obtained during this analysis are significant enough to consider them for further research.

3   Learning from This Experience

Finally, as a researcher, I ask: why conduct this type of investigation using this method? Ideally the answers to that question would lead to identifying some of the benefits of doing facial analysis in the science classroom or any class-room may include:

- Explore how emotions affect our students' behavior, learning and attendance;
- Recognize and label feelings;
- Acknowledge feelings;
- Manage Feelings: Think about feelings and what to do about them;
- Develop strategies on how to manage our emotions and those of our students within the classroom.

Neuroscience studies suggest that the brain has a property called neuroplasticity (Davidson & Begley, 2012). In research that spans several decades, Richard Davidson and other neuroscientists provide ample evidence that the brain can change its ability and function in substantial ways. This neurological change can be attributed to responses to experiences we have (Davidson & Lutz, 2008) as well as the thoughts we have (Davidson, 2012). Neuroplasticity provides new light on the dogma that everything that we are is genetically based. Although our emotional style seems imprinted in us, it does not have to be that way. We are provided with sufficient evidence that the brain is a malleable organ and change is possible. Facial emotion recognition and the tools that are available to help us become aware of our emotions and that of others can be a powerful instrument to build and enhance human relationships of any kind. Although the application to this new concept seems to be more appropriate for cognitive studies, it is a valuable idea to be applied in the classroom. Through this type of analysis, Louise and I became aware of her facial expression and the sociocultural structures that prompt various types of emotional arousal. After my interview with her, we talked about how as much as we want to conceal our emotional expressions, they can escape our consciousness and possibly reveal some evidence of how we feel. We also talked about the significance that the skill of learning facial expression recognition has in our lives and in the way we perceive others' emotional expressions.

The impact that we, as teachers have on students and that students have on us is unprecedented and influences greatly the path in education that students take. Whether our students end up loving a career field or hating anything that has to do with it, is related to the type of relationship and interactive experience we develop in the classroom. The teaching profession is very much ever day filled with emotions. Not only do we deal with our students' intellectual development, but also with their emotional state. More often than not, we distance ourselves from how the issues that we dealt with everyday affect our own emotional state. The fact that we, as science teachers, follow an objective school of thought and scientific philosophy does not make us invulnerable to emotional arousal. Neither does it make science students strangers to positive and negative emotional fluctuations. Facial recognition of emotions can help us, as teachers, become aware of the limitations of our students and also our own emotions.

FIGURE 7.3   Collective effervescence – laughter

"Diffusion" of emotional state can occur in the classroom setting as well as in any other place. How we feel as the facilitator of instruction could very well impact on how that instruction is received. This ripple effect is called *emotional contagion*. *Emotional contagion* was described by Randall Collins (1984) as: "energy which flows through the networks of micro-interaction constituting the macro-structures" (p. 395). Likewise, the term has been described by psychoanalysts as "a process in which a person or group influences the emotions or behavior of another person or group through the conscious or unconscious induction of emotion states or behavioral attitudes" (Schoenewolf, 1990, p. 50). *Emotional contagion* has been shown to influence people's moods in groups and to be important to group life. *Emotional contagion* has also been shown to influence subsequent group dynamics for both the individual and the collective (Barsade, 2002).

In the Brooklyn College research, I experienced a collective mood effervescence during various moments throughout class. For instance, when one of the student-teachers included a funny remark as part of their presentation, the class participants were in synchrony, laughing or smiling with the student-teacher. On the other hand, when the same student-teacher, that same night, presented a video on student bullying, the mood was really somber and unhappy in the class. The student-teacher's facial expression and that of the rest of the class embodied the emotions of the bullied student on the video the class was watching. We captured one of those moments on camera, where the facial expressions were very much the same across the room. This emotional contagion was also reiterated by the class clickers' responses on what students perceived to be the mood of the class at that moment. It is during class events like the bullying episode when some degree of emotional mindfulness in the classroom setting may have positive outcomes for all class participants.

Innately humans have evolved ways to communicate and interpret facial expression of emotions. In an attempt to correct cultural biases during facial analysis, researchers have developed technologies that can aid us in the interpretation of emotions. Computers can repeat tasks reliably and consistently without the encumbrances of nuance. However, the existing technology developed for this purpose is far from being perfected. For instance, resting your head in your hands changes the shape of the face; this change could be misinterpreted by a computer system. The limitation to using computer recognition programs is that each video must be correctly set-up and calibrated to give the researcher the most accurate results possible (Poole, 2016). The largest disadvantages of using computer assisted facial emotional analysis are the physical parameters required for consistent, reliable results. Ultimately, if the file cannot be read, or the face cannot be properly identified within a video using technology, then it is useless; a human can make the determination without minimum specifications (Poole, 2016).

Even though computers can do wonderful things numerically or computationally, it may take many years for a computer to duplicate or even master what humans can presently do. Conversely, a human analyst may misinterpret something he/she sees based on culture, personal experience, or even mental fatigue. Analysis of facial expression may be complex. We must look at nuance factors in the detection of emotion. For example, subjects often change their behavior because they know they are being recorded. This suppression or repression of emotions may manifest in more subtle ways unrelated to the face. Future research could include refinements and improvements to the methods employed in this study. Among them may include a more modular camera setup to ensure the highest possible emotion recognition accuracy, the inclusion of gaze tracking in order to identify stimuli, and the use of prosodic (voice) analysis.

Ekman and Friesen propose that understanding emotional experience does not apply only to relationships you have with others in different contexts. He suggests learning and understanding micro-expressions of yourself can have a significant impact on your life. Learning how to identify micro-expressions in the science classroom can be a powerful skill that may have positive implications for both teachers and students in the science classroom. As teachers learn facial blueprints, they can become aware of students' emotions of attentiveness, confusion, concentration or boredom (Ekman, 1975). Thus, they can cultivate their ability to recognize emotions in students and modify their teaching styles; in ways that can enhance student interest and learning of complex subjects, and that are often the underlying principles of more intricate ones.

Our research on emotional awareness in the science classroom has ramifications for all involved. It was through the analysis and discussion of emotional states that both, the researched and the researchers have come to realize that teacher emotion is the product of cultural, social and political relations (Zembylas, 2005). This concept can have positive and negative implications in the classroom for students, if we as teachers do not know how to regulate and find a balance to deal with both our emotions and those of our students. Fortunately, emotion regulation is part of teacher training and provides teachers with strategies on how to help them with emotion goals (Schutz & Pekrun, 2007). However, the reality is that having gone through emotion regulation training does not guarantee success dealing with emotional stress in the classroom. As teachers, we may set emotional goals in the overall structuring of the teaching environment, yet if a teacher's felt emotions are not congruent with the pedagogical emotional goals, then the teacher will have to put forth great effort to display the desired emotion (Schutz & Pekrun, 2007). Some of the strategies used by teachers when repressing negative emotions is pausing and reminding themselves they are teaching children. Suppression is a type of emotional regulation and while teachers may be able to modify their anger and frustration by forcing themselves to be calm, it may eventually result in negative feedback for the teacher in regards to well-being. Research studies suggest that the use of suppression of emotions as a strategy has been linked to feelings of inauthenticity and depression (e.g., English & John, 2013).

The demand for better and improved technology of facial recognition has increased in the last few decades. A description of the pros and cons of using these programs can be found in Andre Poole's "Seeing emotions: a review of micro and subtle emotion expression training" (2016). Universities, government agencies, and private industry have been utilizing facial recognition programs such as the ones offered by Paul Ekman's Group. Since the analysis presented in this document, other programs such as: The Micro Expression Training Tool 3.0 (eMETT), the Subtled Expression Training Tool 3.0 (eSETT), the Micro Expression Tool Profile, and the Micro Expression Training Tool Plus (eMETT Plus) have been developed and are available for use (Poole, 2016). One of the unexpected outcomes of going through the METT original and METT Advanced training to do the analysis in this study is the new sense of awareness of emotional expressions the trainees experience. When discussed with others that had taken the training, it seems that there is a pattern experienced by trainees. After completing the training, it seems difficult to avoid analyzing the emotional expressions of the people the trainee interacts with on a daily basis. And, monitoring of my own facial expressions too has led me to have a greater awareness of what I may be feeling and displaying making it possible to change either. These are great examples of how research experiences and goals are transformative for all of the participants, including the researchers.

References

Alexakos, K. (2015). *Being a teacher | researcher: A primer on doing authentic inquiry research on teaching and learning.* Sense Publishers.

Arndt, H., & Janney, R. W. (1991). Verbal, prosodic, and kinesic emotive contrasts in speech. *Journal of Pragmatics, 15,* 521–549.

Barsade, S. G. (2002). The ripple effect: Emotional contagion and its influence on group behavior. *Administrative Science Quarterly, 47,* 644–675.

Collins, R. (1984). *The role of emotion in social structure: Emotion as a micro basis for macro-sociology: Approaches to emotions.* Laurence Erlbaum Associates Inc.

Davidson, R. J., & Begley, S. (2012). *The emotional life of your brain: How its unique patterns affect the way you think, feel, and live – And how you can change them.* Hudson Street Press.

Davidson, R. J., & Lutz, A. (2008). Buddha's brain: Neuroplasticity and meditation. *IEEE Signal Processing Magazine, 25*(1), 172–174.

Davis, J. P., & Bellocchi, A. (2018). Emotions in learning science. In S. M. Ritchie & K. Tobin (Eds.), *Eventful learning: Learner emotions* (pp. 9–29). Brill | Sense.

Ekman, P. (1994). Strong evidence for universals in facial expressions: A reply to Russell's mistaken critique. *Psychological Bulletin, 115,* 268–287.

Ekman, P., & Friesen, W. V. (1971). Constants across cultures in the face and emotion. *Journal of Personality and Social Psychology, 17*(2), 124–129.

Ekman, P., & Friesen, W. V. (1975). *Unmasking the face* (Gift ed.). Prentice Hall.

Ekman, P., Friesen, W. V., & Hager, J. C. (2002). *Facial action coding system* (2nd ed.). Research Nexus Ebooks/Weidenfeld & Nicolson.

English, T., & John, O. P. (2013). Understanding the social effects of emotion regulation: The mediating role of authenticity for individual differences in suppression. *Emotion, 13*(2) 314–329.

Izard, C. E. (1977). *Human emotions.* Plenum.

Meyer, D. K., & Turner, J. C. (2007). Scaffolding emotions in classrooms. In P. A. Schutz & R. Pekrun (Eds.), *Educational psychology series. Emotion in education* (pp. 243–258). Elsevier Academic Press. https://doi.org/10.1016/B978-012372545-5/50015-0

PaulEkmanGroup. (2012). *Increase your emotional awareness and increase deception.* Retrieved April 12, 2019, from https://www.paulekman.com

Poole, A. E. (2016). Seeing emotions: a review of micro and subtle emotion expression training. *Cultural Studies of Science Education, 11,* 823–835.

Prosen, S., Vitulic, H. S., & Skraban, O. P. (2011). Teachers' emotional expression in interaction with students at different ages. *C.E.P.S. Journal, 1*(3), 141–157.

Ritchie, S. M., Tobin, K., Sandhu, M., Sandhu, M., Henderson, S., & Roth, W.-M. (2013). Emotional arousal of beginning physics teachers during extended experimental investigations. *Journal of Research in Science Teaching, 50,* 137–161.

Scarantino, A. (2009). Core affect and natural affective kinds. *Philosophy of Science, 76,* 940–957.

Schoenewolf, G. (1990). Emotional contagion: Behavioral induction in individuals and groups. *Modern Psychoanalysis, 15*(1), 49–61.

Sewell Jr., W. H. (2005). *Logics of history: Social theory and social transformation.* University of Chicago Press.

Schutz, P. A., & Pekrun, R. (2007). *Emotion in education.* Elsevier Academic Press.

Tobin, K. (2006). Learning to teach through coteaching and cogenerative dialogue. *Teaching Education, 17*(2), 133–142.

Tomas, L., & Rigano, D. (2018). This is not a sex education class, this is biology! In S. M. Ritchie & K. Tobin (Eds.), *Eventful learning: Learner emotions* (pp. 157–169). Brill | Sense.

Tomkins, S. S. (1995). *Exploring affect: The selected writings of Silvan S. Tomkins* (E. V. Demos, Ed.). Cambridge University Press.

Zembylas, M. (2005). *Teaching with emotion: A postmodern enactment.* Information Age Pub.

CHAPTER 8

An Autoethnographic Account of Heartrate Synchrony in Teaching | Learning

Corinna Brathwaite

Abstract

In this chapter I discuss heartrate synchrony between myself and the instructor in a class in which I was a student. Using event-oriented inquiry and autoethnography, I select four minutes during which time my heartrate and that of my professor were close or matching for analysis. I use a combination of video recordings, inner voice, and oximeter readings to describe and explore emotions experienced in teaching and learning.

Keywords

emotions – heartrate synchrony – inner voice – learning – oximeter – teaching

1　Becoming Aware of Heart Rate

> Corinna: Before class even started, I sat in the lounge area of the Urban Education department here at The CUNY Graduate Center. I tried to pass through the crowds watching the Veteran's Day Parade so I can sit, and prep for the night's class. I started doing the basic set up for the oximeters before moving the laptop, oximeter and my camera upstairs with me to class. It's annoying to carry the laptop around but it isn't much either. So, I carried the laptop open with me to class just to try and avoid having to do it all over again because I didn't want to miss any minute of recording what's happened in class. A classmate offered to help me bring my laptop and bag to class.

Konstantinos Alexakos was my professor for Research Emotions in Teaching and Learning, in a Fall 2014 doctoral course at The CUNY Graduate Center. We both wore finger pulse oximeters in class as part of an emergent and contingent research that we were conducting on emotions in teaching and learning to monitor our heartrates (HR), blood oxygenation (SpO2), and heartbeat strength (PLETHY). Knowing I would wear a finger pulse oximeter did not make me feel anxious; I was able to feel how I would normally feel when I was not wearing an oximeter. There were more things to carry around in addition to the oximeters – the laptop, video cameras, and extra set of batteries just in case.

> Corinna: I was actually pretty excited about this as Alexakos is my Dissertation Committee Chair and expressed in our meetings how comfortable he is with his students using oximeters in the classroom. I have worn oximeters before when I taught, but I was the only person wearing the oximeter. My curiosity was in what would happen when more than one person wore an oximeter in regard to research since we recently had discussions about emotional contagion, emotional climate, synchrony, and emotions. I didn't know what to expect nor did I anticipate what the value of it could be.

I used the HR data readings to look for similarities and found that we had moments where our HRs matched. A four-minute interval revealed that our HRs were close in number of beats per minute (bpm) and that our HRs matched six times within that time interval which was how the events were identified in this study.

2   What Happened Each Minute?

While looking at oximeter readings, I started to look for possible similarities between both my and Alexakos' HRs. Our HRs were in the normal range of 70 to 100 beats per minute (bpm), so I started to look at different time frames if there were any similarities between our HRs. With only the first 22 minutes of the class recorded and saved on video, I started looking at time periods where our HRs matched. I found four minutes where our HRs were very similar and in normal range as depicted in Figure 8.1 and plotted them on a graph. Using italicized font, I discuss how I felt about Alexakos as a professor during that session and how I feel overall about Alexakos as a professor and dissertation advisor, which will provide insight on how I felt both during the event and about the professor overall, which potentially have been causal to the teaching and learning experience, thereby making this study autoethnographic. The italicized font is used to show my thoughts and feelings of the event.

Prior to the class meeting that night, I prepared the laptop to be able to collect data from two oximeters along with two screenshots of video from the laptop to be interpreted later on. Alexakos had set up his own camera on the end of the classroom as well. I did not look at the screen once everything was set up. I participated in the class as I would without the oximeter. However, I did have to make sure the computer was still able to record me and that the screensaver did not get activated. I recorded each class.

The oximeter readings from the entire two-hour class showed that there were times where our HRS were not the same and times where our HRS were the same. In Figure 8.1 the dotted lines show my HR and the solid line shows the HR of Alexakos.

I used that to identify events that occurred within that timeframe which are marked in Figure 8.2.

I chose to explore patterns and contradictions only during the selected four minutes (Figure 8.2). There are six specific events that align with video recordings from the class. There are seventeen moments where our HRS crossed, but that does not mean that our HRS matched at all of those points. According to the transcription of the video recording in Table 8.1, in the appendix, there are six marked, and identifiable, events where our HRS matched on the oximeter screens. This evidence showed that with both our HRS increasing and decreasing, there are other moments where our heart rates intersected. The transcript in Table 8.1 allows insight on what happened in the class during the first minute.

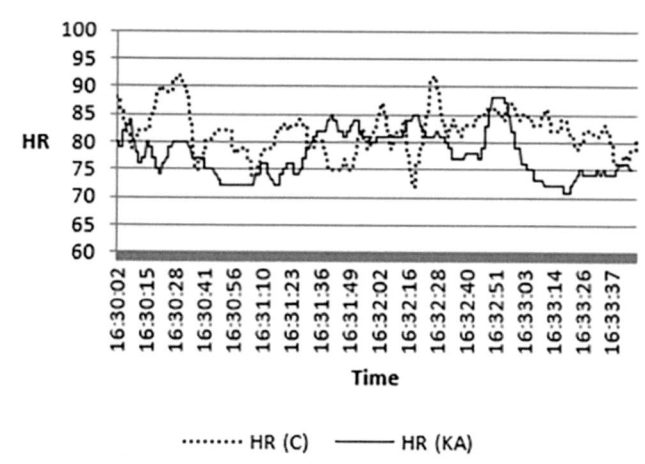

Corinna (C) and Alexakos (KA) HRs

FIGURE 8.1   Four minutes of Veteran's Day class

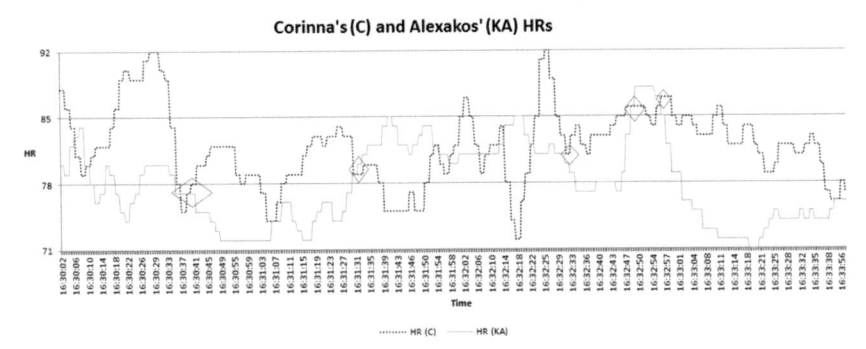

FIGURE 8.2 Six moments where HR matched

2.1 Can You Elaborate on What Happened during This 1st Minute?

Corinna: Hmm ... there's always this sense of relief after successfully setting up the oximeters. You know? Seeing that the oximeters are connected and properly reading, and seeing the video of both of us on the computer screen. I try my best not to look at the computer during the class session so as not to focus on our heartrates to impact it if that is even possible. During this minute – there was like relief ... Then, he goes into Bakhtin. I mean, at that time ... I felt self-conscious about my level of recall about readings and authors because people can start talking about the reading and connect it like a citation mogul. So, when he name dropped Bakhtin, I'm like 'Boom! I know him ... What do I remember? Crap ... Drew a blank!' so it makes sense that I start scratching my scalp. I'm glad my eyebrows look relaxed so I didn't feel too bad about drawing the blank. Then, he continues to talk about Bakhtin. No one really jumped in to add to that part plus he was giving us extra time for doing our work whether it was for our research or for other classes. The class was a mixture of people taking non-matriculated credits and others were at different stages of their doctoral journey. I knew Fergie wanted to ask me about oximeters, but I didn't think she'd ask me during the actual class. She was good though because she records the sessions anyway, but I got distracted. I thought to myself, 'how am I doing this and not paying attention?' I figured, okay, well, I may not actually use this session for research and tried to hurry up and pay attention again to Alexakos. It wouldn't hurt if I didn't drag out the conversation, right? So, I tried to give her the steps to set up and listen again to Alexakos.

TABLE 8.1   Transcript of first event within the first minute of thick coherence

Time	What was said? (KA: Alexakos' HR) (C: Corinna's HR)	What was heard?	What a ction was done?
16:30:00	*Alexakos: after years ... (KA-81)* *(C-88)*		Corinna was looking at Alexakos
16:30:01	*Um ...*		very focused as
16:30:02			eyebrows are
16:30:03	*So I probably wanna*		lowered.
16:30:04	*stay with Bakhtin (KA-81) (C-86)*		Corinna scratched
16:30:05	*and then after that (KA-80) (C-86)*		her scalp and
16:30:06	*we'd be done (KA-79) (C-84). So this way*		eyebrows relaxed.
16:30:07	*you have some time (KA-79) (C-81) to do*		
16:30:08	*Uh ... (KA-82) (C-81)*		
16:30:09	*Whateve r(KA-82) (C-79)*		
16:30:10	*else (KA-83) (C-79) that we (KA-83) (C-80) have*		Corinna rubbed forehead and
16:30:11	*left.*	*Corinna: okay (KA-84) (C-80)*	proceeded to write notes.
16:30:12	*Um. But, Bakhtin*	*Corinna: Thank (KA-80) (C-81) you.*	
16:30:13	*talks a lot (KA-80) (C-82)*		
16:30:14	*about how (KA-78) (C-82)*		
16:30:15	*meaning (KA-76) (C-82) is*		
16:30:16	*Created*		
16:30:17	*in the in (KA-77) (C-82)*		
16:30:18	*betweens. So (KA-77) (C-84),*		
16:30:19	*whatever meaning (KA-80) (C-84) we think we (KA-80) (C-86)*		
16:30:20	*have you know (KA-79) (C-86) – Caitlyn*		

(cont.)

TABLE 8.1   Transcript of first event within the first minute of thick coherence (*cont.*)

Time	What was said? (KA: Alexakos' HR) (C: Corinna's HR)	What was heard?	What a ction was done?
16:30:21	*might have* (KA-79) (C-89)		Corinna clicked her pen as she finished note-taking, sat back, and mushed her lips.
16:30:22	*created* (KA-77) (C-89) *another meaning*		Corinna rocked in her seat.
16:30:23	*between* (KA-77) (C-90) *there. All* (KA-75) (C-90) *those people,*		
16:30:24	*you've seen them.* (KA-75) (C-89)		
16:30:25	*They might have one* (KA-74) (C-89) *meaning,*		
16:30:26	*but then the meaning* (KA-76) (C-89) *that's created*		
16:30:27	*between you and them* (KA-77) (C-89)		
16:30:28	*might be totally different.* (KA-77) (C-91)		
16:30:29	*... and* (KA-79) (C-91) *...*		Corinna swayed her head side to side.
16:30:30	*so* (KA-80) (C-92)		
16:30:31			
16:30:32	*I find that very*		Fergie leaned sideways towards Corinna to ask about oximeters.
16:30:33	*mind blowing* (KA-80) (C-90) *and*		
16:30:34	*Again ... This is probably one of the*		
16:30:35	*first* (KA-80) (C-89) *readings that I read*	*Pen click*	

(*cont.*)

TABLE 8.1   Transcript of first event within the first minute of thick coherence (*cont.*)

Time	What was said? (KA: Alexakos' HR) (C: Corinna's HR)	What was heard?	What a ction was done?
16:30:36	*that I like (KA-80) (C-84). It's easier to*		Corinna is focused on what Fergie is
16:30:37	*understand.*		doing with setting
16:30:38	*(KA-79) (C-78)So just take it.*		up oximeters.
16:30:39	*And, he (KA-75) (C-77) also*		
16:30:40	*talks about laughter (KA-77) (C-77)*		
16:30:41	*and it's filled (KA-77) (C-78)*		
16:30:42	*with things that are*		
16:30:43	*Very*		
16:30:44	*important (KA-77) (C-80).*		
16:30:45	*At least in my work (KA-75) (C-80).*		
16:30:46	*in my (KA-75) (C-81)*		
16:30:47	*understanding.*		Corinna looked at
16:30:48	*So (KA-75) (C-82), take a look at that,*		KA and refocused on the class
16:30:49	*But*		discussion.
16:30:50	*just the creating (KA-74) (C-82) of meaning.*		
16:30:51	*So, for me (KA-73) (C-82)*		
16:30:52	*Um (KA-72) (C-82)*		
16:30:53	*I went*		
16:30:54	*to ... how*		
16:30:55	*many of you know of*		Corinna is focused on what Fergie is doing with setting up oximeters.
16:30:56	*Aviation (KA-72) (C-79) high school?*		Corinna looked at
16:30:57		*Class *inaudible**	Alexakos.
16:30:58	*No? (KA-72) (C-78)*	*Class *inaudible**	
16:30:59	*Right (KA-72) (C-79).*		

Within the first minute, our HRs matched as Alexakos had talked about what we would learn from Bakhtin. According to Table 8.1, our HRs started in the 80s with mine at 88 bpm and his at 81 bpm. While his HR decreased more steadily, mine fluctuated a bit as my attention was taken away from the main discussion. Around this time, I was more concentrated on making sure I was collecting data correctly, as during the past few weeks, the data was either incomplete or the laptop did not have enough memory. When Alexakos dialled back on some of the readings required, I was thrilled and relieved which was where my HR began increasing again to 80. When Alexakos spoke about Bakhtin's work, his voice started to lower when he expressed the importance of Bakhtin's work and its influence on his own work. During that moment, I felt some of the passion as he asked us in the class to really try to absorb the ideologies expressed by Bakhtin as well. After our HRs matched, my HR slightly increased.

2.2   *What Do I Remember Experiencing for Times When Our HRs Matched?*

> Corinna: Where our HRs match, I can't say that I heard what he was saying at that time as I was focused on helping Fergie with getting her computer oximeter ready. I had just finished writing notes, rocking, and swaying. The movement looks to be the cause as to why my HR was increasing. I was no longer rocking and swaying when I was talking with Fergie, so it makes sense that my HR was decreasing.

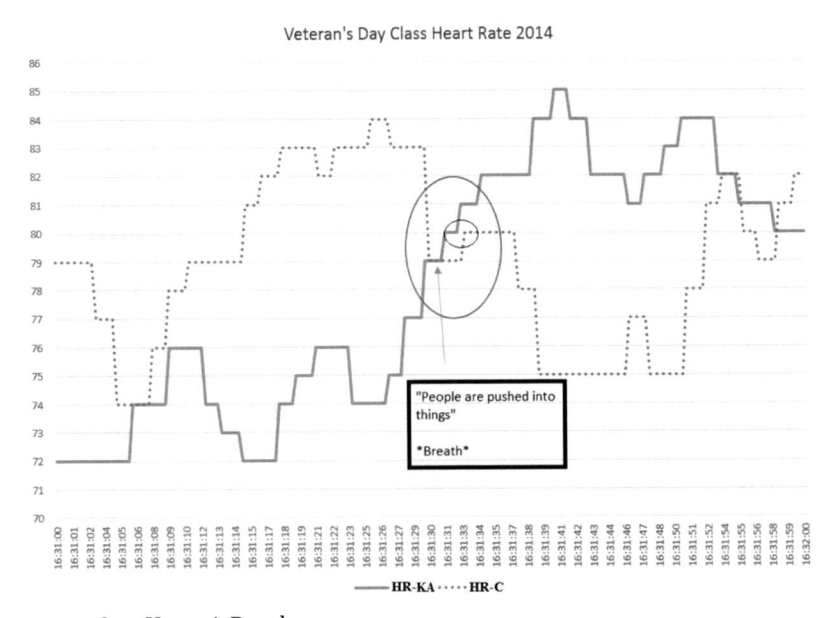

FIGURE 8.3   Veteran's Day class HR

In Figure 8.3, notice that just the second moment is highlighted. If you take an even closer look, you would see that this moment in particular has two points that match in the video, but you can't really see that on the graph. During this particular minute, our HRs not only matched but moved up closely together as you will notice in the transcript better than on the graph. The inner circle that has been outlined shows how close the HRs were.

This class experience was very interesting to me from a researcher standpoint because I was tuning in and out of the lecture. I found that when I tuned in, certain words the professor spoke brought me back into the discussion. This particular minute, I remember hearing three words that you will come across in the transcript detailed in Table 8.2: "ROTC," "race," and "pushed."

2.3   *What about "ROTC" Drew My Attention?*

> Corinna: ROTC, which stands for Reserve Officer Training Corps, caught my attention because one of my best male friends from high school talked very highly of ROTC. When I first met him, I thought he wasn't cool. For me, he was too materialistic. After he was in ROTC, there was a humbler side of him as far as his demeanor, which made him cool to me. So, I had a positive experience with the impact of ROTC on their students in how it builds character. When I heard ROTC, it pulled me back into the conversation because I was curious as to what Alexakos would say about ROTC if anything and I had my own opinions I could share if prompted.

2.4   *What about "Race" Drew My Attention?*

> Corinna: Race, for me, is a tricky matter. When I heard the word "race," my heart sunk to my stomach and my stomach felt really empty. My family is Garifuna, and our roots lie in St. Vincent and the Grenadines. This is the history of Garifuna people from Honduras and Belize. There are Garifuna people also in Guatemala and Nicaragua. My family was born in Honduras. My grandmother's family is from Belize. Our culture is Garifuna which means Black Carib. My mother raised me with the understanding that I am what some call: Black Hispanic or Afro Latina. I knew very well what my identity is. It would draw concern when I would be forced to choose one over the other. When you look at me, you see Black. I don't look like what I quickly learned people stereotyped as Hispanic, which to me became the likeness of a Jennifer Lopez. So, in schools I've attended, I always sat with and was a part of the Black crew. When my last name would be questioned, I would

TABLE 8.2   Transcript of second and third events within the 2nd minute

Time	What was said? (KA: Alexakos' HR) (C: Corinna's HR)	What was heard?	What action was done?
16:31:00	Alexakos: (KA-72) (C-79) and that's the ... that's		Corinna focused straight ahead of her.
16:31:01	the high school I attended		
16:31:02	when I was young (KA-72) (C-77)		
16:31:03	a long time ago (KA-72) (C-74)		
16:31:04	And		Corinna focused on Alexakos right after hearing "ago."
16:31:05	it had the		
16:31:06	what I figured		Corinna focused on what Fergie was doing with oximeters.
16:31:07	just (KA-72) (C-76) by looking at the		
16:31:08	parade (KA-74) (C-76) it (KA-74) (C-78) was that		
16:31:09	this is the		
16:31:10	ROTC (KA-76) (C-79)		
16:31:11	kind of	Margaret: Yea	
16:31:12	groups in the		
16:31:13	in the		
16:31:14	high schools (KA-74) (C-79) or middle		
16:31:15	schools (KA-73) (C-81),		
16:31:16	and (KA-73) (C-82) I mean (KA-72) (C-82)		
16:31:17	it took me back to		
16:31:18	that. But (KA-72) (C-83), also		Corinna refocused on Alexakos.
16:31:19	just by looking at the		
16:31:20	faces (KA-74) (C-83)		Corinna focused on what Fergie was doing with oximeters.
16:31:21	of who (KA-75) (C-82) was in the		Corinna refocused on Alexakos.
16:31:22	Parade		
16:31:23	it (KA-76) (C-83) kinda		
16:31:24	brings up a lot of		

(cont.)

TABLE 8.2   Transcript of second and third events within the 2nd minute (*cont.*)

Time	What was said? (KA: Alexakos' HR) (C: Corinna's HR)	What was heard?	What action was done?
16:31:25	questions(KA-76) (C-84)		Corinna was looking in Alexakos' direction, but her eyes shifted left and right.
16:31:26	in terms of (KA-74) (C-84) race		Corinna looked down upon Alexakos saying "race."
16:31:27 16:31:28 16:31:29	and (KA-74) (C-83) (KA-75) (C-83)Who		Corinna focused on what Fergie was doing with oximeters.
16:31:30 16:31:31 16:31:32	Who's pushed (KA-77) (C-79) into certain things (KA-79) (C-79).		Corinna refocused on Alexakos.
16:31:33 16:31:34 16:31:35	Right? (KA-80) (C-80) ı Uh (KA-81) (C-80)	Margaret: mhm	Corinna looked down.
16:31:36	And so, you (KA-82) (C-80) ...		Corinna straightened up in her chair, took a deep breath, and looked slightly in Fergie's direction.
16:31:37			Corinna shifted in her seat again and remained looking down.

(*cont.*)

TABLE 8.2 Transcript of second and third events within the 2nd minute (*cont.*)

Time	What was said? (KA: Alexakos' HR) (C: Corinna's HR)	What was heard?	What action was done?
16:31:38	(*KA-82*) (*C-78*) *That's why I was* (*KA-82*) (*C-75*) *also*		Corinna was still looking down.
16:31:39	*asking about*		
16:31:40	*emotions. Perhaps some of you noticed* (*KA-84*) (*C-75*)		
16:31:41	*that you didn't want to*		
16:31:42	*go there.*		
16:31:43	*And* (*KA-85*) (*C-75*) *it also brings up*		
16:31:44	*Certain* (*KA-84*) (*C-75*) *emotions*		Corinna focused
16:31:45	*thinking* (*KA-82*) (*C-75*) *okay*		on what Fergie was doing with oximeters.
16:31:46	*you* (*KA-82*) (*C-77*) *know – Why does*		Corinna looked down slightly towards KA.
16:31:47	*society have*		Corinna refocused
16:31:48	*this* (*KA-82*) (*C-75*) *kind* (*KA-81*) (*C-75*) *of*		on Alexakos.
16:31:49	*uh*		Corinna focused
16:31:50	(*KA-82*) (*C-75*) *agenda*		on what Fergie
16:31:51			was doing with
16:31:52	*for* (*KA-83*) (*C-78*) *a certain group of*		oximeters and
16:31:53	*people* (*KA-84*) (*C-81*). *Then other group of*		started speaking to her. They remained
16:31:54	*people* (*KA-84*) (*C-82*) *have a*		in dialogue on the
16:31:55	*different type of agenda*		side.
16:31:56	*or why* (*KA-84*) (*C-80*) *should* (*KA-82*) (*C-80*)		
16:31:57	*Okay* (*KA-82*) (*C-79*) *let's be clear* (*KA-81*) (*C-79*)		
16:31:58	*Uh ...* (*KA-81*) (*C-81*) *students of*		
16:31:59	*color should be*		

lose my Blackness and be considered "Spanish." I didn't fit in with the "Spanish" crew even if I spoke it as well as they did and even danced the music. I then became the Black person that could translate if ever anyone spoke offensively in Spanish. After being insulted the first time by it, I became used to hearing it and shrugging it off never speaking about how it made me feel. So when Black movements would come up, I felt like I wanted a movement that reflected both identities. If I spoke on how I felt, I offended. It was never Black conscious enough or I was denying my own Blackness and only connecting to Hispanic roots. I would no longer want to speak because I felt misunderstood completely and denied the right to express how both are very important. In a flash, hearing the word "race" slapped this in my face.

2.5 What about "Pushed" Drew My Attention?

Corinna: Pushed, since it came soon after hearing "race" further affected my own thoughts of race and I was afraid of where the professor was going with it. I did not want to be positioned to speak in the class about my opinions. I didn't want to offend. I didn't want to express anger, insensitivity, or emptiness on the matter. I was angered about the constant conversation on what's happened wrongly to people and the fact that you have to bring it up for human compassion and get none of it. I was afraid of my current experience of my voice and/or voiceless-ness on the matter. I was saddened by my own lack of interest to partake in the conversation even though I had many emotions and thoughts on the matter. I wanted the professor to switch topics because I didn't want to feel what I was feeling anymore.

I briefly spoke to Fergie about oximeters as she became interested in looking at her own HR readings. While we spoke, I was already not fully tuned into what my professor was even talking about. By the time Alexakos mentioned the word "race," I had only caught that word and I felt like a deer caught in headlights because I did not even know why we were talking about race. I also saw it in my own facial expression during the video. My HR began to decrease steadily, which is what I saw as a contradiction, or change in my HR (Sewell, 2005). This was the second event within the four minutes, according to Table 8.2 as well. By the time Alexakos said the word "pushed," my HR dropped by four to 79 beats per minute (bpm) while his increased by two to 77 bpm. After his statement where he said, "Who's pushed into certain things," Alexakos followed that statement by taking a breath. Since I was not the speaker, I did not want to encourage the conversation either. So, my HR may have decreased as a result of that while Alexakos' HR had increased because he was already making the utterances about such an emotionally charged topic. Alexakos and Pride coined these emotionally charged topics as *thorny issues* (Alexakos et al., 2016). Bakhtin expressed that each utterance had both value and meaning (Bakhtin, 1986). During that breath, our HR continued to follow closely in its increase from 79 bpm to 80 bpm. Alexakos' HR went to 80 just before mine also went to 80. This time around, I leaned to Fergie to talk to her about oximeter software and set up.

2.6 What Made Me so Fidgety?

> Corinna: I was just so nervous during this moment and trying not to get looked at or called on to address this idea of being pushed into the military as a means of opportunity that I just have to do something else. I didn't even think about being caught being rude by having my own conversation with a classmate during class, I was running from the discussion. Trying to avoid hearing or having another discussion on race without even thinking that the issue was more me than anything else. I wanted to not feel the pit in my stomach. I wanted to catch my breath. I wanted Alexakos to switch the subject because I wouldn't dare try to switch a professor's topic.

My only way out of feeling that way was to focus on another conversation, hence I opened my mouth and turned my attention to Fergie. I, basically, distracted and interrupted Fergie's attention in the class. In Table 8.3, you will notice that I just couldn't stay focused on the conversation.

2.7 What Happened during This Minute?

> Corinna: Goodness ... I couldn't believe we were still talking about race there. I was talking to Fergie up until he mentioned "color" and I had started to refocus on Alexakos again. Which is where I see that my HR dropped to the 79 by the next second. That's interesting to me because I noticed when I started wearing oximeters on my own to get used to it. I was either super relaxed or getting angry when my HR would be in the 70s. My HR went back up to the 80s for the few seconds as I focused on Alexakos, but it's interesting that it's almost like I was fidgeting over the next 11 seconds. I find it interesting that while I was going back and forth

TABLE 8.3   Transcript of fourth and fifth events within the third minute

Time	What was said? (KA: Alexakos' HR) (C: Corinna's HR)	What was heard?	What action was done?
16:32:00	*KA: (KA-81) (C-82)marching in step(KA-80) (C-82)*		Corinna focused on what Fergie was doing with the oximeters. They were still in side dialogue.
16:32:01	*You know (KA-80) (C-85) ...*		
16:32:02	*Basically almost*		
16:32:03	*everybody(KA-80) (C-87)*		
16:32:04	*In(KA-81) (C-87) that parade(KA-81) (C-85)*		
16:32:05	*was someone of*		
16:32:06	*color (KA-81) (C-82).*		Corinna refocused on Alexakos.
16:32:07	*Um(KA-81) (C-79)*		
16:32:08	*The fact when you said(KA-81) (C-81)*		
16:32:09	*'Ay um ... Like ...*		
16:32:10	*I didn't see them (KA-81) (C-82).'*		
16:32:11	*Right?*	*Corie laughing*	Corinna looked at the computer that was recording the class and oximeter readings live.
16:32:12	*That must've came out with laughter-*		
16:32:13	*Didn't it?*	*Student 1: yea/ Student2: yea*	Corinna focused on what Fergie was doing with the oximeters and started a side dialogue with her.
16:32:14		*Class *inaudible* (KA-81) (C-84)*	
16:32:15		*Class *inaudible*(KA-81) (C-78)*	
16:32:16	*Yea(KA-82) (C-78)*		
16:32:17	*And(KA-82) (C-74) so(KA-84) (C-74),*		Corinna refocused on Alexakos.
16:32:18	*Well it's(KA-84) (C-72) rather interesting*		Corinna focused on what Fergie was doing with oximeters.

(cont.)

TABLE 8.3 Transcript of fourth and fifth events within the third minute (*cont.*)

Time	What was said? (KA: Alexakos' HR) (C: Corinna's HR)	What was heard?	What action was done?
16:32:19	*To see how(KA-84) (C-76) this*		Corinna refocused on Alexakos.
16:32:20	*Happened(KA-85) (C-76)*		Corinna adjusted the glasses on her face.
16:32:21	*And the kind(KA-85) (C-79) of emotions*		Corinna refocused on Alexakos.
16:32:22	*That ... that have come up(KA-85) (C-82)*		Corinna mushed her lips while still focused on Alexakos.
16:32:23	*Because then(KA-83) (C-82)*		
16:32:24	*At the same time*		Corinna looked at the computer that was recording class and oximeter readings live.
16:32:25	*Crossing(KA-83) (C-85) the street(KA-82) (C-85)*		Corinna refocused on Alexakos.
16:32:26	*You have to deal(KA-82) (C-91) with the*		
16:32:27	*Barricades(KA-81) (C-91), you have to deal with the*		Corinna looked at the computer that was recording the class and oximeter readings live.
16:32:28	*Cops (KA-81) (C-92).*		Corinna looked down when Alexakos said "cops" while nodding her head in agreement
16:32:29	*There was(KA-81) (C-89) somebody who*		Corinna remained looking down
16:32:30	*Assumed(KA-82) (C-85) ... uh*		
16:32:31	*Very correctly(KA-82) (C-83)*		
16:32:32	*I think – that(KA-81) (C-83)*		

(*cont.*)

TABLE 8.3   Transcript of fourth and fifth events within the third minute *(cont.)*

Time	What was said? (KA: Alexakos' HR) (C: Corinna's HR)	What was heard?	What action was done?
16:32:33	*Was a*		Corinna did a hard
16:32:34	*Professor(KA-81) (C-81) here*		blink then leaned in
16:32:35	*Who*		to write on her book
16:32:36	*She(KA-81) (C-83) fit(KA-80) (C-83) the stereotypes*		
16:32:37	*Of(KA-80) (C-84)*		
16:32:38	*White(KA-79) (C-84) female kinda*		
16:32:39	*Dressed(KA-79) (C-82) like an academic(KA-77) (C-82)*		
16:32:40	*You(KA-77) (C-81) know*		Corinna rubbed her brow.
16:32:41	*And she wanted to Cross the*		Corinna continued to
16:32:42	*street(KA-77) (C-83) so the cop said*		write in her book.
16:32:43	*Nope. You can't cross*		
16:32:44	**sound effect :vroop:**		
16:32:45	*She's like, "Why you pushing (KA-78) (C-83) me?*		
16:32:46	*Why you pushing me?*		
16:32:47	*It's like(KA-78) (C-84)*		
16:32:48	*Something you don't do*		
16:32:49	*You know(KA-78) (C-85)*		
16:32:50	*Whole bunch of cops around*		
16:32:51	*You know ... Keep(KA-77) (C-85)*		
16:32:52	*Moving*		
16:32:53	*But the whole(KA-77) (C-86)*		
16:32:54	*Experience(KA-79) (C-86)*		
16:32:55	*Uh(KA-83) (C-86)*		
16:32:56	*I wasn't(KA-86) (C-86) wearing*		
16:32:57	*My oximeter*		
16:32:58	*um (KA-86) (C-88) ... you can see it now, right?*		
16:32:59	*It's (KA-88) (C-85) uh ...*		

between focusing on Alexakos and looking at what Fergie was doing, my HR stayed in the 70s. That's just how uncomfortable I was with the discussion even though I looked outwardly okay. I mean I knew I could talk if I wanted to and that there was nothing wrong with listening. As Alexakos was sharing the experience about the "dealing... cops," my HR went up to 91 and 92 bpm. I more than likely had something to say because when he said cops, I nodded while looking down. I had something to say but didn't want to speak. I needed to address my thoughts somehow. So, I started looking back and forth to the computer. More than likely, I wanted to search something on the internet or quickly check an e-mail but didn't want to stop the screenshots from collecting and recording data. So, I wrote in my book. It couldn't have been notes because this was still anecdotal and had nothing to do with readings.

2.8   What Happened When Alexakos Mentioned "Color"?

Corinna: It was like I could hear him now better than I had wanted to. I started to think about all my relatives who went into the military to run away from home situations and be able to prove to themselves that they could make it for themselves. I thought of how my mother graduated from college but still went into the Navy. She was to be deployed to Germany but didn't because right before being approved for deployment – they found out she was pregnant with me. My mother had refused to give anyone in her family rights over me because she wanted to take care of me herself. She couldn't stay in the military after that.

Alexakos continued the conversation, as detailed in Table 8.4, sharing the story of his colleague's experience with a cop. The professor expressed self-awareness of how he felt shivers while recollecting this event and knew that his HR would be a little higher than expected. Alexakos, at that moment, was very mindful and aware, and called me on it as I was a student-researcher looking at oximeter data (Powietrzynska, 2014).

2.9   What Happened during This Minute?

Corinna: I was still fidgety as class went on, but my HR didn't go back up 90 bpm thankfully. It wasn't until I laughed that my HR went back down to the 70s. I started writing notes because Alexakos was getting back into talking about meaning making and emotions. Towards the end of

TABLE 8.4 Transcript of sixth event within the fourth minute

Time	What was said? (KA: Alexakos' HR) (C: Corinna's HR)	What was heard?	What action was done?
16:33:00	KA: (KA-88) (C-85) Right? (KA-88) (C-84)		Corinna wrote in her book.
16:33:01	Where am I at, uh, Corinna? (KA-88) (C-86)		Corinna looked up at the computer and scratched
16:33:02	I'm at 88.		her head.
16:33:03		Corinna: Yup.	
16:33:04	Just(KA-88) (C-87) going back(KA-87) (C-87) to the		
16:33:05	Experience		
16:33:06	And(KA-85) (C-87) I know the kind of(KA-82) (C-85)		Corinna wrote in her book.
16:33:07	Things		
16:33:08	It's almost(KA-79) (C-84) like		Corinna looked left and right quickly.
16:33:09	Reliving the(KA-79) (C-85)		Corinna refocused on
16:33:10	Experience ... um ...		Alexakos.
16:33:11	And so(KA-76) (C-85)		Corinna looked left and right quickly.
16:33:12	The kind of things that		Corinna looked down.
16:33:13	You tend to box (KA-76) (C-84).		
16:33:14	I think there's meaning(KA-76) (C-83)		
16:33:15	I talked(KA-75) (C-83) about earlier		
16:33:16	How it's created		Corinna focused on what Fergie was doing with oximeters.

(*cont.*)

TABLE 8.4   Transcript of sixth event within the fourth minute (*cont.*)

Time	What was said? (KA: Alexakos' HR) (C: Corinna's HR)	What was heard?	What action was done?
16:33:17	*Based on our*		Corinna rocked her head
16:33:18	*Past(KA-73) (C-83) uh*		back and forth.
16:33:19	*Experiences(KA-73) (C-85)*		
16:33:20	*And our(KA-73) (C-86)*		
16:33:21	*I mean it's funny*		
16:33:22	*I feel(KA-73) (C-84) shivers(KA-72) (C-84)*		
16:33:23	*Going straight(KA-72) (C-82) to the back*		Corinna refocused on Alexakos.
16:33:24	*of my neck*		Corinna rocked her head
16:33:25	*Continuously*		back and forth while
16:33:26	*Um*		looking at Alexakos.
16:33:27			
16:33:28	*And(KA-72) (C-84)*		
16:33:29	*How it's meaning*		Corinna looked down and rocked her head
16:33:30	*And it's emotions*		some more.
16:33:31	*So, I come(KA-72) (C-82) in.*		Corinna wrote in her
16:33:32	*Christine(KA-71) (C-82) is*		book.
16:33:33	*downstairs (KA-71) (C-81). She's like,*		
16:33:34	*'oh(KA-71) (C-79)' you know*		
16:33:35	*'I want(KA-72) (C-79) to talk'*		
16:33:36	*'whatever(KA-73) (C-79), whatever'*		
16:33:37	*I'm like*		
16:33:38	*'yea(KA-73) (C-80), yea(KA-74) (C-80)'*		
16:33:39	*And(KA-74) (C-82) then(KA-75) (C-82) Corinna's there*		Corinna looked up at Alexakos.
16:33:40	*So(KA-74) (C-82) then*		
16:33:41	*You know – my emotions drop*		

(*cont.*)

TABLE 8.4   Transcript of sixth event within the fourth minute (*cont.*)

Time	What was said? (KA: Alexakos' HR) (C: Corinna's HR)	What was heard?	What action was done?
16:33:42	*down. And then(KA-74) (C-81)*		Corinna's eyebrows went
16:33:43	*Who was it? Of course I see*		up while eyes wandering a bit.
16:33:44	*Caitlyn there.*		Corinna looked at Alexakos.
16:33:45	*Who's like'*		Corinna looked at the computer that was recording the oximeter readings and recording the class live.
16:33:46	*'oh(KA-74) (C-82) I(KA-75) (C-82) want to talk to you if you don't mind'*		Corinna quickly looked left and right.
16:33:47	*Of course(KA-74) (C-83)*		
16:33:48	*it doesn't matter*		
16:33:49	*You know(KA-75) (C-82)*		
16:33:50	*I got to put down my own work(KA-74) (C-80)*		Corinna smiled.
16:33:51	*So I start laughing*	Some	Corinna's laughing to
16:33:52	*And(KA-74) (C-77) then my mood changes*	laughter in the classroom from classmates.	herself.
16:33:53			
16:33:54	*Right? (KA-74) (C-76) So.*		Corinna looked at the
16:33:55	*All this (KA-75) (C-76).*		computer that was
16:33:56	*As we look(KA-76) (C-78) at it*		recording oximeter
16:33:57	*As researchers(KA-76) (C-77)*		readings and recording
16:33:58	*I mean*		the class live.
16:33:59	*We can say (KA-76) (C-79), 'okay ...'*		

> the minute, he was getting into researching with emotions. He pulled me back into class by asking what his HR was causing me to respond and it made me pay more attention to what was going on. He made me alert and it made me feel okay with looking at the computer at my HR once in a while. My HR was already in the 80s as I was writing in my book. Alexakos asked me his HR and looked at his oximeter and I looked as well where, just after, my HR went up to 87 and his went down to 87.

In the fourth minute, Alexakos wrapped up the conversation by reconnecting with Bakhtin's ideas of the creation of meaning through experiences. Although in the earlier portion of the minute we matched at 87, he continued to talk about his internal changes (as he was experiencing them) as he relived the experiences he shared with the class.

3 Disrupting a Thorny Issue

This four-minute event uncovered how I react, in a disruptive manner, in a classroom when a thorny issue that I am uncomfortable with is brought up in class. Thorny issue is a phrase used to describe an emotionally charged topic for discussion wrought with pain and suffering that is brought up in a learning environment for a potentially transformative experience (Alexakos, Pride, Amat et al., 2016). In this study, the word "race" triggered emotions for me because I have had experiences where others would quickly validate or invalidate my voice and my identity on the matter based on how they viewed my position as an Afro-Latina, which affected how I would identify myself. As Alexakos continued to talk about the number of *people of color* in the military, as he said it in the transcript, he highlighted opportunity and access or lack thereof. Gloria Ladson-Billings' (1995) Culturally Relevant Pedagogy (CRP) argued that teachers who are successfully culturally relevant and support the success of minority students produce students who are more successful in schools and challenge social order of the existing state of affairs, which is an extension of her argument for Critical Race Theory (CRT) of education (1995). This CRT of education, similar to the CRT found in legal scholarship and defined originally by Derrick Bell in the 1970s, sought to provide a framework of research in education for analysis of racial inequity in the United States – human rights being below property rights, and the two positions combined, which has history, leading back to the Frankfurt School in Germany and DuBois (Martinez, 2015). Alexakos practices CRP in his way of teaching and takes opportunities to open these discussions in his classrooms as he presents thorny issues as topics of classroom discussions, in his research, and in helping his students research emotions in teaching and learning. CRP has three theoretical underpinnings: how culturally relevant teachers view self and others to promote academic success and transformative learning; how culturally relevant teachers structure relations between themselves and students and build a community of learners to make room for collective connected learning; and how culturally relevant teachers view knowledge and how it emerges and develops (Ladson-Billings, 1995).

My narrative was used to explain not only what happened but to also give my voice authority as I am a participant-researcher in this study. Through my narrative, the intent is both hermeneutic, in that I need to explain what happened and why it did, and self-reflective, in that through researching the experience, it may be transformative as I am now aware of my response to race being discussed and could be more aware when thorny issues are discussed in the future, thereby partly making this study a bricolage. Bricolage is using multiple methods to offer an authentic historical account of my way of seeing and creating knowledge in this study for both myself and in general (Kincheloe, 2011). My narrative offers a view as my former, or past, self, and this research expresses the transformative nature of this study through reflexivity. Applying Collins' IR Theory, there are two Interaction Ritual Chains (IRCs) that are occurring. Alexakos is the professor in the course viewed as the expert sharing his knowledge to his students on researching emotions. The second interaction is between myself and Fergie, where at first, I didn't really want to participate, but I found myself initiating disruptive behavior. While I view Alexakos as a culturally relevant teacher, Kincheloe's Critical Pedagogy allows for a broader discussion of culture and power and the effects on marginalized students (Bayne, 2009). I argue that both frameworks apply for this study as the topic shifted to race and limitations and opportunities, which is the part of the conversation where I expressed the most discomfort. I was aware of my discomfort and responded to it by writing in my book, talking with Fergie, fidgeting, and looking around. Alexakos speaking about it did not make me feel threatened. Alexakos is a relatable professor who sets the energy and environment of his classroom. He does try to encourage each student and their voice in the class, so I would say the class was literally a "safe" space for me (Alexakos, 2015).

4   What Happened to My Voice?

There was a parade going on outside prior to class starting. I work a few blocks away from there. I walked through the people to the school building I needed to be in without looking at the people in the parade. I remember looking at the people watching the parade as I walked and thinking that it was cool that families would go to watch the parade together. From my narrative, culture was based on solidarity by race, and power was reflected in lack of capital – be it social or economic. My narrative made me aware that while I identify as *Black Hispanic* or *Afro-Latina*, I still had taken away the importance of my voice in discussions on race. I lost my voice and I didn't realize how important that was. I know that I did not write how I felt about that part of the discussion when I was writing in my notes, because I had refused to be a part of the discussion in general and for myself. My classmates did not jump in to make a point either at that part of the discussion. Now looking at the narrative, remembering how I felt, I question if I needed to really say something at that moment or just call myself to be aware of it. What would be more beneficial for me? Writing this chapter is more difficult than I thought it would be because it calls for this level of truth about a thorny issue that I would never had voiced in any other way. I know who and what I am, and I am confident in that manner; however, in discussing race, I almost feel helpless. No, not almost. I am helpless. I don't know what to do, so it is hard for me to talk about something I don't know how to make an impact on.

4.1 *How My Ontology Transformed through Being Aware*

My views on how to include my perspective with others when it comes to race were questioned, and this research put me in a position to write through it. This paper serves as an empowerment tool for me to not cut myself out of conversations of race. If I have something I find of value to say in a conversation surrounding race, I will say it like in any other type of dialogue. Prior to this investigation, I thought I was in a good enough place to start talking if I felt like I wanted to hear or speak about race. This experience allowed me to acknowledge that while I know who I am and had long validated and accepted myself, I did not always feel right expressing, even in a safe space, who I was to another person or group of people. Even in a safe space, I face having to defend or prove my identity by either speaking the language or describing something native. It gets tiring and is offensive when the person asking you for such proof is also from the same country. Now, I am thinking about how to address these thorny issues even in a safe space. If I am in a conversation where I have the potential of feeling offended or unaccepted regarding how I define myself, I am in a place where I can push back and openly discuss it if I want to. Is it okay that I may not want to? Do I always have to speak? Is my voice always necessary? Being strong in who I am does not require me to always speak in a conversation about race. From this study, I have learned that what I need is to be comfortable being a listener in the conversation too.

References

Alexakos, K., Pride, L. D., Amat, A., Tsetsakos, P., Lee, K. J., Paylor-Smith, C., Zapata, C., Wright, S., & Smith, T. (2016). Mindfulness and discussing "thorny" issues in the classroom. *Cultural Studies of Science Education, 11*(3), 741-769. https://doi.org/10.1007/s11422-015-9718-0

Alexakos, K. (2015). Becoming a science educator | researcher: A personal narrative from a sociocultural perspective. In C. Milne, K. Tobin, & D. DeGennaro (Eds.), *Sociocultural studies and implications for science education* (Vol. 12, pp. 197–209). Springer. https://doi.org/10.1007/978-94-007-4240-6_10

Alexakos, K. (2015). *Being a teacher| researcher: A primer on doing authentic inquiry research on teaching and learning.* Springer.

Bakhtin, M. M., Voloshinov, V. N., Medvedev, P. N., & Morris, P. (1994). *The Bakhtin reader: Selected writings of Bakhtin, Medvedev, and Voloshinov.* E. Arnold.

Calderón, O. (2014). *Transformative science education through action research and self-study practices* (Dissertations and theses, 2014–Present, Paper 22). http://works.gc.cuny.edu/etd/22

Collins, R. (2004). *Interaction ritual chains.* Princeton University Press.

Davidson, R. J., & Begley, S. (2012). *The emotional life of your brain: How its unique patterns affect the way you think, feel, and live – And how you can change them.* Hudson Street Press.

Gayle, B. M., Cortez, D., & Preiss, R. W. (2013) Safe spaces, difficult dialogues, and critical thinking. *International Journal for the Scholarship of Teaching and Learning, 7*(2).

Martinez, A. Y. (2014). Critical race theory: Its origins, history, and importance to the discourses and rhetorics of race. *Frame: Journal of Literary Studies, 27*(2), 9–27.

Pride, L. D. (2018). *Using authentic inquiry to unpack emotions and thorny issues within teaching and learning.* CUNY Academic Works. https://academicworks.cuny.edu/gc_etds/2717

Roth, W. M. (2009). Auto/ethnography and the question of ethics. *Forum Qualitative Sozialforschung/Forum: Qualitative Social Research, 10*(1).

Schutz, P. A., & Zembylas, M. (Eds.). (2009). *Advances in teacher emotion research.* Springer.

Sewell, W. H. (2005). *Logics of history: Social theory and social transformation.* University of Chicago Press.

Tobin, K. (2006). Learning to teach through coteaching and cogenerative dialogue. *Teaching Education, 17*(2), 133–142.

Tobin, K. (2015). The sociocultural turn in science education and its transformative potential. In *Sociocultural studies and implications for science education* (pp. 3–31). Springer.

Tobin, K., & Ritchie, S. M. (2012). Multi-method, multi-theoretical, research in the learning sciences multi-level. *Asia-Pacific Education Researcher, 21*(1), 117–129.

Turner, J. H. (2009). The sociology of emotions: Basic theoretical arguments. *Emotion Review, 1*(4), 340–354. doi:10.1177/1754073909338305

Waldman, P. (2015). *Educating desire: Autobiographical impressions of addiction in alcoholics anonymous.* Springer.

CHAPTER 9

Contemplative, Visual Arts-Based Research Methods for Self-Care and Transformation

Helen Kwah and Gene Fellner

Abstract

In this chapter, I (Kwah) describe how I used contemplative, visual arts-based research methods to reflect upon my experiences as a first-generation Asian-American woman and teacher in relation to students who were also women of color. Applying principles of practice derived from Buddhist meditation, I engaged in drawing and collage-making as visual arts methods to attend to the emotions and thoughts that arose with my reflections. The contemplative process provided a way to better 'see' myself and heal from difficult experiences of racialized injustice, and the visual arts methods of drawing and collage-making enabled me to not only create new representations of myself in solidarity with other women of color, but also to enact forms of resistance to being seen as 'other' by the colonizing gaze of the dominant culture. Thus, I propose that the merging of contemplative and visual arts practices can offer methodologies for autoethnographic research that facilitate self-care and personal and social transformations. I provide explanations in this chapter of the ideas that informed my methods and the details of my process with examples of my visual artifacts. Woven throughout, I engage with a close colleague, Gene Fellner, in a form of responsive dialogue to discuss questions that arose for him concerning my methods and artifacts. We then close the chapter with a metalogue that explores implications and further questions for the use of these methodologies.

Keywords

arts-based educational research – contemplative arts – self-care – decolonization – autoethnography – metalogue

1   Experiences Leading to Art and Contemplation

As a teacher and researcher, I (Kwah) have encountered several students over the years that I had difficulty establishing a connection with; these students were young women of color who were labeled with a disability and not succeeding in school. As an Asian-American female and first generation immigrant who has struggled in school, I felt a bond with these young women in our common objectification as racialized and gendered 'others' within the systems of school and society. After my experiences with these young women, I turned to drawing and collage-making as contemplative, visual arts-based methods for engaging in autoethnographic self-reflection as I recognized the need to know myself better in order to create genuine relationships with other young women of color. Drawing and collage-making helped to facilitate a contemplative process of reflecting upon the thoughts and emotions that attended my own experiences and ways that I had internalized the patriarchal and colonizing gaze (hooks, 1992). Visual arts methods also afforded a means to (re) imagine representations of 'otherness' and the possibilities for solidarity with women of color including the women of color artists whose work I invoked in my own. Framed as an autoethnography with the goal of resonating from the personal to the political, my use of contemplative, visual arts methods functioned as self-care, which I view as a necessity for enabling individuals and communities to heal from racial trauma and injustice (Lorde, 1988).

In this chapter, I describe how I used contemplative, visual arts-based research methods to reflect upon my experiences as a first-generation Asian-American woman and teacher in relation to students who were also women of color. Applying principles of practice derived from Buddhist meditation, I engaged in drawing and collage-making as visual arts methods to attend to the emotions and thoughts that arose with my reflections. The contemplative process provided a way to better 'see' myself and heal from difficult experiences of racialized injustice, and the visual arts methods of drawing and collage-making enabled me to not only create new representations of myself in solidarity with other women of color, but also to enact forms of resistance to being seen as 'other' by the colonizing gaze of the dominant culture. Thus, I propose that the merging of contemplative and visual arts practices can offer methodologies for autoethnographic research that facilitate self-care and personal and social transformations. I provide explanations in this chapter of the ideas that informed my methods and the details of my process with examples of my visual artifacts. Woven throughout, I engage with a close colleague, Gene Fellner, in a form of responsive dialogue to discuss questions that arose for him concerning my methods and artifacts. We then close the chapter with a metalogue that explores implications and further questions for the use of these methodologies.

1.1   *Drawing as a Foundation*

When I was four years old, I started drawing in the blank pages of books. I drew figures of princesses and animals – the companions I didn't have after we immigrated to the United States. My family settled in a town in New York where there were few Asians. Early on I learned that the gaze of others was dangerous as it could bring racial taunts and physical intimidation. I could not yet theorize the gaze as gendered objectification (Mulvey, 1975) or the assertion of regulatory power in postcolonial regimes (Foucault, 1995; Said, 1978).

As a child, I thus coped the way my parents did by looking away and silencing myself. School was no better but as teachers spoke and I was supposed to be taking notes, I found an expressive outlet through drawing. I doodled patterns and pictures all over the margins of notebooks and the white spaces of handouts. Drawing helped me to think and it comforted me; the clutch of the pencil in my hand and the repetitive motions of sketching were an anchor and meditation.

Through drawing I could claim a certain 'right to look' (Mirzoeff, 2011) but I never dared look at myself. I made drawings of things that I saw but I never wanted to draw a self-portrait: I was afraid of something monstrous that might be visible just under my skin, although perhaps it was just how deeply I had internalized the gaze of others. In middle school, my parents urged me to put the drawing away in order to succeed in academics. Similar to the high-achieving young black women that Signithia Fordham (1993) described, I learned to 'pass' through high school, college and post-graduate studies by negating my race and gender, and impersonating the image of the dominant white male subject.

1.2   *Turning again to Drawing*

By the time I was in the last two years of my doctoral education, I had an opportunity to lead and conduct research on an afterschool game design program for middle school girls. The school was located in an urban, low income neighborhood and the students were predominantly Black and Hispanic. While the game design program ran as planned and was successful in many ways, I was struck by the challenges I felt in establishing close connections to my students. At the time, I felt my differences sharply from them – racial, cultural and class differences, and my status as a university researcher – but I also longed to know them better and reach out to them as an older sister. I felt kinship with these young women, with what I perceived to be their desires to express themselves despite the oppressions and injustices they struggled against in their daily lives. However, I acknowledge that at that time I was not ready to address the issues of race, gender, class and power that separated and united us. When the program ended, I was disappointed in not having made stronger connections with these young women.

More recently, I experienced a similar disappointment in connecting with another young Black female student, Alysha (pseudonym). I met Alysha through my colleague, Gene Fellner, who had invited her to co-teach his graduate level Special Education class for pre-service teachers. Alysha's school principal had developed a coteaching initiative with Gene and chose her for this role. Although Alysha had been labeled with an attention deficit hyperactivity disorder and behavioral issues since elementary school, in her final year of high school she was distinguishing herself and had plans for college.

When Gene first introduced me to Alysha, she spoke about her favorite class, an art class, and one of her favorite painters, Frida Kahlo. In particular, Alysha described Kahlo's double self-portrait, titled "the Two Fridas," in remarkable detail from memory, and conveyed her sense of identification with the 'two sides' of Frida: the wounded side and the side that could heal herself. I was moved by Alysha's invocation of the healing power of art-making and her identification with Frida Kahlo. I proposed to develop a digital arts afterschool workshop with Alysha, and both Gene and I were planning to meet with her again to continue our discussions. However, after that initial meeting, Alysha dropped out of contact. Months later we found out from her school principal that Alysha had failed to be accepted by the one college she had applied to and that she had no alternative plans except to work full time at a low-paying job. Gene had also asked Alysha for consent to use her image in research publications, and at that point, Alysha declined.

I had been looking forward to meeting and speaking with Alysha again, and the loss resonated with my earlier failures to reach out to some of the young women in the afterschool game design program. In both cases of failure to reach and the refusal to participate, I did not want to nor could not assume the position of representing these young women. Rather, I realized the need to turn inward before knowing better how to reach outward. The final meeting with Alysha inspired a turn to self-reflection in the form of autoethnography and a return to visual arts practices as my method.

2 Autoethnography and Contemplative Methods

The arts practices I chose were digital collage-making and drawing, and my method was situated within the qualitative research framework of autoethnography. In autoethnography, knowledge is constituted through a process of looking inward to personal experience, which reveals and is shaped by cultural experience (Ellis & Bochner, 2000). Culture does not fully determine the individual though and so by turning inward to see one's experience there is an opportunity to see anew, especially when using arts-based or other nonconventional methods that can access embodied or otherwise implicit aspects of experience (Slattery, 2003).

A process of seeing one's experiences involves a close attention to one's perceptions, thoughts, and feelings. Both artistic practices and Buddhist meditation practices engage such a process, and for this reason, arts practices are often invoked as methods for contemplation (see Walsh, 2015). I viewed my use of the artistic modes of collage-making and drawing as contemplative, and my application was shaped by my own ongoing history of engaging in Buddhist meditation practices. Specifically, I have practiced a form of mindfulness meditation where the goal is to cultivate a non-dual awareness of all phenomena, including one's thoughts and feelings as they arise; such an awareness implies that a subject-object duality no longer structures one's way of knowing and relating to others in the world (Dunne, 2015).

The subject-object dualism can also be understood as the ontological and epistemological framework that underlies all expressions of power and violence enacted by one group (e.g., race/class/gender) over another, including the 'othering' of the imperialist, patriarchal, capitalist, white supremacist gaze (hooks, 1992). I should emphasize though that I did not expect that my efforts to use arts-based methods for contemplative self-reflection would achieve a total dissolution of dualistic subject-object conceptions. Just as with Buddhist meditation practice, the larger goal presents a vision of where one wants to arrive, and the practice is a process for getting there.

2.1   Self-Care and Healing

I emphasize then a contemplative process where collage-making and drawing were methods that helped cultivate a visual form of non-judgmental and compassionate attention to the form, shape, texture and tone of my thoughts and emotions. Further, when difficult emotions such as anger and fear arose, a contemplative process made it more possible to give space to and stay with emotions that would otherwise overwhelm or that I would turn away from. As the renowned Buddhist nun, Pema Chodron (2008, pp. 20–21), explains:

> We stay with the emotion, experience it, and leave it as it is, without proliferating. Thus, we train in opening the fearful heart to the restlessness of our own energy. We learn to abide with the experience of our emotions ... We make the choice, moment-by-moment, to be fully here. Attending to

our present-moment mind and body is a way of being tender toward self, toward others, and toward the world. This quality of attention is inherent in our ability to love.

Thus, the capacity to stay with difficult thoughts and emotions is important to cultivate in order to heal ourselves from our own suffering and to better know how to reach out to others.

2.2 Mini-Metalogue

Gene: I am wondering about the relationship between contemplation and transformation, and maybe especially the relationship of transformation of self to transformation of the world. The concept of contemplation, like the idea of self-care, can seem very self-involved, and yet bell hooks points out that you can't take care of anyone else unless you take care of yourself. How do you see this internal process of contemplation mediating self and other transformation? And is contemplation sealed off from what takes place externally? Can these even be separated?

Helen: In the quote from Pema Chodron above, she urges us to see how our capacity to attend to, hold, and be fully present with ourselves underlies our capacity to love others. As you mention, bell hooks points to the same understanding. However, Buddhist philosophers as well as modern social theorists, such as Pierre Bourdieu, have suggested that self and societal transformations are difficult because the views, ideas, dispositions, and emotional states that prompt our actions operate on an unconscious and habitual level. So it does require some form of on-going practice of genuine, and as even Bourdieu acknowledges, 'embodied' practice of self-reflection in order to get at these unconscious, habitual levels and to manifest as transformation in the way one thinks, feels, and acts toward self and others in the world.

In her epilogue to *A Burst of Light*, Audre Lorde (1988) wrote, "Caring for myself is not self-indulgence, it is self-preservation, and that is an act of political warfare" (p. 130). These often-cited words are testament to the fact that our individual bodies and lives are situated, and for those of us with particular bodies and who are of particular groups, our self-care is a radical action with collective consequences. More recently, Shawn Ginwright (2015) has articulated the need for "radical healing," which confirms the vital political role of self-care in enabling individuals to both heal from racial trauma, violence and injustice, and gather the strength and wisdom to collectively transform their lives and communities. Further, the healing of marginalized individuals and communities needs to take place also at the site of our visual representations. As bell hooks (1995, p. 179) writes:

> All colonized and subjugated people who, by way of resistance, create an oppositional subculture within the framework of domination recognize that the field of representation (how we see ourselves, how others see us) is a site of ongoing struggle. The history of black liberation movements in the United States could be characterized as a struggle over images as much as it has also been a struggle for rights, for equal access.

The use of visual arts for contemplative self-reflection can be significant for self-care and healing in that it provides modes and methods for enacting resistance and re-creating representations of ourselves that assert possibilities for our solidarity.

3   Arts-Based Methods

In the following sections, I describe the process for using collage-making and drawing for contemplative self-reflection and (re)imagining solidarity with other women of color. I began my work by reviewing photos from the afterschool program and re-watching the video recordings of my meeting with Alysha. Selections from the photographs and stills from the video recordings provided starting points for composing digital collages and drawings. Simultaneously, I began turning to the work of several women of color female visual artists (especially, Ana Mendieta and Frida Kahlo) and bringing elements of their work into the collages and drawings.

3.1   The Collage-Making Process
I began the initial collages after finding several interesting moments where three of the young women in the afterschool program, Shana, Michelle, and Lisa (all pseudonyms), were featured. Two examples include the first still below (Figure 9.1a) where Shana's arms are lifted up in a seemingly futile attention-getting gesture and Michelle silently sinks to her desk with eyes closed and hand holding her head. In the second still (Figure 9.1b), Lisa is at the front of the room giving a presentation and with mock anger points at another student who was interrupting her.

FIGURE 9.1   (a) Shana and Michelle; (b) Lisa (stills from video)

Seeing these young women again brought a mix of feelings and thoughts. For example, I remembered being afraid of how 'loud' I thought Shana and Lisa were. I wondered how I had objectified them so that their performativity seemed threatening. I recalled when Shana began making fun of 'Chinese' people within my earshot and how that triggered feelings of fear and shame. And yet, I remembered their expressive energy, and my feeling of joy in seeing them move uninhibitedly around the room.

In place of traditional qualitative methods for analysis, I engaged in a process of contemplation and collage-making. I started by clipping from the still images to bring into PowerPoint, which I chose for its capacity to animate and play images on slides in sequence. I did not record or otherwise write anything down. Rather, as thoughts and emotions arose, I paid attention to the somatic sensations that accompanied them, such as warmth in my chest or a constriction in my throat. Simultaneously or in pauses, I repetitively manipulated images and words on the computer by reclipping, cropping, copying, pasting and juxtaposing until combinations emerged that *resonated* with particular thoughts and feelings.

Throughout my process of collage-making or drawing, I sought a sense of *resonance*, which was aligned with Tom Barone and Elliot Eisner's (2012) definition of *evocation and illumination*. Barone and Eisner (2012) address the question of 'How do we evaluate arts-based research?' by considering the capacity of arts-based artifacts to *evoke and illuminate* a subject so that the subject becomes both familiarized and perceived from different perspectives. Barone and Eisner (2012) acknowledge that this or any criteria for evaluating arts-based research should be seen as a "cue to perception" and not applied prescriptively. Similarly, as I worked on collages or drawings, the moments where I found the artifact to be resonant, or evocative and illuminating, arose organically as I stepped back and forth from the work in progress. There was and is no rubric, and any viewer of the completed works will also necessarily

FIGURE 9.2   Series of images questioning self and viewer (stills from video)

arrive at their own, subjective assessment of the capacity of the artifacts to resonate with their experience and understanding.

As an example of my process, I created a series of images from the video stills where the words, "I don't know ... you" were projected (Figure 9.2). Each collaged image appeared on separate PowerPoint slides with pauses before the words appeared on the screen. This allowed for a moment where the young women in the classroom could be (re)presented as a question for seeing until words appeared that challenged or made ambiguous any answer to the question. This series of images, which both invited and questioned the viewer's seeing of the young women, resonated with my sense that I both did not know them and did not know myself.

3.2   *Mini-Metalogue*

Gene: I like how the series of images in this collage juggles multiple meanings. It does so by: 1. Joining images that are seen and text that is read (two different and non-redundant ways of conveying meaning); 2. Contesting through images the periods that are part of the text-image; 3. Showing two different girls in different positions accompanied by identical text; and 4. Creating a border that separates the images but at the same time connects them. From where I stand, I find the collage unsettling and challenging because it exposes the chasm between these young black girls and me which might be aligned with your own interpretation of them.

But images even without text are polysemic and polyphonic in that the viewer brings their own experience to their interpretation. Without your explanatory text, the viewer might see the words as representing what the girls in the images are saying rather than what the artist is contemplating. Additionally, I could see the experiences the viewer brings to the images might leading to deficit narratives about the girls who are shown. Does it at all bother you that once the images are out there your control over their interpretation disappears?

Helen: To a certain extent artists address this issue with labels and artists' statements when their work is shown in a gallery. It doesn't bother me that I don't have control over how the images are interpreted because images invite polysemia. Images do not specify their referents in the way that words do, and this is why they are in some ways a more appropriate language to not only evoke one's own experience but also to communicate with multiple viewers whose experiences may differ. Whatever others may read into the images, even deficit meanings, can provide the starting point for discussions. The question then becomes how to have those discussions with viewers because the context for showing and sharing the images (for example here, through a published chapter in a book) does not afford the discussion as easily.

During the collage-making process, I also brought in images from certain women artists that I found myself thinking about. In particular, I was drawn to the Cuban-American artist, Ana Mendieta, and her "Silhueta" series. In these works, she traced her silhouette and imprinted or left other traces of her body behind to occupy spaces and places temporarily until they disintegrated or merged back into the environment. From a copy of one of Mendieta's Silhuetas, I clipped the straw outline of Ana Mendieta's figure and brought this image into my final sequence of collages. The collaged images (Figure 9.3) resonated with my longing to assert myself and be seen, and with the pain of being invisible, the reality in my experiences of feeling silenced and absent.

3.3 *Mini-Metalogue*

Gene: I am moved by the way you've enlisted Ana Mendieta as an ally both in your explorations and in your struggles toward solidarity with women of color. The girls you've included in the collage don't know Mendieta at all, and yet you have joined their conditions with your own. In the world of words, the texts of others are often joined in thematic unity by writers and scholars of all sorts, and images created by visual

FIGURE 9.3   Series of collaged images

artists are often appropriated by other visual artists. And yet, this intuitive joining of Mendieta's images with your own and with images of your students seems as if you are engraving the connections between the three of you as a subtle political statement about the enduring oppression of women of color? Is this an example of contemplative practice, of work on the inside reverberating on surround planes?

Helen: Yes, that is how I see the inner work of contemplative practice moving through and vivifying, or giving presence to the experiences and understandings that connect me to other women of color across time, space, place, culture. That is a beautiful image of contemplative practice working from the inside-out by "reverberating on surrounding planes."

3.4   *The Drawing Process*

After working on collages, I decided to move to drawing as my arts medium. I recognized that I had not literally put myself, my own image, in the collages and I felt that drawing would be a more immediate and tactile way to bring my embodiment and representation into the work. The medium of digital collage also seemed unsatisfactory because of its immateriality. As I described from my childhood, I found pleasure in the materiality of drawing: the movements, the gestures, and sensory engagements with materials. Even more so than collage-making, drawing afforded an entry for my body to become more visible in the work. The assertion of my pleasure in drawing could be seen as a move to reclaim and re-occupy the field of representation. I also found a sense of calm in drawing; I had always experienced the repetitive motions and attention that drawing required as a contemplative practice.

I decided to turn to drawing around the time that I found out that Alysha was no longer available to meet any more. I intended the drawings to not only make the traces of my hand and body visible but to also literally (re)present images of myself in the genre of self-portraiture. Similar to the process of starting my collages, I began reviewing video recordings of my meeting with Alysha and pulling stills from the video to linger over. The video stills were a starting point for attending to the thoughts and feelings that arose as I considered my interactions with Alysha. I then began drawing my self-portrait as I saw myself through the frame of my interactions with Alysha, and as a way to imagine solidarity with Alysha and other women of color. The criteria I used for evaluating the process of drawing and the artifact itself was again an appeal to a quality of resonance or evocation (Eisner & Barone, 2012).

For an initial drawing, I began with a video still of Alysha at a moment where I recalled how I began talking too much from my class privilege of being an academic researcher, and how she began looking away into the distance. With the thoughts and emotions from that moment present, I started drawing a self-portrait based upon Alysha, but not with the intention to represent Alysha so much as to dwell with the thoughts and feelings in that remembered moment – for example, the longing to connect with her, the anxiety as I watched her tune out, and even a sense of aesthetic pleasure in seeing how the oranges and pinks in her shirt were echoed in her fingernail color and fruit drink. I began sketching the shirt she was wearing and then began drawing in a face with my features merged with hers. Unlike in the earlier digital collages I had made, I was trying to situate myself directly in the picture but still in relation, if only imagined relation, to Alysha (Figure 9.4).

FIGURE 9.4
Self-portrait 1

In subsequent drawings based upon contemplating the same video still, I explored similar tensions but found myself wanting to erase or blur the face. I started drawing my face in charcoal but as I began to smudge and wipe out the features (Figure 9.5). In a second drawing, I again began drawing my face but allowed it to become blurred beyond recognition and also eclipsed by the hair (Figure 9.6). I wondered about this move to erase or blur the face as an act of resistance, a refusal of the viewer's gaze, which could be the colonizing gaze or maybe even Alysha's refusal of my own gaze as a researcher.

FIGURE 9.5   Self-portrait 2

FIGURE 9.6   Self-portrait 3

3.5   *Mini-Metalogue*

Gene: Did you decide to use this technique of 'blurring' the face intentionally in advance of drawing or did the intention emerge from the actual act of blurring?

Helen: No, the move to blur the face came about intuitively. I was of course using an eraser as usual to erase and refine. As I began to draw and erase certain elements on my face, the traces of what I had drawn remained and evoked feelings of sadness and longing. Around this time I was also reading about the notion of the 'object's refusal' in essays by the Black critical theorist, Fred Moten (2003). He identifies the political necessity to refuse representations of 'otherness (being seen and treated as an object), and especially representations that replicate and further proliferate the spectacular forms violence enacted on Black people.

Gene: My friends who are artists have all been attracted to these drawings of yours; they find them mysterious and beautiful. Interestingly though, a friend of mine was disturbed by the drawings. He told me, "We are human. We are attracted to faces. It is someone's face and their expression that creates empathy in a painting of a human figure. I don't really like looking at these drawings."

Helen: Yes, I agree that the connection we make with each other through looking at and reading each other's faces is profound and something that I longed for. Precisely for these reasons, I think the capacity to 'look' was what I wanted to frustrate or refuse in order to see it anew. As Nicholas Mirzoeff (2011) puts it, there is a 'right to look' that those in power exercise over 'others. By blurring the face of my portraits, I was questioning this hegemonic relation and also trying to evoke the longing that we have to look at and know each other.

Also, as I drew the hair, I experienced feelings of joy in making the marks and allowing the strands to swoop wildly. The imagery and the drawing motions and sensations conveyed the feeling of a force that could not be contained any more, the force of desire for material presence, desire to be seen, and desire to move untamed. In these ways, this self-portrait in relation to Alysha resonated with the thoughts and emotions that stirred from my encounter with her, and it also explored ways to enact an oppositional gaze (hooks, 1992) and (re)present my connections to Alysha.

4 Metalogue

I have collaborated with Gene Fellner on other arts-based work involving alternative modes for sensing and knowing (Fellner & Kwah, 2018). Gene and I engage in a metalogue here to consider in more detail the ideas and implications of using visual arts-based contemplative methods for research and transformations of self and community.

4.1 Another Form and Way of Knowing

Gene: When listening to you I can't help but think of the contrast to the methods of Arendt's Socrates who tried to give birth to the truth in someone else's opinion through logical argument. Scholarly tradition, though not dialogic in the selfless way that Socrates was, largely affirms intellectual interrogation as an approach to finding truths, as if intellectual comprehension of one's own contradictions is the path to enlightenment. In your case, your first path is not to interrogate someone else's opinions, to define truths, or to study 'others' as most researchers do, but to interrogate yourself (thus blurring object-subject dualities) and your unease with your experience. You do so not through argument of any type but through a (re)presenting of your own ideas to yourself in a form – drawings, collages – that are not literal but affective; you are seeking emotional resonance rather than logical understanding.

Helen: Yes, you could say I am seeking an emotional resonance or an understanding of how I construct my experiences and relationships to others through my thoughts and emotions. This is not an understanding that can be generated or assessed through logical, positivist, Cartesian epistemologies or methods. Rather, I am suggesting in my work that contemplative, arts-based methods can help bring forth and (re)present this alternative form and way of knowing.

4.2 Understanding Contemplative Practice

Gene: However, methodologically, you are trying to identify less with your feelings (and so maybe facilitating empathy with others) through a deep immersion in those very same feelings. Is this correct? I get confused with the idea of not being attached to your thoughts and feelings since these are the catalyst for your explorations. Not being attached is supposed to be central to the Buddhist approach to wisdom, but I don't see how the non-attachment leads to emotional understanding?

Helen: Although I'm generalizing, in the Buddhist approach, it is the attachment to the 'self' that leads to suffering. Attachment means identifying very strongly with one's own thoughts and feelings in order to define and defend your sense of self in opposition to others. Usually these attachments are habitual and unconscious, so that they arise in reaction to situations and interaction with others without your conscious awareness. For example, every time you look at your own child, a whole host of subtle thoughts and feelings might arise about how the child looks and behaves that you don't consciously pay attention to but that influence how you speak to your child and what you say. The problem is that most of those thoughts and feelings reflect ideas about yourself and what you want to be identified with rather than ideas about your child based upon genuinely listening to their needs. Thoughts and feelings that are constantly being generated in this unconscious, self-centered way, and they push and pull you to act without any awareness. The detachment that is promoted through methods such as meditation is not so much a rejection or negation of thoughts and feelings so much as a move to detach from their grip. By becoming more able to see what you experience fully and without judgment, you then become more open to and able to attend to the experience of others. This is how cultivating a non-attachment leads to emotional understanding or resonance within yourself and with others.

4.3 Questions about Arts Methods

Gene: So how does your arts-based methodology reflect that process? And would you address further your process of assessment, how resonance and evocation, the criteria for evaluation that you mention, appear to you as you are working?

Helen: My arts-based method started with looking at images, whether the video stills from recordings of the afterschool program or recordings of my meeting with Alysha. As I described earlier in this chapter, as I look at the images, I notice and attend to what thoughts and feelings are arising, and how they are experienced somatically in my body. Similar to an insight or mindfulness meditation practice, I do not judge or elaborate on the thoughts or feelings or sensations. Both simultaneously and in pauses, I also engage my hands and senses in the craft of collage-making or drawing. Of course thoughts and feelings are now arising as I work with image-making, but I am again trying to notice and pay attention without judgment. I would say then that this methodology or practice is a visual form of contemplation.

As for assessment or knowing when any artifact that I'm making is successful, I agree with Tom Barone and Elliot Eisner (2012) in looking for the work's capacity to evoke and illuminate. I refer to this capacity more as a sense of 'resonance,' though. As I am working on a collage or drawing, there are always moments of stepping back to assess the work. However, I don't methodically or purposefully engage in another contemplation of the work at that point. Rather, there is an intuitive sense of whether I need to, for example, manipulate a shape, soften a line, or add a new element to the work. I continue in this way until I feel that the work is resonant or evocative of the range of thoughts, feelings, and understanding of my subject of focus.

Gene: So how would someone who is not involved in your process assess the artifacts you make?

Helen: In the case of arts-based methods and artifacts, it is hard to prescribe criteria for assessment. Again, as Barone and Eisner (2012) suggest, one can only proffer 'cues' to guide the viewer's perceptions. The challenge is that a particular artifact that I've made may or may not resonate with particular viewers. Arts-based artifacts operate similar to works of art in relying on outside viewers to bring their own experiences and capacities for noticing, sensing and attending.

Gene: You have always used art to mediate your relationship with the world and to help you to find your way within it, but what about the person who does not see herself as artistically inclined or has no particular desire to engage in artistic activity? Do you think the arts-based methods for understanding could be useful for such a person as well?

Helen: Each of us has to choose the methods that align with our views of knowledge and reality, our values and our sensibilities. Maybe an arts-based method will be more useful and appeal to someone who consciously identifies themselves as an artist or as having artistic sensibilities. Nevertheless, there are some people who may have artistic sensibilities but who have never had an opportunity to find out. In fact, it may be interesting to try an arts-based method from the standpoint of its difference from traditional methods; it's very unconventionality might provide opening for new insights.

4.4   Positionality and the Dialectics of Transformation

Gene: When you were a child, drawing was a means of survival; without it you would have sunk into despair at being and feeling 'othered' in an unfriendly world. Drawing was like a companion to you; it helped you imagine a different world and possibilities. Though possibility is still central to your arts-based projects, it seems to me that in this particular project you weren't drawing to survive in the same sense.

Helen: You could say I was drawing to survive when I was younger – even then, it was a way of healing and making sense of my situation, but drawing was also something I abandoned in high school as I attempted to assimilate to the standards, values and practices of the dominant culture. The way I engage with drawing now, at least in this arts-based research work, is as a mode for contemplating, reflecting, and re-imagining. However, perhaps I am still using drawing as a means of survival in that the contemplative self-reflective process is a way to know myself better and thus to heal from the thoughts, emotions, and experiences of racial/class/gender conflicts that had remained unseen, or insufficiently seen.

Gene: Yes, in this work you are using drawing to understand your situation with young black women, to come to terms with your experiences with them that left you feeling incomplete and longing for something more vital. You are engaging the need to be seen, the need to feel that "bodily presence," the absence of which has accompanied you since you've been young. In the digital collages you include here, your students' echo your desire, but at the same time you are aware of their vivacity, their seemingly "uninhibited movement," which you also want for yourself. When you then add Ana Mendieta's image to the collage, my impression is that you are visually joining these girls' claims to be seen with the needs and desires of a historic demand to be seen that embraces all women, third world women in particular, and you specifically. In the drawings of Alysha, your merging of your image with hers and your erasing of both your image and hers is a continuation of that process. It is also an act of refusing to be seen according to the "colonizer's gaze" and yet asserting your presence.

Helen: Yes, and what you are describing are the ways that a single visual arts-based work can resonate and evoke different thoughts, emotions and ideas, sometimes reflecting not-yet resolved tensions, and sometimes addressing different audiences. I think this multiplicity and multi-vocality is particularly made possible through a visual arts medium. Also, in terms of social and political significance, I think visual arts practices, and as I've suggested, especially contemplative visual arts practices, provide tangible routes towards the healing and transformation of individuals and communities.

Gene: Still, maybe that leap to talking about transformation needs to address the obstacles more directly. With all that unites you and the young women with whom you have worked, they nevertheless appear different from you and indeed suffer oppression in materially different ways, often severely so. Though being excluded lies at the base of both your experience and theirs in this country, anti-blackness is inextricable from the history of the United States on a root level. You don't deny this history, but you feelingly need, desire and choose to focus on the common core of your experiences, that of exclusion based on race and gender. The drawings don't get rid of the types of barriers you face in this goal, but for yourself first and then with others, they serve to illuminate the essence of solidarity – the common experiences and interests – that unite you as a sisterhood and in that emphasis, recognition and understanding there is hope and possibility which seems to me essential to personal self-healing while also opening up the opportunity for collective self-healing. Though you write about working from the inside out, transformation is never unidirectional, which is why transformative work on any level mediates transformation on other levels. You do not expect your drawing meditations to suddenly lead to revolutionary transformations, but they continue the discussion on a level beyond personal contemplation. As you change yourself, you cannot help but change the world in which you are living. And the drawings are beautiful. There is hope and possibility in that as well.

Helen: There were obstacles to relating to the young women in the after school program and Alysha, and the ones that I brought with me had to do with class differences as you point to, and also the ways that we each – they as well as I – had internalized the gaze of the dominant culture. There were many moments where we each saw each 'other' as irretrievably and sometimes dangerously different. The self-healing and transformation that I was seeking for myself and for these young women needed to address these obstacles and I believe that contemplative practices played this role. In my case, contemplative arts-based methods, whether collage-making or drawing, allowed me to sustain a non-judgmental attention to these ways that I had internalized oppression as they manifested in the thoughts and feelings that arose for me in those moments. There was the beginning of a process of self-healing and personal transformation, but to make the leap to actualization, there is a need for lots of practice. Contemplative, visual arts-based research methods helped me to sustain a practice of becoming more aware of and better able to let go of the harmful ways that I internalized and viewed others through the gaze of the dominant culture. Finally, yes, I agree that as one is always situated in and creates a world with others – personal transformation already always has an impact on transforming that world.

5   Final Words

I hope this chapter and metalogue make apparent some of the ways that contemplative, visual arts-based research methods can generate knowledge and care for the self and other, and especially for women of color or other individuals who are marginalized and seen as 'other.' By bringing a contemplative view and approach to visual arts practice, I hope it is clear how such methodologies enable a caring visual attentiveness to the emotions and thoughts that arise when reflecting upon one's experiences. Contemplative practices can help individuals and by extension, communities, heal from the emotional damage and internalized oppressions imposed by the dominant culture; and visual arts practices can provide the means for enacting resistance and (re)presenting new images of ourselves and our collective solidarity. In these ways, contemplative, visual arts-based research methods can offer profound possibilities for personal and social transformation.

References

Barone, T., & Eisner, E. W. (2012). *Arts based research.* Routledge.

Bateson, G. (1972). *Steps to an ecology of mind: Collected essays in anthropology, psychiatry, evolution, and epistemology.* Chandler Publishing Co.

Chodron, P. (2008). *Comfortable with uncertainty: 108 teachings on cultivating fearlessness and compassion.* Shambhala Publications.

Ellis, C., & Bochner, A. P. (2000). Autoethnography, personal narrative, reflexivity: Researcher as subject. In N. K. Denzin & Y. S. Lincoln (Eds.), *Handbook of qualitative research* (2nd ed., pp. 733–768). Sage.

Fellner, G., & Kwah, H. (2018). Transforming the embodied dispositions of pre-service special education teachers. *International Journal of Qualitative Studies, 31,* 520–534. https://doi.org/10.1080/09518398.2017.1422291

Fordham, S. (1993). "Those loud black girls": (Black) women, silence, and gender "passing" in the academy. *Anthropology & Education Quarterly, 24*(1), 3–32. https://doi.org/10.1525/aeq.1993.24.1.05x1736t

Foucault, M. (1995). *Discipline and punish: The birth of the prison.* Random House.

Ginwright, S. (2015). *Hope and healing in urban education: How urban activists and teachers are reclaiming matters of the heart.* Routledge.

hooks, b. (1992). *Black looks: Race and representation.* South End Press.

hooks, b. (1995). *Art on my mind: Visual politics.* The New Press.

Lorde, A. (1988). *A burst of light: Essays.* Firebrand Books.

Mirzoeff, N. (2011). The right to look. *Critical Inquiry, 37*(3), 473–496.

Moten, F. (2003). *In the break: The aesthetics of the black radical tradition.* University of Minnesota Press.

Mulvey, L. (1975). Visual pleasure and narrative cinema. *Screen, 16*(3), 6–18. https://doi.org/10.1093/screen/16.3.6

Said, E. (1978). *Orientalism.* Pantheon Books.

Slattery, P. (2003). Troubling the contours of arts-based educational research. *Qualitative Inquiry, 9*(2), 192–197. https://doi.org/10.1177/1077800402250929

Walsh, S. (2015). *Arts-based and contemplative practices in research and teaching: Honoring presence.* Routledge/Taylor & Francis Group.

CHAPTER 10

Stitching a Wound: Exploring Memories, Loss, Empty Nest, Embodied Emotions through Arts Based Research and Narrative

Anna Malyukova

Abstract

In this narrative tale I explore memories, loss, the empty nest, and embodied emotions of letting go of my children as they grow up. The methodologies I used to explore these issues are arts-based research, hermeneutic phenomenology, and heuristics; specifically use of images as a heuristic. I explore memories not as a thing of the past, but as an active part of becoming, in the present and future. The article is divided into three acts. Each ACT has BACKSTAGE sections (4 in total), which are used to present theoretical implications. There are SCENES in each of ACT, in which, in narrative form, I describe the different points in time, exploring my memories. I choose deliberately to separate narrative sections from theoretical parts to keep the description of my memories separate from the analysis.

Keywords

memories – loss – empty nest – embodied emotions – arts-based research – heuristics

1   A Konvert

When I was 20 years old, and pregnant with my son, my mother sewed for me a traditional swaddler blanket (in Russian called konvert – an envelope). On the day of leaving the hospital, mothers place their swaddled babies into a blanket, just like the one my mother made for me, and step outside to meet the rest of the family. I only used it once, but back in 1999 my mother thought it was important for me to have it. Eighteen years later, it re-emerged from the closet where it has been since my son moved here from Russia in 2005. As I let go of my son, who left for college in the fall of 2017, I dealt with the pain of being left behind. As I worked on an art-based project in a graduate class, I selected images of my children walking in different moments of their lives (in a sense away from me) and printed them out on fabric. I chose the blanket, sewed by my mother 18 years ago, to connect three generations by stitching images of my children to the blanket.

2   Conducting Arts-Based Research

2.1   *Act 1: Sets up the Stage for Conducting Arts-Based Research*
2.1.1   Backstage 1

Inspired by Carolyne Ali-Khan's (2016) creative writing style and Peter Waldman's (2015) narrative tale, I adapt their models to tell a story of how using arts-based research helped me explore memories and embodied emotions in experiencing loss and empty nest. John Van Maanen (1988) uses "impressionist tales" as a way to draw a reader into a world. Such impressionist tales allow authors and readers to sneak a peek into another's consciousness, which, for Van Maanen (1988), requires "standards [that] are not disciplinary but literary ones, the main obligation of the impressionist is to keep the audience alert and interested" (p. 106). With the goal of keeping the reader alert and interested, and also to provide a glimpse into what my experiences were like in the process of using arts as a research methodology, I use Ali-Khan's (2016) theatrical structure of a play to tell my story. Ali-Khan (2016) uses Joe Kincheloe's (2008) idea of radical listening in her piece, especially in terms of radically listening to yourself. She writes about listening to her body as she teaches, as well as paying attention to the bodies of her students, which provide her a new vantage point to understand teaching as embodied praxis (Ali-Khan, 2016). Our bodies always carry an extraordinary amount of trauma and we carry that pain in our bodies, in our minds, in our skin. As I embarked on the journey of conducting research using visual arts, I had to, first, listen to myself and notice what needed my attention, and, second, allow this embodied trauma and pain to spill over into my work. This process became transformational for me. Waldman (2015) writes about the fluid framework of narrative, how the stories of our lives change as we change. As I explored my memories, I went through what Anna Stetsenko (2017) calls, "[the] dynamic process of thinking about the past that links past memory processes to the self" (p. 306). Memories explored in the process of arts-based research became my present and my future. I also argue that reflecting on these memories allows me to "change" the past, or at least how I feel about it, which then shapes the present and the future as well.

Tom Barone and Elliot Eisner (2012) state that using arts in research is a way to evoke and compel viewers to encounter an issue or issues introduced by a research project. Barone and Eisner (2012) also write that, "Painting is an activity and the artist will therefore tend to *see* what he paints rather than *paint* what he sees" (p. 4). While taking a journey of creating an art-based research project, the process of creation is based on seeing what I create, as I learn from my creation what it is that I am actually seeing. Barone and Eisner (2012) write that arts-based research becomes a heuristic through which we deepen and make more complex our understanding of some aspects of the world. I realize that in my project, the images become a heuristic where I (and possibly others) reflect on our lives by viewing the images.

Carolina Rodrigues De Souza and Mauricio Pietrocola (2016) also write about using images in their research. De Souza and Pietrocola (2016) use photographs as a type of heuristic, in which photos and images are a way to trigger insights and also engage participants in discussions. Using images in research, according to De Souza and Pietrocola (2016), plays an important role in a process in which participants learn something about themselves by reflecting on

FIGURE 10.1
Walking along Central Park

their own experiences, prejudices in their behavior, or in their way of thinking and assessment. My research has become a personal heuristic as I try to
become aware of my own state of being as my son leaves for college. Hopefully,
it can be a heuristic for others who reflect on their own experiences of letting
go of their children, of separation, of an empty nest.

Moreover, such cultural production in social interactions, as Kenneth Tobin
(2015) argues, reproduces culture while transforming it, where culture always is
a system of reproduction | transformation (I use the Sheffer stroke, as in "repro-
duction | transformation," to express the dialectical relationship between the
two constructs, which, as Konstantinos Alexakos states (2015), present mutu-
ally contingent and emergent characteristics, which mediate and are mediated
by the other). By working on creating an art project, I learn from the research
and then represent my work in cultural production, in my case – a piece of art.

2.2   Scene 1: Getting Groceries at the Store

For the longest time, everyone had been asking me if I was ready for my son
to leave. I believed I was. At least that was what I thought until the day of his
actual leaving. I asked him what he would like for his last dinner before going to
take the bus to go to college, and then I went to the store to get a few things to
cook the meal. Standing in the middle of the vegetable aisle, I suddenly found
myself gasping for air, as I felt my chest tightening at the thought that my son
is indeed leaving. As I picked out the carrots for chicken plov, his favorite meal,
tears started falling down my cheeks and sobs wracked my whole torso. "My
boy is leaving me," was all I could think. "My boy …"

Chaotically, I gathered items from the shelves, grabbing things I did not
need and forgetting items I came for. I walked home, crying all the way. By the
time I made my way home, I was a mess. My son opened the door and saw me
completely disheveled, with red eyes, runny nose, and tears streaming down
my face.

"What happened?" he asked with a concern in his voice.

"You are leaving," I responded.

"Did you just realize this?" he asked, his voice trailing off giving away his
surprise.

"Did I?" I thought. How did it happen that I was completely unprepared for
this moment?

2.2.1   Backstage 2

> Remembrance of things past is not necessarily the remembrance of
> things as they were. (Proust, 1996, p. 120)

What are memories? Abandoning a typical view of memories, where our memories are recorded, processed, and saved within the unknown storehouses of our brain, I choose to view memories differently. Memories exist in more than our brain – our bodies remember things, just as we never forget how to ride a bike, once we learn how to do it. Exploring memories is not looking in the files of our brain, where each and every memory has been securely stored until the day of retrieval. Memories, especially strong memories, only exist, as argued by Stetsenko (2017), if this past is relevant to the present and the future. Stetsenko (2017) writes about the continuous work of keeping the past alive through meaningful projects. To remember, according to Stetsenko (2017), is to never forget, to never completely leave behind our memories, but to keep them alive in the very fabric of our active projects of becoming. Memories are then never a thing of the past, but are constructing both the present and the future. As we hold on to our memories, both with and without awareness, these memories change as well. Some memories do fade away as they recede in the multilayers of our reality, which is ever changing and transforming by our agentic | passive participation in the social world. Forgetting is then also an active process, not just simply a natural process of "filing away" memories, but letting go of memories that are not relevant to our present and to our future. Memories are also a social process, since our lives are, in essence, a social process, even if we are alone in the process of remembering, which may be possible physically (being alone), but can never be attained conceptually. In a radical sense, we are interconnected with all social objects, living and non-living, material and non-material. Our lives, following Vygotsky's teachings, are shaped by the sociocultural world, where each individual is shaped by the world and is also shaping the world back. Our memories are shaped by a variety of resources, as argued by Stetsenko (2017) – historical, material, social, technological, bodily – and each includes their own histories and dynamics. Inventing an artifact object to support and guide memory, according to Vygotsky (cited in Stetsenko, 2017), is an operation that is exceptionally complex and instructive. Memory relies on materializing the process of remembering in objects and patterns of activities (Stetsenko, 2017). When speaking about one's memories, the use of language will serve as a medium for exploring the past, as argued by Benjamin (1999), and not as an instrument. "It is the medium of that which is experienced, just as the earth is the medium in which ancient cities lie buried. He who seeks to approach his own buried past must conduct himself like a man digging" (Benjamin, 1999, p. 576). In my search for memories both distant and recent, but especially for those that were buried deep, I needed to do some digging, some searching, and some reflecting. This process became a very active, agentic pursuit, but even in that I was not doing it alone. Acting, Stetsenko

(2017) writes, is always collaborative, even when acting alone. Memories are carried out by a person and his agency in the fullness of one's embodiment and interactivity with the social practices in the world.

2.2.2   Scene 2: Classroom, Memories, and Arts-Based Research

> The actual work of art is what the product does with and in experience.
> (Dewey, 1934, p. 204)

"Pick an image on your phone or laptop that means something to you," asked Gene Fellner (hereafter Gene), the professor of my arts-based research class. Gene asked this question to start us thinking about visual arts, whether it is a painting, photograph, or anything else that could potentially inspire us. I pressed the unlock button on my phone and there it was – a photograph of my

FIGURE 10.2
Walking through the Cloisters

kids as my screensaver. In the image they are walking down a path in the Cloisters, a park in Washington Heights, Manhattan. This is an image of them walking away from me – literally *and* figuratively. I felt a dull, lasting pain inside my chest. "My boy ...," I thought to myself. "Far away from me ..." My daughter in the image is looking back at me as if to symbolize that she is still with me – for now – but she too will someday be moving on and will leave me behind.

I explained why I picked the image. I described feelings of melancholy, of sadness, my memories of joy (being with them) and gloom (them growing up) flooding me completely. Until that day, I had not really thought about why I chose the image to be my screensaver, the first thing I see when I pick up my phone. Putting my thoughts and feelings into words and sharing them with the class was a revelation to me. I thought I had simply picked the image because I liked it. But there is more to it. Talking about the image in class allowed me to speak about my pain, which until then I had kept to myself and those very close to me. Speaking to others about it was both scary and liberating. I felt raw after each class. Everything I was trying to hold back, to ignore, was now right on the surface, flowing right through me like a wild, cascading mountain stream.

2.2.3   Backstage 3

As we contemplated, in the beginning of the semester, what to create, we stared onto a blank canvas, a blank page, a blank space in our minds (if there is such a thing), feeling terrified as to whether what we wanted to produce had any value, worried that we were not competent enough as artists to make anything "good." Maya Pindyck (2017) suggests looking at a blank page differently, not as "the page that is a blank surface upon which to project your ideas and plop down words, but as a dynamic text with its own volition that can manifest in relation to a reader" (p. 58). The text or the blank page is no longer an inanimate thing, which brings to mind Heesoon Bai's work (2013) in which she problematizes the modern everyday ontology of separating the animate from the inanimate, showing that such separation has not just ethical implications for our environment, but also has connections to our everyday life, where we interact with "things" both animate and inanimate. In this case, when we contemplate creating something, it puts a lot of pressure on us as the "creators." However, if we see our projects as alive, as dynamic, as something that communicates to us (and to others) something out of its own volition, it helps us feel instead as collaborators, lifting away much of the pressure. Pidnyck (2017) states that writing should not be viewed as putting thoughts 'down on paper,' but rather as a process of relation to what the page already carries, both its visible (its texture, its stains) and invisible (its history, and its text) elements. Pidnyck writes about the process of literacy and erasure. "The only way I can describe it is like this: the words rise above the page, by say an eighth of an inch, and hover there in space, singly and unconnected, and they form a kind of field, and from this field I pick my words as if they were flowers" (Pindyck, 2017, p. 60). In that sense, as we each contemplate our work, we allow our thoughts, our memories, our experiences to rise above, to hover over us, and as we reflect on them, we actively create a project by picking the most salient elements, as they, in turn, actively interact with us in a dynamic process. One can argue that at the moment when the words and experiences rise above, they become objectified, meaning they become what I perceive them to be by observing them. Suddenly, there is tension in that process, in which I see my experiences as something other, even though they are mine. As subject and object continuously change places, the process of research becomes, what Pierre Bourdieu (2004) refers to, a process of reflexivity, where I am casting an ironic gaze on the social world, including myself in it. I am the object of research but also the one who is conducting the research, and as a result, my work continuously evolves and with it my thinking and feeling about my experiences evolves as well.

I began with photographs as a mode of visual art in my arts-based research project. Sarah Pink (2011) writes about the use of photographs stating that they allow us to see modes that are visual: including characteristics such as color, shape, size, position, and light. But they also cannot show us everything, leaving our other senses uninvolved, such as touch, smell, hearing and taste, bodily movement, texture, three-dimensional shape, and sounds. As my project grew, week after week, I chose to add other modes, in addition to photographs, to express my experiences of separation and loss and also to evoke something in the viewer. Pink (2011) writes about the practice of sensory ethnography, which involves the researchers' empathetic engagement with the practices and places that are important to the people participating in the research. I wanted my project to embrace Pink's notions of empathetic engagement – by highlighting and exploring the issue of raising children, watching them grow, and then letting them go – by engaging with my children, and by speaking to them about my work. I recorded conversations with my children as we looked at the images of them walking in different moments in time. Together, we explored our memories, co-constructed new memories, learned about our differences (of how we remembered these moments and how we felt in them). Later in my art project, I included the ability to listen to our conversations on an audio recorder, which was one of the ways I connected multiple modes of expression to create a fuller, more nuanced, and more complete picture, thus allowing for greater reflexivity and transformation.

3   Continuous Work – Opening of the Arts-Based Research Exhibit

3.1   *Act 2: Follows Reflection after the Art Exhibit Where We Presented Our Work*

3.1.1   Scene 1: Opening of the Exhibit

"This is interesting," said one of the visitors to the exhibit, as I shared my experiences and presented my art project. "That was not my experience." At first, I thought that it is perfectly normal that it does not represent everyone's experience. Each family that raises children eventually has to say goodbye to them in some way, and each family experiences their own 'empty nest' differently. But then I thought, "Was my experience really that different from others?" And if so, why was it different? Why did I feel so much pain?

3.1.2   Scene 2: Memories of Separation

It was a warm July night. I read a book to my boy, sang his favorite lullaby, tucked him in with a blanket (even though he did not need tucking), and sat with him, stroking his hair until he was asleep. Reluctantly, I got up and walked away from his bed. I glanced back on my way out – blonde curls all over the pillow, my sweet, two-year-old boy whom, without knowing it, I would not see again for three and a half years.

3.1.3   Backstage 4

Looking back at my earlier experiences pushed me to consider how important they are in my present and my future. David Jardine (2006) writes about hermeneutics and how rich and memorable experiences catch our attention and ask things of us. Working on the arts-based research project brought out these memorable experiences of separation with my son and called for me to pay attention to them. Understanding, Jardine (2006) argues, begins when something addresses us. The pain that I experienced when I had to leave my son 16 year ago, was hidden away from the surface, because I was not ready to address it (perhaps because it was too painful, or for some other reason), but it was present in me, in my body, in my life. It came up to the surface, when a new separation was imminent. I had to use words to express these embodied emotions to myself, my family, my research community. Words are never separate from the experiences and are born, according to Mikhail Bakhtin (2010), in a dialogue with them. Meanings of words are then realized only in the process of active, responsive understanding, Bakhtin writes (2010). Working through finding words to articulate my experiences through an active process of understanding these experiences became transformative for my family, because we all had to engage in the process of reflection and learn from each other's pain.

Bakhtin (2010) also writes about a plurality of consciousness, where there is never a single transcendent consciousness or truth, but multiple meaning systems – polysemia, and multiple voices – polyphonia. What emerged in the process of revisiting these memories was a polyphonic composition, where each "melody" streamed independently and yet together created a "musical" piece – a piece about separation, reunification, coming of age, and saying goodbye.

4   Arts-Based Research and Healing

4.1   *Act 3: Follows Reflection after the Art Exhibit Where We Presented Our Work*

4.1.1   Scene 1: Arts-Based Research

We were working on our projects in class. I had brought the photographs of my children printed out on fabric that I then began to stitch onto a blanket. This was a blanket my mother made for me 19 years ago when my first child was about to be born. The blanket was soft and delicate. My mother sewed it for me before we knew that I would be having a boy, so she chose a soft and

FIGURE 10.3
Walking on the street in Washington Heights on graduation day

neutral yellow color. As I stitched the images of my kids onto the blanket, I looked at the stitches that my mother made. I realized that she must have also been thinking about her child growing up when she was making it for me. I was only 20 years old at the time, not that much older than my son is now. Gene asked me how I felt as I worked on making the stitches. Strangely, I felt good. I touched the fabric, its texture caressed my fingers, calming, soothing. I thought of my mother holding the blanket in her hands almost 20 years ago and, as I touched it now, it almost felt that we connected across time.

FIGURE 10.4   Working on the art project: stitching the blanket

My son's first year of college came to its end and eventually he was back home for the summer. Working on this project, watching my children walking away from me in the pictures, stitching their images printed on fabric on the blanket made by my mother, placed into perspective many strong emotions I experienced when my son first left. A long time ago, I walked away from my mother, and now I am thousands of miles away from her still. Yet, her presence in my life, in my thinking, and in my academic work is very strong. I may have walked away, but she is always walking by my side. My memories have been transformed and so were my emotions in the healing process of art making.

Gene later told me that this work of stitching was almost like stitching a wound. Looking back at it now, I understand that it was therapeutic. Looking at the images of my children, I now feel joy, nostalgia for happy memories, and not the raw pain I felt when I initially chose the image for this project.

5   Epilogue

When I shared this arts-based research with other students and researchers at a our monthly research meeting, many related to the experience I describe above. Some related to it because their own children grew up and left for college, or because they too have been separated with their loved ones. For others it was because, like myself, they have strong embodied emotions (like pain, sadness, loss), which they carry with them and their emotions resonated with mine. I practiced my presentation many times before the event, hoping that it would help me keep it together during the actual presentation. Once I was done, my adviser, Konstantinos Alexakos, said this, and hearing him say it, I let go of shame and cried:

> We can always rewrite our past ... We can rewrite our past ... Speaking to our children is one way to bring healing and not just to you. I am sure your son had to do some healing as well. It is very important to send love to our earlier selves, because we all have one thing or another that needs healing. It is important to love ourselves, not to blame ourselves. Because of the choices we had to make for whatever reasons. Not just rewriting our future, but also our past. (Alexakos, USER-S forum, The Graduate Center, CUNY, October 2018)

On the path of "now, knowing myself," which has become my mantra, introduced to me by Ken Tobin (personal communication, September, 2018), I had

FIGURE 10.5
Collection of all the images used in the art project

taken this journey of knowing, understanding myself. First, I examined myself using arts as a medium, situating myself in a larger context, nuancing the context with meaning from multiple perspectives, then, I uncovered very strong emotions present in my very existence and finally, I found a way to bring healing, which is still an ongoing process. Alexakos (2017) states that change is the point of learning and in order to change it is often necessary to unlearn and let go of fears. I would add letting go of pain and guilt to the list necessary for learning. In the process of exploring issues of importance in an arts-based research class, I was able to address something that needed to be addressed, but I was also able to find a place where I could speak about it, both though art, art making, writing, and speaking to others, which included both my family and my research community. And it all started with a now serendipitous image of my children walking away from me.

References

Ali-Khan, C. (2016). Dirty secrets and silent conversations: Exploring radical listening through embodied autoethnographic teaching. *The International Journal of Critical Pedagogy, 7*(3), 13–33.

Alexakos, K. (2015). *Being a teacher| researcher: A primer on doing authentic inquiry research on teaching and learning.* Sense Publishers. https://doi.org/10.1007/978-94-6351-182-7_14

Alexakos, K. (2017). Mindfulness and sexual wellness. In M. Powietrzynska & K. Tobin (Eds.), *Weaving complementary knowledge systems and mindfulness to educate a literate citizenry for sustainable and healthy lives* (pp. 215–234). Sense Publishers. https://doi.org/10.1007/978-94-6300-570-8_8

Bai, H. (2013). Peace with the earth: Animism and contemplative ways. *Cultural Studies of Science Education, 10*, 135–147. https://doi.org/10.1007/978-94-6300-570-8_8

Bakhtin, M. M. (2010). *The dialogic imagination: Four essays* (Vol. 1). University of Texas Press.

Benjamin, W. (1999). Excavation and memory. In M. W. Jennings, H. Eiland, & G. Smith (Eds.), *Selected writings, 1931–1934* (Vol. 2, p. 576). Belknap.

Bourdieu, P. (2004). *Science of science and reflexivity.* University of Chicago Press.

De Souza, C. R., & Pietrocola, M. (2016). *Mindfulness in education.* In M. Powietrzynska & K. Tobin (Eds.), *Mindfulness and educating citizens for everyday life* (pp. 115–133). Sense Publishers. https://doi.org/10.1007/978-94-6300-570-8_8

Dewey, J. (1934). *Art as experience.* Putnam.

Eisner, E. W. (2001). Concerns and aspirations for qualitative research in the new millennium. *Qualitative Research, 1*(2), 135–145. https://doi.org/10.1177/146879410100100202

Jardine, D. W. (2006a). 11. On hermeneutics: "Over and above our wanting and doing." In K. Tobin & J. L. Kincheloe (Eds.), *Doing educational research* (pp. 269–288). Sense Publishers.

Kincheloe, J. L. (2012). Critical pedagogy in the twenty-first century: Evolution for survival. *Counterpoints, 422*, 147–183.

Pindyck, M. (2017). Teaching literacy as and through erasure. *English Journal, 106*(5), 58.

Pink, S. (2011). Multimodality, multisensoriality and ethnographic knowing: Social semiotics and the phenomenology of perception. *Qualitative Research, 11*, 261–276. https://doi.org/10.1177/1468794111399835

Proust, M. (1996). *In search of lost time* (Vol. 6). Vintage.

Stetsenko, A. (2017). *The transformative mind: Expanding Vygotsky's approach to development and education.* Cambridge University Press.

Tobin, K. (2015). *The sociocultural turn in science education and its transformative potential.* In C. Milne, K. Tobin, & D. DeGennaro (Eds.), *Sociocultural studies and implications for science education* (pp. 3–31). Springer. https://doi.org/10.1007/978-94-007-4240-6_1

Van Maanen, J. (1988). *Tales of the field: On writing ethnography.* University of Chicago Press.

Waldman, P. (2015). *Educating desire: Autobiographical impressions of addiction in Alcoholics Anonymous.* Sense Publishers. https://doi.org/10.1007/978-94-6300-145-8

Self-Reflection Methods to Study Emotional Experiences in Science and Mathematics Preservice Teacher Education

Arnau Amat and Isabel Sellas

Abstract

This chapter describes how two preservice teachers' initial views of teaching and learning science and mathematics are shaped by their prior emotional experiences as students. From a hermeneutic phenomenological approach, this study highlights how the emotions that they felt while studying these courses as students have affected their perceptions as teachers and how these perceptions shift reflexively thanks to the Didactics courses, which themselves are based on reflexivity. Both cases presented in the study uncover authoritarian structures in science and mathematics teaching that use unpleasant emotions to constrain student agency. These cases reflect how interpretive research can allow teacher educators not only to improve their understandings of their students' views, but also how interpretive research can help these preservice teachers reflect on and change their mental structures and practices with regard to teaching and learning.

Keywords

preservice teacher education – reflexivity – science education – mathematics education

1   **Research on Teaching Science and Mathematics Perceptions in Elementary Preservice Teacher Training Courses**

Eugènia: It's a good thing that children have the chance to learn science with hands-on activities and discover things for themselves (...). Children learn about physical and natural phenomena in their close environment when they experience it, live it and identify it. From their observations, they form some ideas, they show interest in these phenomena and want to discover things ... (March 2016)

Eugènia: First of all, I would like to clarify my first explanation that for children to gain scientific knowledge, teachers must design activities to work on not only facts and observations, but also ideas (...). Teachers' guidance is characterized by asking good questions. These questions must be productive, which means that students must think about their answers. Inquiry does not always have to be free, because teachers must offer children some models to think about. If teachers only promote observation, without any other help or ideas, explanations will be difficult to construct for students. (June 2016)

Miquel Àngel: When I went to school everything was very different. Each class was like an adventure where you could take part or you were left behind. In that moment, studying math was like being at the North Pole. In other words, with each task and new concept you can feel the cold more, because there was no empathy with the subject (...). At university, everything was completely different for me. Cold became warmth, because of the good explanations and the good connection with different topics (...). In elementary school there was only one way to do and solve the mathematics problems and only some students were able to do that; the others who weren't, were just 'present.' (June 2016)

The first two quotes that open this chapter were written by Eugènia, an elementary preservice teacher in the first author's (Arnau Amat) Didactics of Science course, while the third quote was from Miquel Àngel, an elementary preservice teacher in the second author's (Isabel Sellas) Didactics of Mathematics course. Both of these undergraduate classes took place at the Universitat de Vic – Universitat Central de Catalunya. The courses were taught in Catalan as were the responses of the two participants. Using these two case studies, in the following pages we (Amat reflecting on Eugènia and Sellas on Miquel Àngel) illustrate our particular ways of conducting research, and how collaborative methodologies based on preservice teachers' reflections can be applied.

Eugènia and Miquel Àngel were selected because their views of teaching underwent a noticeable shift. For instance, in the case of Eugènia, the second quote above was her own answer to her first quote four months earlier. Eugènia's two comments, as was the case with her classmates, reflect a change in her understanding of how scientific knowledge is built with elementary students. Her view evolves from an empiricist conception, in which students learn directly from their senses without differentiating between observations and inferences (Lederman, 2007) to a more constructivist view (Carey & Smith, 1993). From Miquel Àngel's quote, we gain some sense of how mathematics learning was experienced by him when he was an elementary school student, where mathematics was taught only for the "good" students who were taught that there was only one correct way to solve mathematical problems. Miquel Àngel changed his initial idea about how mathematics should be taught from a narrow view, where the truth only came from the teacher, to a broader view, where understanding is built through the process of reflection and communication (Hiebert, Carpenter, Fennema, Wearne, Murray, Olivier, & Human, 1997).

Our approach on preservice teacher education is framed by reflexivity (Alexakos, 2015); our main goal is to uncover conscious and unconscious social structures that are framing our student's mental schemas and practices. For this reason, our preservice courses are inspired by reflection orientation as suggested by Sandra Abell, Ken Appleton, and Deborah Hanuscin (2010), who claim that preservice teachers arrive at teacher education courses with their own personal theories about teaching and learning. Therefore, "the goal of the science [and mathematics] methods instructor who holds a reflection orientation is for students to confront and change their view of science [and mathematics] teaching and learning through various opportunities for reflection" (Abell et al., 2010, p. 54). Even though these didactics courses discussed here are developed in different ways, both courses are designed to provide different learning contexts to promote student reflection on: (a) the science and mathematics teaching by others; (b) their own science and mathematics teaching; (c) their own science and mathematics learning; (d) expert opinions. Konstantinos Alexakos (2015, p. 5) writes that

> We change as we interact with ourselves, with others, and with our environment. The experiences we have change us as we, too, change our experiences. What is and how we experience an event or an interaction is refracted through who, we are, our emotions, and how we think.

Our belief is that when awareness is brought to the unconscious structures of students' ways of thinking, students will be aware of such views and will be able to transform them.

The main goal on these two courses is the development of Pedagogical Content Knowledge (PCK) on science and mathematics education, which was defined by Lee Shulman (1986). According to him, PCK goes beyond content knowledge because science and mathematics teachers should have the specific knowledge to make the content comprehensible, in order to promote students' learning. Therefore, the most useful forms of representation of those ideas, the most powerful analogies, illustrations, examples, explanations, and demonstrations – in a word, the ways of representing and formulating the subject that make it comprehensible to others. (Shulman, 1986, p. 9)

However, as teacher educators, we also keep in mind that emotions are an essential part of any teaching and learning process (Tobin, 2006). From our perspective, cognition and emotion are related to a dialectical relationship: we cannot understand reason without emotion, and vice versa, because as it is argued by Michalinos Zembylas (2014, p. 543): "the reason has been produced as the effects of culturally and historically specific power relations that always entail an array of human faculties. The emotions that are identified as aspects of the affective domain have also been constructed by historical power relations." Zembylas (2007) also pointed out the inclusion of the emotional dimension in the PCK, in particular, "how teachers and students develop emotional understanding of each other or the subject matter that they are exploring" (p. 355). This understanding may be produced in different planes: firstly, on an individual plane, or how teachers experience their own emotional knowledge; secondly, on an interactional plane, or how teachers use emotional knowledge in their relationship with students; and finally, on socio-political plane, or how sociocultural context of schooling affects teachers' curricular decisions and actions. Such emotional contagion was investigated in previous work (Amat, Zapata, Alexakos, Pride, Paylor-Smith, & Hernandez, 2016), on how emotions can be contagious in a science teacher course using student heart-rates in a discussion on race. It is through being mindful of the emotional effect of these issues and by showing compassion to the others, that it is possible to create a safe space, where students can express their own feelings about challenging topics (Alexakos, Pride, Amat, Tsetsakos, Lee, Paylor-Smith, Zapata, Wright, & Smith, 2016).

Because we are mindful of the understandings on emotions, in our didactic courses we did not want to reflect on only the cognition dimension of PCK, but also to promote reflection on the emotional dimension in the teaching and learning processes. For this reason, from the very beginning, preservice teachers were asked to express their initial ideas and emotions about what teaching and learning science and mathematics meant to them.

Students were asked to design a lesson plan about a particular science or mathematics curricular topic. These lesson plans, apart from informing the instructors with regard to the students' views of teaching, became a powerful educational resource throughout the course, because, as shown by Isabel Jiménez (2016), from the criteria introduced during the course, students analyzed their own initial proposals in order to re-shape them. In addition, preservice teachers filled out a questionnaire that asked them about: (a) interest in science and mathematics, (b) how science and mathematics are understood, (c) how teaching and mathematics are viewed. In the last part of the survey, based on Steven Ritchie, Peter Hudson, Alberto Bellocchi, Senka Henderson, Donna King, and Kenneth Tobin's (2016) previous studies, they chose three emotions out of ten, for two different situations: emotions that they were remembered when these participants were studying science or mathematics; and emotions that the participants feel when they think about teaching science or mathematics in the future. A justification for the answers was required in both of these cases.

In our view, designing our courses based on reflection fits very well with hermeneutical phenomenology research, whose main aim is the description and the interpretation of educational phenomena (Tobin, 2015). As described by Tobin (2014, p. 135):

> A hermeneutical-phenomenological perspective adopts a stance that you can learn about social life understanding participants' experience in social life. Furthermore, the approach emphasizes that experiences should be represented by participants' voices.

Thus, in this research approach self-reporting methods described by Ritchie et al. (2016) – such as personal and emotional diaries, cogens, surveys or recall interviews – are useful tools in doing research about, as well as in promoting preservice teachers' reflection.

If the educational research process is understood from a classical, or even from a mainstream view, then we could have analyzed and compared all the student teachers' initial opinions with their own final opinions in the Didactics of Science and Didactics of Mathematics courses. We could have categorized and quantified all data, and we could have inferred whether or not our didactics courses had led to a change in the preservice teachers' views with regard to how science and mathematics should be taught. According to Joe Kincheloe and Kenneth Tobin (2009), if we had followed such a positivistic or the crypto-positivistic paradigm, we would have reduced the complexity of the teaching and learning processes to cause and effect. Thus, without a hermeneutic research approach, we would not have gained insights as to why Eugènia and Miquel Àngel held their initial views on teaching science and mathematics and how their stories of transformation occurred. From our point of view, positivistic approaches promote a black box approach of what is going on in a classroom – in comes teaching and out goes learning – without asking what is happening in this process.

What the sociocultural theoretical framework and hermeneutical research approaches allow us to do is open the black box to inquire about social phenomena that are taking place in it. As argued by Mikhail Bakhtin (1986), the key is the idea that meaning making is always situated and a context dependent process: "All words have the 'taste' of a profession, a genre, a tendency, a party, a particular work, a particular person, a generation, an age group, the day and hour. Each word tastes of the context and contexts in which it has lived its socially charged life" (p. 293).

Thus, the place, the learner, the teacher, the specific moment, in other words, all the educational context with all of its complexity enact at the same moment when learning is constructed. In the case of our preservice teachers, if we want to know how their view changed, we must do the same as biologists in the lab and increase the zoom lenses of microscopy, in order to look at our research object more closely (Tobin & Ritchie, 2011). Furthermore, to comprehend how they changed their minds we must listen to their voices, and that means, to engage them in the research. For this reason, our research is a collaborative research approach because preservice teachers' views are listened to and considered during our courses, to build up and write down our interpretations.

Our research is also framed in the four authenticity criteria described by Tobin (2015) and Alexakos (2015), who claim that education research must benefit those who are involved in the research while the research is being enacted. The first authenticity criterion is ontological, which is to ensure that all the participants, researchers included, should learn from the research, or in other words, that by being engaged in the research they should change their perceptions. The second criterion is educative, which is related to understanding difference as a main value to promote learning. The main point is encouraging all participants to voice the views, without favoring any of them. The third criterion, catalytic change, is associated with the crystallization of any improvements as a result of being involved. The participants' social life is transformed as an outcome of the research. Finally, the fourth, tactical authenticity, addresses social injustices and any disadvantages that were found throughout the research process.

In our opinion, following these criteria allow those of us working on the stance of collaborative research methodologies to interpret educational phenomena with and for the participants; because researchers not only build the research from the participants' voices, but also allow them to learn thanks to their involvement in metacognition processes, in which they have to reflect on their own learning process.

2   Eugènia, or How the "Mysticism" of Science Shapes Her View on Science Teaching

The first case that is presented in this chapter revolves around my (Arnau Amat's) experience, as a professor of the Didactics of Science. Here I focus on

Eugènia. She is an elementary preservice teacher who is fond of literature and the scenic arts. Throughout the course she showed special artistic creativity and how art can be applied in science teaching at different moments. When she was a teenager and had to choose which courses to take in high school, she skipped as many science courses as possible. Even though in college she majored in the music teaching program, she had to face the challenge of the obligatory Didactics of Science course in the third year of the elementary teaching degree. As Eugènia said at the end of the semester, she was really scared when she started the course.

> *Eugènia*: I felt fear because I thought my scientific knowledge was very poor, terrible ... For this reason, I though this subject could be very bad for me and I was a little bit scared of not being at the cutting edge of this subject.

Eugènia's case provides an interesting example because her story was unique in our class and might have been overlooked with a different method of statistical analysis. The uniqueness of Eugènia's case lies in that while she started out with huge resistance and fear towards science she ended up not only with one of the best grades in the class but also with a huge change of attitude towards teaching science. Learning from her situation allowed me, as the course professor, to learn and empathize not just with her but also with my other preservice teachers who may also attend my courses with associations to unpleasant or negative emotions such as fear, disappointment or anger.

2.1   *Eugènia's Experiences in Science in School: "It's Such a Drag ..."*
When Eugènia recalls memories of science classes in elementary and high school, she feels only unpleasant emotions. In general, these emotions are not shared by her classmates. As was explained earlier, in the initial questionnaire, which was filled out by 26 preservice teachers, they were asked to choose three out of ten emotions to define how they felt in two different contexts: when they remembered their science classes as students and, how they would feel if they had to teach science as elementary teachers. In both cases, they were invited to provide an explanation of why they had chosen these emotions. Even though I am aware that their memories are just simplified opinions about how they have experienced their science schooling, they are another approach to students' emotions concerning science and mathematics.

As can be seen in Figure 11.1, a significant number of my preservice teachers related science classes to positive emotions, such as happiness, enthusiasm, and wonder. When their reflections are analyzed in detail, the majority of the preservice teachers justified these positive emotions because they felt engaged

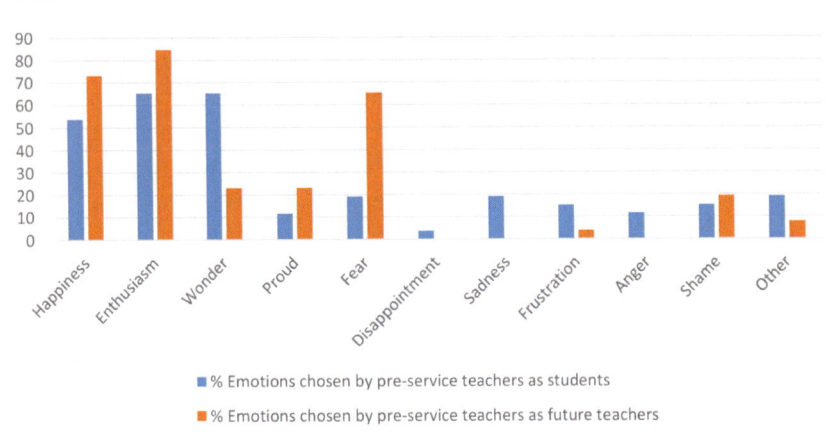

FIGURE 11.1   Preservice students' emotions regarding the teaching and learning of science

in the learning process. Thus, of the preservice teachers who had chosen wonder and enthusiasm, 16 and 8 respectively, mentioned that they felt this when
they were learning science content. Many of these participants connected
happiness and enthusiasm with active pedagogical methodologies which are
typical in science education, such as outdoor school activities in natural settings or laboratory experimentation. Having said that, Figure 11.1 also reveals
some students who chose unpleasant emotions to describe their experience as
science students, such as Eugènia. Approximately, 19% of students, for example, chose fear or sadness, and 15%, chose shame and frustration. With regards
to fear, preservice teachers who picked this emotion did so because they had
found it difficult to learn some scientific knowledge or how scared they were
of science exams.

From our point of view, these descriptive results are very useful to frame
Eugènia's case, because she was a part of this group, but our aim is not to generalize. If we just look at the whole class group data with this aim, we would
be focusing on the research in such a reductionist way that we would miss the
chance to construct a full understanding of specific cases. Therefore, we would
miss a great opportunity to understand why Eugènia was the only student who
picked these three unpleasant emotions to describe how she learnt science.
Moreover, if we want to interpret why she chose anger, sadness and disappointment, as more relevant emotions when she studied science, we must listen to her voice. Thanks to self-reporting methods, we are able to incorporate
the participants' own reflections in the study.

In this regard too, Eugènia remembers feeling sadness and disappointment
because of the traditional educational methods based on memorization she
experienced as a student: "I didn't find science interesting and I was so bored ...

When I looked at the class schedule and I saw science class, I thought it's such a drag ..." She also remembers feeling anger. Anger because science was presented as a superior field of knowledge. In the initial questionnaire, she explains how the science teacher in her high school made fun of students who were not enrolled in science courses and she wrote down in the initial questionnaire "students who chose science courses were the cool group. I suppose he was kidding, and had no ill intentions, but he repeated the same thing every other day ... And I was sick of him".

Eugènia was especially angry because her science teacher claimed the superiority of science: "He always said that science is above everything and the other disciplines don't have any kind of relevance."

In some cases, like Eugènia's, the school science that preservice teachers are taught is presented from a very authoritarian and narrow-minded point of view. Eduardo Mortimer and Philip Scott (2003) wrote how science education lessons can often be described as having two communicative approaches: authoritarian or dialogical. In authoritarian communicative approaches, power belongs only to the teacher, because only the teacher's views, opinions and ideas are taken into account. On the other hand, since the students and teachers' views, opinions and ideas are interacting in dialogical communicative approaches power is more evenly distributed. Science by definition is dialogical because scientists must contrast, discuss and construct their hypotheses and theories with other scientists. However, in schools, sometimes science is presented as a monolithic, non-historical and true knowledge that students have to memorize and reproduce. In addition, apart from this authoritarian way of presenting science, Eugènia suffered what is described by Jay Lemke (1990) as the mysticism of science; presenting science as a superior discipline, enforces even more this idea that science is a finished body of knowledge that must be reproduced, becoming a dogmatic thing. However, this approach can provoke resistance towards science, as in this case.

2.2 Eugènia's Views on Teaching Science: A Rebel's Answer

The way that Eugènia experienced science, so traditional and dogmatic, has alarming consequences for a future elementary teacher as well. As was presented at the beginning of this chapter, Eugènia expressed her view of teaching science because she wants to teach it differently than how she remembers science being taught to her:

> *Eugènia*: [As a teacher,] I put a lot of emphasis on experimentation and manipulation activities because when I filled out the initial questionnaire

> I remembered my science classes were based on memorizing exercises,
> basically using text books. So, I thought that the best way to teach science
> would be the opposite: doing a lot of experimentation and hands-on
> activities to promote learning and, at the same time, to enjoy yourself
> through inquiry.

To enjoy oneself through inquiry is exactly what she had not experienced in
school. For this reason, when she was asked which emotions came to mind if
she thought about having to teach science, she confessed she would feel enthusiasm. She picked this emotion because she would like to have the chance to
teach in a completely different way than she had been taught in school; she
would provide her students with "the opportunity of learning without boredom." Eugènia shares this enthusiasm with her classmates, not only to promote better science knowledge in their future students, but also to promote
pleasant emotions in them.

However, from my view, the main difference between Eugènia and her classmates is her explicit will to change her view of science education. She felt a
rebellious anger as a student and an engaged enthusiasm as a future teacher.
According to Zembylas (2011), "emotions in the classroom, then, are not only a
private matter but also a political space in which students and teachers interact with implication in larger political and cultural struggles" (p. 33). Despite
Eugènia's enthusiasm, this emotion would be accompanied by unpleasant
emotions. From Figure 11.1 it can be seen how in contrast, many preservice
teachers in my class felt more unpleasant emotions when they thought as
future teachers than when they remembered their science classes in school.
When Eugènia thought of her emotions as a teacher, she picked shame and
fear, as did most of her classmates. When we look closer at the main reasons for
choosing these two emotions, most student teachers reported that they were
due to the difficulty of learning and teaching some scientific content.

In particular, Eugènia would feel shame as a science teacher because she
thinks she does not remember anything from elementary and high school,
because she only memorized, and then forgot, all the scientific concepts. "I
don't remember a lot of things about elementary school. I can only say that we
studied science using textbooks. Moreover, I don't think I have much scientific
knowledge and I have some kind of difficulty learning it." In a similar way, she
would feel fear because she is afraid of her future students asking her something with regard to science which she will not be able to answer.

Even though this low self-esteem in elementary preservice teachers regarding science knowledge has been described by other authors previously (Abell
et al., 2010), we must look at Eugènia's story from a historical viewpoint to

comprehend why she would feel such emotions. Therefore, both emotions arose because she really thought she had a lack of scientific knowledge. As is described by Lemke (1990), the mysticism of science presents science as difficult knowledge, only available to people who possess special talents and intellect and "when students fail to master it, they are encouraged to believe that it is their own fault: they are just not smart enough to be scientists" (p. 138). Eugènia experienced a school science that was understood as non-historical knowledge, where she only had to memorize some content and reproduce it in the exam, and the implicit message was: 'you do it this way or you are going to get left behind.'

2.3   Searching for Significant Events in the Didactics of Science Course

I wonder, however, why did Eugènia's view of science change? How could she go from a very empiricist way of teaching to a more socio-constructivist method?

It could be considered that it was precisely the Didactics of Science course that helped this shift in her teaching opinion. From a certain point of view that may be so, but for us (the authors) it is a very reductionist way to look at the phenomenon, because then the subject would become an unproblematic black box. The only way to learn and to improve from and for our courses is by studying what is going on in them; we must comprehend how our students are learning, feeling and experiencing all the activities that are designed for them.

Thus, in my view, the Didactics of Science course is understood like any other social phenomenon, which follows a historical flux, as described by Sewell (2006), which are built for different events, which are always contingent: present events will affect future ones, but at the same time, present events are affected by past ones. Some of these events are more meaningful than others, because in some of them social structures are transformed. Therefore, to comprehend what was going on in the course it is important to figure out which events helped to change preservice teachers' mentalities. In other words, if I wanted to understand how Eugènia changed her mind, from a more empiricist way of teaching science to a more constructivist way of teaching science, it will be necessary to break this historical flux into several meaningful discrete events.

As a researcher, I could have chosen which events were more transformative. However, if my view is understanding learning processes from a situated and context dependency, then I must consider that each preservice teacher feels his or her transformations in a particular moment and place; and experiences each one in a unique way. Therefore, the best option to figure out what the meaningful events are is to engage participants in their selection. For this reason, in the final exam, preservice teachers had to reflect on two meaningful moments in the course that helped to change their mind about science teaching. Eugènia confessed how difficult it was to choose only two moments, but she described the sessions in the Didactics' lab as the most meaningful ones. In fact, the majority of my preservice teachers picked them.

The Didactics of Science course is structured in two different kinds of session per week. Once a week half the group worked in the Didactics lab. In these sessions, preservice teachers experience, as science learners, an eight-week project to inquire about the internal structure of matter, inspired by the work of Andrés Acher, Maria Arcà, and Neus Santmartí (2006) and the Model Centered Instruction (Schwarz, 2009). During the project, student teachers are organized in cooperative groups, and they are involved not only in experiments into the interactions of matter states and heat or dissolutions, but also how to create coherent explanations of different scientific phenomena using different kinds of representation. In contrast, the other weekly session is developed for the whole group and is focused on the reflection of methodology features of the lab session class, such as the teacher's role, nature of science, and the key importance of modeling.

Nevertheless, Eugènia was able to point to a particular session: "I would say the last session when we summarize the matter experiments." To understand why she chose this last session, it is absolutely necessary to describe the first session, when preservice teachers started to work on the internal structure of matter. In the first session, four different experiments on the internal structure of matter were presented. All groups had to do the four experiments and in order to guide the activity a Prediction – Observation – Explanation (POE) question structure was provided in each experiment. My aim was to work on the empiricist view of science; the idea that scientific knowledge is built only from the direct observation of data to transform this view into a more socio-constructivist one.

Thus, as argued by Lederman (2007), it is important to differentiate as clearly as possible between observations and inferences: on the one hand, observations are descriptions of natural phenomena that are elaborated using the senses; on the other hand, inferences go beyond the senses because they include the 'invention' of explanation. Throughout the session, student teachers looked frustrated, because they were able to answer the prediction and the observation questions, but not the explanation question. My intervention was as passive as possible; when a group asked me about the scientific explanation, I smiled at them and went to visit another group.

When the experiments were finished, we discussed what was going on from a didactics perspective. At a certain point in the discussion, I asked them what they had learnt from the experiments. They were aware that they had observed a lot, but they had not really learnt many things, because they could not answer the explanation question in the experiments. Then I told them that we had reproduced a science teaching activity based on a radical empiricist view, where the main idea is that we can comprehend natural phenomena using only the senses, without any theory as scaffolding or any teacher support. Finally, I closed the session by saying that we would revisit all the experiments in a few weeks, after the model of matter was constructed to show them that they would be able to answer the scientific explanation without too much help.

However, Eugènia's reflection was not about this first session, but the final one when initial experiments were revisited, six weeks later. In this particular session, from the model of matter that had been constructed and agreed by all of them, student teachers were able to construct explanations through different kinds of representation, such as drawings, plasticine models, corporal performances and writing.

It is important to point out that in the first session, when the matter experiments were presented, Eugènia experienced some of the unpleasant emotions that she had felt as an elementary and a secondary student. On the one hand, she felt happiness because she was very comfortable with her classmates in the cooperative group. On the other hand, she felt frustration. "I didn't have the faintest idea why the thing that we were observing was happening. I couldn't explain anything in most of the experiments," but she was disgusted because "I didn't like not having as much scientific knowledge as my classmates." However, when it is focused on what Eugènia thought in the final session, she only picked pleasant emotions. Firstly, happiness and enthusiasm that she related to the dynamism of the session and she wrote again about the importance of her classmates. "I liked listening to my classmates in the cooperative group talking about the topic. I liked to listen to their opinions and arguments because they helped me to understand the scientific explanation."

The role of representations was also very important for her. In the final session, each group had to propose their own explanation using different kinds of representation and between groups they had to co-evaluate each other. Finally, they had to reach an agreement about what the most coherent explanation was. It is important how the construction of representations, as concrete constructions of her mental models, were important for her to promote the understanding: "For people like me, with visual memory, this kind of representation eases the understanding process."

This session was designed to promote a dialogical approach to science and science teaching, through the dialogue and the discussion in the cooperative groups and between groups. About this session, she said, "I was enthusiastic to see how science could be in a way that I hadn't expected; different, enjoyable, interesting and I was able to understand too." She confesses that in that moment she felt more self-confident and her attitudes towards science were already different from the beginning of the course. For this reason, in this last session she was proud of herself because "I was able to explain all the things that we worked on in this session."

Finally, it is important how her view of what science is shifted from the first questionnaire, in which an empiricist view is stated, to the final class, when she expressed a more constructivist view, as follows: "Working cooperatively with my classmates, I realized that inquiring, modeling, questioning and communicating emotions are indispensable elements in the science process."

3   Miquel Àngel, or a Reconciliation Story

The second case is about a Didactics of Mathematics course, in which I (Isabel Sellas) was the professor. The focus of this case study is a preservice student: Miquel Àngel. The authoritarian way of experiencing science in school as discussed in the first case study is shared by some mathematics preservice teachers and can promote alarming consequences for their views on mathematics teaching.

Miquel Àngel is a preservice teacher in his forties, who had not studied for a long time before enrolling in the elementary education degree. A year ago, his personal life changed direction. After doing a Catalan course for adults, he decided to start higher education studies at university. How he experienced mathematics in school had a lot of influence on his final decision; he decided to study a degree based on avoiding mathematics. "That year, I had to choose a degree. I discarded all the degrees and courses with mathematics in the syllabus because I had bad memories of it, and at that moment, I was more confident with language courses, which would allow me to seek new challenges." As in Eugènia's case, this case study was chosen because it is a great example of a transformation story. I believe that, as the professor of the Didactics of Mathematics course, this case allows me to reflect on how narrow views on mathematics learning are associated with unpleasant emotions and with a reproductive way of teaching it.

3.1   *The Reencounter: Fear and Anxiety*
Even though he would have liked to discard all mathematics courses, Miquel Àngel had to take Didactics of Mathematics in the first and the second year of his elementary education degree. He was quite anxious:

> *Miquel Àngel:* I had to started new courses and one of them was Didactics of Mathematics. I expected a nightmare. At the beginning, in every single class I was nervous and tense. And it was not for nothing: I was attending mathematics sessions!

From the very beginning, I noticed how he was suffering. One day, Miquel Àngel came to see me and said that he wanted to talk to me. In a private meeting, he confessed that he was not sure about passing the course because it had been a long time since he had done anything related to mathematics. Furthermore, as previously stated, he had not had particularly positive experiences with mathematics in school.

These negative experiences were obvious when I looked at their initial questionnaires. Similar to the Didactics of Science course, on the first day of the course preservice teachers had to fill out a questionnaire, in which they had to pick three emotions to describe how they felt when they thought about their learning experiences as students in school. The three emotions chosen by Miquel Àngel were: happiness, sadness and fear; happy memories were chosen when "you had learnt to perform a calculation successfully"; sadness was felt "because in certain moments, you weren't able to learn the mechanism and, then, perform the calculation successfully"; finally, fear "when I had to do tests because if you knew how to solve the task, there wasn't any problem; but if you didn't, then you were anxious about having to solve it."

Miquel Àngel's emotional response when he remembers mathematical learning, as in Eugènia's case, was associated with evaluation and, mostly, with the idea of doing something right or wrong. These emotions of sadness and fear which arose when they were not able to solve certain tasks proved how mistakes are not viewed as an important element to promote learning and comprehension (Hiebert et al., 1997) but as learning setbacks. In some cases, evaluation tasks are used as tools, and even emotional instruments, to control and constrain students' agency.

3.2   *His Memories: Procedures and Operations*

How Miquel Àngel explained his emotions provided me with a clue to understanding his point about how he had been taught mathematics in school. Performing calculations played a major role in whether the emotion was pleasant or unpleasant for Miquel Àngel. That is, from his point of view, doing mathematics is merely the ability to perform mechanical procedures and solving some operations. This idea is associated with how mathematics was taught in his elementary school, where problems had a single solution, and where mathematics is synonymous with achieving the correct result:

> *Miquel Àngel*: When I was an elementary student, mathematical prob-
> lems were always closed. It didn't matter how you tried to figure out the
> solution, because there was only one way to solve it. So, if you did them
> well, then it meant that you were able to understand the procedure.

Like Eugènia, this view of teaching mathematics provides an authoritarian
communicative approach, in which only the teacher has the valid truth and in
which the voice of students is not listened to.

Before starting the study of teaching and learning methods in mental calculation and fractions in the Didactics of Mathematics course, preservice student
teachers designed a lesson plan for elementary students. In Miquel Àngel's
group, their view on the teaching of mathematics was mechanical: first, teaching theory, and then applying this theory in practical activities. "Firstly, we are
going to give them the theory about fractions and how they work; elementary
students could participate at any time and express any doubts." The same pattern occurred when their lesson plan was analyzed: the teacher explains while
students are listening, then students must reproduce what was taught by the
teacher. In their initial lesson plan Miquel Àngel and the other members of his
group reproduced how they had experienced mathematics in school, as did
the rest of the class. Sometimes this approach was more or less explicit, but
they had in common designing one-answer activities with one-way methodology to be resolved in as little time as possible.

3.3   *The Discovery: A New Model of Teaching Mathematics*

Based on National Council of Teachers of Mathematics (2000), my aim in
this course is to reflect on student teachers' views on learning mathematics,
which should go further than simply repeating procedures. I want to promote
a new view in which learning mathematics implies solving problems, reasoning, justifying, providing arguments, communicating and representing mathematical ideas and linking mathematical ideas to other disciplines. Therefore,
the course was designed to promote first-hand experiences in my preservice
teachers, a new view of learning mathematics, and to provide them with some
moments of self-reflection on their learning.

With all these tenets in mind, in different sessions of the course different
problems were proposed and preservice teachers had to solve them as elementary students. Therefore, problems from different mathematical topics
were suggested: fractions, multiples, lowest common multiple, etc. They were
worked on in class promoting reasoning, communication and the connection
between different mathematical ideas. In order to analyze how the problems
were solved and how the methodology was applied, the preservice teachers'

individual reflections were discussed in class and connected with the main authors in mathematics education, such as Carpenter, Fennema, Franke, Levi, and Empson (1999), Hiebert et al. (1997), NCTM (2000), Sullivan and Lilburn (2002) or Van de Walle, Karp, and Bay-Williams (2008).

In some of these sessions in which preservice teachers solved problems as elementary students, I realized how Miquel Àngel, who sat in the front row, was puzzled and surprised. On numerous occasions, he said that he had never seen mathematics presented in this way and he had never considered that mathematics could be learnt with more than one answer, with different ways to solve the same problem or, even, the possibility of communicating mathematical ideas. In the final interview, which was conducted when the course was over, it was clear how Miquel Àngel had changed his mind about open problems and the communication process in mathematics education:

> *Miquel Àngel*: Now, thanks to the problems that we did, I realized that if a closed problem is given to elementary students, only a few will be able to solve it. However, if they are given an open problem, then all of them will be able to do it, and this is very important. Moreover, students have to justify how they have solved the problem, which means not only becoming mindful of their learning and new things, but also because they are engaged in the class and feel part of it. And for me, this is like a miracle.

Apart from that, Miquel Àngel revealed the connection with mathematical ideas as the great discovery in the mathematics course. At the beginning of the course, mathematics was an accumulation of unconnected topics: "In that moment, I felt like each concept was completely new and a new challenge. For example, I can be good at multiplication, but when you start division it was like starting from scratch. Teachers didn't promote thinking, because they taught concepts without showing connections." For this reason, Miquel Àngel was fascinated when he discovered the connection between some different mathematical topics. For the first time in his whole life, he associated topics that he had never thought about: "I realized that in multiplications, actually, you simplify addition. So, if you have to add the same number repeatedly, it is more convenient to multiply to go faster. And I realized that division is related to distribution which, at the same time, is related to fractions."

3.4   *The Transformation: Reconciliation*

When Miquel Àngel started the elementary education degree, his view of mathematics was a compartmentalized discipline with no connection to other topics. In addition, his opinion was that mathematics teaching meant finding the correct answer by reproducing a procedure that the teacher had proposed just before. Moreover, his memories of learning mathematics were not positive:

> *Miquel Àngel*: In school, studying mathematics was like being at the North Pole; in other words, with each task and with each new concept you can feel the cold, because there was no empathy with the course. However, it was possible to engage in the course only if you were able to understand the concepts; only then did you become a lucky person because you could enjoy it.

From his explanation, we can see that Miquel Àngel's aim was to pass the mathematics exams without looking for any kind of engagement with the course. However, after the Didactics of Mathematics course, he changed his mind about mathematics and how it is learnt:

> *Miquel Àngel*: At the university, everything was completely different. The cold became warmth, because of the good explanations and the connections made to different topics (...). In school there was only one way to do and solve the mathematics problems and only some students were able to do that; the others who weren't, were just 'present.' These things didn't happen on the Didactics of Mathematics course because I learnt different ways of solving mathematical problems.

When the course finished, Miquel Àngel said he had a better relationship with mathematics. He stopped blaming himself because he realized that it was not because of his inability or his attitude, but because of how mathematics was taught to him. Currently, his involvement in learning and teaching mathematics goes beyond the Didactics of Mathematics course. He now regularly attends other courses on teaching and learning mathematics outside the university and he works as a volunteer in extra-curricular mathematics activities in an elementary school. He is also considering the possibility of taking another optional course on mathematics education in the elementary education degree. Therefore, not only did Miquel Àngel change his view on teaching mathematics, but he also emotionally and intellectually reconciled himself with it.

4   Implications in Science and Mathematics Teacher Education

As professors of Didactics of a Science and Mathematics, our pedagogical knowledge was enriched by the experience. Without conducting this research, we would not have had the chance to reflect on how the authoritarian approaches experienced in school can affect our preservice teachers' emotionally.

Abell et al. (2006) pointed out that we can understand that preservice teachers are newcomers to the community of elementary science and mathematics teaching, but they are old-timers as members of school culture. Therefore, the school culture that preservice teachers experienced as students has an enormous influence on how science and mathematics teaching is viewed. In the cases of Eugènia and Miquel Àngel, the methodology used when they were taught before taking our courses, was based on the transmission of knowledge, its memorization and reproduction. However, the authority of science and mathematics should derive, in Lemke's (1990) words, "from evidence and logical argument rather than from the power relations between people or groups in a society" (p. 142).

In their prior experiences, Eugènia and Miquel Àngel were taught using an authoritarian discourse approach, in which the power was not distributed and was held only by the teacher. When the instructor following an authoritarian discourse rationality, listening to other voices or understanding other perspectives was not allowed. As described by Bakhtin (1986):

> authoritative discourse permits no play with the context framing it, no play with its borders, no gradual and flexible transitions, no spontaneously creative stylizing variants on it. It enters our verbal consciousness as a compact and indivisible mass; one must either totally affirm it, or reject it. (p. 343)

The answers arising from the activities were correct or incorrect according to the teachers' perspectives, but not for the inner rationale of the discipline.

When science and mathematics are built within the framework of authoritarian discourse, the mysticism of science and mathematics knowledge is, sometimes unconsciously, fostered. Sometimes, teachers who adopt this stance understand students' mistakes not because of their views on science and mathematics, but because of a lack of knowledge or their inability. In this respect, teachers attempt to control and constrain students' agency through the use of evaluation tools as weapons which have an emotional impact on students. Punishments or making fun of students' ideas or mistakes, and the unpleasant emotions that the teacher spreads to students with these practices, can be seen as a way to control their opinions, beliefs, and acts.

Furthermore, when science and mathematics are taught with such a dogmatic view, we can be under the illusion that these disciplines possess a special truth, completely different to common sense and accessible only to experts

and privileged minds (Lemke, 1990). This approach alienates students from science and mathematics because these students, like Eugènia and Miquel Àngel,
think they will not be able to understand scientific and mathematical content.
In the case studies described in this chapter, dogmatic views of science and
mathematics generated emotions such as fear, anger, sadness, and frustration.

From our point of view, how they felt as students is important to understanding why these students changed how they felt about science and math.
The word 'emotion' comes from the Latin '*emovere*,' which is related to movement. Emotions push human beings not only to physiological reactions, but
also to act on a social plane. According to Zembylas (2011), this action can be
produced in two different directions: emotions can either act to reproduce
social control or to transform existing power relationships. Thus, experiencing
an authoritarian methodology in school also has, in our case studies, two different responses: on the one hand, in Miquel Àngel's case, this authoritarian
methodology is reproduced in the same way the discipline was taught to him;
on the other hand, in Eugènia's case, anger acted as a fuel to react against this
authoritarian way of teaching science because she did not want to promote the
same emotions that she had felt as a student.

Even though their initial positions were different, after experiencing our
preservice teacher courses their views changed. Didactics of Science and
Didactics of Mathematics are based on a more dialogical approach: the preservice teachers' views are considered, the discipline constructs are built together,
and there is a broad range of possible answers that are coherent with the discipline's rationality. As described in both cases, this new approach in teaching increases students' self-confidence and self-esteem, because they are not
under as much pressure as they were in their elementary schools, where they
had to provide the 'right' scientific or mathematical explanation. Therefore,
emotions such as enthusiasm, pride and happiness can appear in this context.
For this reason, students became engaged in this discipline, because a new way
of teaching science and mathematics was experienced, without the unpleasant emotions that they had experienced as students.

In our opinion, students' views of what science and mathematics are, and
how science and mathematics could be taught were transformed thanks to
their self-analysis and awareness of how they felt on the course and how they
learnt scientific and mathematical content. We, as instructors and researchers, feel that, without reflecting on their own learning and feelings, the students probably would not have changed their mind in such a drastic way. Using
their own emotional experiences to reflect on how they felt in school and on
how they would feel as future teachers, but also using their own view of how

science and mathematics were taught to them and how they would teach the courses to others, were shown to be good strategies to transform their mental schemas and their practices.

5   Implications in Collaborative Research Methodologies

The purpose of this chapter was not only to provide two cases to illustrate how critical self-reflection of authoritarian power structures can be used as a powerful tool for teacher education, but also as a tool to inquire about collaborative research methodologies. As pointed out by Alexakos (2015), research approaches are framed by a particular understanding of how knowledge is built (epistemology), what the nature of reality is (ontology), and what the main values of the research are (axiology). Collaborative research is framed within interpretive and socio-critical research paradigms, in which it is possible to comprehend reality in the form of social constructs which are context-dependent. Therefore, the constructs are not true, but more or less sophisticated (Guba & Lincoln, 1995).

We agree with Tobin (2014) that there are many advantages to respecting the complexity of the cases and considering the experiences of the participants, rather than producing reductionist models and defining significant variables. Our research approach allows us to open the black box of teaching and learning phenomena, in order to build a comprehension of what is going on in our Didactics courses. In this study, for example, focusing on our participants' unique experiences provides us with the opportunity to enter an unexplored field. Thanks to their cases we, as professors and researchers, can comprehend better how students with quite dogmatic and authoritarian experiences felt when preservice teachers arrived in our courses; and, moreover, we have the chance to reflect on the role of emotions as transformative forces.

Not only did Eugènia and Miquel Angel's views and emotions on teaching science and mathematics change because of their engagement with the course and in the research, so did ours. Eugènia, for instance, told us how filling out the emotional diary every single session was useful in helping her to "be more aware of which moments in the session were meaningful for us." Moreover, being mindful of her own emotions will be important to her as a future teacher:

> *Eugènia*: I think it is absolutely necessary to know which kind of emotions my students will feel when they study science, because emotion could influence their learning processes. If we, as teachers, don't know

how they feel, it is pretty unlikely we will be able to teach them and to make them comfortable in class.

A similar notion was expressed by Miquel Àngel. When the course and most of the research was finished, he sent us an e-mail, in which he said:

> *Miquel Àngel*: I would like to thank you for the opportunity that being involved in the research gave me because I took advantage of it to reflect on my view of teaching mathematics and to continue with my learning.

These two outcomes of the research are consistent with the two first criteria, ontological and educative criteria, in authenticity research as defined by Tobin (2016) and Alexakos (2015). In our opinion, this research is also catalytic because it not only changed participants' perspectives, but also catalyzed improvements in us (the instructors) and how we approached and taught these courses. After researching emotions during the courses, rather than one we began to use multiple research and self-reported methods, such as emotional diaries and self-reflections on student teachers' school memories which also became part of our syllabus. This research is tactical as well, because the research aim is to reveal the disadvantages caused by power relationships. In our opinion, authoritarian and dogmatic views on science and mathematics are an abuse of the teacher's power. Thus, a lot of students get left behind, sometimes because they really think that these disciplines are only for an elite. If we really believe in science and mathematics for all students, social structures and the power relationships behind these ways of teaching must be uncovered, in order to address them.

Acknowledgements

The authors would like to thank all the students who collaborated in this study. The authors' thanks are also extended to our colleagues of the CODI research group and Montserrat Prat for their insights and recommendations throughout the research. Finally, we appreciate the assistance of Milford Edge for his linguistic assessment.

References

Abell, S. K., Appleton, K., & Hanuscin, D. L. (2010). *Designing and teaching the elementary science methods course*. Routledge.

Abell, S. K., Smith, D. C., & Volkmann, M. J. (2006). Inquiry in science teacher education. In L. B. Flick & N. G. Lederman (Eds,), *Scientific inquiry and nature of science. Implications for teaching, learning and teacher education* (pp. 173–200). Springer.

Acher, A., Arcà, M., & Sanmartí, N. (2004). Modeling as a teaching learning process for understanding materials: A case study in primary science education. *Science Education, 91*, 398–418.

Alexakos, K. (2015). *Being a teacher | researcher: A primer on doing authentic inquiry research on teaching and learning.* Sense Publishers.

Alexakos, K., Pride, L. D., Amat, A., Tsetsakos, P., Lee, K. J., Paylor-Smith, C., Zapata, C., Wright, S., & Smith, T. (2016). Mindfulness and discussing "thorny" issues in the classroom. *Cultural Studies of Science Education, 11*, 741–769. doi: 10.1007/s11422-015-9718-0

Amat, A., Zapata, C., Alexakos, K., Pride, L. D., Paylor-Smith, C., & Hernandez, M. (2016). Incorporating oximeter analyses to investigate synchronies in heart rate while teaching and learning about race. *Cultural Studies of Science Education, 11*, 758–801. doi:10.1007/s11422-016-9767-z

Bakhtin, M. M. (1986). *The dialogic imagination: Four essays.* University of Texas Press.

Carey, S., & Smith, C. (1993). On understanding the nature of scientific knowledge. *Educational Psychologist, 28*(3), 235–251. doi:10.1207/s15326985ep2803_4

Carpenter, T. P., Fennema, E., Franke, M. L., Levi, L., & Empson, S. B. (1999). *Children's mathematics. Cognitively guided instruction.* Heinemann.

Guba, E. G., & Lincoln, Y. S. (1994). Competing paradigms in qualitative research. In N. K. Denzin & Y. S. Lincoln (Eds.), *Handbook of qualitative research* (pp. 105–117). Sage.

Hiebert, J., Carpenter, T. P., Fennema, E., Fuson, K. C., Wearne, D., Murray, H., Olivier, A., & Human, P. (1997). *Making sense. Teaching and learning mathematics with understanding.* Heinemann.

Jiménez, I. (2016). *Preservice teacher knowledge application: From model-centered instruction to lesson plan design* (Unpublished doctoral thesis). Universitat de Vic – Universitat Central de Catalunya, Vic, Spain.

Kincheloe, J. L., & Tobin, K. (2009). The much exaggerated death of positivism. *Cultural Studies of Science Education, 4*, 513–528. doi:10.1007/s11422-009-9178-5

Lederman, N. G. (2007). Nature of science: Past, present and future. In S. K. Abell & N. G. Lederman (Eds.), *Handbook of research on science education* (Vol. 2, pp. 831–879). Routledge.

Lemke, J. L. (1990). *Talking science: Language, learning, and values.* Ablex Publishing Corporation.

Mortimer, E. F., & Scott, P. H. (2003). *Meaning making in secondary science classrooms.* Open University Press.

National Council of Teachers of Mathematics. (2000). *Principles and standards for school mathematics.* NCTM.

Ritchie, S. M., Hudson, P., Bellocchi, A., Senka, H., King, D., & Tobin, K. (2016). Evolution of self-reporting methods for identifying discrete emotions in science classrooms. *Cultural Studies of Science Education, 11*, 577–593. doi:10.1007/s11422-014-9607-y

Schwarz, C. (2009). Developing preservice elementary teachers' knowledge and practices through modeling-centered scientific inquiry. *Science Education, 94*, 720–744. doi:10.1002/sce.20324

Sewell Jr., W. H. Jr. (2005). *Logics of history: Social theory and social transformation.* University of Chicago Press.

Shulman, L. S. (1986). Those who understand: Knowledge growth in teaching. *Educational Researcher, 15*(2), 4–14. doi:10.3102/0013189X015002004

Sullivan, P., & Lilburn, P. (2002). *Good questions for math teaching. Why ask them and what to ask [K-6].* Math Solutions.

Tobin, K. (2006). Aligning the cultures of teaching and learning science in urban high schools. *Cultural Studies of Science Education, 1*, 219–252. doi:10.10007/s11422-005-9008-3

Tobin, K. (2014). Using collaborative inquiry to better understand teaching and learning. In L. Bencze & S. Alsop (Eds.), *Activist science and technology education* (pp. 127–147). Springer.

Tobin, K. (2015). Qualitative research in classrooms. Pushing the boundaries of theory and methodology. In K. Tobin & S. R. Steinberg (Eds.), *Doing educational research* (2nd ed., pp. 33–75). Sense Publishers.

Tobin, K., & Ritchie, S. M. (2011). Multi-method, multi-theoretical, multi-level research in the learning science. *The Asia-Pacific Educational Researcher, 20*(3), 117–129.

Van de Walle, J. A., Karp, K. S., & Bay-Williams, J. M. (2010). *Elementary and middle school mathematics. Teaching developmentally* (7th ed.). Pearson Education.

Zembylas, M. (2007). Emotional ecology: The intersection of emotional knowledge and pedagogical content knowledge in teaching. *Teaching and Teacher Education, 23*, 355–367. doi:10.1016/j.tate.2006.12.002

Zembylas, M. (2011). Teaching and teacher emotions: A post-structural perspective. In C. Day & J. C. Lee (Eds.), *New understandings of teacher's work* (pp. 31–43). Springer.

Zembylas, M. (2014). Making sense of the complex entanglement between emotion and pedagogy: Contributions of the 'affective turn.' *Cultural Studies of Science Education, 11*, 539–550. doi:10.1007/s11422-014-9623-y

Improving Place-Based Environmental Education Using Cogenerative Dialogue and Photovoice

Amy DeFelice

Abstract

In this chapter I explore how using a place-based approach in a science class mediated students' science identities, and potential interest in science. I describe how I learned with my ninth-grade students about our experiences in the Field Studies class through using cogenerative dialogues that incorporate photovoice. Students' reflections from our cogenerative dialogue on the science fair and students' digital photographs that sparked additional dialogues are incorporated as examples of how to learn about students' science identities. The examples described here illustrate that teacher-researchers can utilize the methods of cogenerative dialogue and photovoice to listen to students' voices and improve place-based teaching and learning.

Keywords

environmental education – place-based science – science identities – cogenerative dialogue – photovoice

1   Teaching and Learning in Familiar Places

Urban students' daily lived experiences are often disconnected from science experiences at school, which can result in students not seeing the importance of science in their lives. This leads to students being unengaged and disinterested in science (Basu & Calabrese Barton, 2007). One way to overcome this challenge is to link students to learning about their local environment through environmental education programs that engage students in real-world science experiences in the places that are familiar to them (Calabrese Barton & Berchini, 2013). Traditionally, environmental education programs have not generally focused on connecting urban students to their local environments, but instead examine global scale environmental issues, such as climate change and rainforest destruction. This approach does not recognize that it is important for students to connect with and appreciate their local environment before they are asked to think about and offer solutions for global environmental issues (Sobel, 1996). As an alternative to traditional science and environmental programs, a different approach to teaching and learning uses the local environment as a framework within which students can construct their own learning, guided by teachers (Lim & Calabrese Barton, 2006). Place-based education can be designed so students and teachers encounter the physical place, and the people and living and non-living factors, that define that place to develop a relationship, or sense of place (Adams & Branco, 2016). When learning experiences are designed and facilitated to enhance students' sense of place of the urban environment all learners can increase awareness and sensitivity to the environment and to each other (Adams et al., 2017).

The Field Studies class for ninth grade students at an Environmentally Themed High School in Brooklyn, NY approaches environmental education with a place-based perspective and strives to connect students to the local environments to increase students' engagement in science learning. While I was a teacher at this school I became very interested in understanding how my ninth-grade students perceived and engaged in science activities in the required place-based environmental science course called Field Studies. I was particularly interested to learn when, and how, my students felt like they were enacting their science identities during Field Studies in an effort to improve environmental science teaching and learning and make the learning relevant to their lives. Science identities are described as any aspect of one's life that is recognized by oneself or others as enactment of science practices, or contributes to one's desire or interest to pursue scientific endeavors (Carlone & Johnson, 2007). For example, developing knowledges about the physical, biological, and social world through observing, questioning, seeking answers through designing experiments or systematic inquiry, and reflecting on experiences.

In this chapter I describe how my students and I researched the teaching and learning in Field Studies together. Students were invited to participate in cogenerative dialogues (cogens) held weekly after school. Cogens are a space where teachers and students engage in dialogue as equals with a goal of improving teaching and learning in the class (Tobin, 2006). Cogens were digitally voice recorded and later transcribed to look for patterns and contradictions (Sewell, 2005). Student researchers were provided with digital cameras during class to document their Field Studies experiences. We utilized photovoice (Wang & Burris, 1997) where students shared their stories and described their teaching and learning experiences depicted in their photographs.

2 Place-Based Environmental Education

Place-based education engages students in cross-curricular, or multidisciplinary, methods where knowledge is co-constructed through hands-on, real-world learning experiences (Sobel, 2005). The local community and environment are the contexts for student engagement in language arts, social studies, mathematics and science learning. A place-based teaching and learning approach to environmental education increases students' understanding of the physical, cultural, historic and socioeconomic meanings of local places (Semken, 2005). Woodhouse and Knapp (2000) note that place-based education: emerges from the particular attributes of a place, is inherently multidisciplinary and experiential, is reflective of an educational philosophy that is wider than "learning to earn," and connects place with self and community. The concept of curriculum emerging from a particular place is an alternative to current positivistic views and trends in education of testing, global standardization, competitiveness and career training (Lieberman & Hoody, 1998). According to David Sobel (2005):

> This approach to education increases academic achievement, helps students develop stronger ties to their community, enhances students' appreciation for the natural world, and creates a heightened commitment to serving as active, contributing citizens. (p. 7)

Place-based education emphasizes and provides the needed context for learning through real experiences, such as local environmental issues, to capture student interest (Loveland, 2003).

One of the goals of place-based science teaching and learning is to increase student engagement in the curriculum through connecting science to the local community and showing the relevance of science to students' lives (Sobel, 2005). It is challenging as an educator to determine what real-life science projects will resonate with students and engage them in critical thinking considering the diverse population of students. Place-based education recognizes that ecosystems and communities vary around schools, therefore schools should design their own programs to take into account the natural ecosystems and sociocultural systems specific to their location, resources, and needs (Lieberman & Hoody, 1998). Field Studies was designed to engage traditionally underrepresented students, who may see themselves as outsiders to the field of science (Brickhouse, 1994), in real-world science activities where they had opportunities to develop questions and design investigations of local ecosystems. The demographics of the students in the school and the class described include 90% black, 5% Latino/a and 5% Asian American, with a high percentage of students from families with low-incomes. When planning and coteaching Field Studies, my colleagues and I had the overarching goals of providing students with hands-on ecological learning experiences to observe and understand the ecosystems of the local urban park and engage students in authentic science research projects about the local environment. Later in this chapter I explain how I learned about the implementation of Field Studies with my student researchers and share what I think can be done to improve these kinds of learning experiences for underrepresented students.

3 Science Identities

Identities are always transforming and individuals have multiple identities that overlap with their science identities (Brickhouse et al., 2000). Aspects of our identities are expressed to varying degrees in different fields of culture and include factors such as gender, ethnicity, race and economic class (Calabrese Barton, 1998). Jean Lave and Etienne Wenger (1991) explain that students' identities transform by participating in communities of practice. Through engaging in activities that are perceived as scientific and demonstrating competence that is recognized by meaningful others, students develop a sense of themselves as someone who does science (Carlone & Johnson, 2007). One's science identity transforms as they find their place among other people engaged in these social activities and find a way to contribute to the social practices of science (Stetsenko, 2008). This participation also is influenced by the places where the activity happens (Adams & Gupta, 2013). It has been shown that conducting authentic science research in an urban park can enhance students' science identities as they felt a sense of belonging to the science community as they participated in science practices (DeFelice et al., 2014). Places such as urban parks can become an important teaching resource since places and identities are interconnected (Adams & Branco, 2016). It is also necessary to create a more diverse understanding of what communities of practice are considered scientific, beyond that of research scientists, but to include, for example, healthcare workers, ecologists, citizen scientists and gardeners (Brickhouse et al., 2000). With this understanding of science identities, Field Studies students participated in authentic science experiences about the local environment with the intention of fostering personal relevance of science, and supporting a sense of care and appreciation for the natural world.

4   Methods for Learning with Students

As a researcher I recognize that I have reached my inquiries through my personal experiences. I also realize that my students have their own prior experiences that influence their learning in the Field Studies program. Because of this theoretical framework a hermeneutic phenomenological (Van Manen, 1990) approach was necessary in that it allowed me to reflect on my own stories and juxtapose them with my students' stories in order to circle events and narratives with meaning. When a researcher is passionate about her work, at some point she will reflect on her own experiences and realize that her experiences have led to her research topic. Max Van Manen (1990) stresses that reflection on lived experiences is always recollective because it is reflection on experience that is already passed or lived through. Reflection on a recent event will include memories and other past experiences as well. Through reflection, thoughts are deepened, thinking is radicalized, and action will eventually flow from this revolutionary thinking (Van Manen, 1990). Cogens, as a methodological approach, allowed space for my students and me to share our experiences in the Field Studies course and co-interpret the events therein.

5   Cogenerative Dialogues for Reflection

Cogens have been used in a variety of educational settings to investigate teaching and learning (Bayne, 2009). Gillian Bayne found that using cogens and informal interviewing techniques can support a variety of students and be especially beneficial in urban science classrooms, where there are often cultural misalignments between students' and teachers' knowledges and experiences. Bayne explains that the open discussions of cogens create a forum, or field of culture, where the "teacher, students, and others, work together to improve the quality and efficacy of teaching and learning" (p. 517). These spaces create a new learning environment where the object of inquiry is the classroom environment, or in this case the Field Studies class (Tobin et al., 2005). This provides a structure for students and teachers to share ideas and opinions in a non-judgmental environment where participants are listening and receptive to allow for reflexivity about experiences to develop higher quality teaching and learning (Tobin & Roth, 2006).

Cogens provide a space for reflecting on how my life experiences and knowledge of science is similar to and different from my students. Such an example arose in a cogen where my students and I were discussing an activity where we collected macroinvertebrates using nets to scoop the leaf litter from the bottom of the lake in the park. Students described how they enjoyed physically interacting with the water and using the nets. One of my students shared how this was like their childhood experiences using a seine net to catch fish at the beach. I shared my childhood memories of making "aquariums" at my family's cottage by using a small net to collect minnows from the lake and put them in into a large glass jar with sand, rocks, and sticks to observe for the afternoon. Although catching minnows in Canada is different than searching for macro-invertebrates in leaf litter in Brooklyn, or catching sea creatures at the beach, there is still a similarity of catching living things from the water. Cogens afford students and teachers a field of culture to generate recognition and respect for multiple ways of knowing and different knowledge systems.

I invited approximately 30 students in my Field Studies class to attend cogens that were held once a week after school during the 2011–12 school year. Students who participated in the cogens and took digital pictures during the Field Studies class were asked to complete assent forms and their parents completed consent forms. Students were made aware that their participation was completely voluntary; they could join or withdraw from the group at any time and students' grades in the course were not impacted in any way from attending cogens. Generally, cogens included a group of one to four students and myself each week. Occasionally the Field Studies instructor and an assistant both hired by the park and botanical garden attended the cogens as well. Cogens were used instead of interviews because the cogens created a space where, to the extent possible, an equitable space was created where students felt free to share what they were really thinking, either positive or negative, about the class, without feeling like it affected their grade. Cogens were digitally voice recorded and later transcribed to look for themes of science-related identities and to assess place-based science lessons.

As a teacher-researcher I hoped to understand my students' reactions to the Field Studies course in order to improve the Field Studies teaching and learning activities for future classes. I also wanted to learn in what ways the Field Studies class mediated students' science identities. Students who participated in the cogens were considered student researchers because of their contributions to the study. We did not aim to reach consensus within the group, but were aiming to arrive at consensus in our understanding of differences. Everyone had an equal opportunity to speak. We employed radical listening (Tobin, 2009) in the cogens as we were learning to view difference as a resource. We strived to focus on what others were saying, and learn from each other about how our science identities were forming and transforming through the learning experiences (Alexakos & Pierwola, 2013) without passing judgments or letting our minds wander.

5.1   *Digital Photography and Photovoice*

Photovoice is a form of action research in community development and education where marginalized social groups use images to express their concerns and increase awareness to hopefully initiate change (Wang & Burris, 1997). Photovoice can allow urban youths to become more familiar with their communities from an ecological perspective and add an "ecological layer" to their identities (Bellino & Adams, 2014). I prompted student researchers to take digital photographs during Field Studies of anything that they found interesting, inspirational, or relating to science. Student researchers shared two digital cameras each week and were not pressured to take photos if they did not feel like participating. I also took photos during the class. I downloaded students' photographs and organized them into folders by student and date. Photographs taken during class were shared in cogens using a laptop computer to elicit dialogues as student researchers described and discussed their photographs. These photographs provided a starting point for our discussions and helped us to explain and tell our stories of our experiences from our own individual perspectives. Cogens did not always focus on the photographs but since details of experiences or events are often forgotten, or not noticed, the photographs reminded us of topics to discuss that we may have otherwise overlooked. I later returned to students' photographs to look for developing themes of science identities.

6   Reflecting with Photovoice and Cogen

6.1   *Field Studies Photovoice*

6.1.1   Alexia

Alexia expressed her science identity in the digital photographs she decided to take during class. She specifically chose to photograph her peers collecting samples and discovering "new" organisms. The photographs Alexia and others took allowed me to understand their perspectives of the class activities as they shared their stories about what the photographs were depicting. Figure 12.1 is of a student in Alexia's group looking for macroinvertebrates in the urban park's water system. Figure 12.2 is of a student's discovery of a small snail found in the leaf litter.

During the cogens, Alexia presented her photos and reflected on her Field Studies experiences.

> *Alexia:* At first I didn't like [the urban park] because of all of the bugs and it makes you feel itchy. Aquatic bugs weren't as bad. I would have rather

FIGURE 12.1   Students used dip nets to collect leaf litter from the bottom of the water source to identify macroinvertebrates

FIGURE 12.2   Snail found in the leaf litter of the lake at the urban park

> been in the water chemistry group because the macroinvertebrates were running away from us ... My group liked scooping with the nets and interacting with the water but not necessarily picking through leaves for macroinvertebrates ... My group members would find the macroinvertebrates and I would identify them. I tried to make the data as accurate as possible.

Alexia's science identity is present when she wanted to have accurate data for her project. Her photos and explanations of them indicated this. Students in her group were not as interested in investing the same level of focus or accuracy with the project and this was frustrating for Alexia. The Field Studies teachers and I tried to help students determine projects that would interest and inspire them to carefully collect data and feel that their data are important, like Alexia, through completing place-based projects about the local environment. However, even if the projects are about the local area where students live, it is difficult to reach all students' interests with every project. I value discussing with students what activities they found useful or interesting about the local natural world so that I can replicate and improve these activities with future students. Alexia's photovoice reflections of her photographs and discussions in cogens enabled her to express her science identity as well as help me improve the learning experience.

6.2   *Appreciating the Beauty of Nature*
6.2.1   Kim
One of the goals of Field Studies was for students to appreciate the natural world and develop a sense of care or stewardship for the environment. Education should focus on caring for nature and when students recognize that nature has an intrinsic value this can emerge into an aesthetic relation to nature (Postma, 2009). Kim's photographs of the landscape throughout the park (Figures 12.3– 12.7) have an aesthetic quality and depict the beauty of nature. The aesthetic component of science is often disregarded because science education is concerned with standards, conceptual change, and inquiry (Pugh & Girod, 2007). However, "science aesthetics" guides and encourages people to open up to the beauty of nature and allows people to perceive things in meaningful new ways (Pugh & Girod, 2007). Mark Girod (2007) terms this "re-seeing" where deep observation is a means for deepening the aesthetic experience and, in turn, the learning of science. Kim's photovoice of Field Studies expressed how she "wanted to take pictures of beautiful things in nature."

Kim was given the same directions for using the camera as Alexia and other student researchers, which were to take pictures of anything that interested them or reminded them of science. Interestingly, Kim chose to take nature

FIGURE 12.3   New leaves on a tree in spring. Woodchips are covering the ground because it is a high foot traffic area and soil is compacted preventing the growth of grass

FIGURE 12.4   Lullwater Bridge showing part of the aquatic ecosystem in the park

FIGURE 12.5   Walkway in early spring

FIGURE 12.6   Reflection at the surface of the water showing duckweed growth

FIGURE 12.7   Binnen Falls, near one of the data collection sites for students' science fair
projects

photos of the places where students were conducting science activities and
did not take pictures of the actual science activities they were conducting.
Kim's sense of place for the park as an area of natural beauty and serenity are
expressed in her photographs. The photos show the natural surroundings of
the urban park as an oasis of nature in the middle of the city and express her
feelings of appreciation for the natural world. I did not engage in a discussion
with Kim about the scientific ideas that are expressed in her photographs. At
the time I viewed Kim's photos as aesthetically pleasing, and listened as she
expressed an appreciation for the natural beauty of the area, but I did not make
the connection between aesthetics and science. We could have used "re-seeing" and analyzed her photos through a scientific lens. "Re-seeing irrevocably
transform one's vision and understanding of the world in aesthetic yet scientifically important and accurate ways" (Girod, 2007, p. 51). Although aesthetics
theory in science education was not a focus of this study, Kim's photographs
have inspired me to pursue this topic in the future. I am curious how aesthetics
and re-seeing expand our sense of place and how I can utilize these ideas in
my teaching and my everyday experiences as I wonder about the natural world.

Kim described in a cogen that she does not normally go to the park on her
own because it is not very close to where she lives and her mother wouldn't
let her go there alone. Other students have also expressed that they do not

regularly go to this urban park because it is too far from their homes. Going to the park for Field Studies class opened Kim's mind to the idea of this natural place where she could experience nature and made her feel more comfortable in these surroundings. I do not encourage students to go to the park alone for safety reasons, but I do encourage them to go there with friends and family outside of Field Studies. I think that many students in Field Studies developed a sense of place in relation to the park that expanded to include a place for learning science, in whatever ways science learning happened for them. In Kim's example, her sense of place was expanded to include the beauty of nature that is available in her urban environment. Her experience of the park also confirmed her aesthetic notions of nature—as being a place of beauty and reflection. Kim's reflections, both through the photos and her description of her photos on the park, demonstrate how she developed an appreciation for this natural space and formed a sense of care for the park. I hope that as time passes students appreciate and enjoy the natural landscape and are more likely to protect this natural space and return to the urban park.

6.3 Science Fair Cogen

Students in Field Studies spent the majority of the class in the spring semester planning and carrying out field observation projects, and then presented their work at the school's science fair. In one of the last cogens of the school year we focused our discussion on the annual science fair. I asked students, "What did you think of the science fair?" Nicholas, normally a quiet and reserved student who rarely attended cogens, called out with more enthusiasm than I had ever heard him express before: "It was awesome!" I asked why he thought it was awesome. Nicholas said: "Because we got to show off everything we learned and studied and researched in the park." This was Nicholas's first science fair and seemed to be a pivotal event for him that year.

The Science Fair offered a chance for students to demonstrate what they learned in Field Studies to a larger audience. Staff from the landscape management department of the local urban park, educational staff from the botanical garden, cooperating scientists from the local community college, and teachers served as judges. It was also a time for students in other classes, like Geology, Advanced Placement Biology, Chemistry in the Community, Conceptual Physics, Marine Biology and Science Research to display their work in science. Student projects were displayed on tri-fold poster boards and judges circulated through the projects while students presented their work. All students received a certificate of participation and rubrics were collected and tallied to determine first, second, and third place in each category.

Nicholas's response that the science fair was "awesome" was very encouraging for me as a science teacher. Although he is a very quiet and shy student,

Nicholas's group determined what each group member was going to explain to the judges during the science fair ahead of time and he felt prepared to participate. Nicholas said that he felt like a scientist while completing the science fair project and presenting because he was sharing his group's findings. Nicholas was encouraged by his peers beyond his normal "comfort zone" to participate in presenting to the judges. Nicholas described his group's research question and results:

> *Nicholas:* How does pH affect phytoplankton and zooplankton at three sites in the park? We found a higher pH at the lake and more plankton there. This didn't support our hypothesis because our hypothesis was that water had to be neutral for there to be plankton.

Nicholas enacted his science identity during the science fair and also in the cogen where he reflected on his learning and science fair experience as he shared his understanding of the project. The other students participating in the cogen said they were surprised to hear Nicholas open up and talk since he was usually so shy. I too was pleasantly surprised to see Nicholas trying on this identity and encouraged him to continue to share with the group. An important aspect of identity development includes being seen as a "kind of person" by others. Other people are important in the development of identities because our identities are shaped by how others see us and the roles we have in a field of culture as we work towards reaching a goal (Stetsenko, 2008). Nicholas was viewed as a quiet student by other students and me and this probably added to his shyness in class. The science fair and cogens were places for Nicholas to transform and expand his identities by speaking up and moving past his "shy" label. As others start to see Nicholas in different ways it will further encourage his emerging science identity.

Not all students in the cogen had as positive reactions to the science fair projects. For example, Alexia said:

> *Alexia:* I guess we did OK. It was a little nerve-wracking. I didn't like when one of the judges asked my group member a question and they didn't know the answer. I tried to answer for him but they were like, 'No, let him answer.'

Alexia felt that her group could have done better presenting and that their display could have been better. She shared that creating the poster boards felt rushed and that if they had more time their board might have looked nicer. She also said that since she is a strong science student most of her group just expected her to do all of the work and answer all of the judges' questions during the science fair. For Alexia, being correct is an important part of her identity as a student and this is enacted in her science class. Other students respect her for being a good science student and she identifies as a scientist by saying that she likes science and wants to study science in college. It was difficult for her to work in a group with peers who were not as invested in the project as she was. Alexia's science identity was encouraged somewhat by the science fair project despite her frustrations with her group.

As we continued reflecting on the science fair, Kim shared her challenges working with her group:

> *Kim:* I felt stupid while presenting with my group. One of my group members was saying stupid stuff on purpose ... the judges had a fake smile on their face when they looked at our board because we didn't really have anything on our board ... The judges would ask questions and afterward we would think 'oh I should have included that.' I had high expectations for my performance. When I went home and thought about it I was like, 'I should have thought about that' and that's why I felt stupid.

Kim participated in science fairs in 6th, 7th, and 8th grade. Her prior experiences with science fairs in middle school may have made her have higher expectations of herself and her performance in the 9th grade science fair. The Field Studies science fair project did afford Kim an opportunity to enact her science identity however she was not proud of her performance during the science fair. In the cogen Kim was reflecting upon how she was learning science and how her performance did not match up with her knowledge or her own expectations.

Overall the science fair projects created an opportunity for students to enact their science identities by participating in a community of practice as they learned about the aquatic ecosystem of the park and presented what they learned to others. The cogens provided me and the other Field Studies teachers with valuable feedback about how to improve the project for future classes. For example, students requested that we provide more time to prepare their posters. Students also suggested we better explain the rubric so that they could be ready for their presentations. Some students were "annoyed" that they didn't get into a group with their first topic of choice and it wasn't enjoyable to do research on something that they didn't really want to study. Alexia said she would have rather studied a different topic altogether, such as "researching how people interact with the park, how they treat the park and if they litter or pick plants or what they come to the park to do." I had not considered studying a social science topic in the Field Studies class however this would be an interesting subject to pursue with future classes and made me think about redefining environmental related studies for urban students in urban contexts. This topic of inquiry also indicated to me that Alexia's sense of place of the park included an appreciation for the natural area because she wanted to learn more about human impacts on the park. Students' suggestions and reactions were shared at the end of the year Field Studies meeting with other teachers and the park and garden education directors.

7   Field Studies as Place-Based Science Education

The theme for the Field Studies science fair projects was how do humans impact the urban park? The park is widely used and hosts more than ten million visitors a year. Topics for human impact projects have included: soil compaction from people walking on shortcuts between paths, or playing ball in the open fields, thus creating dirt paths where vegetation can't grow, dumping charcoal near trees altering the soil chemistry, volunteering to monitor the spread of invasive species, such as garlic mustard, and helping landscape management pull out the invasive species, monitoring water quality, or comparing air quality inside the park with air quality along a busy street. In the fall semester students engaged in lessons in the different ecosystems of the park and were introduced to field research techniques and issues of concern for the urban ecosystem. The spring science fair projects engaged students in the most significant place-based lessons because they selected a topic of inquiry about the park (with some logistical constraints), formed a plan to research their topics, and then reported their findings to the school community during the science fair. The other teachers and I assumed that students would be more interested in the science projects because they were about the local environment and we thought that would bring more relevance to the students' lives. Although students were participating in scientific endeavors to investigate the park, which is in close proximity to the school, this place was not necessarily viewed by the students as their local environment.

I was surprised when I learned that many of my students never went to the urban park outside of the time we spent there for class. Most students did not feel that this urban park was part of their community, although they began to think of the park as part of the school community. I was less surprised to learn that students rarely went to the botanical garden, where class was also held, outside of class time. Yet, students also came to view the botanical garden as an extension of the school community. It was evident to me through our cogens that students did make connections between their Field Studies experiences in the park and garden, to what was familiar to them in their lived experiences elsewhere, thus expanding their understandings of these places. Perhaps if the projects were more closely tied to students' concepts of their local communities, then they would have felt an increased relevance of science to their lives. Gruenewald (2003) says that educators should follow critical place-based pedagogy where students are critical of their community and work to better the lives of those in their community. Field Studies students reported their findings from their science fair projects to the school community and made recommendations to the park's landscape management department based on their findings from their projects, however actions for improvement were not fully enacted. The practicality of this aspect of place-based education must be considered and remains a challenging goal for educators and students. If our goal of instilling appreciation and developing a sense of care for the environment are reached through the place-based Field Studies curriculum then students will hopefully view these places as their community and become advocates for the park and garden, and seek action to improve these parts of their community in the future.

8   Connecting through Place-Based Learning

As a teacher-researcher, it was important for me to learn about how the place-based environmental science Field Studies course impacted (or not) my students' relationships to and perceptions of science which I refer to as transforming their science identities. Kim affirmed the importance of place-based environmental education when she said: "A connection to the natural world can still be made in the classroom but it won't have the same effect as when you're actually outside and visualizing it first-hand." Individuals experienced investigating authentic science questions in the urban park differently as we enhanced our knowledges of a local place. Students transformed their science identities as they participated in scientific communities of practice where they: observed, wondered, collected and interpreted data, collaborated with peers, and shared findings with a larger audience.

An example of this science identity transformation was how Nicholas confidently described his Field Studies project and clearly demonstrated to the participants in our cogen that he is someone who can "do science." Alexia, already viewed by herself and peers as someone who "does science," overcame her fear of "creepy crawly insects" to complete her project, with little help from her group. She also provided feedback to me on how to improve the experience for future students. Kim expressed her appreciation for being outdoors observing the natural world and the aesthetic beauty of nature in her photographs. Participating in cogens where we reflected on our photographs and the teaching and learning in our class also influenced my science identities. For example, I expanded my views of scientific communities of practice and considered alternative ways we can study human impacts on the urban park. Cogens with students also inspired me to question our relationships to local places and how we see our communities. My students also critiqued and challenged me to move beyond criticality towards action. I had the opportunity to work with students and other educators to revise the Field Studies curriculum to make the course more engaging for students while providing them a strong science foundation. The revisions to the curriculum demonstrate action as an outcome of this research. However, more action for improving and protecting our local environments is needed. This research surrounding place-based environmental science demonstrates how teacher-researchers can be responsive to their research findings, so a course can incorporate science that is more relevant to the lived experiences of their students.

References

Adams, J. D., & Branco, B. (2016). Extending parks into the classroom through informal learning and place-based education. In P. G. Patrick (Ed.), *Preparing informal science educators* (pp. 337–354). Springer International Publishing.

Adams, J. D., Greenwood, D. A., Thomashow, M., & Russ, A. (2017). Sense of place. In A. Russ & M. E. Krasny (Eds.), *Urban environmental education review* (pp. 68–75). Cornell University Press.

Adams, J., & Gupta, P. (2013). "I learn more here than I do in school. Honestly, I wouldn't lie about that": Creating a space for agency and identity around science. *International Journal of Critical Pedagogy, 4*, 87–104.

Alexakos, K., & Pierwola, A. (2013). Learning at the "boundaries": Radical listening, creationism, and learning from the "other." *Cultural Studies of Science Education, 8*, 39–49. https://doi.org/10.1007/s11422-012-9470-7

Basu, S. J., & Barton, A. C. (2007). Developing a sustained interest in science among Urban minority youth. *Journal of Research in Science Teaching, 44*, 466–489. https://doi.org/10.1002/tea.20143

Bayne, G. U. (2009). Cogenerative dialogues: The creation of interstitial culture in the New York metropolis. In W.-M. Roth & K. Tobin (Eds.), *The world of science education: Handbook of research in North America* (pp. 513–527). Sense Publishers.

Bellino, M., & Adams, J. D. (2014). Reimagining environmental education: Urban youths' perceptions and investigations of their communities. *Revista Brasileira de Pesquisa em Educação de Ciências, 14*(2), 27–38.

Brickhouse, N. W. (1994). Bringing in the outsiders: Reshaping the sciences of the future. *Curriculum Studies, 26*(4), 401–416. https://doi.org/10.1080/0022027940260404

Brickhouse, N. W., Lowery, P., & Shultz, K. (2000). What kind of a girl does science? The construction of school science identities. *Journal of Research in Science Teaching, 37*(5), 441–458. https://doi.org/10.1002/(SICI)1098-2736(200005)37:5<441::AID-TEA4>3.0.CO;2-3

Calabrese Barton, A. (1998). Teaching science with homeless children: Pedagogy, representation, and identity. *Journal of Research in Science Teaching, 35*(4), 379–394. https://doi.org/10.1002/(SICI)1098-2736(199804)35:4<379::AID-TEA8>3.0.CO;2-N

Calabrese Barton, A., & Berchini, C. (2013). Becoming and insider: Teaching science in Urban settings. *Theory into Practice, 52*(1), 21–27. https://doi.org/10.1080/07351690.2013.743765

Carlone, H. B., & Johnson, A. (2007), Understanding the science experiences of successful women of color: Science identity as an analytic lens. *Journal of Research in Science Teaching, 44*, 1187–1218. doi:10.1002/tea.20237

DeFelice, A., Adams, J. D., Branco, B., & Pieroni, P. (2014). Engaging underrepresented high school students in an Urban environmental and geoscience place-based curriculum. *Journal of Geoscience Education, 62*(1), 49–60. https://doi.org/10.5408/12-400.1

Girod, M. (2007). A conceptual overview of the role of beauty and aesthetics in science and science education. *Studies in Science Education, 43*, 38–61. https://doi.org/10.1080/03057260708560226

Gruenewald, D. (2003). Foundations of place: A multidisciplinary framework for place-conscious education. *American Educational Research Journal, 40*, 619–654. https://doi.org/10.3102/00028312040003619

Gruenewald, D. (2003). The best of both worlds: A critical pedagogy of place. *Educational Researcher, 32*(4), 3–12. https://doi.org/10.3102/0013189X032004003

Lave, J., & Wenger, E. (1991). *Situated learning: Legitimate peripheral participation.* Cambridge University Press.

Lieberman, G. A., & Hoody, L. L. (1998). *Closing the achievement gap: Using the environment as an integrating context for learning.* State Environment and Education Roundtable.

Lim, M., & Calabrese Barton, A. (2006). Science learning and a sense of place in an urban middle school. *Cultural Studies of Science Education, 1*, 107–142. https://doi.org/10.1007/s11422-005-9002-9

Loveland, E. (2003). Achieving academic goals through place-based learning: Students in five states show how to do it. *Rural Roots, 4*(1), 6–11.

Postma, D. W. (2009). *Why care for nature? In search of an ethical framework for environmental responsibility and education.* Springer.

Pugh, K., & Girod, M. (2007). Science, art and experience: Constructing a science pedagogy from Dewey's aesthetics. *Journal of Science Teacher Education, 18*, 9–27. https://doi.org/10.1007/s10972-006-9029-0

Semken, S. (2005). Sense of place and place-based introductory geoscience teaching for American Indian and Alaska Native Undergraduates. *Journal of Geoscience Education, 53*(2), 149–157. https://doi.org/10.5408/1089-9995-53.2.149

Sewell Jr., W. H. (2005). *Logics of history: Social theory and social transformation.* University of Chicago Press.

Sobel, D. (1996). *Beyond ecophobia: Reclaiming the heart in nature education.* The Orion Society and The Myrin Institute.

Sobel, D. (2005). *Place-Based education: Connecting classrooms and communities.* The Orion Society.

Stetsenko, A. (2008). From relational ontology to transformative activist stance on development and learning: Expanding Vygotsky's (CHAT) project. *Cultural Studies of Science Education, 3*, 471–491. https://doi.org/10.1007/s11422-008-9111-3

Tobin, K. (2006). Learning to teach through coteaching and cogenerative dialogue. *Teaching Education, 17*(2), 133–142. https://doi.org/10.1080/10476210600680358

Tobin, K. (2009). Tuning into others' voices: Radical listening, learning from difference, and escaping oppression. *Cultural Studies of Science Education, 4*, 505–511. https://doi.org/10.1007/s11422-009-9218-1

Tobin, K., Elmesky, R., & Seiler, G. (Ed.). (2005). *Improving Urban science education.* Rowman and Littlefield.

Tobin, K., & Roth, W.-M. (2006). *Teaching to learn: A view from the field.* Sense Publishers.

Van Manen, M. (1990). *Researching lived experience: Human science for an action sensitive pedagogy.* SUNY Press.

Wang, C., & Burris, M. A. (1997). Photovoice: Concept, methodology, and use for participatory needs assessment. *Health Education & Behavior, 24*(3), 369–387. https://doi.org/10.1177/109019819702400309

Woodhouse, J. L. & Knapp, C. E. (2000). *Place-based curriculum and instruction: Outdoor and environmental education approaches.* ERIC Digest EDO-RC-00-6. ERIC Clearinghouse on Rural Education and Small Schools, Appalachia Education Laboratory, 2 pp.

CHAPTER 13

Places That Matter: Collective Exploration of the Meaning of Neighborhood Places Using Mental Mapping with Youths

Marissa E. Bellino

Abstract

In this chapter I introduce mental mapping as a participatory methodology along with its implementation in an environmental science class. Anchored in a participant's map and in the follow up discussion in her group, the methodology of mental mapping and some of the analytical constructs identified by students are presented. How mental mapping was introduced to students in the class, the overall methodology, student maps, and student analysis are all discussed. I end the chapter with a summary of the affordances and experiences cited in student final reflections on the mental mapping process and how it can best be utilized with young people to critically explore local environments.

Keywords

mental mapping – youth participatory action research – environmental education – critical pedagogy – critical pedagogy of place

1 An Overview of What's to Come

Youth participatory action research (YPAR) situated in the lived experiences of youth, can illuminate the influence of globalization and neoliberalism on local environments in urban contexts and support youth in developing a critically conscious environmental identity. This critically conscious environmental identity is conceptualized as an application of one's understanding of socio-environmental issues that incorporate critical reflection and action on the understanding of these conditions. YPAR methodologies, like mental mapping, can be enacted and adapted for multiple contexts, uncover the questions most important to youth, and privilege the knowledge they bring with them from their individual and collective experiences.

In this chapter I discuss mental mapping as a YPAR methodology and share how it was utilized in a high school environmental science class. I begin by introducing one student, Kathy (a pseudonym), along with her map and dialogue, as a way to illuminate the potential mental mapping has for exposing socio-environmental issues experienced by youth. I then describe the methodology of mental mapping, including some of the analytical constructs that can be utilized with mental maps and how these appeared in the student maps. Next, I explain how mental mapping was introduced to students in the class, sharing the methodology, student maps, and student analysis. I end the chapter by summarizing the affordances and experiences cited in student final reflections on the mental mapping process and how it can best be utilized with young people to critically explore local environments.

The mental mapping methodology, as I outline it in this chapter, was introduced to students in an elective, college-credit environmental science course at a public high school in New York City. Students in the course were juniors and seniors and paid a subsidized tuition fee to receive four college credits. The class drew upon critical and participatory pedagogies throughout the year. This style of teaching the course was chosen to engage students in a relevant urban environmental education that was based upon their personal and collective experiences of neighborhood and place. In addition to mental mapping, students also conducted participatory research in their neighborhoods, including neighborhood reflections, critical advertising projects, and photovoice (Bellino, 2015) research to further investigate and document relationships to place. Mental mapping occurred a third of the way through the year and was the second of the neighborhood participatory projects conducted.

While this work occurred in a high school environmental science course, the applications for teaching and learning can cut across disciplines and grade levels. Mariah Kornbluh, Emily Ozer, Carrie Allen, and Ben Kirshner (2015) present a diversity of YPAR projects done in schools and show how they work to create a sense of empowerment for students by developing their sociopolitical consciousness and promoting civic engagement. However, they add that YPAR also has the potential to address many of the new national and state standards (Common Core State Standards, Next Generation Science Standards, College, Career, and Civic Life: C3 Framework for Social Studies State Standards). In the use presented here, mental mapping was conceptualized as a YPAR methodology that can illuminate the diversity of experiences young people have with place, both positive and negative, in order to address specific questions of interest to youth. Maps and associated dialogue were also understood through the process of participatory data construction and analysis. Both Caitlin Cahill (2009) and Pennie Foster-Fishman, Kristen Law, Lauren Lichty, and Christina Aoun (2010) found participatory analysis specifically enhanced students' ability to think critically about local issues and helped make visible, often hidden structures, which assisted youth to develop counter narratives to their more common understandings of experience. This versatility and reflexivity speaks to the value of mental mapping as both a participatory methodology and a critical and place-based pedagogical orientation.

The application presented in the chapter was inspired by and adapted from the work of environmental education researchers as well as geographers who have forwarded the notion that people and places have complex relationships that include social, cultural, economic, religious, and ecological factors (Gieseking, 2013). Alex Kudryavtsev, Richard Stedman, and Marianne Krasny (2012) did an extensive review of the literature on sense of place in environmental education, teasing out the two dimensions of place attachment and place meaning. Place attachment refers to ways individuals relate to place and the bond described between an individual or group and a place. Place meaning is more of a symbolic and representational meaning that an individual or group ascribes to a particular place. Mental mapping, as used in the context I present in this chapter, was conceptualized as a tool to uncover both place meaning and place attachment for youth. Allowing students to reflect upon and critically analyze their complex relationships to place, can open up space in classrooms for youth voice in ways where their knowledge is privileged and their experiences are used as the vehicle for teaching and learning (Loebach & Gilliland, 2010).

2 Kathy's Map

Kathy's map (Figure 13.1) is full of life. When you look at it, it is colorful, there are hand drawn components mixed with magazine cutouts. It feels active and alive. According to Kathy, this map shows "how I perceived my neighborhood as I grew up, and its surroundings. My map includes pictures of things that were essential components to my upbringing and childhood." In conjunction with her map, her conversation about the places she included was animated and she was excited to share it. She spoke at length about one fire hydrant, "the pompa," which brought such strong emotional memories back to her when she began speaking of it. Here is a brief excerpt from a recording of Kathy talking about the pompa with another student Jay (a pseudonym) and me, while she shares her map with her group during class.

FIGURE 13.1   Kathy's mental map of her childhood neighborhood

Kathy: For us, you guys know what a pompa is?

Jay: Yeah

K: So like Spanish people, this pompa was originally at the corner

J: Fire hydrant

K: Yeah Fire Hydrant, but we call it a pompa. This fire hydrant has a lot of meaning to me because as a little girl this fire hydrant was in the corner of this street. And you know how I said we would have barbeques like in the summer, we would open it and play.

J: I hate that so much

K: We would play for hours just in water. Have so much fun, I don't even understand.

J: I like feel like that water, all that good water is being wasted on a hot summer day. They just open it cause it's hot and it's all this water going to waste. I feel like there's people in other places that need that water and it's just like 'Hey let's open the hydrant.' Like we don't care about the water. And then like in order to get out of my house, I would need to, if the fire hydrant was open, I would have to go all around the park. 'Cause they have a tendency ...

Marissa: Who are they?

J: Um the people who open the fire hydrant, so the teens and kids on my block, on my whole block, would open it to play in it and it would be open for a whole week and it's all that water being wasted, and then I don't get hot water.

K: I understand where you are coming from, like it's completely understandable and I'm not saying it's justifiable the fact that we had fun
or partook in this. But for me it kind of brought my community
together. Like back in the day, we would all come together, have fun
in the pompa.

Kathy's explanation of the pompa gets to the meaning that this place, the
pompa, had in her environment as well as the tensions that she knows exist
around her experience with it when another student (Jay) challenges her experience with an experience of her own. In Kathy's reflection about the mental
mapping process she writes about the specific experiences and feelings she
had in her neighborhood and how those have changed now that she has gotten
older and the neighborhood has changed. But she also writes, "These things
were hard for me to express to my group because I felt a bit ashamed of my
circumstance, but once I focused on the positive aspects of my neighborhood a
little Spanish girl burst right out of me. I became so happily overwhelmed with
the memories of my childhood that my current situation flew out the window"
(Mental Mapping Reflection, December 2013).

Kathy's experience reveals many aspects of the methodology of mental
mapping and what mental mapping can afford us as researchers; the map as
an artifact, the conversations that emerge from sharing the map with others,
and the relationship between the physical place and the meaning that Kathy
makes of it. In this case, we can hear and see the complex relationships that
Kathy has with her childhood neighborhood. And Kathy's experience is not
unique to other youth that I have worked with in classrooms where over and
over we have seen the tensions and contradictions they have with the places
they live, particularly in urban environments where there is so much disparity
between neighborhoods, and youth like Kathy move around a lot.

3   Mental Mapping in an Environmental Science Classroom

Mental mapping, as conceptualized in this chapter, is a participatory methodology that generates visual representations of places that hold meaning to participants. This method offers both the physical representations of places in the
form of a map, as well as recorded conversations about the maps. Information
about the meaning of places in mental maps is based on respondents' views of
the relative importance of places in their daily lives (Trell & van Hoven, 2010).
Mental maps are a way for participants to engage with places in both spatial
and verbal ways. This allows for the exploration of places as well as behaviors and emotions associated with places. Again, this is something we see in

Kathy's map as she describes the physical place, the pompa, that is represented on her map but also, the behaviors associated with the pompa, turning it on and playing with the water on a hot summer day, and the emotional meaning associated with both the place and the behaviors, having fun and bringing the community together. Geographers and urban planners have used mental mapping to better inform how cities are organized and planned, but more recently environmental psychologists have found value in the method as a way to "visualize other dynamics of human-environment relations, such as sense of place, movement, environmental perception and cognition, and even illuminating socio-spatial inequalities" (Gieseking, 2013, pp. 713–714).

Jack Jen Gieseking (2013) discusses over 50 analytical techniques and components, which she groups into four categories including mechanics of method (e.g., time limit, use of entire paper, text labeling), drawing elements (e.g., shapes, scale, borders, color, symbols), narratives of place (e.g., built environment elements, physical environment elements, discussion of emotions through physical space), and personalization (e.g., including what possess personal meaning, includes depiction of self in map, first and last drawn elements). For the purposes of our course and this study, we were interested in learning more about youth relationships to place in order to better understand the lived experiences of youth in urban environments, looking for patterns and contradictions across neighborhoods and producing a youth-centered urban environmental education course that privileged these lived experiences. With these goals in mind, the most salient analytical components of the mental mapping process for students were the built and physical environmental elements and the discussion of emotions and personal meaning in maps.

4   Mental Mapping Methodology in Our Participatory Classroom

4.1   *Making Mental Maps*

Mental mapping has many ways it can be executed but there are typically two components, the creation of a visual map and the discussion of the map. This adaptable methodology allows it to be readily incorporated into a participatory research project. Mental mapping was introduced in response to class analysis of community reflections where new research questions emerged.

For the construction of the map, students were asked to generate quick maps of their neighborhoods, focusing on the places that have meaning to them (both good and bad). They were given big chart paper, markers, post-its, magazines, scissors, tape and were able to construct their maps in any way they wanted. Students had 30 minutes to construct their maps, which were

TABLE 13.1   Research questions generated by students for mental mapping

Do you have a place(s) in your neighborhood that is/are comfortable?
What meaning do you ascribe to these places?
What are the characteristics of those places?
Are young people dis(placed)?
What is lacking in your neighborhood?
How do young people perceive their neighborhoods and the larger city?
What spaces are attractive to them, why?
How do they move in their neighborhoods? The city?

then used as springboards for critical discussions. The map, as a data artifact, acted as a prompt for students to begin sharing their experiences growing up in their neighborhoods. Because of the ability to refer to the spatial components on their maps, students were able to make meaning of the places they live and reflect on the ways these places have shaped them. Students worked in mixed neighborhood groups of four and recorded their conversations about each map. The class decided on mixed grouping because students in the class came from all over the city and this grouping would allow them to look across neighborhoods for similarities and differences. Conversations lasted approximately 30 minutes per map and audio files were uploaded to a shared site for students to access. In this way, all of the data were available to students to go back and listen.

4.2   *Sharing Mental Maps*

We did multiple rounds of coding beginning with each image on the map being coded along with the meaning ascribed by the mapmaker. Within groups, common themes were generated across the maps building from the physical codes to more of the cognitive and emotional meanings that places had for youth. Each group presented their themes to the class and together we documented common themes and new questions. Finally, students reflected on the methodology and their overall learning from the mental mapping data (see appendices for the analysis handouts and samples of individual and group analysis).

5   Experience and Learning from Mental Maps

As a class, we had many research questions that we wanted to address including, from a methodological standpoint, how mental mapping was interpreted by students and deemed a useful way to address their questions. By analyzing the physical maps, we were able to begin to see the ways youth interpreted the construction of the maps and addressing some aspects of Gieseking's (2013) four components and techniques associated with mental mapping: mechanics of method; drawing elements; narratives of place; and personalization.

5.1   The Physical Maps

Some maps were drawn towards more scaled and realistic representations of their neighborhoods while other maps use images as more symbolic representations of places that have meaning. These examples reflect a continuum in how students interpreted the task of constructing a mental map, from spatially accurate to purely symbolic. Gieseking (2013), in summarizing some of the mechanics of the methods, includes how some participants tend to mirror a standard physical map while others create more symbolic representations of meaningful places. One of the values of mental mapping is that there are many points of analysis which enhance the ability of the methodology to privilege the experiences of youth.

5.3   Student Research Questions

In this use of mental mapping, students set out to answer research questions about how they experience their neighborhoods. Through the multiple layers of analysis including their final reflections on the process of mental mapping, youth synthesized their ideas about their neighborhoods and in the process revealed their collective thinking about these questions. Table 13.2 summarizes student responses to one of their collective research questions. From these responses, students generated larger themes and new questions emerged.

5.4   Collective Themes and Emerging Questions

Many of the themes that emerged from the mental mapping have surfaced in previous years of work with youths (Bellino, 2016). In discussing the themes as a class, it was clear that they are interconnected and part of larger narratives about youths' experiences in places; narratives they tell about themselves and narratives that are told about them and their neighborhoods. Table 13.3 reveals themes that emerged from student and whole class discussions with descriptions and/or quotes as to how students understood these emerging from the data.

In the analysis, students began to uncover the larger notion that their experiences in neighborhoods are a product of larger historical, economic, and societal factors and when bringing that critical lens to their analysis, complicates their experiences with these places. Analysis begins to reveal the tensions and

TABLE 13.2 Youths' research question and student responses from analysis

Do you have a place(s) in your neighborhood that is/are comfortable?	"A lot of people do not feel any connection to their neighborhood." (Raymond)
	"The idea of an escape was evident in almost everyone's maps and thoughts when the idea was presented to the class. When we came together and talked about the different themes that came up within people's maps, the idea of having a place (physical or not) to run to when one does not want to be at home." (Leyva)
	"I discover that I use places to escape reality and imagine myself in a better place. I also realize that I enjoy going on walks and seeing nature which is ironic since I'm not much of an environment person, I was able to connect with views such as the G.W. Bridge to help me think of other things either when I was sad or happy, I looked up to it." (Anastasia)
	"What I can also take out is that many people aren't as connected as their family like I am. It honestly really makes me appreciate the fact that I have a group of people that I can go to for help or comfort. A lot more people didn't feel comfortable in their neighborhood like I did." (West)

contradictions that are present for youths and is particularly visible in the new questions that emerged for them throughout discussions (Table 13.4).

When reading these questions, and these are just a few representative ones around some of the prior themes, we can hear the tension youths are expressing as they navigate their own identities in relation to these neighborhoods and the larger city that is rapidly changing. And again, the questions are interconnected, speaking to issues and concerns most salient to youths in investigating environments.

6 Student Reflections on Learning and Methodology

As a final part of the mental mapping process students were asked to reflect on what they learned from the process of mental mapping as well as their critique

TABLE 13.3   Two student thematic analyses and quotes from class discussion that relate to
              themes

Theme	Quote
Neighborhoods influence your sense of identity (personal, cultural, social)	"Young people are often caught in power struggles between their own identity and society, family, and other expected norms." "It is stressful when you don't have a good sense of who you are because you don't get to explore other aspects of your identity. Are you only one thing?" "I like it here (Manhattan) better. I am sick of seeing Dominicans." "It is an American thing to say we are going to be independent when we are older." "Image is really important. If a neighborhood looks bad, people are embarrassed to go live there. Name brands are associated with better off people. But this also promotes sameness."
Neighborhood change influences how you see your neighborhood. Gentrification makes our neighborhoods more homogenous.	"Some of our neighborhoods are isolated by transportation, like bridges, highways, and railroads. These isolate our neighborhoods while bringing in people from outside the city." "The South Bronx is being glamorized now, it is being called SOBRO. When we give a new name to a neighborhood it is a sign of gentrification. That people who have more money are moving into poorer neighborhoods causing housing prices to rise, corporations move in, and family establishments move out." "Gentrification brings jobs but I wonder about these jobs. Are these high paying jobs that require lots of skill and education or are these minimum wage jobs?" "When white people move in, corporations seize on the demographic changes, rent increases and people are displaced."

of the methodology. Here I present the three intersecting themes that emerged from the student reflections on learning and the affordances and challenges expressed by the students about the methodology. In reflecting on the learning process, students cited the multiple levels of classroom dialogue that incorporated new and other perspectives, the diversity of experiences of youths, and a stronger sense of classroom community. The mental mapping methodology we utilized in the classroom afforded students the opportunity to critically analyze their neighborhoods through the larger collective experiences

TABLE 13.4   A sample of new questions that emerged during whole class discussion of themes
             revealed during the mental mapping project

Student questions

Why does gentrification make places feel safer?

Do we really want diversity or do we feel more comfortable in homogenous groups?

Where do stereotypes about our neighborhoods come from and how do they
influence us?

How do we define a "connection to our community" and in what ways do
communities come together?

Are we disconnecting ourselves from neighborhoods or are our neighborhoods
disconnected from us?

What happens when you feel excluded from your neighborhood?

How do we judge our neighborhoods as "good" or "bad"? Is it white people
moving in?

that were being cited in the data. The development of this critical lens allowed
students to integrate the diversity of neighborhoods and experiences of youths
during an engaging and fun introduction to participatory research. However,
this level of research was overwhelming at times for the students as it was their
first experience collecting and analyzing data in a systematic way on this scale.
We dedicated a few weeks to working on this project and students cited that
the process got tiresome and repetitive (as data analysis can be) however, we
discussed the challenges of data analysis as part of the research process and
the importance of documenting at multiple levels of experience (individual,
group, whole class).

6.1   *Opening up to New Perspectives*

One of the largest themes that emerged for the students as part of the mental mapping process was how it served as a way to expose them to new experiences and perspectives of their peers in the classroom. Students claimed
that the mental mapping process opened up their eyes to the experiences
and perspectives of other students in the class. Audrey writes, "The mental
mapping process helped me better understand why things are how they are in
my neighborhood in my classmate's neighborhoods. It gave me an inside look
because, for example, some of my classmates live in Midtown or the Upper
West Side and I was able to see things from their perspective instead of an outsider's point of view" (Mental Mapping Reflections, December 2013). Another

example from Sarah is specifically about the importance of family and its potential association with connection/disconnection to neighborhood. "I realized that family and family opinions are very important to a lot of people in the class. As a result, a lot of people did not feel any connection to their neighborhoods. When we were discussing this in class, I wondered why people feel this way? For me it was hard to believe" (Mental Mapping Reflection, December 2013). We can hear how Sarah is thinking more about the collective experience in relation to her own experience and it is in her questioning of why students don't feel that connection, she related it back to her own experience. Her difficulty in believing that other students would feel disconnected was new for her as she had a strong connection to her neighborhood, however, this new perspective allowed Sarah to also think beyond her limited experience in place to incorporate the experiences of others. Another student, Natalie, writes, "I was able to connect with people from different neighborhoods and realized I am not alone in feeling disconnect with my neighborhood. People from my neighborhood seemed very connected and involved with it, so I thought that I was one of the only ones who did not connect with her neighborhood. This whole process helped me connect with people all over the city" (Mental Mapping Reflection, December 2013). In this case we can see how the experience of mental mapping allowed students across neighborhoods to share similar experiences and interrogate why those experiences exist for them. In particular, the feeling of disconnect from one's neighborhood was a common theme for many students and speaks again to the kinds of opportunities for dialogue that mental mapping can open up in a classroom, allowing everyone in the classroom environment to learn more deeply about the lives and experiences of others.

6.2   *Valuing the Diversity of Experiences*

Closely tied to an increase in perspective of others is how students noted that there is no singular experience for youths. This challenged youths to expand their ways of thinking about experience towards a collection of experiences in order to incorporate the diversity of meanings and relationships all youths had with their neighborhoods. Sophia recognizes that there are both common experiences and no single story for young people growing up in New York City. "I also learned that we had a lot of common themes between groups, which shows how similar our experiences as young adults can be in a busy metropolis; however, as Taylor pointed out, there is no one single story of what it is like to be a teenager in NYC" (Mental Mapping Reflection, December 2013). Another student, Maria writes, "I learned new things about the places that others lived. Places that I have never been or that my parents told me were unsafe.

I feel as if this was most people's reactions seeing as learning about the different places was one of the big topics that we had discussed as a class. Because of this many new ideas were generated that I would not have thought about before this. For example, that people can feel disconnected from their neighborhood even though they live there" (Mental Mapping Reflection, December 2013). Similar to Maria, West writes, "After looking at other people's maps, what I took away is that many people have different views in and of their community, both good and bad. What I can also take away is that many people aren't as connected to their family like I am. It honestly really makes me appreciate the fact that I have a group of people that I can go to for help or comfort. A lot more people didn't feel comfortable in their neighborhood like I did. But honestly, there was a lot of meaning behind these maps that I would have never thought about and honestly makes me think about all the flaws of the community and in New York in general" (Mental Mapping Reflection, December 2013). We can hear in both student accounts the way that their perspectives have been broadened and challenged by learning about the diversity of experiences of their classmates. Exposure to this diversity of experience can lead to empathy and compassion. We hear Maria recognize the way her parents labeled other neighborhoods as "unsafe" but how through learning about the lives of those in those neighborhoods there is a greater awareness of why one might feel disconnected. West recognizes how lucky he is to have a supportive family and that this is not something everyone has. We hear his gratitude and empathy for those who don't have this kind of connection between family and place. Developing empathy and compassion through the process, I believe, leads into the final theme around safety and sense of community.

6.3   *Safe Classroom Environment*

Students felt that by learning about the neighborhoods and experiences of others it allowed for a stronger sense of classroom community and safety. Leyva, a student who struggled throughout the year with her sense of place and identity writes about her fear of sharing about her neighborhood in her group. "The three members of the group I was in all lived in really 'nice' neighborhoods that most people wanted to go to – I didn't. So, it was definitely hard for me to want to describe my neighborhood and the events that occur in my neighborhood because it's not the type of environment most people would want to be in. I had to get out of my comfort zone and talk about this with other people that I thought would judge me because I lived in this 'bad neighborhood.' When I was presenting, I felt myself shaking and choking up because out of the 1,300 students in our school, only two people have been to my neighborhood. It was scary to think that another 3 people would know the secret of where I lived and why I kept it a secret. In the end, although I still kind of regret the fact that I didn't make up some neighborhood that people liked and would appreciate and not judge, I am proud of myself for actually facing one of my fears and going through with this research and ending it successfully" (Mental Mapping Reflection, December 2013). Here we can see the physical and emotional response that mental mapping had on Leyva and the ways in which she had to trust her classmates to not judge her and her neighborhood. While this takes incredible courage on the part of Leyva, it also takes a safe classroom environment to take those steps towards trust.

6.4   Affordances of Mental Mapping

Because mental mapping included both visual and oral discussions of place, it afforded students the opportunity to remember the places they grew up in a way that was more nostalgic but also more critical. Some students cited that the discussions brought out both positive and negative feelings that they had either forgotten about or chose to forget. As a result, the maps raised awareness about issues in neighborhoods that were otherwise not visible as they were able to both spatially see these places and discuss their place attachment and place meaning to them. The sharing of their stories in place allowed students to recognize the ways in which their shared struggles in neighborhoods (or positive experiences) are a product of a larger system of domination. This helped them understand the many ways their individual experiences were being shaped by social constructions of place filled with specific ideologies about urban youths, urban environments, the urban experience, and the value of different urban neighborhoods (Haymes, 1995). The opportunity for criticality that mental mapping, as practiced in this chapter, is a representation of David Gruenewald's (2003) conceptualization of a critical pedagogy of place. In response to the 'placelessness' of much of our standardized curriculum in schools, a critical pedagogy of place directly responds to the social and ecological contexts of our lives and as such creates a uniquely relevant learning opportunity for youths.

Many of the students also cited that as a research methodology, mental mapping was fun and interesting in a way that they did not expect research to be. Embedded in the epistemology of participatory action research is the assumptions that all people hold knowledge of their lived experiences and mental mapping allowed for the voices and experiences of youths in urban environments to be privileged. Julio Cammarota and Michelle Fine (2008) recognize that YPAR has educative potential and is aligned to popular education as it focuses on the development of knowledge and skills that allow youth to "speak back and organize for change" (p. 5). These commitments embedded in YPAR make it an ideal pedagogical tool for youths, as it is engaging, relevant, and empowering. Student research questions, dialogue, and analysis all speak to a powerful experience for this group of students as they had not necessarily questioned the ways in which knowledge about youth was produced.

6.5 Critiques of Mental Mapping

In reflecting upon the research methodology students articulated the following critiques of mental mapping the way we introduced it and utilized it in our course. Time was an overall issue for students. Some students cited that they wished they had more time to make the maps, while others wished they had more time to share the maps. Analysis was a struggle for students as this was their first encounter with analyzing qualitative research and doing it in a collective. Some students wanted to hold tightly to their personal experiences and felt like those were sometimes lost when larger themes began to emerge while others felt like there was too much focus on personal experience. Students also wrestled with the notion of meaningful and what meaningful places were and how to represent them. Finally, while the ability to engage in difficult discussions was something that mental mapping allowed students to participate in, it also brought up discomfort about places and at some moments students said they were holding back ideas because they were either difficult or uncomfortable to discuss. One student even brought up the levels of guilt that doing this made her feel because she lives in a very privileged part of the city compared to her classmates.

7 The Power of Mental Mapping

Returning to Kathy, her reflection is telling about the power of the experience of utilizing mental mapping in the classroom and opportunities it afforded her on a very personal and emotional level. When she reflected about the mental mapping process she writes about the specific experiences and feelings she had in her neighborhood and how those have changed now that she has gotten older, moved away, and the neighborhood has changed. But she also writes, "These things were hard for me to express to my group because I felt a bit ashamed of my circumstance, but once I focused on the positive aspects of my neighborhood a little Spanish girl burst right out of me. I became so happily overwhelmed with the memories of my childhood that my current situation flew out the window." Kathy and the other maps and conversations highlight the ways that youths' experiences in place are dynamic, relational, and can generate a sense of collective experience of being in a place (Travlou, Owens, Thompson, & Maxwell, 2008, p. 320). From Kathy and other student responses we can see how mental mapping, as a method to visually represent and voice the experiences of youths in place, has multiple strengths that can inform teaching, learning, and educational research. These include the following:

- Mapping can document the unique spatial components and experiences of all participants
- It is applicable to diverse contexts (e.g., neighborhoods, schools, homes)
- The dialogic nature of the methodology speaks back to dominant narratives of urban communities
- Participants are conducting multiple layers of analysis on data artifacts they created
- Mapping and dialogues have the capacity to illuminate shared experiences across diverse contexts
- Through dialogue, new, researchable questions, and civic actions can emerge

The power to create maps and engage in collective dialogue, storytelling, and reflection on youths' interactions in place, challenges existing spatial narratives that circulate in urban environments. The spatial relations of everyday life are tied to both the unique and similar experiences of being a young person living in a dynamic city characterized by extreme inequality. These experiences often remain invisible, unquestioned, normalized, and outside the scope of conventional classrooms and disciplines. However, the places our students live are constantly marking them, making them question their value, their identity, and their social relations with and within place. We cannot ask our students to bifurcate these parts of themselves when they walk into our schools. By bringing the subjectivity of youths and their social positions within schools and communities to the forefront, opportunities to develop investigative research skills (e.g., creating artifacts, coding and analyzing data, interpreting data) as well as critical social knowledge (e.g., why is my neighborhood labeled "unsafe?") are honed. Much of the work in the critical geographies is happening outside of formal school spaces (Skelton, 2013) and as a result its reach and influence on educators is minimal. In this paper I present a critical spatial analysis for and by youths in a formal environmental science high school classroom. Therefore, the implications for teaching and learning are at the forefront of this work. Through exploration at the intersection of life experience and place, youths' recognition of forces impacting urban environments as well as the knowledge of underlying critical and social theories shaping these urban environments are illuminated and explored.

References

Bellino, M. E. (2015). Using photovoice as a critical youth participatory method in environmental education research. In K. Tobin & S. R. Steinberg (Eds.), *Doing educational research: A handbook* (pp. 365–380). Sense Publishers.

Bellino, M. E. (2016). *Critical youth participatory action research to reimagine environmental education with youth in Urban environments* (Unpublished doctoral dissertation). CUNY, New York. http://academicworks.cuny.edu/gc_etds/1448

Cahill, C. (2009). Participatory data analysis. In S. Kindon, R. Pain, & M. Kesby (Eds.), *Participatory action research approaches and methods: Connecting people, participation and place* (Reprinted, pp. 181–187). Routledge.

Cammarota, J., & Fine, M. (2008). Youth participatory action research: A pedagogy for transformational resistance. In *Revolutionizing education: Youth participatory action research in motion*. Routledge.

Foster-Fishman, P. G., Law, K. M., Lichty, L. F., & Aoun, C. (2010). Youth ReACT for social change: A method for youth participatory action research. *American Journal of Community Psychology, 46*(1–2), 67–83. https://doi.org/10.1007/s10464-010-9316-y

Gieseking, J. J. (2013). Where we go from here: The mental sketch mapping method and its analytic components. *Qualitative Inquiry, 19*(9), 712–724. https://doi.org/10.1177/1077800413500926

Gruenewald, D. A. (2003). The best of both worlds: A critical pedagogy of place. *Educational Researcher, 32*(4), 3–12.

Haymes, S. N. (1995). *Race, culture, and the city: A pedagogy for Black Urban struggle.* State University of New York Press.

Kornbluh, M., Ozer, E. J., Allen, C. D., & Kirshner, B. (2015). Youth participatory action research as an approach to sociopolitical development and the new academic standards: Considerations for educators. *The Urban Review, 47*(5), 868–892. https://doi.org/10.1007/s11256-015-0337-6

Kudryavtsev, A., Stedman, R. C., & Krasny, M. E. (2012). Sense of place in environmental education. *Environmental Education Research, 18*(2), 229–250. https://doi.org/10.1080/13504622.2011.609615

Loebach, J., & Gilliland, J. (2010). Child-led tours to uncover children's perceptions and use of neighborhood environments. *Children Youth and Environments, 20*(1), 52–90.

Skelton, T. (2013). Young people, children, politics and space: A decade of youthful political geography scholarship 2003–13. *Space and Polity, 17*(1), 123–136.

Travlou, P., Owens, P. E., Thompson, C. W., & Maxwell, L. (2008). Place mapping with teenagers: Locating their territories and documenting their experience of the public realm. *Children's Geographies, 6*(3), 309–326. https://doi.org/10.1080/14733280802184039

Trell, E.-M., & van Hoven, B. (2010). Making sense of place: exploring creative and (inter) active research methods with young people. *Fennia-International Journal of Geography, 188*(1), 91–104.

CHAPTER 14

Bring Us Back: Photographs for Meaning Making and Knowledge Production

Kate E. O'Hara

Abstract

In this narrative, I relate the process and pedagogical methods for engaging students in critical reflection, meaning making, and knowledge production through the use of visual and textual heuristics. Context is developed through autoethnographic accounts of teaching practices and instructional activities aimed at guiding students in articulating and challenging their own beliefs, values, attitudes, and assumptions related to service learning experiences.

Keywords

teaching – learning – heuristics – photographs – service learning – critical reflection – knowledge production

Kate: I stopped ordering the prints. I didn't want to, but I had to. And, there was another option. Not necessarily one I liked, yet an option just the same. I have an affinity for taking photographs, and looking at them too. But I miss my 35 mm film camera that was with me for decades, capturing moments in time: my cousins crowded around the Thanksgiving table, the sun setting behind the landscape of New Hampshire pines, the glistening, wet fur of an old dog, a honey bee eating the rotting fruit of a Macintosh apple, the graffiti filled seat of the 1 train. All the moments were printed vividly on thick paper, with a depth of color and texture. After a forced hiatus, I made the transition to digital photography, and despite the online photo storage, I continued to print all people, places, events, or moments in time I captured. However now, the plastic storage bins are accumulating and they take up living space. The small cardboard folders are rarely, if ever, taken out to view those 4" × 6" rectangles of memories. No more passing them around. No more pointing to the details. No more shared reminiscing evoked by the images. I now share photos with family and friends on a smartphone, viewing them with a swiping motion, speedily moving past moments, stopping periodically to move my thumb and forefinger to zoom in and look at the detail. I am nostalgic for the printed experience, however the tradeoff for no longer printing is that I can retrieve a moment, a memory, whenever and wherever I go.

I teach an undergraduate course, *Foundations of Inquiry*, at a private, urban research university. The course is part of the University's core curriculum and one every undergraduate is required to take. The core courses serve as grounding in critical thinking, the scientific process, writing, and effective speaking. *Foundations of Inquiry* introduces students not only to the fundamentals of critical thinking, but also an overview of qualitative and quantitative research methods used in academic disciplines such as philosophy, history, economics, sociology, anthropology, and psychology. In addition to course content, I have also chosen to implement service learning in my curriculum.

Service learning is a form of experiential education where learning occurs through a sequence of action (service) and reflection (learning) as students work both independently and collaboratively. Unlike volunteerism, community service, or internships, service learning is connected to course content and is framed around clear learning goals. The service activities provide students with opportunities to apply course content and discipline specific knowledge to address real-world issues. Perhaps, most importantly for me, is that service learning also provides students opportunities for critical reflection about their unique experiences. I broadly conceptualize critical reflection as an extension of critical thought; a meaning-making or knowledge production process, with reflective thought as an "active, persistent and careful consideration of any belief or supposed form of knowledge in the light of the grounds that support it, and the further conclusions to which it tends" (Dewey, 1910, p. 6).

Our community partner for service learning is a New York City elementary school. Our undergraduate students meet weekly with 3rd, 4th, or 5th graders to create learning activities that draw from our course content, as well as their own talents and passions. Throughout the semester we engage in whole class discussions about the skills they are acquiring through their service experience, and how those skills are valuable and applicable in future professional endeavors. I encourage my students to take risks, serve as leaders, work collaboratively, and problem solve.

An integral component of service learning is reflection. Through reflection journals, students express their perceived connection between their service activities and the content of the course. In preparation for the journal writing we talk about critical reflection and the importance of details; but details beyond the superficial to those rich with descriptions and analysis. We talk about reflection as a means to question their own beliefs, values, attitudes and assumptions about their experiences. And, I explain the importance of reflection as cyclical, with the aim of gaining deeper understanding of their experiences, making meaning from their experiences, and to both constructing and applying knowledge.

We also talk about the reflection journals in relation to qualitative research, in particular, field notes for documenting. As one would do in the writing of field reports, students observe and accurately record details, but they are again reminded to analyze their superficial observations. We also talk about analyzing within the interdisciplinary context of the course: what would a philosopher, historian, economist, sociologist, anthropologist, or psychologist notice about the people, places, or events observed?

In class, students share stories of their experiences as I guide them in thinking critically about their work, asking them questions, and offering differing perspectives. After each service learning experience, students are required to complete a reflective journal entry. But, when they are tasked with the written reflections, they struggle.

> Kate: I always bring my camera when I visit the elementary school. My phone is convenient for capturing the working groups of college and elementary students, however, my camera, with a telephoto lens, can document even the smallest of details; the muted green of a germinated seed poking out of a wet paper towel, the repurposed vegetable can filled with crayons, their wax tips dull and rounded from use, or the smooth skin of a small hand clapping. My students look forward to the days I share my photos in class. They joke with one another about their expressions and poses, and fondly recall the interactions they had with the elementary students. They also proudly comment on the elementary students' expressions; inquisitive and joy filled.

After each service experience, I recognized that students struggled with writing the corresponding reflection so I decided to implement the use of writing prompts. A colleague used prompts and found them effective. After reading through the prompts used by my colleague, and after conducting research related to reflective writing, I created 35 writing prompts. After introducing the prompts, I fielded the usual questions about the journal entry: How long does it have to be? Does it have to be a paragraph or can I just add a sentence below the questions? Do I have to write anything if my teammates weren't there and I really didn't do anything?

I asked students to begin each entry with: What worked? What didn't work? What did you learn? Additional prompts included: How is your service learning experience related to the readings, activities, and discussion in class? What have you done this week to make a difference? Did you hear, smell, or feel anything that surprised you? How is your experience different from what you expected? Identify three strengths you demonstrated in your service. Explain. How have you been challenged? During your service learning experience, have you felt like an "outsider"? Why or why not? How does being an "outsider" differ from being an "insider"? What makes you feel uncomfortable during your service experience? Why? What new skills have you learned since you began your service?

I then waited to read the insightful, reflective thoughts and opinions, with descriptive words capturing moments that were of significance during their experience. Instead, I poured through pages of surface descriptions of observations. A positive aspect was that in the spirit of qualitative research, the entries served as excellent field notes, detailed, with descriptions of information such as the students' physical environment, including the people they encountered. But, the prompts did not produce my intended results. In many instances, student responses were brief, fact recordings with limited sensory impressions. As I alternated from reading journal entries to downloading, saving, and uploading to cloud storage the photos I took during my elementary school visit, I had an idea. What if we used photographs as prompts?

> Kate: I'm melancholic about my grandmother's albums, filled with photos of days that I had been part of, or wished I had been part of. A visit to my grandmother's apartment almost always included looking through her photo albums, large heavy binders filled with plastic pages that held black and white photos, Polaroids, and small square color prints with white borders, the indentation of an ink pen leaving fading dates and names along the bottom horizontal. Who's that? Where was that? Was I alive then? Look at what they are wearing! My comments and questions were often met with stories that brought not only the picture to life, but also meaning, and intertwined memories, to my life.

How do we teach someone to become critically reflective? I'm reminded of the concept of praxis: reflection and action upon the world in order to transform it. Students' experiences cannot be merely observational or ones that include planned activity, or for some students, even activism; they must engage in "serious reflection" for change, and for learning (Freire, 2005). In my work I continuously aim to effectively implement high-impact teaching practices (AAC&U, 2019), engaged teaching practices (PassageWorks Institute, 2014), problem-posing education (Freire, 2005) and a culturally sustaining pedagogy (Paris, 2012). Through class discussion, I problem pose, encourage the sharing of diverse perspectives, and identify and question assumptions in relation to service learning. These discussions had a positive impact. The level of criticality increased in the reflections but there were still students providing only brief, surface accounts, with little or no connection to their own learning or real-world applications. So, I introduced my idea of using photographs.

We began by recalling traditional methods employed by researchers in various disciplines, and then discussed the idea of a photograph as a method of collection and analysis. We discussed ethical implications of taking photographs, as well as the need for consent from those photographed. I asked that during their next visit to the elementary school they take one, or even several, pictures. I explained that the photos need not be of the students, but rather any aspect of their experience including those related to their travels to and from the elementary school. I then added to their list of prompts: Why did you decide to take this picture? I asked that in addition to their explanation they reflected critically, using the photo as a writing prompt to examine their own beliefs, values, attitudes, and assumptions, questioning their perspectives of meaning, as well as articulate the knowledge they constructed, and applied.

It has been theorized that when people stop to take a photograph, they temporarily disengage from the moment they are in. One study in particular found that when participants took photographs of objects after viewing them, they remembered fewer details about the objects than when they only observed the objects without photographing them (Henkel, 2013). However, I did not want the photos taken to aid in a recall of details or specific facts, but rather use the photo as means for making an association, a connection, recollecting a memory. I wanted the use of the photos as a reflective prompt to be interpretive and fluid. I wanted the photograph to enhance awareness of what was experienced, as well as why it was experienced in the way that it was. The photograph, in this instance, would serve as a non-textual characteristic of a construct, or a heuristic (Tobin, forthcoming). Or so I thought.

When I asked the students, "What is your preference when writing your reflection; using a photograph you took, or using one of the writing prompts?" the responses varied. Some students preferred both, "I like the prompts as a guide, but I can definitely write a lot about a picture." Or "I prefer the prompts because I can't write a full reflection about a picture." Phrases such as, "about a picture" seemed to me an indication that I again missed my mark. This was confirmed as I continued reading student responses: "I only went to the elementary school once, and my group only met once so there was not much to take a picture of." "I didn't take a picture because I don't like getting my picture taken so I just assume the kids don't either." "I like the prompts because the prompts address the experience in a more direct way. The prompts are more of a direct question that I can answer." "When I look at the picture I can't describe a lot. I'd rather just answer questions."

From students' responses it was evident that I needed to further explain the intended use of the photograph, and its purpose as a prompt. I reiterated and elaborated:

> The picture you take does not have to be of a person. The picture is not meant to 'explain' or definitively capture a person, place, event, or moment in time. It is meant to be a writing prompt; a creative way to facilitate critical reflection. If you are using a picture do not merely describe the picture. Use the photo as a reminder or a cue in which you reflect on your own feelings, beliefs, values, attitudes and assumptions about the related person, place, event, or moment in time. Reflect on the meaning the photograph holds for you in relation to that particular aspect of your experience. Reflect on the shared, or practice based, knowledge associated with your photograph, as well as thinking about knowledge that has been created.

I introduced the idea that the preconstructed is everywhere (Bourdieu, 1992) and requested that they ask themselves, "What are my thoughts, ideas, or perceptions behind this construct?" I also discussed the idea of "photograph as beyondness" suggesting they reflect on the reality beyond the image, to one that continues in a time and space beyond the frame (Mjaaland, 2017). I again implored to go beyond the superficial.

When I was finished sharing my clarifications and suggestions, a student in the back of the room fittingly exclaimed, "Wow, that's deep." Amidst the laugher I replied with a wide grin, "Let's hope so."

> Kate: My living room is now freshly painted and ready for the walls to be adorned with photographs. I've been collecting frames that seem suitable to accent the new décor and color palate, but the selection of photos has come to a standstill. How could I possibly decide which ones to display? Would the framed photographs be more important than those still in the cardboard folders? Which memory would I take out of the plastic sleeve and make public?

While students began to take photographs during their service experience, I reflected on my own practice. My reflections are autoethnographical in that I critically reflect on my lived experience (Ellis et al., 2011), with narrative accounts that are analyzed and interpreted (Chang, 2008). I thought about the question I had asked the students regarding their preference of writing prompts; was it a photograph they took, or was it one of the text prompts? Then I thought, was it important that students prefer one over the other? Or, was it useful to understand the role of both heuristics? I realized by asking the question, I was creating a value laden or hierarchical relationship between visual and textual, when in fact I wanted visual and textual representations to have their own inherent values. I wanted to create "dialogical space" (Mjaaland, 2009).

By creating space, the students began to create meaning for themselves about their experiences. "It was interesting to wonder, why did I take that picture? I realize that I'm kinda drawn to the kids' paintings. I miss doing things like that [painting]. I feel kinda old." "The picture of the garbage, the litter, makes me think why am I seeing that every day? Why are we putting garbage in our neighborhood? Maybe that'll be something I ask the 4th graders. We could do some sort of an activity to [sic]. It would be good with the recycling stuff their [sic] learning."

As students continued to incorporate the use of their photographs in their reflections, I also asked that they simply share thoughts on the journaling process. They responded that they frequently used text prompts with the addition of photos, but also solely used the photographs. "I really like using the picture. It's less restrictive." "My journal entry isn't directly related to what's in the picture so I feel more 'free' with my writing." "I like writing from my pictures. It's more story-like than just answering the questions." "My picture allows me to draw inspiration from it." "I've been taking pictures and using them for my reflections. I feel like they activate my memory."

With the use of photographs students were also able to discuss the commonalities in the fields of study we explored. From weekly lessons, students recalled that historians use photographs as primary sources and examples of material cultural, and sociologists view photographs as social artifacts. They began to understand how they themselves had engaged in weekly research, with their photography serving as a method for data collection and analysis. They also identified the association of the photographs with their critical reflections, as non-textual characteristics of a construct. With the realization of this interconnectedness, they began to contextualize their experiences in relation to their photographs, and their photographs in relation to memories, meaning making, and the production and representation of knowledge. A freshman student commented:

Freshman student: Last week we used our phones to take selfies with the [elementary] students. But today was our last day and my teammate brought her Polaroid camera. The students were so excited. We didn't have any activity planned. We just used the time to say goodbye and share the projects from last week. I enjoyed every last minute of being together with them. The students that I had worked with previously started hugging me and became really close. Even though I was not feeling good, seeing them and hugging them really made my day. I took two Polaroid pictures with me back home for memories.

I read the final sentence and I thought to myself, yes, I would have too.

1   Afterword: Multilogicality of the Bricolage

In the spirit of critical refection, I have read through this chapter with the aim of articulating the methodologies I employed; methodologies employed both consciously and unconsciously. Using a multilogical approach of several research methods was something Joe Kincheloe introduced to me during my doctoral studies. Joe and I would discuss the limitations of monological thinking, opposed to the valuing of diverse perspectives, methods, and insights of multimethodological research. This multilogicality was the underpinning of Joe's concept of bricolage. For Joe, bricolage involved "the process of rigorously rethinking and reconceptualizing multidisciplinary research" (2008, p. 4). We would talk about research in terms of meaning making, and then using that meaning in practical, ethical, and socially just ways. In a multimethodological approach, bricolage is concerned not only with divergent methods of inquiry but with diverse theoretical and philosophical understandings of the various elements encountered in the act of research (Kincheloe, 2001, p. 679).

I'll begin with my use of critical reflection as a research method. As mentioned earlier, I broadly conceptualize critical refection as an extension of critical thought; a meaning-making or knowledge production process, with reflective thought being an active and ongoing consideration of any held belief or form of knowledge (Dewey, 1910). But, also within my broad conceptualization I draw from the work of Paulo Freire and Pierre Bourdieu. Freire speaks of critical reflecting on one's practice as a "requirement of the relationship between theory and practice" and as a teacher, being an agent of knowledge production; continually "confirming, modifying, and amplifying" knowledge (1998, p. 30). Formal and informal feedback from my students related to their service experiences provided ongoing opportunities for me to connect my work, and their work, to theory. With this knowledge, I was able to revise content and implementation strategies as needed. The cyclic process of reflecting, revising, and acting lends itself to Bourdieu's concept of reflexivity or the systematic examination of the unconscious thought of our social selves, or our habitus. Habitus includes our preferences, propensities, perceptions, and our ways of knowing (Bourdieu, 1994). The use of visual and textual heuristics for critical reflection allowed gateways for students to examine their thoughts. The critical reflection exemplified in this chapter is a transformative method that can result in a sense of agency by linking the personal learning with the possibilities for change, and thus action (Fook, 2011).

Because I critically reflect on my lived experience, I define my personal accounts as autoethographical. As an autoethnographer, my personal accounts are those that are reflected upon, analyzed, and interpreted within a broader sociocultural context (Change, 2008). Autoethnography as a method "expands and opens up a wider lens on the world, eschewing rigid definitions of what constitutes meaningful and useful research" (Ellis et al., 2011).

When defining lived experience, I draw from the work of van Manen (1992) and his approach to human science research, which is textual reflection on lived experience and everyday actions. This approach is "phenomenological, hermeneutic, and semiotic, or language oriented" (p. 2). I use this approach with the aim of describing, and making interpreted sense of the phenomena of learning. In this instance, my own learning, as well as that of my students. The textual reflection in this chapter is comprised of narrative accounts. These accounts are more than mere recorded stories. Narrative is both phenomenon and method. "Narrative names the structured quality of experience to be studied, and it names the patterns of inquiry for its study ... the phenomenon "story" and the inquiry "narrative" (Connelly & Clandinin, 1990). My narratives are interwoven with autoethnographic accounts, critical reflection, and reflectivity. The narratives, as a writing activity, are a hermeneutical phenomenological research approach with the "research and writing as aspects of one process" (van Manen, 1992, pp. 7–8).

The interconnectedness of my methodologies is evident. In social science research what emerges from a multilogical approach, or the multiple perspectives of the bricolage, are new ways of thinking about teaching and learning. And, new ways of researching. In welcoming the complexity of the bricolage, we can move beyond the limitations of monological knowledge, to the creation of new and diverse research designs and methods, along with new narratives to represent them.

References

Bourdieu, P. (1992). The practice of reflexive sociology (The Paris workshop). In P. Bourdieu & L. J. D. Wacquant (Eds.), *An invitation to reflexive sociology*. University of Chicago Press.

Chang, H. (2008). *Autoethnography as method*. Left Coast Press.

Connelly, F. M., & Clandinin, D. J. (1990). Stories of experience and narrative inquiry. *Educational Researcher, 19*(5), 2–14.

Dewey, J. (1910). *How we think*. D. C. Heath and Company.

Ellis, C., Adams, T., & Bochner, A. (2011). Autoethnography: An overview. *Historical Social Research/Historische Sozialforschung, 36*(4(138)), 273–290.

Fook, J. (2011). Developing critical reflection as a research method. In J. Higgs, A. Titchen, D. Horsfall, & D. Bridges (Eds.), *Creative spaces for qualitative researching*. Sense Publishers.

Freire, P. (1998). *Pedagogy of freedom: Ethics, democracy and civic courage*. Rowman & Littlefield Publishers.

Freire, P. (2005). *Pedagogy of the oppressed* (M. B. Raos, Trans., 30th anniversary ed.). Continuum International Publishing Group.

Henkel, L. A. (2013). Point-and-shoot memories: The influence of taking photos on memory for a museum tour. *Psychological Science, 25*(2), 396–402. https://doi.org/10.1177/0956797613504438

Kincheloe, J. (2001). Describing the bricolage: Conceptualizing a new rigor in qualitative research. *Qualitative Inquiry, 7*(6), 679–92.

Kincheloe, J. (2008). Critical pedagogy and the knowledge wars of the twenty-first century. *International Journal of Critical Pedagogy, 1*(1). http://freireproject.org/wp-content/journals/TIJCP/Vol1No1/48-38-1-PB.pdf

Mjaaland, T. (2009). Evocative encounters: An exploration of artistic practice as a visual research method. *Visual Anthropology, 22*, 393–411. https://doi.org/10.1080/08949460801986145

Mjaaland, T. (2017). Imagining the real: The photographic image and imagination in knowledge production. *Visual Anthropology, 30*(1), 1–21. https://doi.org/10.1080/08949468.2017.1255079

Paris, D. (2012). Culturally sustaining pedagogy: A needed change in stance, terminology, and practice. *Educational Researcher, 41*(3), 93–97. https://doi.org/10.3102/0013189X12441244

PassageWorks Institute. (2014). *Engaged teaching*. http://passageworks.org/engaged-teaching/

Tobin, K. (forthcoming). Authentic inquiry as a constituent of methodological bricolage. In C. Siry, C. Schreiber, R. Gomez Fernandez, & B. Reuter (Eds.), *Critical methodologies for researching teaching and learning*. Brill | Sense.

van Manen, M. (1990). *Researching lived experience: Human science for an action sensitive pedagogy*. SUNY Press.

CHAPTER 15

The Spectrum of Teacher Action Research Projects in Science Classrooms

Marissa E. Bellino and Jennifer D. Adams

Abstract

In this chapter, we examine the experience of new teachers engaged in Teacher Action Research (TAR) and Teacher-Participant Action Research (T-PAR) in science classrooms. With the pressure of neoliberal school reform that favors quantitative measures and data driven inquiry, teachers have little time for self-reflection towards the improvement of their own practice. These education reforms leave little time and space for creative action research endeavors by teachers to reflect on their teaching practice and address the multiple inequalities that are embedded in these reforms. However, TAR and T-PAR, with a critical framework, could provide teachers the space to engage in inquiry in the context of their practice. We look at the variation in action research projects conducted by secondary science educators in a teacher education program. Action projects ranged in participation with some projects embracing participatory action research (PAR) principles of increased participation of stakeholders aimed at transforming unjust school structures to projects that were teacher focused and uphold the education reforms of high stakes testing, Common Core Learning Standards, and teacher evaluation systems. Reflections on the action research process revealed the power of research, the assumptions science teachers hold about research, and the challenges that conducting action research presents in the classroom.

Keywords

teacher education – action research – participatory research – reflective practice

1   A Brief Review of Teacher Action Research

Currently, many new teachers experience pressures of accountability based on narrow measures of standardized assessments. This leaves little room for teachers to be reflexive about their own teaching through systematic data collection and analysis, thus limiting their ability to contribute to the knowledge production of what we know about teaching and learning (Cochran-Smith & Lytle, 1990). This is especially critical for new teachers who are developing their teaching identities while concurrently teaching and learning to teach in their own classrooms.

Early on, Lawrence Stenhouse (1975) championed the notion of teachers studying their own practice. He claimed that teachers are the best researchers of their own classrooms because they know the history and background of their pupils and have the experiential knowledge of the unfolding of social life in the classroom. Many teacher preparation programs have moved beyond the traditional literature review-based thesis and now include Teacher Action Research (TAR) as a part of their professional training. In general, this is viewed as a way to merge theory with practice (Honigsfeld, Connolly, & Kelly, 2013), and create reflective practitioners (Vaughan & Burnaford, 2015), however some teachers may view it only as a hurdle to clear on the path to certification. TAR can be empowering as praxis as it allows teachers to make decisions based on their experience within the demands of practical situations that emerge in the classroom (Postholm, 2009). As researcher-practitioners, teachers systematically collect and analyze data in ways that are both integrated in and inform classroom practice in ongoing ways. Furthermore, TAR with a social justice framework enables teachers to work with their students towards creating equitable learning environments. While TAR is valuable as an ongoing praxis, it is unclear if teachers continue to use any aspects of action research beyond that which is required for certification or a Master's degree.

TAR is a form of practitioner inquiry that empowers teachers to study their own classroom situations based on specific and immediate needs. It generates knowledge and practices that work best in their given contexts and can be shared with other teachers. TAR "provides teachers with opportunities to build and sharpen the dispositions that create reflective and collaborative teacher leaders" (Vaughan & Burnaford, 2015, p. 286). Embedded in action research is the ideology that the person who has the problem has the solution (Freire, 2013) and it involves the study of a problematic situation in an ongoing, systematic and recursive way in order to take action to improve the situation (Pine, 2009). Problem does not necessarily entail a negative situation, for example in many classrooms an ongoing concern is continuously improving teaching in ways that meet the needs of diverse learners in the classroom. Through action research teachers could frame questions and design their inquiry in ways that allow them to learn about meeting the learning needs of their students as situated in the design and enactment of lesson plans and related activities.

Action research has a long history in social justice movements and has been enacted and utilized by educational practitioners in diverse setting and for various purposes. Action research emerges from the epistemological stance that knowledge generation does not have to come solely from academics with limited experience in education, schools, or classrooms, but that all stakeholders have valuable knowledge and that collaborative methodologies can be leveraged in research and practice to improve and transform schools (Tobin, Elmesky, & Seiler, 2005). The purpose of action research is to improve social formations by involving participants in a cyclical process of fact-finding, planning, exploratory action, and evaluation (Lewin, 1948, pp. 202–206). With its emergent and contingent nature, TAR challenges traditional forms of research and involves teachers conducting research with students and other stakeholders as opposed to academics conducting research on participants (Savaskan, 2013). Action research incorporates multiple goals, including the democratization of power differentials in educational settings, the improvement of student education, and professional growth and identity formation of teachers through self-reflection (Pine, 2009).

2 Approaches to Action Research

There are several forms of action research determined by the inclusion of multiple stakeholder and challenging existing power structures. Participatory action research (PAR) emphasizes the local cultural, political, economic, and social contexts of the research milieu with a commitment to the transformation of schools. By partnering with multiple stakeholders (i.e., students, administrators, parents) PAR is inherently an approach that begins with the needs of those most affected by an oppressive situation and works with them to improve and change their situation. Critical Participatory Action Research (Critical PAR) is an epistemology that engages research design, methods, analyses and products through a lens of democratic participation (Torre et al., 2012, p. 1) that engages all stakeholders in addressing an area of concern. In this paper, we discuss both teacher action research and action research as enacted by teachers in science classrooms, which we refer to as T-PAR.

In recent years, under the strong influence of neoliberal education policies, teacher action research has been used to serve the purpose of promoting narrow

reforms aimed at improving scores on high stakes tests or examining the effec-
tiveness of federal curriculum mandates and instructional methods (Somekh &
Zeichner, 2009). Using action research within this climate does not challenge
current education policies and dilutes the historical and political nature rooted
in action research (Cochran-Smith & Lytle, 1999). As a result, equity and social
justice issues that are at the heart of the purpose of action research are left
out of many practitioner inquiry courses and texts. Instead, action research is
framed as a formulaic strategy that does not challenge underlying social and
economic inequalities that influence the classroom experiences of students
(Brydon-Miller & Maguire, 2009). While teacher action research has become
central in many university teacher education programs and attempts to be
more robust in implementation (Vaughn & Burnaford, 2015), it often does not
challenge the deeply embedded historical and political hegemony that shape
school policies (Cochran-Smith & Lytle, 1999).

Science classrooms are spaces where teachers often struggle with meeting content requirements while motivating and engaging learners, many of
whom may not like science. In addition, as new teachers, they are also navigating learning to teach while creating and maintaining safe learning environments and being responsive to school culture and administrative demands. All
of these factors contribute to multiple issues that influence the teacher and
her classroom. The focus of this chapter is to describe an in-service teacher
education course that is designed around TAR. We describe how a cohort of
in-service secondary science teachers utilized the action research model of
practitioner inquiry in various settings and reflected on their experience as
teacher researchers. More specifically, we looked at the spectrum of action
research projects conducted to begin to uncover the ways that science teachers positioned themselves with respect to dominant education paradigms and
current education policy.

We also describe T-PAR, teacher action research that is conducted with students using a PAR framework. Recently, Sarah Stapleton (2018) posed T-PAR as
a methodological approach to empower teachers as a marginalized group in
schools and schooling. This is in response to the lack of teacher voice in larger
pedagogical and policy decisions, especially those who work in school with
high poverty and higher populations of black, brown and immigrant students.
Stapleton's operationalization of T-PAR emphasized the marginalization of
teachers and is done in the context of a researcher working together with
teachers to learn more about their roles as teachers nested within the contexts
of schools, districts, policies, etc. Our conceptualization of T-PAR differs from
Stapleton's in that (a) it is done in the context of a year-long, credit-bearing
graduate thesis course (as opposed to a discrete collaborative project between

a researcher and teachers) and (b) it describes teachers enacting PAR with students as a methodology in their own action research projects. However, we do feel that Stapleton's approach provides an equity-oriented collaborative approach for researchers who desire to do ongoing or longitudinal work with teachers.

3 Overview of a TAR-Centered Course

This course, situated in an urban public liberal arts university, is a seminar in science education research and takes place over two semesters. Teachers enrolled in this course are all second-year science teachers working in middle and high school classrooms in a large urban school district. They entered the teaching profession through an alternative certification program and completed their Master's in Secondary Science Education over 2 years while teaching full-time. The subjects taught range and include biology, Earth science, general science, forensic science, and environmental science.

The course focuses on issues around teaching science in diverse urban settings and with children of diverse abilities, socioeconomic, and cultural backgrounds. The first semester centers on familiarizing teachers with current science education and urban education research literature and emphasizes readings with a critical, social justice and equity framework. The literature also supports the development of basic tools/methodology to collect and analyze data on classroom practice, with an emphasis on qualitative methods and participatory, student-centered approaches. At the end of the first semester teachers generate a comprehensive literature review in an area of concern, initial research questions, and a literature supported plan to pursue a reiterative cycle of action research data collection and analysis during the second semester.

Teachers begin initial data collection at the beginning of the first semester in the form of "mini observations" where they spend ten-minute segments observing their classroom around their area(s) of concern, jotting field notes or memos of their observations and sharing their impressions with peers both in an online forum and during class meetings. This process helps to initiate the iterative action research cycle and helps teachers to hone their research questions in light of what they learn from class readings and dialogues with their peers around the readings and mini observations. Throughout the course, the reiterative cycle of inquiry, data collection and implementation of action is emphasized fostering an ongoing addressing of the issue with lessons learned from data (Figure 15.1).

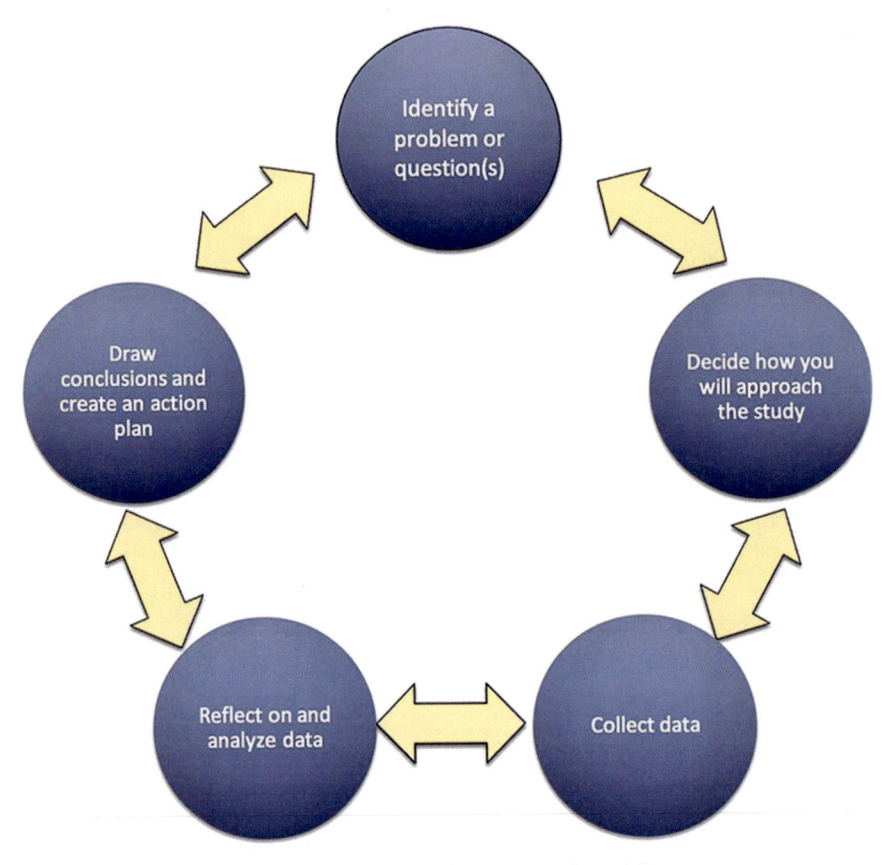

FIGURE 15.1   The cycle of teacher action research as presented to teachers

During the second semester teachers independently enact the action research cycles in their classrooms and focus on data collection, analysis, and communication as a praxis of critical reflection on teaching and learning. Although they work independently, they have regular small group meetings and virtual reflection prompts that allow the class to engage in ongoing dialogues about their emergent and ongoing learning from their data. These dialogues also provide opportunities to ask for suggestions and receive feedback about their emerging research claims and continuing data collection plans. With the emergent and contingent nature of action research, teachers are encouraged to adjust their data collection plans as they learn more about their research questions. This ongoing communication helps to foster a culture of peer critique and relevance of research, an essential component of building community around the action research approach.

Since many of the course participants had a natural science background, they often expressed concern about research validity and tended to default to a more positivistic approach with a control and experimental group. We addressed this by first discussing ethical and practical concerns with such approaches in classrooms (i.e., individual class differences, not all students benefiting from potentially transformative practices, planning two different lessons for the same content). Secondly, we emphasized qualitative descriptive research that allows them to gain a more nuanced perspective of their classrooms and thirdly, we discussed Guba and Lincoln's (1989) authenticity criteria as a way of assessing the quality of the research.

4   A Praxis of Relevancy in Educational Research

The final product for thesis courses is traditionally a full-length research paper. However, we learned that the research paper only served as a source of grades for the course and served not much more beyond that. Keeping with the spirit of having as many stakeholders learn from the research as possible, we adjusted the final products to include: a one-pager of the most critical aspects of their research that they wish to share with other teachers and stakeholders. The challenge is that they have to condense a year-long project into the most salient information for other urban science educators. For this document, they are prompted to (a) provide a brief overview of their research, and (b) describe key take-away points from their research and literature and include any helpful resources for other practitioners who want to implement any aspects of their research in their classrooms. The one-pager accompanies a collaborative PowerPoint presentation of the research project. The action plan is more comprehensive as this emphasizes a description of the data analysis and findings of the research in relation to a plan that outlines how they intend to enact what they learned from the research in their classroom. For this assignment, they are prompted to use both their data analysis and existing literature to support their action plan. The action plan also includes a final reflection that provides a space for the teachers to discuss their growth as educators and teacher researchers, the comfort and challenges experienced while conducting action research, and ways action research informed their teaching praxis. The other two products include an end-of-term poster presentation where people outside of the course are invited to interact with them around their research, and a public presentation that requires them to either present at a conference or facilitate professional development within their school or district in relation to their research. All of these final products serve to allow the teachers' research to be communicated to broad range of stakeholders and feel empowered that their research impacts others outside of the scope of the course.

5   Collecting Data about TAR and T-PAR

For the writing of this chapter we accessed a variety of assignments that the teachers completed throughout the year and included weekly informal reflections using an online course management program, final research action plans, critical research reflections, and small group meetings. We also held a small focus group with a group of teachers who implemented T-PAR with their students in the context of this course. Aside from the focus group meeting, most data artifacts were a part of the course assignments. Additionally, we sent out a short questionnaire to teachers one year later asking about the long-term impacts of the action research course and project on their practice. We received an ethics approval to conduct this research during the implementation of the course, however we did not analyze the data until after the end of the term.

The T-PAR group met together five times throughout the spring semester to discuss their ongoing research. During these meetings, they shared their successes and struggles and discussed any practical issues that needed to be addressed in order to complete their research. The group met one final time after the completion of projects to reflect and dialogue about the overall experience with PAR in the science classroom. The discussions were semi-structured and centered around the uniqueness of PAR as an epistemology for conducting research in the science classroom, the specific constraints and tensions that emerged from the methodology, as well as the impact of the research process on both teachers and students.

Almost one year later, all 24 teachers were asked to complete a short questionnaire through Google Forms to reflect on their experience conducting action research as part of their graduate coursework. There was a total of 6 questions (see Appendix A for questionnaire) that focused on ways that their teaching practice was impacted by the action research. Teachers were also asked if they still utilize action research methods in their classrooms and if they were to conduct an action research project today, what issue or concerns they might address.

6   Examining the Impacts of TAR

We first examined the range of action research projects across the class. We based our examination on the same categories that outline the TAR projects for the teachers: (1) area of investigation, (2) type of investigation, (3) use of students as co-researchers and (4) methods used to conduct investigation.

Because we were also in the impacts of TAR on teaching practice and notions about research and teaching, we developed the following prompts to analyze the final reflections: (1) impacts on teacher practice, (2) shifting ideas about research and (3) challenges to conducting action research. Focus group data with the teachers who utilized PAR methods with their students were analyzed for the unique experiences of the teachers and students involved and the unique challenges associated with conducting PAR in a classroom environment. The questionnaire data was analyzed for lasting impacts on teacher practice; ways teachers still draw on aspects of the action research process in their classrooms, and other teacher learning outcomes in relation to conducting the action research.

5.1 The Range of Teacher Action Research Projects

The teacher action research projects ranged along the participatory spectrum from projects that were primarily teacher centered to ones that were more student-centered. The area of investigation data (Table 15.1) shows that of the 24 projects, 5 drew on the local experience of students through the incorporation of community places including school gardens, neighborhoods, and local parks; 3 focused on student experiences that occurred outside of the classroom, such as afterschool clubs; and the remaining 16 projects focused on examining specific pedagogical issues and interventions such as grouping, literacy, incorporation of arts or technology, mindfulness/breathing, journaling. The teachers identified and planned investigations based on their specific needs and/or intellectual curiosities about learning and classroom behavior.

In Table 15.2 we outline the types of investigation, use of students as co-researchers, and methods to highlight variation in the ways teachers approached the action research project. We differentiated it based on the larger theoretical

TABLE 15.1   General categories of action research projects

Area of investigation	Number of projects
Local environments (school gardens, neighborhoods, local parks)	5
Grouping strategies	5
Arts and technology integration	5
Literacy techniques	3
Inside classroom interventions (breathing, journaling)	3
Outside classroom (clubs, school failure)	3

TABLE 15.2   Types of investigations conducted by teachers and methods utilized

Type of investigation	Number of projects	Number of projects with student researchers	Methods utilized
Positivist (causal)	14	0	Surveys, interviews, journals, focus groups, test scores
Interpretive	5	2	Cogenerative dialogue, journals, focus groups
PAR	5	5	Photovoice, narrative, field investigations, surveys

paradigm associated with the action research project. Positivist (causal) projects had a scientific view of teaching and learning, interpretive projects sought understanding and meaning in teaching and learning, and PAR projects embraced a critical stance to education research by forming research collectives with the aim of investigating an issue central to the school community.

Fourteen teachers approached their research as a search of a causal relationship between two variables in the classroom. For example, some representative foci included the effect of breathing strategies on student focus, the effect of journaling on student test scores, and the effect of using video reviews on student test scores. These projects were narrowly focused on issues facing many teachers within the current education reform movement, specifically student achievement on high stakes exams, implementation of Common Core Learning Standards, and teacher evaluation systems. Not only do these projects represent concerns of the teacher but are also indicative of a way of thinking that is evident in science teachers coming from an academic science background that privileges causal relationships. Joe Kincheloe and Ken Tobin (2009) argue that this type of positivistic research, while oftentimes masked, can strongly influence what constitutes objective knowledge. In our work with engaging science teachers in TAR we have found this shift in thinking – from the causal to the interpretive – to be a challenge. Of the 14 action research projects that investigated causal factors in the classroom none utilized students as co-researchers in any aspect of the research project. Using students as co-researchers could have been at any stage in the research process, from determining the research investigation to aiding in data collection and analysis. All of these projects involved teachers conducting research *on* students as opposed to *with* students. Even with the utilization of mixed qualitative and quantitative methods (i.e., surveys, interviews, focus groups), the focus of the research was always unidirectional, beginning with issues identified by the teacher and guided by the teacher research question.

In contrast, 5 T-PAR projects all incorporated students in the research process. This included allowing students to shape the research question, create data collection tools (i.e., surveys, questionnaires), and collect and analyze data. The T-PAR projects used a mixed methods approach, including cogenerative dialogues (Roth & Tobin, 2004), student journal reflections, and focus group dialogues. These 5 interpretive investigations attempted to uncover meaning in multiple school contexts and included topics like, the impact of school failure on student perceptions of their school, and the impact of using students as co-developers of final projects and 2 of the 5 projects incorporated students as co-researchers in some capacity during the inquiry process.

6 Action Research Final Reflections

In the following sections, we describe what we gleaned from analyzing the final research reflections, focus group and survey.

6.1 The Power of Action Research in Urban Science Classrooms

The process of participating in TAR contributed to personal and professional growth by allowing teachers to look at their practice more reflexively, learn about their students in unique ways, and see how research directly benefited students. Engaging in action research afforded teachers structured opportunities to reflect on their practice; almost all teachers cited a newfound reflexivity in their teaching that was either absent before or was under the conscious surface. Conducting action research over the course of the year allowed teachers to hone this reflective practice and incorporate this way of thinking into their teaching approach. One science teacher wrote, "The results of my action research not only generated a sense of pride in my vocation but are also extremely useful to a second-year teacher, like myself, whose curriculum and teaching persona is still evolving." Teachers also cited the ways that TAR allowed them to learn about their students in new ways, particularly on a more personal level that shifted the ways that teachers thought about their students. In a final reflection, a teacher stated "Now I feel empowered to include all my students regardless of their academic limitation in the science classroom experience." This is an especially powerful point of learning because it speaks to the notion of equity in learning opportunities by not excluding students with real or perceived academic deficiencies. This is important in urban science classrooms where economically marginalized and racialized students are often perceived as not being capable of doing science.

6.2   Assumptions about Conducting Education Research

In reflecting upon the research process many teachers discussed the ideas they held about research prior to conducting action research in their classrooms. Upon being introduced to the theory and methodology of action research teachers expressed high levels of discomfort in ways that action research challenged their views about scientific research. Adam, a high school biology teacher wrote, "At the start of this research project I was stuck on developing a methodology that could point to causality ... It bothered me that I could not control the many variables within my classroom." Mostly all teachers expressed tensions between the ways they were taught to think about science and research and the more emergent and grounded nature of action research. Furthermore, because many teachers teach the scientific method to their students in class they were more comfortable with generating clear hypotheses, controlling variables, and collecting quantitative data that would lead to valid results. Some of them even used similar language in their reflections, as one teacher noted, "My results were inconclusive." Coming from natural science backgrounds, many of the teachers were unfamiliar with the qualitative approaches utilized in social science and education research. Another wrote, "I have realized the importance and use of qualitative data. I have always valued quantitative data, however this project showed how this type of research necessitates an interpretation of quantitative data with the insights of qualitative data." In these instances, not having variables to "control" is an important metaphor for the lived urban science classroom. The notion of control over students as opposed to learning with students is one that dominates urban science teaching pedagogy specifically and education in general. Through engaging in TAR with a qualitative approach, teachers began to see that it is impossible to control student learning but rather learn to expand the different opportunities that students have to engage in science learning. Through using interpretive data, teachers learned the nuances of social life in the classroom and how this influences science teaching and learning.

6.3   Challenges to Conducting Action Research in the Urban Science
Classroom

Almost all teachers cited multiple challenges to conducting action research in their classrooms. The main challenge that almost all teachers discussed was the time commitment to conducting research atop multiple demands placed on them as new teachers. This comment from one teacher was echoed by many others in the class. "While I truly enjoyed the experience it also was an added source of stress. Balancing all of my responsibilities inside and outside of teaching, action research was another job to take on." Another common challenge cited was the dual role as teacher and researcher and how to be both at the same time. Reflecting upon this tension, one teacher stated, "It was difficult to observe students while teaching." More specifically, the teachers who conducted T-PAR experienced tensions between their role as teacher and researcher. Additionally, they experienced ontological dissonance around the purpose of education in terms of education for critical consciousness or for higher test scores. This is more explicitly revealed in the focus group interview with the group of teachers who conducted T-PAR projects in their schools.

7   T-PAR Focus Group: A Powerful Experience

All of the T-PAR projects had salient aspects of research in common. All five of the teachers conducted their work with a group of students who investigated an issue that was locally situated in the school or neighborhood environment. Projects occurred in local parks, school gardens, and school neighborhoods. T-PAR projects utilized the expertise and knowledge of students in co-researcher roles at multiple points along the research process. This aspect of the work differs from more conventional TAR projects in that the T-PAR included multiple stakeholders throughout the project versus using it solely as a tool for reflective practice. Student co-researchers helped develop research questions, design data collection techniques, and aided in collective data analysis.

T-PAR as an alternative pedagogical choice turned out to be a positive experience for both students and teachers. Teachers noted that both they, and their students, experienced a sense of empowerment throughout the research, an increase in confidence around taking risks in the classroom, particularly after teachers observed the ways that T-PAR allowed for student voice in both describing who they were and how they view their world both in and out of the classroom. Multiple teachers spoke about ways that T-PAR allowed for students to find a balance between the individual leadership roles typically valued in schools and the collective experience that was happening in the classroom. A middle school teacher stated that the project "gave more voice to students who don't usually feel they have a space for their voices." The T-PAR projects were place-based focused and examined relationships between students and their contexts. The value of learning in local places was a powerful theme for all teachers as they cited ways that the research was directly able to connect content and skills to the experiences of students.

While teachers cited this alternative teaching experience as liberating in many ways, they also discussed the difficulty of doing T-PAR work with many institutional constraints placed on them and their students. One teacher asked, "What am I supposed to be doing when this (referring to the T-PAR experience) is how we learn, but this is not valued in schools?" She went on to express frustration with the ways that education today stresses testing, standardization, and time management, all of which run counter to the experiences and learning that happened in her classrooms as a result of conducting a PAR project with students. All five of the teachers expressed the tensions of giving up power in the classroom and how, while they felt it was important for the authenticity of the research, it challenged their ways of thinking about their roles during the research process. A high school teacher reflected, "it is about what works for the students, not for us as teachers." Related to this was the need for teachers to constantly be reflexive in their classrooms about their role. Teachers' struggles with the ways in which T-PAR work needed to be heavily structured but unstructured enough to allow room for students' ideas and needs to emerge. This frustration was also linked to their notion of being a good teacher and researcher as they all agreed that in order for the research to be as authentic as possible it had to be both emergent and contingent where they were, as one high school teacher noted, "always looking for resources to continue the conversation in class."

8   Impacts of Action Research: One-Year Later

Apparent during the entire research process was a constant tension between the search for clear answers to a specific issue and the learning of the process to becoming a reflective practitioner. Many teachers talked about wanting the answer to what makes for the best grouping strategy, literacy strategy, or test taking strategy as opposed to having a deeper understanding that there is no one right answer due to the shifting context in schools and classroom. The struggle between wanting a solution to an immediate issue overlooks the value of action research as a process of observing, reflecting, asking questions, taking actions, assessing actions, and asking new questions. Most teachers cited some aspect of the action research process or an outcome from their action research that they valued and still continue to utilize in their classroom. These included a constantly reflective teaching identity, the incorporation of students into decision making which teachers feel empowers students, facilitating relationships building between students and teachers, and allowing teachers to draw upon students' experiences. Teachers cited broad strategies or ethics they learned from their action research that they still draw upon, including the importance of creating a safe and caring classroom environment, incorporating varieties of grouping strategies, and specific projects that worked well with students. Many teachers still utilize research methods (surveys, cogenerative dialogues) and conduct research in some capacity in their schools and classrooms. When asked what issues they might address today if they were to conduct action research, most teachers continued to discuss the day-to-day issues they face (assignment completion rates, problem-solving ability, collaborative teacher planning) without addressing the deeper issues as to why these situations exist. Most of the teachers look for solutions to problems without a critical investigation of the larger education system and/or the context in which these situations are arising.

9 TAR as a Challenge to Education Reforms

The current movement in educational research privileges "scientifically based education research" calling for "narrowly defined quantitative data to drive decisions to improve teaching with little critique of the contexts or purpose of schooling" (Brydon-Miller & Maguire, 2009, p. 85). Constrained by educational and institutional demands, much action research, as utilized by the group of teachers in this chapter, tended to focus on ways of supporting reform movements towards improvement of standardized test scores, implementation of the Common Core Learning Standards, and new teacher evaluation systems. In these instances, the action research supports the status quo and does not challenge the oppressive social structures that exist in the classroom, school, community. However, when more participatory methodologies were incorporated into the research process the projects embraced the more critical and emancipatory aspects of action research. The incorporation of students' communities and neighborhoods allowed the research to flow from the students challenging traditional education research resulting in a sense of agency for both students and teachers.

For science teachers, the enactment of action research is compounded by narrow views of what constitutes valid research. New science teachers bring with them many assumptions about research drawing from their own experiences with science learning and as teachers of "the scientific method." For science teachers, education action research can challenge and unsettle these assumptions. Many science teachers in this course wanted very clear experimental methods that yield "valid" results and their action research projects reflected this tension. Therefore, it is not only important to acknowledge this tension with science educators in the process of introducing action research, but it is also critical to make them aware of the history and political roots of action research as well as the distinction in education research paradigms.

Equally important is to create space that allows them to explore and discuss these tensions in the action research process.

We realize that while employing the action research framework in this course allowed for teachers to make immediate and ongoing, albeit small changes in their practice, seeking to ensure that systemic structures did not occur at a deep level. As mentioned, perhaps it was because the same structure places excessive demands on teachers that impede them from examining the complex sociocultural issues underlying classroom teaching and learning, thus preventing them from uncovering and advocating for changes that center teacher knowledge and student learning. Perhaps one way to overcome this is by embedding aspects of action research in general and participatory action research throughout teacher education. While we are not advocating for a thesis-level project in each course, maybe allowing in service and/or pre-service teachers the space to read (literature that unpacks the hidden curriculum in schooling), observe, question, investigate, practice and reflect on their teaching and student learning with others, in collaborative spaces, would be a start in developing critically conscious teachers.

The focus of this chapter on action research with in-service teachers in a teacher education program and more specifically the use of action research methods to conduct teacher research speaks directly to what it means to be a science educator in our current era of global science education reform. We attempted to provide one answer to the larger question of what it means to be a next generation science educator, the opportunities and challenges that exist, particularly in our urban schools. We shed light on the ways that teacher action research can incorporate the social, cultural, epistemological, ontological, linguistic, personal, and moral dimensions of learning science into science education while at the same time opening up space for emerging and shifting personal and professional identities among science educators.

References

Brydon-Miller, M., & Maguire, P. (2009). Participatory action research: Contributions to the development of practitioner inquiry in education. *Educational Action Research, 17*(1), 79–93. https://doi.org/10.1080/09650790802667469

Cochran-Smith, M., & Lytle, S. L. (1990). Research on teaching and teacher research: The issues that divide. *Educational Researcher, 19*(2), 2–11. https://doi.org/10.3102/0013189X019002002

Cochran-Smith, M., & Lytle, S. L. (1999). The teacher research movement: A decade later. *Educational Researcher, 28*(7), 15–25. https://doi.org/10.3102/0013189X028007015

Freire, P. (1973). *Education for critical consciousness* (Vol. 1). Bloomsbury Publishing.

Guba, E. G., & Lincoln, Y. S. (1989). *Fourth generation evaluation.* Sage Publications.

Honigsfeld, A., Connolly, M., & Kelly, S. (2013). Demystifying teacher action research: Lessons learned from a graduate education capstone experience. *Delta Kappa Gamma Bulletin, 79*(2), 15.

Kincheloe, J. L., & Tobin, K. (2009). The much exaggerated death of positivism. *Cultural Studies of Science Education, 4*(3), 513–528. https://doi.org/10.1007/s11422-009-9178-5

Lewin, K. (1948). *Resolving social conflicts: Selected papers on group dynamics* (G. W. Lewin, Ed.). Harper & Row.

Pine, G. J. (2009). *Teacher action research: Building knowledge democracies.* Sage.

Postholm, M. B. (2009). Research and development work: Developing teachers as researchers or just teachers? *Educational Action Research, 17,* 551–565. https://doi.org/10.1080/09650790903309425

Roth, W. M., & Tobin, K. (2004, September). Co-generative dialoguing and metaloguing: Reflexivity of processes and genres. *Forum Qualitative Sozialforschung/Forum: Qualitative Social Research, 5*(3).

Savaskan, I. P. (2013). Readiness for action research: Are teacher candidates ready to become an agent of action research? *International Journal of Innovative Interdisciplinary Research, 2*(12), 49–63.

Somekh, B., & Zeichner, K. (2009). Action research for educational reform: Remodelling action research theories and practices in local contexts. *Educational Action Research, 17*(1), 5–21. https://doi.org/10.1080/09650790802667402

Stenhouse, L. (1975). *An introduction to curriculum research and development.* Heineman.

Tobin, K. G., Elmesky, R., & Seiler, G. (2005). *Improving Urban science education: New roles for teachers, students, and researchers.* Rowman & Littlefield.

Torre, M. Fine, M., Stoudt, B., & Fox, M. (2012). Critical participatory action research as public science. In P. Camic & H. Cooper (Eds.), *Handbook of research methods in psychology.* American Psychology Association. https://doi.org/10.1037/13620-011

Vaughan, M., & Burnaford, G. (2015). Action research in graduate teacher education: A review of the literature 2000–2015. *Educational Action Research,* 1–20. https://doi.org/10.1080/09650792.2015.1062408

Appendix A: Questionnaire for Teachers One Year Later

1. How has your teaching changed as a result of your action research project? Please explain.
2. How has the way you think about your teaching changed as a result of engaging in the action research project?
3. What have you implemented in your teaching practice that you learned from your action research?
4. Do you continue to conduct action research (in any modified form) as part of your classroom practice? Please explain.
5. If you had to do an action research project in your classroom today, what issues would you want to explore?
6. Is there anything else you would like to add about your experience conducting action research and how it influenced/influences your teaching practice?

CHAPTER 16

The Double-Edged Sword: Walking the Line between Ethical Research and Regulatory Overreach

Mitch Bleier

Abstract

Research of all kinds is conducted to make sense of our world, explore phenomena, solve problems, and improve life ... at least for some. In conducting research, particularly in the realm of the human sciences, ethical issues arise, and ethical norms may be violated or exposed as problematic.

While there always have been advocates for principled treatment of fellow human beings, several egregious abuses of the rights and wellbeing of research subjects in the twentieth century have precipitated concentrated efforts at identifying, codifying, and implementing standards and practices for ethical treatment of all participants in research endeavors.

Institutional review boards (IRBs) have been established within universities, government agencies and other large institutions involved in biomedical and behavioral research. These organizations are charged with ensuring that activities of students, staff and faculty at their institutions comply with ethical and legal standards for conducting research. It is not uncommon, however, for the IRB to overstep its authority and challenge (or even block) proposed research on grounds clearly outside of its purview.

In the Spring of 2017, I applied to the institutional review board (IRB) at the Graduate Center of the City University of New York (CUNY) for approval of research that I was conducting in pursuit of a PhD in Urban Education. In this chapter I briefly explore the reasons for and historical development of official protections for human participants in research, discuss my own challenges in applying for approval from my institution's IRB, and address the idea of generalizability in social science research – the particular area of conflict under which the IRB challenged in my own research.

Keywords

IRB – institutional review board – generalizability – ethics

1   Why an IRB?

The noble purpose of the IRB is to ensure that all research involving human subjects is conducted ethically and in such a way that no, or only minimal harm comes to these subjects. According to the Belmont Report (1979), whose ethical standards are a "primary concern for many IRBs" (Alexakos, 2015, p. 66), research involving human subjects must adhere to three basic ethical principles: respect for persons; beneficence; and justice. The report provides guidance on satisfying "adequate standards for informed consent," assessing and making appropriate decisions about the benefits and risks of participating in the research, and equitable criteria for selection of participants.

The work of the IRB is both necessary and important. Origins and development of codes for the adaptation of ethical practices in biomedical and behavioral research involving human participants was, in part, informed by, and in response to such events as Nazi medical experimentation during World War II, the U.S. Public Health Service's Syphilis Experiments at Tuskegee, and the medical research conducted on Henrietta Lacks and on tissues removed from her body (Skloot, 2011).

While ethical questions always have been considered in the execution of public policy, the mid-twentieth century saw a series of increasingly focused efforts to construct ethical standards and rules for conducting biomedical and behavioral research, and to make these regulations both more uniform across institutions, and unbounded by national borders. Major efforts in this direction include the Nuremburg Code (Nuerenberg Military Tribunals, 1949) in the late 1940s, and the Declaration of Helsinki (World Medical Association, 2018) in 1964, which periodically has been amended in response to considerations of ethics and international law. The modern IRB system was established and codified by the National Research Act of 1974 (Brandeis University, n.d.). In 1991, a Federal Policy for the Protection of Human Subjects was adopted across multiple US federal agencies. Generally known as the Common Rule, this set of guidelines, regulations and laws has been revised periodically through 2017 and is the basis for monitoring and regulating research with human subjects (U.S. Department of Health and Human Services, n.d.).

The collaborative efforts required to establish principles and legally codify guidelines and enforceable protocols and regulations have been undertaken to protect human beings from being harmed in the course of biomedical or behavioral research, and to ensure participants are afforded the opportunity to make informed decisions about their participation in such research. IRB approval protects all research participants including principal investigators and the institution itself. Research approval carries the weight of professional scrutiny, ongoing monitoring and a set of agreed-to practices that guide participants' behavior and, when challenged, are used resolve issues and disputes between and among all concerned. However, many students and faculty at my university (Bleier, Lopez & Powietrzynska, Chapter 17, this volume) and at other institutions (Gunsalus, 2004; Schrag, 2016) experience difficulties in getting approval for their research when IRBs reach beyond the limits of their purview and challenge research design, methods and other aspects of proposed research unconnected to ethical concerns.

2   The Work of the IRB

A quick search of any university's website will turn up information on the institution's Human Research Protection Program (HRPP) and guidelines on the conduct of human research as well as procedures for submitting proposed research and, subsequently, working with the IRB to ensure that the research, when approved and carried out meets both institutional ethical standards and complies with federal law.

One of the first web pages ("Human research protection program," n.d.) a potential CUNY researcher is likely to encounter contains the following statement:

> The CUNY Human Research Protection Program (HRPP) is responsible for the protection of the rights and welfare of human subjects in research projects conducted at CUNY or by CUNY faculty, staff and students and RF CUNY staff. The program provides oversight, administrative support and educational training to ensure that CUNY research complies with federal and State regulations, University policy and the highest ethical standards. The CUNY HRPP comprises of 5 University Integrated Institutional Review Boards (IRBs) and 19 on-site HRPP offices.

Some of the potential difficulties experienced by researchers – particularly in the social sciences – may be foreshadowed by the language regarding human research found in the guidelines on my (and most other) university's websites. Identifying participants in a research project as "subjects" already places them on paper, and in the minds of the researcher, the IRB and the university, in the position of being researched *on* rather than *with* – of being the passive, less-powerful *topics* of the research rather than full agentic partners in the enterprise.

3 A Description of My Research

In order to provide background for assessing the matters raised by, and my responses to the IRB, particularly around issues of sample size and generalizability, I offer a brief, but detailed, description of the relevant aspects my Doctoral research – an investigation of one young woman's efforts and experiences as she creates and follows a dynamic, contingent plan of self-education in the professional making, aging and distribution of cheese.

3.1 *The Proposed Research*
Finding light in the caves: Achieving professional and personal bliss on a journey in Cheeseworld (Bleier, 2018) is a phenomenological, hermeneutic study of the professional education of Ashley, a young cheesemaker/affineur/cheesemonger. She had had an unremarkable but respectable K-12 career as a student. However, she found that formal post-secondary schooling was not providing her with the things she wanted or needed. She found herself directionless and unsure of what to do with herself and her life. Then, happenstance and a series of choices led her to become involved in a community of practice centered on the production and sale of cheese, a career possibility about which she was largely unaware until she stumbled upon it, and within which she began to forge a professional educational program for herself comprised of a dynamic group of mentors, as well as workplaces and other fields within and among which she could move toward central participation.

Ashley and I became partners in this research. Identification of, and commitment to our inquiry as hermeneutic and phenomenological in nature means that our research (which is ongoing) focuses on the particular lived experience of the participants. It is interpretive – characterized by attention to difference and the embracing of contradiction. We always intend for our work to be both truthful and transferable but make no claims of generalizability in the positivistic sense that Western science practice hegemonically demands of *all* attempts at sense making (Guba & Lincoln, 1986).

The doing of research – making observations, collecting, organizing and analyzing data, and the statement of conclusions – is inseparable from interpretation.

This is most glaringly apparent in the human sciences. It is merely an illusion – one that is both actively promoted and passively accepted – that the design, carrying out of that design, and the analysis of data are objective and that the research and its findings are somehow separable from and independent of the researcher(s). We disagree and contend that these elements are not merely *sub*jective. This study (as with all research, and all human activity for that matter) exists within a social context – a matrix of beliefs, traditions and understandings – that is highly *inter*subjective (Schwandt, 2007). The participation of multiple researchers guarantees the highlighting of this intersubjectivity, but, even where a lone researcher is recognized, the phenomena, the existing literature and the researcher's own experiences all mediate the interpretations – the knowledge – generated during the course of the investigation and the sharing (via text and presentation) of the research findings (Tobin & Steinberg, 2015).

3.2   *The Characteristics of the Research*
If we are successful in addressing the ontological, epistemological and axiological positions that initiate, guide and continue to shape this project, we can characterize this research as emergent, contingent and authentic. It also is distinguished by a commitment to polysemy, polyphony and multilogicality (Alexakos, 2015).

3.2.1   Dynamic and Evolving
Our research is both emergent and contingent We do not start with an initial, inflexible question that is, in some way, answered at the end of the research. Whatever the initial plan, the progress of the research and the questions pursued continuously respond to the research itself. Each "step" is both a result of and a response to knowledge produced during the course of the research.

3.2.2   Multiple Voices – Multiple Meanings
We value and seek to employ, respect and promote polyphony and polysemy. In polyphonic research, the "story" of the research is told in the voices of *all* participants. An effort to affect a recursive sharing and dialogue around the work helps to realize this goal. As this research is polysemic, it is not just the voices, but also the perspectives of the participants with which we seek to infuse the text. Both polyphony and polysemy tap into difference and contradiction. This, we believe is where the meaning of the narrative can be most interestingly made subject to sense making. Through this process, all participants' voices, and all meanings mediate each other. As the reader joins the

research participants, knowledge production expands and a complex, contradictory story emerges that informs and serves each member of this expansive partnership differently and complementarily.

Polysemy is not merely a feature of our human-centered research, it is a feature of life itself. Any research that is not polysemic is by default reductive and simplified, often to the point of meaninglessness. All human activity is experienced in different ways by each individual. The realities and meanings these individuals perceive and construct are all viable. Each individual's understanding and social interaction is enriched and rendered more meaningful when she is able to empathize – to understand, if not adopt/adapt the ideas of the other.

Nor is polysemy solely within the purview of the "soft" sciences. Near the beginning of the twentieth century, Albert Einstein upended our understanding of the physical world. The orderly and retrospectively simple ways of the universe as conceived by Newton now were not so fixed, not so orderly, and certainly not so simple. Einstein hadn't negated the Newtonian view of the universe, rather, he provided us with a complementary lens for making sense of physical phenomena, both every day and extraordinary. However, I believe that if Einstein played tennis, he would have functioned within the Newtonian constraints as if these accurately describe the workings of the universe. This simplified model describes a limited set of physical phenomena in ways that allow us to make sense of a small slice of our world – a model that becomes all the more powerful as we recognize its limitations (what it can and, to a great extent, what it can't illuminate for us). [Disclaimer: I don't know if Einstein played tennis.]

3.2.3 For the Benefit of All Involved and Even Those Who Are Not

Our research is shaped by an axiological stance that informs, both overtly and passively, decisions we make at every juncture.

Among our goals in engaging in this study is that the research be authentic. That is, we intend for the work to be meaningful for all participants (including the readers), and to do good in the world. Authentic inquiry is situated "in the world of lived experience" and is transformative for the researchers, the researched, and for the research itself (Alexakos, 2015). We have made efforts to insure the legitimacy and efficacy of this work by attending to authenticity criteria originally developed by Yvonna Guba and Egon Lincoln (1989), adapted by Ken Tobin (2015) and evolved over years of use in research in the Learning Sciences strand of the Urban Education program at the CUNY Graduate Center

Briefly, the four authenticity criteria that guide us are *ontological authenticity* – the research is characterized by its support/encouragement for all participants to be changed through their participation; *educative authenticity* – the research provides opportunities for all participants to learn from one another. This criterion embraces diversity and difference as strengths. It recognizes difference as a resource rather than an obstacle; *catalytic authenticity* – the research becomes a catalyst for positive change in the world enacted by the participants, and *tactical authenticity* – participation in the research is potentially beneficial to all participants.

Changes in the ways we have come to work together reflect both ontological and educative authenticity criteria. Tactical authenticity is grounded in the questions raised and the particular threads of the story that we (both together and as individuals) choose to pursue. Catalytic authenticity in our research derives from our belief(s) that our sharing of this particular and unique path of self-directed education can live in the world as an example, a model, and a potential guide (for decision makers: learners, educators and policymakers) to successful, satisfying participation in a community of practice. Catalytic authenticity in our work is largely aspirational, may be realized only in time, and may never rise to our (the researchers') awareness.

Taken together, the authenticity criteria and the authentic inquiry which embodies them provide a framework that "explicitly incorporates and values multi-representation, multiple voices (polyphonia), and multiple realities (polysemia), is holistic, encourages inclusivity and embraces otherness" (Alexakos, 2015, p. 45). The adoption and adaptation of these criteria is the result of an axiological stance that includes our belief that our research should, at least potentially, do some good in the world.

It is important to note that we are not always consciously applying these authenticity criteria, but rather the criteria, through constant reflexive and recursive intersubjective interactions within our community of practice centered on education and education research at the Graduate Center, are infused into our axiological stances. Although most of the time we are not explicitly evaluating our work in the context of the authenticity criteria – in fact, all four authenticity criteria are not achieved at all stages of the research – the criteria mediate our conversations, our writing, and the discussions we have with colleagues, associates and coworkers in the Learning Sciences strand of the Urban Education program at the CUNY Graduate Center.

3.2.4 Multilogicality

Methods and processes employed during the course of this research are not chosen up front. They are considered and selected when and as suggested by the research (Berry, 2015). Observation and participation in cheesemaking, affinage, cheesemongering and classes raise questions and present opportunities that, if perceived as potentially fruitful, are pursued. Discussions, interviews, correspondence via written texts are used when and as they arise as possibilities. It is not only the *selection* of an approach or method that is decided upon through the period of the research, but also the jettisoning of such activities. No particular method is included or excluded permanently – assessment and reassessment of research activities is ongoing and continuous. This bricolage approach often is a challenge to established, learned, inertia-laden views of educational research largely driven by positivistic and crypto-positivistic stances held by both consumers and producers of the research (Berry, 2015; Kincheloe & Tobin, 2009). However, multilogicality in education research enables researchers to follow the story and to produce rich, contextualized knowledge that is provocative of further questioning and demanding of further investigation.

3.3 *What Can* This *Tell Us about* That?

Among the hegemonic, positivistic imperatives of Western science is its demand for repeatability and generalizability (Kincheloe & Tobin, 2009). Again, I think that this is more of an issue of the practitioners and even more of the acolytes than of science itself. Of course, statistical generalizability is a perfectly reasonable expectation. If cause and effect relationships are sought while, for example, exploring the relationship between radiation and various aspects of DNA replication, scientists should document all experimental procedures and conditions so that their work can be replicated, confirmed or refuted, and built upon. A problem occurs, however, when this kind of thinking is applied to the investigation of social life.

This may be an artifact of inappropriate science instruction. Even the commonly used words "teaching" and "instruction" reveal a pervasive one-way, transmission perspective. In this banking model of education (Freire, 1970), the learner – the aspirational member of a community of practice – is a passive vessel in these constructions. Agency is, if not forbidden, at least delayed or put off to a time and place where the learner has been assimilated, indoctrinated, trained in the dogma, the canon, the Truth.

Recently, in discussing this idea of generalizability in the social sciences, the question arose, how can you expect to make generalizations and predictions about social phenomena from a single person's experience? I bristled, then realized (not without some embarrassment) that this is a question *I* might have asked in the not-too-distant past.

How *do* we do meaningful research on social life? How can we mount an objective study of social phenomena? The short answer is, we can't. However, this is as unenlightening an answer as the sample size issue is a question.

Here is an example: Informal (even unaware) social science investigation is done within the most common of social groups – the family. Raising children is almost universally done with "sample sizes" of n < 5 … and, objectivity is not claimed, nor aspired to, nor achieved. The family "researcher" is deeply involved in every aspect of the project of understanding, learning from/with, and making choices and performing actions that benefit both individuals and the group as a whole.

But even the language used to discuss these issues is hegemonic and heavily laden with subtext and supertext that must be challenged. Social science is not necessarily done with samples, with "n"s. The participants in social science research (like the members of a family) are not representative of a larger population to which our findings can be applied. Family resemblances and the ability to use knowledge produced by this research in other settings is part of why this work is done, but much of this research focuses on difference, contradiction and complexity.

Of course, the living of family life, or any aspect of social life is hardly considered research. However, social science research often exists within the same constraints and affordances associated with the living of social life. In fact, for the research documented in this dissertation and for most hermeneutic phenomenological research, engagement in social life and research of social life are so inextricably intertwined as to be inseparable. This renders demands for and claims of (or even attempts at) objectivity untenable.

Attempts at and claims of universality in this type of research also are unsound and unproductive. Generalizability, however, is a somewhat more nuanced issue and warrants further discussion. Although the bricolage of much phenomenological, hermeneutic research may include quantitative elements and methods that may well be statistically generalizable beyond the participants in the research to some broader population, many researchers and authors commonly dismiss the idea of generalizability in social science. Margaret Eisenhart (2009) cites numerous instances of researchers rejecting the existence of generalizability in "qualitative" research and characterizing as unwarranted and inappropriate, criticism of this research for lack of this generalizability.

3.4   *Methodological Dissonance: The Question of Sample Size*

As stated earlier, in preparation for the proposed research, I was challenged in the process of applying for IRB approval to explain how, given my intention to focus on a single research participant, I would be able to "assess meaningful (statistical) data based on an n of 1? How does one individual predict a societal change?" I was taken aback as it became clear to me that the question was meant to be rhetorical because, in the next sentence, without allowing for any response from me, the reviewer included a directive to "revise projected enroll-ment based upon statistical power analyses" (CUNY Graduate Center IRB, per-sonal communication, 2017).

No longer was I merely explaining my methods to a genuinely puzzled and interested Western-science-oriented colleague, I was now justifying my pro-posed work to a gatekeeper. This required a thoughtful response that bridged very different and, perhaps, incommensurable ways of making sense of the world. It required a response that would educate and convince someone whose knowledge and belief systems reflected my own professional origins in the sciences. This was a valuable exercise for me as well and reflects the impor-tance of polysemia in research: constant challenges to one's ontological and epistemological positions and the infusion and acceptance of the coexistence of contradictory truths. If all partners in the enterprise are acting in good faith, the work becomes deeper, more nuanced and more meaningful.

Prior to this challenge, I, like many researchers engaged in what often is referred to as qualitative research, made the argument that our work was not generalizable ... period (Eisenhart, 2009). Social life is complex, and each indi-vidual is unique. Transactions and relationships between and among multiple individuals increase the complexity exponentially. Therefore, the claim that any individual is representative of a larger population is likely to be both unre-alistic and misleading. However, I was embarking on this project for a purpose. My story and Ashley's story were to be told and explored for a reason. My col-leagues and advisors were investing in my work because it meant something to them, and they were incorporating our collaborative thinking and investi-gation of my writing about the research into their own thinking and their own work. If not generalizability in the quantitative, statistical sense, I was certainly striving for some meaning, value and relevance to others' work as I embarked on my own. My response, encouraged by my faculty advisor and informed by his own work (Tobin, 2009), reflects my efforts to educate the gatekeeper and have my research greenlighted, but also my own grappling with the generaliz-ability of this kind of work.

I had already made several adjustments to my research proposal in response to IRB concerns. For example, my original plan was to conduct conversations with my research participant on videotape. The IRB was concerned that, with only a single participant, I would not be able to maintain her anonymity. Although I had thought that it might be valuable for some, as yet unidentified future purpose, to have a record of the full proxemic and prosodic richness of the conversations that video *and* audio would afford, this type of data was not necessary to the current research, so I agreed to collect only audio from our conversations. However, the anonymity that precipitated this modification was not an issue as my research participant and co-researcher, Ashley had already waived anonymity and agreed to be identified via the informed-consent form.

This latest demand (to "revise projected enrollment") was a threat to the fundamental tenets of my research. In addition, increasing the number of participants in the study (the sample size) was impractical and would likely derail my entire study. I reached out to my dissertation committee advisor, Kenneth Tobin for advice. He, a former physicist and I, a science educator, had discussed these issues before and I knew that his familiarity with research in both the natural and the human sciences as well as his years of working within academic settings would lead to a solution that would satisfy both me and the IRB. I forwarded Ken the relevant part of the correspondence from the IRB and he responded:

> This is dreadful. But here is what I would do. I would say that you are NOT seeking statistical generalizability, but instead are seeking theoretical generalizability. I would then cite the attached book [(Ercikan & Roth, 2009)]. The chapter by Eisenhart is a good one to cite and of course there is a chapter by me. Other chapters in this book are excellent.
>
> I was going to write to all levels of CUNY about this appalling issue and now I am very motivated to do so – next semester though. Maybe you can join me in writing a paper on the problems of monosemia and adherence to crypto-positivism and its embracing of reductivism and statistical generalizability. (Personal communication via email, April 20, 2017)

The resources and encouragement provided by Ken enabled me to respond to the IRB in a way that would both preserve my research plan and, perhaps, educate those whose judgement determines, to some extent, what research is done (and not done) at our institution.

4 My Response to the IRB

Representatives of the IRB were generally helpful throughout the application process. I felt that they were on my side and wanted to approve the research as soon as possible. The IRB process can be irritating. Small details are questioned and must be explained with clarity and to people from other fields who don't speak the same specialized language associated with the researcher's area of study. Ultimately, though, this process can broaden and deepen the expertise of both researcher and IRB member. In acknowledgement for the generally helpful and supportive interactions I had had with the IRB, and with the hope that the relationship I had established with my contact person would serve me well, I attached my response to the recent, disturbing query to this cover letter.

4.1   *The Cover Letter*

> Mr. Entredeux (a pseudonym),
>
> The most recent reviewer comments from the IRB to my proposed research raised an issue that (a) did not come up in previous responses, and (b) seems unrelated to the ethical issues that I thought were the focus of the IRB approval process.
>
> I am including a response with this email.
>
> As these most recent reviewer comments seemed to come not from you as in previous rounds, and your communications have thus far been clear and helpful, I wanted to speak with you before formally attaching my response to the protocol and submitting it.
>
> I hope that the attached document clears up any misunderstanding about the nature of my proposed research and can assist you in guiding me in my next (and, I hope, final) steps toward IRB approval.
>
> Is it possible for us to speak on the telephone after you have had a chance to examine the attached document? My contact information is included.
>
> Thank you in advance for your time and expertise.

Within a half an hour, Mr. Entredeux called me and explained that mine was an unusual situation and that he wasn't sure why this issue had arisen at this late stage in the IRB process. He suggested that he felt that I had made a good case and that I was likely to receive one of two decisions in short order: a favorable response to my request for approval; or a statement that my work fell outside of the scope of the IRB's oversight – in effect, that it was not considered research and, therefore, not subject to IRB approval.

4.2   *My Response to the Reviewer's Query*

The reviewer's query. The most recent review of my IRB application raised an issue that had not arisen during earlier preliminary submissions:

As per the Expedited Reviewer, "how does the PI propose to assess meaningful (statistical) data based on an n of 1? How does one individual predict a societal change? Please revise projected enrollment based upon statistical power analyses."

My response. The proposed study is phenomenological and interpretive in nature and as such is not intended to produce statistically generalizable findings or to make predictions about societal change, but rather to explore and document a particular and unique case of a person seeking out and appropriating a variety of resources including apprenticeship, learning on the job, and formal educational opportunities to create an effective program of professional learning in order to build a career in artisanal cheese production. However, it is hoped that this work will provide an example that learners, teachers and policy makers may use, in combination with their experience and understanding, to inform their own decisions about educating themselves and others in this and other fields.

4.3 Generalizability, Sample Size and the Selection of Research Participants

Statistical generalizability or application of the findings of my research to some "general population" from which the participant(s) are drawn and of which they are representative is not the goal here. Eisenhart (2009), quoting Howard Becker, points out that the research on small samples (e.g., the inclusion of only one or a few participants) is entirely consistent with claims that *theoretical generalizability* in social science research can provide a "refined understanding of a generic process" – in the case of the proposed research, apprenticeship, learning on the job, or formal employment-related "training" – that has "wide applicability in social life" (p. 60).

The participant(s) in my research are chosen not randomly, but *specifically for* differences and individuality that will poke at, interrogate and challenge the efficacy of the very types of broad, uniform, one-size-fits-all educational experiences that have not worked for so many people. Participant(s)' experiences help to shed a light on how individuals encounter and engage with structures that help them produce the professional knowledge required of them. Eisenhart (2009) explains:

> In striving for theoretical generalization, the selection of a group or site to study is made based on the likelihood that the case will reveal something new and different, and that once this new phenomenon is theorized,

additional cases will expose differences or variations that test its generalizability. The criterion for selecting cases from which one will generalize
is not random or representative sampling but the extent to which the
cases selected are likely to establish, refine, or refute a theory. (p. 60)

Kadriye Ercikan and Wolff-Michael Roth (2009) have asserted that, in social
science research, it is often the case that "generalizability of research findings cannot be judged based on sample size." Ercikan further points out that,
in the case of phenomenology (which characterizes the currently proposed
research), where small samples are the norm, research may "identify universal
relationships that have great degrees of generalizability," while other research
"may use very large samples but focus on overall group results and have very
little generalizability for key sub-groups" (p. 211).

Kenneth Tobin (2009), grappling with the ideas of generalizability and sample size in interpretive, phenomenological research in education, argued that:

> ... designing a study with generalizability as a goal can lead to serious
> distortions in the focus of the research, the methods used, the outcomes,
> and the perceived relevance of the work to those involved in the study
> and the education community in general. (p. 158)

Tobin is concerned that his research always is conscious of participants as
human beings rather than subjects or a randomly selected, representative
sample of a larger population to which his research findings could be generalized. As to sample size, Tobin (2009) writes:

> It was necessary for me to carefully consider the humanity of partici-
> pants and my purposes for involving them in research. Among the puz-
> zles that needed to be resolved were how many participants to include in
> a study, when to include them, the nature of what could be learned from
> research, and how to handle diversity within a data set. (p. 158)

Integrity of the research and its purposes as well as logistics are considerations
when determining the number of participants and when to include them.
Tobin advocates careful and deliberate selection of participants both serially
and contingently. These decisions are made based on what is being learned
and what new questions arise during the course of the research. Participants
are chosen not randomly for purposes of assembling a representative sample,
but specifically because of their differences from each other in order to explore
contradictions, puzzles and new, unanticipated questions that arise.

4.4   *The Upshot*

Mr. Entredeux was right. The next day, when I checked the status of my online application to the IRB, I found that my research had been approved – no explanation, no comments, no back and forth. While I was pleased to have cleared this hurdle, I was now wanting to discuss this issue and understand how, in an institution where the kind of work that I was proposing was not rare, the possibility of a denial due to a misunderstanding so fundamental to the conducting of social science research could exist.

I proceeded with my research, completed my degree, and published, with Ashley, an account of the study (Bleier & Morton, 2019). This chapter represents my efforts to contribute to that conversation about the essential role of the IRB and its responsibility to the research community.

4.5   *Balance and the Road Ahead*

Ultimately, the imperative to protect human (and other living) participants in all kinds of research justifies the sometimes-irritating restraints imposed by the IRB. The never-ending task of the entire research community – researchers, research participants, administrators and federal regulators – is to assess and support as much research as possible. This necessitates a constant assessment and reassessment process for simultaneously maximizing high-quality research and minimizing harm. The borderland between benefit and risk of harm often is plied by those unfamiliar with the territory and is fraught with opportunities to make detrimental decisions. Although these decisions generally are well-intentioned, they may at times be malicious and unethical by design. A diligent effort to visit and revisit ethical principles and to engage in honest and thorough scrutiny within a diverse community of interested parties will provide us with our best shot at respecting persons, ensuring beneficence and encouraging justice. In the end, the result should be that students, staff and faculty at institutions where research is conducted engage in knowledge production that provides the most benefit while minimizing the harm done in the world.

The necessary work of the IRB must be conducted in ways that protect research participants while not unnecessarily impeding research. All stakeholders must be fully informed and educated as to the rights, responsibilities and limitations of everyone involved.

Faculty members who sit on the IRB serve the university community over and above their obligations as employees. This activity is a professional responsibility for which they are not compensated and for which they are sometimes not fully prepared. In their roles as gatekeepers, IRB members sometimes overreach and attempt to expand the scope of their powers. Inexperienced researchers also not fully informed of the rules and of their rights may not feel empowered to challenge this very-official body.

My encounters with the IRB described in this chapter were generally positive and supportive of my work. However, an unexpected response from the IRB at a critical moment in my timeline had the potential to derail my work and progress toward my degree. It was only with the help of a very supportive cadre within my own department that I was guided to respond in a detailed way that enlightened the anonymous reviewer, obtained approval for my research, and, I both hope and imagine, smoothed the way for future researchers.

References

Alexakos, K. (2015). *Being a teacher | researcher: A primer on doing authentic inquiry research on teaching and learning.* Sense Publishers.

Belmont Report. (1979). *Ethical principles and guidelines for the protection of human subjects of research.* The National Commission for the Protection of Human Subjects of Biomedical and Behavioral Research. Retrieved May 8, 2018, from https://www.hhs.gov/ohrp/regulations-and-policy/belmont-report/read-the-belmont-report/index.html

Berry, K. (2015). Research as bricolage: Embracing relationality, multiplicity and complexity. In K. Tobin & S. Steinberg (Eds.), *Doing educational research – A handbook* (2nd ed., pp. 79–110). Sense Publishers.

Bleier, M. (2018). *Finding light in the caves: Achieving professional and personal bliss on a journey in Cheeseworld* (Doctoral dissertation). City University of New York, Graduate Center. https://academicworks.cuny.edu/gc_etds/2773

Bleier, M., & Morton, A. (2019). Adventures in Cheeseworld: Learning in the world and on the job. In L. Bryan & K. Tobin (Eds.), *Critical visions for science education: The road ahead* (pp. 75–99). Brill | Sense. doi:10.1163/9789004389663_05

Brandeis University. (n.d.). *IRBs: A brief history.* Retrieved May 16, 2018, from https://www.brandeis.edu/ora/compliance/irb/101/history.html

Eisenhart, M. (2009). Generalization from qualitative inquiry. In K. Ercikan & W.-M. Roth (Eds.), *Generalizing from educational research* (pp. 51–66). Routledge.

Ercikan, K. (2009). Limitations in sample-to-population generalizing. In K. Ercikan & W.-M. Roth (Eds.), *Generalizing from educational research* (pp. 211–234). Routledge.

Ercikan, K., & Roth, W.-M. (Eds.). (2009). *Generalizing from educational research.* Routledge.

Freire, P. (1970). *Pedagogy of the oppressed.* Continuum International Publishing Group.

Guba, E., & Lincoln, Y. S. (1989). *Fourth generation evaluation.* Sage Publishing.

Gunsalus, C. (2004). The nanny state meets the inner lawyer: Overregulating while underprotecting human participants in research. *Ethics & Behavior, 14,* 369–382.

Human Research Protection Program. (n.d.). http://www2.cuny.edu/research/research-compliance/human-research-protection-program-hrpp/

Kincheloe, J., & Tobin, K. (2009). The much exaggerated death of positivism. *Cultural Studies of Science Education, 4,* 513–528. doi:10.1007/s11422-009-9178-5

Nuerenburg Military Tribunals. (1949). *Trials of war criminals before the Nuerenberg Military Tribunals under control council law No. 10* (Vol. II, pp. 181–182). U.S. Government Printing Office. https://www.loc.gov/rr/frd/Military_Law/pdf/NT_war-criminals_Vol-II.pdf

Schrag, Z. (2016, May 8). Texas A&M IRB imposed review for surveys of public officials [Blog post]. Institutional Review Blog. http://www.institutionalreviewblog.com/2016/05/texas-irb-imposedreview-for-surveys-of.html

Schwandt, T. (2007). Judging interpretations. *New Directions for Evaluation, 114,* 11–14.

Skloot, R. (2010). *The immortal life of Henrietta Lacks.* Crown Publishers.

Tobin, K. (2009). Repetition, difference, and rising up with research in education. In K. Ercikan & W.-M. Roth (Eds.), *Generalizing from educational research* (pp. 149–172). Routledge.

Tobin, K. (2015). Qualitative research in classrooms: Pushing the boundaries of theory and methodology. In K. Tobin & S. Steinberg (Eds.), *Doing educational research – A handbook* (2nd ed., pp. 33–75). Sense Publishers.

Tobin, K., & Steinberg, S. (Eds.). (2015). *Doing educational research – A handbook* (2nd ed.). Sense Publishers.

U.S. Department of Health and Human Services. (n.d.). Retrieved May 16, 2018, from https://www.hhs.gov/ohrp/regulations-and-policy/regulations/common-rule/index.html

World Medical Association. (2018). *Declaration of Helsinki: Ethical principles for medical research involving human subjects.* Retrieved May 16, 2018, from https://www.wma.net/policies-post/wma-declaration-of-helsinki-ethical-principles-for-medical-research-involving-human-subjects/

CHAPTER 17

Encounters with the Institutional Review Board: A Metalogue

Mitch Bleier, Manny Lopez and Malgorzata Powietrzynska

Abstract

Every encounter with the the Institutional review board (IRB) is unique. Each of the three authors of this chapter has had limited experience in getting institutional approval and support for her/his research. In the following conversation, our invidual stories are brought together in the expectation that the contradiction, complexity and diversity of our experiences will begin to make each of our accounts more meaningful to us and will provide the beginning of a rich exploration of these issues to which readers may bring their own experiences into the conversation.

Keywords

Institutional Review Board (IRB) – ethics – research participants – crypto-positivism – teacher-researcher – overreach

1 Broadening the Discussion

The preceding chapter (Bleier, Chapter 16, this volume) sprung from one researcher's (the first author's) encounter with the institutional review board (IRB) approval process in pursuit of a PhD. We (Mitch Bleier, Manny Lopez and Malgorzata Powietrzynska) now engage in a metalogue among three current and former doctoral students from the same institution that addresses similar issues. Our hope is that each of our experiences will augment the meaning of each of the others' and leave the reader with a broader, richer, more complex understanding. We further hope that our conversation will resonate with both researchers and policy makers at our and at other institutions, and provide context, encouragement and guidance for decision makers to construct and advance institutional policies that will better support a full and diverse universe of research methods, methodologies and genres even as these policies continue to protect all participants in research activities to the greatest extent possible (Tobin & Bryan, 2018).

Three aspects of the IRB process that we discuss here are (a) the necessity and importance of the IRB, (b) IRB overreach or, as Lynn Bryan calls it, IRB "mission creep" (Tobin & Bryan, 2018, p. 12), and (c) a rethinking and enhancements that will make the IRB process more viable, more responsive, and more relevant to the broad range of research conducted within our own and other institutions.

2 Importance and Necessity of the IRB

2.1 *Mitch*

Recently, a statue of James Marion Sims was removed from its pedestal on Fifth Avenue in New York City. It was placed there in 1894 in recognition of Dr. Sims' part in the development of medical advances, techniques and practices in the field of gynecology (Flynn, 2018). The statue's departure, the result of increased public awareness and public protest, was not universally welcomed, but was triggered by a recognition of research methods and practices that, by today's standards are deemed unacceptable. (I suspect that practicing coerced medical procedures on enslaved women in the absence of anesthesia was likely seen by some, even at the time as barbaric, but the voices of the powerful often quiet or even silence the voices of the less-powerful.) It is important to note that Sims' work was not questioned on the merits of its efficacy or scientific methodology, but rather because it violated modern ethical norms and standards.

Today, we have a system of laws, protocols and practices at the Federal and institutional levels with the stated aim to ensure that the protection of the rights and welfare of human subjects in biomedical and behavioral research projects is addressed in the design and adhered to in the conducting of the research. These rules often are perceived as an obstacle for researchers, but in the end, they result in a system that is meant to protect both researchers and other participants in research from harm.

3 IRB Unbound

3.1 *Mitch*

The first submission of my research proposal to the IRB yielded 26 questions that had to be addressed before I could continue with my application. Many of the questions were nearly identical. At least three quarters of these seemed so unrelated to my research that I wasn't sure how to proceed.

I emailed, Ken Tobin, my advisor, "I can't simply write 'N/A' for virtually every question."

"Why not," was his reply. "Just make sure they understand what you are doing and why you are doing it."

So, I set out to do just that.

Several of the questions concerned how I was planning to select research subjects. The reviewer wanted to know what my selection criteria were, how I would approach potential subjects, how I would make sure that no one was coerced or dissuaded from participation, and how I would affect random selection. I told my liaison with the IRB that I already had one participant for my research and that there were likely to be no additions, so I don't have selection criteria. He said, you can't select anyone *before* you receive IRB approval.

I explained that my planned study arose from the work of my co-researcher (participant). The study would not have existed but for her work. Her participation predated and precipitated the idea of the research.

When the liaison said you'll have to come up with some criteria ... and a selection process I realized that the IRB review process was not designed for the kind of research I intended to do, nor for the research of most of my colleagues at the Graduate Center.

I was determined to get approval, so I constructed a selection protocol that I *might* use when choosing any *additional* participants – although, my process would most likely involve carefully selecting non-random participants both serially and contingently as the study progressed. These participants would be chosen specifically for their interesting uniqueness and for differences from those already involved.

Then I proceeded to write N/A in most of the boxes ... and I resubmitted.

That the process is so positivistic, so scientist, and so exclusionary is bad enough, but it is not merely forcing a Western science research framework on *all* types of research, that is the problem. It is the crypto-positivistic assumption that there simply is no other valid way to investigate *anything*.

3.2 *Manny*

I recently submitted a research application for IRB review and approval for the first time. After reading the reviewer's feedback, I question their influence over my research design and methodology. Still, the IRB application process, including the reviewer's comments, were informative.

The feedback that I received on my IRB application was mostly practical. In some cases, I simply needed to add information that was not in my initial application. As an example, including my advisor in the short list of individuals who will have access to the audio recorded interviews is clearly necessary, but I neglected to check the box near his name to authorize his access. Also, I am grateful that the reviewer provided useful guidance with examples. "Contributions to scholarly research" is one example of a potential benefit to society that I will add to my revised application. I accept most of the IRB's review and will easily address their comments.

While updates to my original application are straightforward, I am wary of the IRB's influence on my research design and methodology. For instance, I am not yet sure how to address the reviewer's following comment regarding my study: "... the research reads as if the PI is simply interested in soliciting answers regarding the items contained inside the questionnaire." This feedback is neither objective nor for the purposes of protecting the rights and welfare of human participants.

As a novice IRB applicant, it seems to me that the reviewer is attempting to be helpful, but may be overstepping his role in that the feedback on my research design is unrelated to ethics, rights, or the welfare of human participants. My doctoral dissertation committee reviewed and approved my study design prior to IRB application submission. It is not clear to me if the IRB's involvement should influence my approved research design, particularly since there is no violation to the rights or welfare of human participants.

3.3   Malgorzata

I must admit that compared to your respective bumpy roads traveled with our institutional IRB, mine have been relatively smooth. Coincidently, I have just completed an entire cycle of an IRB-approved research study; from filing an initial application and receiving an unconditional approval in 2012, through submitting an amendment and completing continuing review at a three-year mark, to now "handing in" a final report. So far, at none of these steps, have I been asked to provide additional information regarding the study protocol. Admittedly, my project, which aimed at developing and validating research tools (i.e., heuristics) through mostly anonymous online communication with adult participants (Powietrzynska, 2015), was deemed to pose "very minimal or no risks" and thus met the criteria for exemption status. In addition, the proposed methodology that included both "qualitative" and "quantitative" approaches as well as an anticipated large participant pool (500 individuals) had a semblance of and might have been perceived as conforming to mainstream research paradigms that privilege objectivism and the scientific method. Accordingly, I might have appeared as a "typical" researcher whose main goal was to collect data and use it to advance her own agenda with the research "subjects" acting as mere sources of that data. Taken together, this set of circumstances might have resulted in the lack of scrutiny of my protocol in contrast to what you appear to have experienced.

This is not to say that I have been immune to having my research designs challenged; sadly, the academic community is fraught with judgment. Overreaching practices by IRB panels are but one instance of a more pervasive problem of overtly privileging one paradigm over another often enacted through what is referred to as a peer-review process. Other examples include submissions of manuscripts to publication outlets, proposing conference presentations, applying for grant funding, or earning tenure or promotion. The high stakes nature of outcomes as well as power dynamics associated with each of these activities are quite clear. Therefore, some researchers who adopt "unconventional" frameworks may resort to using undesirable tactics that aim at placating those in power. Such was the case with Mitch who felt compelled to comply with the IRB reviewer's request to devise a participant selection protocol. I, too, found myself proactively "bending" in anticipation of potential problems. For example, the IRB application requires that the researcher specifies research questions and/or hypotheses associated with her project. This may be problematic for those (me included) who adopt designs that are responsive to the emergent and contingent nature of social life and are generally not driven by some a priori assumptions (see Guba, 1981). However, in order to comply with the IRB mandate, I (and possibly others who subscribe to similar research paradigms) do construct potential research questions to be included in the application. Having witnessed similar situations, Ken Tobin (2007) laments,

> To gain IRB approval to do research, accommodations have to be made to align with incommensurable framework and its associated method. The result is distortion and, in some cases, deception to get through the IRB. (p. 709)

3.4   *Mitch*

That three researchers in the same program within a relatively short time frame should have such different experiences seeking IRB approval for their work reveals many of the issues that should and must be addressed if what we seek is a vibrant, diverse, eclectic, enlightening research environment. Beyond this, the disparities between institutions further contribute to a more broadly uneven research landscape that magnifies and exacerbates pressures that may attenuate innovation and diversity in the generation of knowledge. We must ask: Is there privilege? Are values and practices outside of the purview of the IRB being imposed on researchers? How does this play out in terms of what research actually occurs and what research is discouraged?

Of course, each research project is unique and must be evaluated as such. The variability of proposed research activities renders problematic any attempts at streamlining or standardizing the approval process. Therefore, the community at our institution and, perhaps, cross-institutional organizations need to continually examine and reexamine guidelines for review of proposed research projects and how to educate IRB members, and apply guidelines wisely, fairly, and equitably in ways that both comply with federal law and protect the rights and wellbeing of all participants. It also is important that we do not sow the field with deception as Ken warns in in the quote included by Malgorzata (above). It is a perverse situation where the very body designed to promote ethical research practices suborns deception from its institution's researchers.

3.5 *Malgorzata*

When thinking about fairness and equitability as exercised by IRB panels, another set of questions may need consideration: Are research proposals submitted by (doctoral) students treated differently than, say, those of tenured professors? Might the IRB reviewers feel obligated (perhaps even in good faith) to educate the assumed fledgling researchers on the "right way" to conduct their studies? Indeed, Robert J. Amdur (2006) who argues that "scientific quality is a criterion for IRB approval," notes, "in organizations where a large volume of social science research is done by students, it is not unusual for the IRB to review protocols where the scientific design is not optimal, but the risk to subjects is virtually zero" (p. 153). At the same time, as remarked by Manny, the reviewer's questioning of his study design may be viewed as an attempt at undermining the legitimacy and qualifications of the dissertation advisors who must be assumed to have provided a stamp of approval for the research proposal prior to its submission for IRB review. As was demonstrated in Mitch's case, the wisdom and unwavering support of one's advisor in navigating through the academic labyrinth is crucial particularly when faced with power differentials. We have been fortunate to be guided by an advisor who exhibits courage to confront situations he perceives as unfair. I also found it beneficial to seek guidance from colleagues (including other doctoral students) who had been successful in going through the IRB approval process. Having a model to follow is helpful particularly to someone who is an IRB novice.

3.6 *Mitch*

Several times during this discussion, the idea of the IRB approval process being instructive for both the researcher and the members of the IRB has been recognized and advocated for. It seems that, at least for students, advisors, dissertation committee members and others who possess "specialized expertise in the area that is being evaluated in the study" (Amadur, 2006, p. 153) are in the best position to advise on research design and methodological matters. The advice and, in some cases, approval might precede submission of a proposal to the IRB. Part of the IRBs charge is to weigh risk and benefit in determining if a research protocol is ultimately to be approved. This leads the IRB to evaluate proposed methods and practices to determine what benefit if any at all is accrued by virtue of participation in the research. In deference to the active involvement of advisors, committee members, and colleagues in the field of study, the IRB should provide the researcher and her team with as much leeway as possible in determining what constitutes beneficence as well as what constitutes productive research design.

Although the process may be difficult to nail down and to codify, it seems reasonable that researchers, professional colleagues, advisors and the IRB, working in partnership will go a long way toward generating research that is both ethical and meaningful.

3.7 Malgorzata

What Mitch's experience teaches us as well, is that making an effort to build a relationship with at least one member on the IRB panel may prove useful. As may be the case with any number of human transactions in social life, an in-person meeting or even a phone call may go a long way in counteracting the faceless nature of a "blind" review and hopefully minimizing what amounts to methodological bullying. Prompted by Ken's long-time collaborator, Konstantinos Alexakos, who actively engages and encourages teachers to conduct research into their own practice (Alexakos, 2015), I recently used a face-to-face approach when interacting with IRB at our sister institution. At the time, my co-PI and I were preparing to file an application for our project to be conducted with high school students. Having overcome some scheduling challenges, we met with the IRB representative who was very helpful in answering our questions, providing clarifications, and making useful suggestions. Subsequently, our project was approved with no questions asked. The problem we did encounter, however, was a long waiting period before the approval was formally granted. Unlike my earlier experiences, it took 3 months to approve the project that ironically met the conditions for an "expedited review."

4 Imagining a Better Future

4.1 Mitch

Kenneth Tobin (Tobin & Bryan, 2018) makes the case for "IRB processes to be reconstituted to legitimize present-day research methodologies and methods"

(p. 11). He calls for guidelines that (a) are more relevant to the many ways that social science research is conducted, (b) address the ethical use of the many technologies (e.g., smartphones and video) that are in regular use in class-rooms and other venues where research occurs, and (c) address the kinds of research, researchers and research participants that increasingly populate the world of social science research.

In my encounters with the IRB, my difficulties seemed to stem not from a resistance to my research on grounds related to ethical treatment of partici-pants – the domain of the IRB – but from a complete incongruence between *my* view and *their* view of what research is. The guidelines used by the IRB don't oppose my research, they simply do not recognize it as research at all. Ideally, IRB members, individually or as a group, should be able to recognize the whole gamut of research genres they may encounter, but the most import-ant issue is that they understand their role in ensuring the ethical conduct of research within their own institutions.

When one's only tool is Western science, everything looks like a collection of variables to be controlled, manipulated or measured in the quest of cause and effect relationships, or ... it looks like quackery.

4.2   *Manny*

I am struck that the IRB does not recognize your work as research. I reviewed the "Criteria for IRB Approval" as spelled out in our institution's (CUNY) HRPP Policy and Procedures (2016) to learn why this is the case. Specifically, para-graph 14.2, *Experimental Design and Scientific Validity*, reads in part, "When necessary, the IRBs may seek expert consultants to assist in the review of research that requires expertise beyond or in addition to that available on the IRBs" (p.36). Clearly members of the IRBs have the authority to seek subject matter consultation when their knowledge is limited.

4.3   *Mitch*

This raises questions about both the composition of the IRB and communica-tion among its members. Does the IRB draw from, represent and benefit from the diversity of expertise and experience among the faculty of the institution? The availability of outside experts certainly is an option that can enhance and strengthen the activities of the IRB and, by extension, the research program of the institution, especially when extremely specialized projects are being undertaken. However, in most cases, it seems that large organizations such as CUNY generally should be able to provide the professional capability to assess and advise on the vast majority of proposed research endeavors using entirely internal resources.

4.4   *Malgorzata*

Ken's good suggestions as quoted above by Mitch might be long overdue and if/when implemented, they could help move us in what we consider a desirable direction. However, it is hardly a secret that academia suffers from high levels of institutional inertia that generally stifle change or at least the speed with which it occurs. The state of affairs is quite ironic when we consider that one major purpose of academia is to generate knowledge. As remarked by Lev Vygotsky (1997) below, our search for new knowledge may necessitate explorations of novel methodological approaches.

> In studying any new area, it is necessary to begin by seeking and developing a method. In the form of a general position, we might say that every basically new approach to scientific problems leads inevitably to new methods and ways of research. (p. 27)

In addition, as noted by Egon Guba (1981), when deciding on (or evaluating) a research paradigm (e.g., choosing between *rationalistic* and *naturalistic* approach), the issue should not be assumptions of which paradigm are "true" (i.e., superior) but rather which offer the best fit to the phenomenon under study. Already, at the time his article was published, Guba pointed to the increasing number of investigators who "have become convinced of the relative utility of the naturalistic paradigm for studying that class of phenomena that often is called social/behavioral" (p. 77). Still, too many of our colleagues continue to be challenged by the academic "establishment" for engaging in research that does not conform to positivist (rationalist) paradigms. Among them are Gene Fellner, Helen Kwah, and Peter Waldman (in press) who use narrative and visual forms of expression to explore possibilities for alternative ontologies or ways of knowing and argue for the role of arts-based explorations in challenging positivism and contributing to post-humanist frameworks of being in the world. The tendency to guard the traditional ways of "doing education" certainly spills over to its other dimensions including pedagogical approaches. As we remark elsewhere (Powietrzynska & Noble, 2018), in the context of shared teaching space, my co-teacher, Linda Noble, and I are consistently chastised by our academician colleagues for "upsetting" the physical classroom setup when we convert rows of desks into a semicircle in an effort to facilitate multi-directional interactions among the participants of our graduate level course in teacher education. That to us is yet another manifestation of privileging one paradigm over another.

These undesirable experiences should not (and, so far, did not) discourage us from pursuing educational practices (including the lines of investigation) in which we believe and are passionate about. Linda and I certainly continue teaching in a semicircle and accommodate our less progressive colleagues' demands by returning the classroom set-up to the traditional form at the end of each class session. Likewise, despite the misguided IRB probes, neither Mitch's nor Manny's research efforts have been compromised or derailed. It is possibly our resilience and support by like-minded colleagues that keeps us going. However, there are ways in which an IRB may adjust its functioning to advance a more, in Mitch's words, "vibrant, diverse, eclectic, enlightening research environment" and to avoid potentially applying a single yardstick to all applications. For example, as you remark earlier and as proposed by Lynn Bryan (Tobin & Bryan, 2018), "a responsible IRB panel" should strive for having "adequate representation so as to be able to evaluate qualitative methods – grounded in diverse frameworks such as hermeneutics, phenomenology, and ethnomethodology – in terms of ethics and risk to human participants/ co-researchers" (p. 11). Alternatively, as noted by Manny above, absent such representation, an IRB panel has an option (an obligation?) to recruit relevant expertise whenever such is warranted. The question is what possible structures might need to be reckoned with in order to accomplish such changes: funding, institutional hierarchies, administrative red tape, etc. Amdur (2006) actually admits that a practice of asking for consultant opinions on a case-by-case basis is likely to be "awkward and inefficient." Instead, he provides solutions enacted in some institutions such as having a representative(s) of the investigator's department review the protocol prior to it being forwarded to IRB.

University IRBs may actually learn a lesson or two from the manner research review process is enacted by none other than the New York City Department of Education (NYC DOE) – at least in the way I experienced it. When, following my university-based research projects, an opportunity presented itself to conduct a study in a public high school setting, I needed to secure an approval from the NYC DOE IRB. Contrary to my expectations, I found the process to be fairly straightforward and consistent with the intended objectives of IRB. The advantages of the NYC DOE approach include: (1) availability of clear guidelines (particularly helpful for the first-time application filers like me)[1]; (2) an intuitive and relatively easy-to-navigate on-line application system[2] which, in my view, is superior to that currently used by our university; (3) high levels of responsiveness by the IRB representatives and a quick turnaround time from application to approval; and (4) most important, an exclusive focus on ensuring protection of the research participants rather than questioning the proposed methodology. The two DOE IRB members with whom my co-PI and I interacted requested a few adjustments that appeared to have been prompted by the fact that high school students are minors and are therefore considered by federal regulations as part of "vulnerable" or "special" classes requiring particular protections. Taken from our email correspondence, the following quote by one of the panel members appears to aim at ensuring that a potential risk of coercion is minimized:

> Parent consent and student assent should be handled separately. The assent form should not be sent home with students. It should be administered at another time in the school. Students have the right to not participate even if parents give consent. The concern is that parents would influence the student's decision.

This instance illustrates that, as pointed out at the beginning of this piece, IRBS play an important role in ensuring that research participants, particularly those within vulnerable populations, enjoy protections from undue harms. At times, well-intentioned researchers like my co-PI and I may need guidance in making certain that no aspect of our planned investigation creates a potential for adversely impacting our recruits. No matter how noble our intentions may be and who or what may drive our epistemological quests, there is no doubt that IRBS are there to prevent anyone from ever again attempting to use (concentration camp) prisoners or enslaved peoples, or *any* group – vulnerable or otherwise – as "subjects" of inhumanely conducted medical, surgical, or other forms of experiments "for the benefit of science." Furthermore, while I'm not an expert in the laws regulating animal-based research, I would hope that protections similar to those enjoyed by humans are ultimately also extended to all sentient beings.

4.5 Manny

We must take every opportunity to illuminate our important research activities which are conducted at our institutions. It has been my experience that budding researchers want to learn about the various alternate and complementary research methodologies and methods used to contribute to theoretical generalizability (Eisenhart, 2009). I remain excited to participate in discussions with the academic community about event oriented inquiry, heuristics, and cogenerative dialogues (Tobin & Richie, 2012). Certainly, my university's vice chancellor for research and the director for research compliance must be aware of such various diverse methods and frameworks, as should the appropriate administrators at every other institution where research is done. It is especially important to continue to conduct research and produce knowledge for ontological, educative, and catalytic beneficence (Tobin & Ritchie, 2012).

4.6 *Mitch*

I think that each of us has considered elimination of the IRB or strictly confining it to the evaluation of researchers' methods for ethical practice. Perhaps, however, a more viable approach to institutional interaction with research that takes place under its auspices is called for.

First and foremost, all institutions should be actively concerned with the ethical treatment of research participants. But, institutions could and should bring their resources to bear in the support of students, faculty and staff who engage in the scholarship and professional work that constitute part or the entirety of their work at those institutions. Rather than a process of semi-anonymous approval via electronic application, committees of colleagues (perhaps, heavily weighted to members within the researchers' fields, and, perhaps, nominated or selected by the researchers) could evaluate and advise before and during the active period of the research projects. Of course, unless clear (but not rigid) guidelines for these committees (entities) are set, we will not avoid the kinds of problems we've been discussing here. Committees would not approve, but provide non-binding written and/or face-to-face advice recommendations. In addition, the committee also would evaluate the work for ethical practices. The recommendations concerning ethical practices in their work may be obligatory, but also subject to an appeals process that would include additional institutional personnel beyond the members of the committee.

Such a rethinking of the role of institutions in supporting research would see the IRB, in consultation with the researcher(s) and, in the case of doctoral students, the committee, fulfill the narrow function of ensuring that any research conducted under the auspices of its institution, maintains ethical practices and preserves and protects the rights of all research participants. In order to accomplish this wisely and thoughtfully, it is necessary that the IRB as a whole encompasses the general and specific expertise of its members *and* exercises the ability to consult with the committee and outside resources to develop a level of understanding that will enable them to make informed and sensible recommendations.

In the case of much social science research, this transformation must include reinterpreting, or better revising and expanding evaluation criteria so that the IRB no longer finds itself appraising naturalistic research using guidelines (along with a shoehorn) intended for very different work.

The questions about generalizability I encountered when applying for IRB approval are emblematic (but by no means constitute the totality) of this problem. My phenomenological inquiry was challenged as to its generalizability and its predictive value. Of course, one goal I have for my work is that it provides value and benefit both to participants and to the broader universe of readers and professionals. But concepts of generalizability that bow to a rationalistic paradigm do not promote and support the kinds of inquiry that are widely employed in social science research. Viability, dependability, fittingness are among the utility criteria cited by Guba, Lincoln, Tobin, Fellner, Kwah, Waldman, Powietrzynska, Noble (all referenced elsewhere in this chapter) and a growing body of social science researchers, as more appropriate measures of the value of social science research than traditional notions of generalizability. Of course, utility of research often materializes only after it is in the hands of the reader long after the researchers have published their work, letting it go into the world to partner with future researchers and consumers who breathe life into it and use it to generate knowledge about the world beyond what the authors could even have conceived.

In short, I suggest that the IRB should be more of a supportive and advisory body in addition to its function as an ethical gatekeeper. This leads me to believe that the minimal condition of ethical arbiter should be a requirement, but institutions may and should choose to expand the advisory (but not gatekeeping) role of the IRB. Some, perhaps many of my colleagues believe that my vision of an expanded and supportive structure for review and approval of research is both desirable and unlikely to ever materialize. They offer as support for their position the difficulties and lack of agreement that can happen even now within a doctoral candidate's committee or among the IRB as it is now structured. This may be true, but it is an idea with such a potential for benefit that it is well worth struggling toward.

Notes

1   See http://schools.nyc.gov/NR/rdonlyres/A20C1F79-E3CC-4734-B704-A62C93487896/0/
Proposal_Guidelines_Revised2242014.pdf
2   See IRBManager.com

References

Alexakos, K. (2015). *Being a teacher | researcher: A primer on doing authentic inquiry research on teaching and learning.* Sense Publishers.

Amdur, R. J.(2006). Evaluating study design and quality. In E. A. Bankert & R. J. Amdur (Eds.), *Institutional review board: Management and function.* Jones and Bartlett Publishers.

City University of New York. (2016). *CUNY HRPP policies and procedures.* http://www2.cuny.edu/wp-content/uploads/sites/4/page-assets/research/research-compliance/human-research-protection-program-hrpp/hrpp-policies-procedures/2016.09.09-HRPP-Policy-master-doc-FINAL.pdf

Eisenhart, M. (2009). Generalization from qualitative inquiry. In K. Ercikan & W.-M. Roth (Eds.), *Generalizing from educational research* (pp. 51–66). Routledge.

Kwah, H., Fellner, G., & Waldman, P. (2020). After positivism: Three scenes in a bricolage. *Taboo: The Journal of Culture and Education, 19*(2), 6–21.

Flynn, M. (2018, April 18). Statue of 'father of gynecology,' who experimented on enslaved women, removed from Central Park. *Washington Post.* https://www.washingtonpost.com/news/morning-mix/wp/2018/04/18/statue-of-father-of-gynecology-who-experimented-on-enslaved-women-removed-from-central-park/?utm_term=.9533c01c21da

Guba, E. G. (1981). Criteria for assessing the trustworthiness of naturalistic inquiries. *Educational Communication and Technology, 29*(2), 75–91.

Powietrzynska, M. (2015). Heuristics for mindfulness in education and beyond. In C. Milne, K. Tobin, & D. Degenero (Eds.), *Sociocultural studies and implications for science education: The experiential and the virtual* (pp. 59–80). Springer.

Powietrzynska, M., & Noble, L. (2018). Mindfulness – Seeping through the cracks in the American context of teacher education. *Learning: Research and Practice, 4*(1), 66–77. doi:10.1080/23735082.2018.1428140

Tobin, K. (2007). Research with human participants. *Cultural Studies of Science Education, 2*(4), 703–710. https://doi.org/10.1007/s11422-007-9073-x

Tobin, K., & Bryan, L. (2018). Bold visions for science education: A metalogue. In L. Bryan & K. Tobin (Eds.), *Critical issues and bold visions for science education: The road ahead* (pp. 1–15). Brill | Sense.

Tobin, K., & Richie, S. (2012). Multi-method, multi-theoretical, multi-level research in the learning sciences. *The Asia -Pacific Education Researcher, 21*(1), 117–129.

Vygotsky, L. S. (1997). *The history of the development of the higher mental functions.* Plenum Press.

CHAPTER 18

Purposeful Research for Transformation and the Greater Good

Kenneth Tobin and Konstantinos Alexakos

Abstract

We begin this chapter with a review of where our research started and foundations which are intuitive, emergent, contingent, and oriented toward transforming practice in ways that empower learners. We address evolution of our multilogical methodology, which includes authentic and event-oriented inquiry and embraces high value for transformative research with the intention of serving the greater good. Benefits of our research are expected to catalyze changes in the lives of all those who participate and those with whom they interact.

Challenging present times call for research that educates the citizenry to change lifestyles for the purpose of knowing ourselves and changing practices to enhance wellness and well-being. Changes extend beyond individuals who need to know and act to sustain harmony in fragile ecosystems that include living and nonliving components.

Keywords

multilogicality – emergence and contingence – transformative research – wellness – well-being

1   Research Purpose

What am I here for? What is the meaning of life? We only speak for ourselves, but these are questions that are with us now, and as variants, have been with us from the beginning. Clearly, the questions are context dependent. Who's asking them, and in what circumstances? Every moment of life, every now, has the potential to generate a different array of responses. How do education researchers, and more generally researchers in the social sciences and humanities, respond to the two questions today? In this chapter we work our way back to these questions as first we look at the roots of our research practices, examine emergence and contingence as overarching schemas for our research, look into some trends that tend to stagnate research and researcher roles in a quagmire of insignificance, review a pathway toward research that makes a difference, and study the potential of a focus on know myself, as a mantra for research in contexts that are arguably some of the greatest worldwide threats to humanity – the Covid-19 pandemic, poverty and social inequities, racial and social injustice.

2 Genesis of Our Multilogical Research

From the very beginning of our journey into academic research, which for Ken was 1973 and with Konstantinos in the early 2000s, we were driven by a desire to improve the quality of teaching and learning. Ken was inspired by the revolutionary aspects of Mary Budd Rowe's research on wait-time and her willingness to understand spikes in the curve. Rowe listened to approximately 300 audiotapes of classrooms that were trialing the Science Curriculum Improvement Study (Rowe, 1969). Only three of the tapes exhibited evidence of verbal inquiry. Rowe set out to ascertain what it was about those three different tapes that led to the highly desirable patterns of inquiry that were the goal of so many curriculum projects developed in the 1960s. She became aware that in those classes, the average wait-time was more than three seconds (Rowe, 1974a, 1974b). In contrast, the average wait-time in a vast majority of classes was less than one second.

What appealed to Ken about Rowe's research was that her mode of inquiry differed radically from research designs used at the time. Indeed, her approach was unique and involved a great deal of what we have portrayed in this book as emergent and contingent, interpretive, event-oriented, and authentic inquiry (Rowe, 1974c). Furthermore, Rowe's research was overtly theoretical. She recognized effective teaching and learning and used her own theoretical lenses to view and analyze what was happening, why it was happening, and what more was there.

Unfortunately, although the exemplary nature of her research was recognized by many of her colleagues, the mainstream was not publishing much research of this type. It was a credit to her that Rowe found ways to disseminate what she learned from her research and inspired others to follow in her footsteps. Unfortunately, the social context of the time did not support a quest to develop her research further within a multilogical frame, such as we have been privileged to develop, use, and expand. Our methodologies | methods are grounded in an intuitive, emergent, and passive approach we have pursued after Ken was drawn to research by Rowe's willingness to learn from what she and others experience in their practice, in this case teaching and learning science.

For Konstantinos, his beginning in academic research would probably be in taking classes with whom would later on become his dissertation advisor, Angela Calabrese Barton. Calabrese Barton's emphasis on her doctoral students having a voice allowed and encouraged Konstantinos to go beyond the traditional dissertation research and begin to align his research with his own interests in sociocultural questions. Ken was a guest speaker in one of her classes and this is where they first met. It was Ken's interests in mindfulness and wellness for teachers and their students that brought us together as research partners and coteachers and ultimately close friends, collaborators and companions in our life journeys. Our research has grown to beyond just observe or test questions to exploring the "so what?" what more is there, and much more important; how do we intervene and transform once we decide that change is what we want or what is necessary?

3   Emergence and Contingence as Overarching Tenets of Our Multilogical Design

Is my design all right? One of our doctoral students, who was involved in cutting-edge research, sent Ken some examples of what she was receiving from participants she had selected to write a journal to capture their narratives about lived experiences. The journal entries provided deep insights into issues that emerged as the study progressed. Ken's email response to her indicated the pleasure he experienced as he read her message and excerpts she provided from the journal i.e., "this is fantastic!" The student replied with humor, almost immediately: "but is the design okay?" Although her response to Ken was partially in jest, it underlines the pervasiveness of ever-present doubts, fueled by crypto-positivism (Kincheloe & Tobin, 2009) – that cast uncertainties on central issues such as what counts as "scientific" research? We have used emergence and contingence as overarching tenets for a multilogical approach to social inquiry for more than 20 years. Newcomers, often delighted to engage emancipatory methodologies that involve use of flexible designs, often get swamped by concerns that colleagues may regard their work as nonscientific. As we have illustrated in the chapters of this book, and two companions to be published in the months ahead (Tobin & Alexakos, forthcoming-a, forthcoming-b), our research identifies new avenues to investigate, and provides insights that are potential catalysts for transforming both the personal as well as the social dynamics of teaching and learning, not only in schools and colleges, but also in myriad institutions, throughout the lifeworld, in which teaching and learning occur, with and without conscious awareness (e.g., home, workplace, leisure, hospital, nursing home).

Here we use a construct of passivity as a dialectical partner with agency. That is, within a cultural field, the passivity | agency (dialectical) relationship is ever present (Roth, 2007). Passivity is to open up to learn from the structures of the field – to radically prostrate and learn from myriad schemas and practices that are continuously flowing in a dynamic flux, through the field (Lévinas, 1999). Continuously flowing culture in which all participants reproduce | transform culture (i.e., learning). To be passive is to be receptive, to open oneself to the field's cultural flux without seeking to appropriate structures to pursue particular goals. The purpose is to notice what is happening without reacting, avoiding, or appropriating. This approach is similar to Vipassana meditation and mindfulness, as described earlier by Rhoda Wong (Chapter 6).

Emergent and contingent designs are flexible, adaptive to contingencies associated with answers we obtained to broad questions, including: What is happening? Why is it happening? What have we learned so far? And what do we want to learn next?

3.1   *Quantitative, Qualitative, and Mixed Methods*

Jennifer, a doctoral student, requested an interview with Ken, as part of an assignment for one of her courses. She sent three questions that would provide a basis for the interview. The third question was: do you have any advice as I consider a qualitative case study or look to add to that and include a quantitative measure for a mixed methods approach?

In Ken's response, that welcomed a forthcoming interview to discuss the questions she raised, he attached Chapters 2 and 3 from this book and, in the following manner, addressed some aspects associated with the third question:

> Ken: I am very much opposed to the term "mixed methods" since everything we do involves mixed methods and yet people who like to use the terms qualitative and quantitative research find it useful to muddy the waters even further with the use of a term like mixed methods. At the Graduate Center we have spent a lot of time developing authentic inquiry and event-oriented inquiry as important components that embrace multilogicality.

Here in this closing chapter for this volume on doing purposeful, transformative research, we explore three issues in greater depth. First, as Ken and Joe Kincheloe noted in 2006, continued use of labels qualitative and quantitative research are limiting and obfuscate the logics of inquiry, often moving forward in ways that are consistent with crypto-positivism. From our standpoint, qualitative and quantitative refer to datatypes that are appropriate for many approaches to research. It seems imperative that researchers adopt a reflexive approach when explaining the core principles of their research – be aware of these principles and explicit about how they play out in a particular study. For example, the methodologies | methods we employ in our ongoing social inquiry include many data forms if and as desirable. What we consider to be paramount is why we find particular data forms useful in our research and how each affords insights into emergent questions we seek to answer. Accordingly, we strongly recommend that those who include research methods courses in their programs desist from a pervasive practice of labeling what is in the courses as qualitative and quantitative research. In taking this strong stance we acknowledge the historical rationale for use of qualitative research by pioneers of the use of ethnography, narrative and autobiography in educational research. These researchers suffered many forms of social violence as they sought to disseminate what they had learned at conferences and when they submitted their work for peer review to publish in journals and books. Of course, when published, the hostilities continued and, in some cases, intensified in crypto-positivistic critiques from mainstream academics.

Ken lived through these times when he commenced his early research. Scientism was pervasive and randomized selection and assignment of subjects to treatment groups were considered a gold standard. Quasi-experimental research was accepted as a probable approach to research that most education researchers would engage. Indeed, Russell Yeany Jr., a leading science educator of the time, taught his doctoral students that they should sleep with the ubiquitous text by Donald Campbell and Julian Stanley (1963) under their pillow. He joked that perhaps some of the text would be absorbed into students' brains during a good night of sleep. Since the 1960s this slim 84-page textbook has morphed into a mammoth volume of 656 pages (Shadish, Cook, & Campbell, 2001) – too fat to sleep on!

From our standpoint, it is well past due for doctoral studies curricula to be revamped so that outmoded ideas are not perpetuated in requirements. For example, when the doctorate in Urban Education, at the Graduate Center, was revised, the faculty voted to require that in addition to a core course, entitled Introduction to Research Methods in Urban Education, students are "required to take 9 credits of courses related to methodology, one in quantitative research, one in qualitative research methods, and an advanced research methods course." Just prior to this revamp of the curriculum, a required core course entitled Logics of Inquiry and another entitled Structure of Social Knowledge were deleted from the curriculum. To our way of thinking, these curricular changes were regressive and, at least for our students, did not provide theoretical and methodological | methods foundations needed to engage cutting-edge research in our ongoing research. Obtaining the required knowledge necessitated participation in research from the very beginning of the doctoral program, active involvement in seminars, and regular research squad meetings. Of course, the question to address is why is it necessary to do the courses if they are not aligned with a candidate's goals for doing doctoral education?

A critical issue to be considered in relation to doctoral degrees concerns the relative importance of coursework in what is regarded a terminal degree. How much coursework is actually needed and what is the justification for core courses? How are they of use to the students? The US model for PhD typically involves coursework – with the nature of the courses varying quite a lot, even within PhD programs in the same university. In contrast, in many other countries, a PhD is a research only degree – with no required coursework. We imagine for some students one or the other of the two would be preferable while for many others the need will be somewhere in between. We think it is time for education PhD programs to reconsider the virtues of these different structures and create new models that educate doctoral students to meet the challenging times we face today.

Mixed methods also is a label that started out as a compromise between those advocating for quantitative and qualitative research respectively. In fact, Ken has several well cited publications from the 1990s that advocated for utilizing both qualitative and quantitative methods (Fraser & Tobin, 1991, 1992; Tobin & Fraser, 1998). However, that was many years ago and the tools we have to do educational research are superior in many ways in 2020. Also, since we began our collaboration with Joe Kincheloe, we have employed methodologies | methods that are mixed, in much more sophisticated ways than is encapsulated in the commonly used label of mixed methods. Like Corinna Zapata's discussion on oximeters in her chapter (Chapter 8) we see methods as tools for a particular job. Rather than the artificial dichotomy between methods such as quantitative, qualitative, ethnographic, etc., we prefer the term multilogical, employing multiple methods as needed to get multiple perspectives, understandings and "truths" about what we are researching. We see the future of social inquiry in terms of research methodologies | methods that remove the shackles from researchers so that an expansion occurs to include fresh ways of theorizing what is happening and why it is happening.

The recently announced Age of Anthropocene (e.g., Maslin & Lewis, 2020), draws attention to the extent of human's influence include myriad ways that necessitate things like habitat destruction due to climate change, pollution, and ecosystem instabilities and destruction that threaten mass extinctions, including that of humans unless reversals occur. Is the citizenry (here we mean not a particular, official, nationalistically exclusive category but all members of society) sufficiently well-educated to face a pandemic that threatens human life and social institutions such as employment, education, health and the stability of the food supply? How can we expand the lenses for researching interactions that are salient to wellness and sustainability that involve humans interacting with other humans, other animal species and plants, as well as those, like mountains, air, water, oceans that are presently classified as inanimate?

Furthermore, the two of us are strongly influenced in our ways of thinking about research now and in the coming years by our personal experiences and interests with healing arts – experiences that push the boundaries on how to be in the world, understand what is happening, and contemplate ways of sustaining and enhancing the quality of being – not just for humanity, but for the ecosystem as a whole – harmony and cooperation being overarching tenets for the research we value for today and tomorrow.

4   Research That Makes a Difference

In 1978, Ken began his doctoral degree at the University of Georgia, which, at the time, he judged to be the preeminent institution in the world for research in science education. Within a month or so of his arrival, Ken was speaking with James Okey, who informed him that the faculty was considering a change in the dissertation requirements. A recent publication in *Bioscience*, by Malcolm Reid (1978), addressed an issue of whether the dissertation had become "an academic anachronism" (Chernin, 1975). Reid explained that some faculties had advocated abandoning dissertations entirely. He explained that dissertations are rarely read and cited, the number of publications from dissertations is relatively low, and writing a dissertation does not prepare researchers to publish papers. Other noteworthy points raised by Reid include dissertations increasing in length, often including material that is of little use to others, and graduates not reworking and submitting papers for publication of important research in the dissertation. Reid recommended that "requirements that a candidate must produce an expansive traditional-style dissertation for a PhD degree in the sciences must be abandoned (p. 653). As a solution, Reid proposed a journal style dissertation. In making a case for journal style, Reid indicated it had been used at the University of Georgia for 10 years, but that faculty resistance was a major obstacle, some arguing that "education, in order to be good, must be painful and difficult ... Training of the mind occurs through disciplined academic studies" (Tronsgard, 1963).

The Science Education faculty at the University of Georgia rejected the idea, of a journal style dissertation, but left open the door to consider cases based on individual merits. A year or so later, Okey approached Ken with the suggestion that he apply to submit a journal style dissertation. In 1980 Ken defended his dissertation, consisting of 11 chapters – 9 manuscripts book ended by an introduction and a conclusion. Each of the manuscripts either was good to go, or needed only minor revisions before submission. One paper was published in 1980, three in 1981, three in 1982. In 1987 too, an expanded version of the literature review from the dissertation was published. In addition, Ken was encouraged to write derivative papers for teachers, teacher educators, and researchers. One derivative paper was published in 1981, three in 1982, one in 1983, six in 1984, and one in 1985.

As a contrast, Ken submitted a master's degree thesis at the West Australian Institute of Technology, in 1977 without being aware of the importance, indeed the obligation, to publish what is being learned from the research in journals. He only published one manuscript from his thesis that contained considerably more publishable material. This manuscript was published in 1980 at the urging of his advisors at the University of Georgia. This is a clear example of the points made by Reid. If Ken had written a manuscript style dissertation for his master's degree it is likely that 4–5 additional manuscripts would have been published in international journals. We note that failure to publish was not indicative of not publishing in journals. Prior to 1980, Ken published eight papers – none from research in his master's thesis or doctoral dissertation.

When Ken began to supervise doctoral students in 1987, he advised them that the default structure was manuscript style (i.e., for journals and book chapters). Since then 64 doctoral students have graduated with Ken as advisor/major professor and only a small number deviated from manuscript style. Most of the exceptions opted for a monograph style, these being published as books. None of the 64 followed a traditional five-chapter standard form for writing the dissertation.

4.1   *And 20 Years Later ...*

Nell Duke and Sarah Beck (1999) reviewed doctoral dissertations in education. They reported that in 1991, the Council of Graduate Schools stated that 9 out of 48 graduate schools surveyed (i.e., 19%), provided alternative optional structures for a dissertation. Duke and Beck offered several alternative formats for the dissertation. Their primary goals were to disseminate in ways that reached a wider audience and use a format that would prepare graduates for the type of writing they need to do throughout their career. The first option they provided was a manuscript style dissertation. Depending on the goals of the PhD candidate, the structure could include emphases on any of the following: articles for researchers, teachers, teacher educators, and policymakers. The dissertation could provide a sampling of chapters featuring each category and an emphasis on one of the categories. For example, three chapters featuring research, and one each focusing on teacher education, practice teaching, and policymaking.

After also reviewing strengths of the traditional format, Duke and Beck conclude that (p. 35):

> It is incumbent upon this field to adapt the dissertation to meet the professional demands faced by its members and thus to make the best possible use of this enduring institution.

When Ken did his doctoral degree in 1978, the idea of a journal style dissertation was already used by a small number of faculty in PhD programs, mainly in the sciences. It was a big leap for educators to move away from traditional approaches, and Ken was the first person to deviate from the traditional style in the science education program at the University of Georgia. As often is the case, ripple effects afforded changes wherever Ken taught, and most, but not all of his students also advocated manuscript style dissertations when they became professors. However, as Duke and Best show in their article, even by the end of the 20th century there were still calls for fresh options for the traditional monograph that has been standard fare for doctoral dissertations.

The situation described by Reid, in 1978, is somewhat similar to that which has occurred in the 20-year history of the Urban Education PhD program at the Graduate Center. In order to get a feel for the trend in dissertation structure over the past seven years, Ken examined all 100 dissertations written by graduates in the period from 2014–2020. Fifty three of the 100 dissertations were traditional in structure. That is, most students wrote a traditional 5–7-chapter dissertation (i.e., introduction, literature review, methods, results, conclusions). Furthermore, another 20 dissertations (bringing the total to 73 out of 100) also were traditional in their structure, just a few chapters longer. The additional chapters focused on reporting different sets of results. Aligning with the trend Reid noted, these 20 dissertations involved bigger studies and were lengthier.

Ken observed a trend for faculty advisors – each of their advisees has much the same dissertation style. We (Konstantinos and Ken) fit this pattern since we both advise all, or almost all, of our students to write a manuscript style dissertation. Most other advisors recommend that their students write a traditional style dissertation. The analysis showed a pattern very similar to that described by Reid.

Only three faculty members were associated with students writing manuscript style dissertation (Ken, Konstantinos, and Jennifer Adams). Seventeen dissertations featured manuscript style. Finally, four manuscripts were monographs, two of them published as books (i.e., in total, 73% traditional, 17% manuscript style, and 2% monographs published as books, 2% monographs not published. The remaining 6 (6%) were not available online.

Issues associated with writing a dissertation intersect with our values and preferences for multilogical methodologies | methods and associated ways of seeing, valuing, and being in the world. Our research journey, the recent parts of which are represented in this volume and two to be published companion volumes have moved the focus of our research to embrace social research on learning, teaching, and being, outside of the traditional institutional framework (e.g., schools, colleges, museums, zoos). For a good number of years, we have advocated for research along the birth through death continuum, situated in diverse contexts/institutions, such as monastery, cheese cave, nursing home, hospital, hospice, dojo, ashram, home, workplace, and garden.

Change has been slow to come for a variety of reasons, the primary reason being that the vast majority of colleagues support the status quo. Within our institution a relatively small number of like-minded individuals, usually tenured and fully promoted, forged new pathways and attracted a steady stream of students. That said, we frequently felt oppressive forces that limited resources, diverting them toward mainstream projects. Those who were untenured felt vulnerable and many were deterred from moving away from the center – a center supported by crypto-positivism and a long tradition.

4.2   *Moving beyond Standard Form and Manuscript Styles*

One of Anthony Paré's (2017) recommendations, with which we resonate, is to study a multidisciplinary team of academics and non-academics. The activity is an internship which includes an action research that is situated at the site of the internship. This suggestion gives priority for educators to engage more with society and on a birth through death continuum. Sites for internships would include nontraditional institutions (i.e., beyond the Academy), such as hospitals, churches, hospices, nursing homes, healing arts centers, and sports organizations. Paré addresses an issue of learning to write active, living texts that focus on, "just-in-time instruction, delivered at the very moment when they matter and when their import is obvious" (p. 414). Paré noted that,

There is a growing sense that a key academic text, the monograph dissertation, no longer does the work it needs to do. And even its main alternative, the manuscript dissertation, fails to engage doctoral students in the range of rhetorical activities that have become commonplace in contemporary scientific and scholarly life. Moreover, its decline as an effective genre has been precipitous – largely within a single generation – and many scholars and institutions are struggling to catch up with the times. (p. 416)

Paré calls for a multimodal approach that provides the scope for students to produce a portfolio in which artifacts, such as the following are included: papers of various genres, such as book reviews, newsletter articles, blog posts, conference papers, and grant proposals. In addition, relevant poems, innovative theater, in visual arts might be included. Multimedia also can be incorporated to include creative magazines for selective audiences, an interactive website, documentary film, radio show, and a YouTube channel.

Similarly, in a White paper, the Institute for the Public Life of Arts and Ideas, at McGill University, exhorted graduate programs to consider a portfolio as a replacement for the doctoral dissertation:

The contents of the portfolio, which could be negotiated with a student's committee initially and revised as the work progressed, could include single- and multi-authored projects in a variety of media and modes, including academic and non-academic articles, edited book chapters, a blog, conference papers, video productions and other projects ... Each project aims toward a form of publication – an essay in an academic journal, a long article in a public affairs or arts magazine, an interactive website, a documentary film or radio show, an innovative theatre or visual arts program, etc. (2013, p. 15)

We endorse the portfolio idea because it is a critical next step in authentic inquiry. As we enact authentic inquiry, it is imperative for catalytic authenticity and social justice (i.e., tactical authenticity) that appropriate media are used to educate as many stakeholders as possible about what we are learning from research. Using approaches such as those listed above (e.g., YouTube channel or Zoom-based seminar), researchers are not deviating from the research design, instead they are diligently following an emergent and contingent pathway that creates ripples, disseminates what is being learned to those involved in the study, while expanding those who are involved by reaching out in ways that are accessible to particular participants. In this way, research is not anchored in the 1970s, or even earlier, but is responsive to now, and those who are collaborating with us on the grand challenges of life in this world now.

Paré's advocacy for change has many admirable aspects. Researchers should have facility with the day's tools, and employ them as appropriate, most often in an emergent and contingent way. Accordingly, we should see blogs, tweets, wiki sites, webpages, podcasts, and videos as integral parts of disseminating what we learn from authentic inquiry. Furthermore, creating a documentary for the purposes of disseminating research is a powerful way to educate a population that accepts streaming from smart TV, smart phones, and laptops as part of everyday life. As we tackle crises of representation we should move beyond single authored, print-based texts to incorporate collaborative and digital media as a matter of routine.

5   Expanding Possibilities and Curiosities

It is difficult to see how science education can survive for much longer. Arguably, the need for science education has never been stronger. In a context of global warming, climate change, and a Covid-19 pandemic, Glenn Kessler, Salvador Rizzo, and Meg Kelly (2020) noted that:

> It took President Trump 827 days to top 10,000 false and misleading claims … an average of 12 claims a day. But on July 9, just 440 days later, the president crossed the 20,000 mark – an average of 23 claims a day over a 14-month period, which included the events leading up to Trump's impeachment trial, the worldwide pandemic that crashed the economy and the eruption of protests over the death of George Floyd in police custody.

The president's false claims about medical science in the pandemic are legendary as is his inability or unwillingness to interpret data correctly. Cable TV channels and programs, many of which run 24×7, are compelled to report most of what Trump says and does, exposing a litany of lies throughout every day, and providing consumers a choice of believing a president or believing panels of experts. Every TV channel has its own set of experts – intensive care physicians, epidemiologists, and University medical staff of all ranks, for example. Occasionally, scientists are called to join the panel, respond to questions, or speculate on endless what if scenarios. However, in all our time in the United States, we are yet to see a science educator on one of the panels, or for that matter author an Op Ed piece for one of the leading newspapers. When it comes to the grand challenges that face us now, science education is silent when it comes to educating the public at large. We point out that it is not a question of the agency of science educators, but rather their lack of esteem in society.

If an expert on education is needed every now and then, a school superintendent, principal, or public-school teacher will appear – but such occasions are rare. Basically, whatever it is that science educators do, it is not valued highly or perceived to be relevant to the pandemic. So, who has the responsibility and the will to seize the initiative to educate the citizenry for life now? What do citizens need to know to identify a president's false science claims as lies, and what must they do when they know the president is lying? Questions such as these are at the heart of a democracy.

Ever since the beginning of March it has been well-nigh impossible to get medical treatment for non-life-threatening ailments. This situation draws attention to a mantra we have strongly supported as a crucial role for literate citizenry – know yourself. We value highly the idea that from birth until death all people should learn continuously to monitor their body, notice signs of illness, and understand how to address minor symptoms such as body aches and pains, colds and flu, and other projects such as coughing, elevated temperatures, and excess discharges from the body. What we have in mind extends far beyond anatomy and physiology. Whereas it may be useful to name and locate organs, bones, and muscles, for example, we emphasize personal knowledge that can tie to lifestyle decisions and ways to facilitate the body growing, restoring, and replacing cells, organs, and systems.

We see education of the type needed to know our body as occurring in myriad institutions, not only schools, colleges, museums, and zoos. Indeed, we see a good beginning in the earlier conversation about University faculty and PhD graduates being highly educated to use YouTube channels, wikis, Zoom-type seminars, blogs, podcasts, and focused news releases. By active participation in spreading what we know through media and genres like these, the ripple effects associated with our ongoing research will be enhanced – thereby affording an accumulation of transformations that will, over time, be perceived as significant societal change. We emphasize that science educators in particular, and educators more generally, have to effectively communicate with the entire citizenry to attain the status of being considered relevant in today's universe and all that it entails.

A second aspect of know myself is the mind. In our research, we have been involved in meditation and mindfulness practices for more than a decade. Recently we studied Vipassana meditation and mindfulness with a former monk as our teacher. The Vipassana approach was in the Thai forest tradition that passed through Luangpor Pramote. In this practice, as Yau Yan Wong

(Chapter 7) made clear, practitioners notice changes in the body and in the mind and come to realize the salience of impermanence. As anger arises in the mind, the meditating person does not try to prevent it from rising, but simply notes its rise and fall. Similarly, any changes in the body are noted, and there is no effort to prevent such changes or to force the mind to focus on the breath. Instead, the meditator becomes a stable observer who watches and notices changes in the body and the mind.

We regard meditation and mindfulness as core practices that are likely linked to wellness of all humans. We see additional research on different approaches to meditation and mindfulness and its infusion into everyday life as fertile grounds for research and education for the citizenry.

There is more we can do. Our research has shown various links to emotions and the body's physiology. Already there is much we can disseminate to the citizenry in the ways to which we have alluded earlier in this section. For example, we know that breathing in softly (inhalation and exhalation) can increase the oxygen flow to the cells. Similarly, nasal breathing, in and out, can promote parasympathetic functioning of the body and thereby operate the body in ways that facilitate social communication and collective tools needed for cooperation and group success. Hence, educating children and adults to breathe, when awake and asleep, through the nose is a high priority. We feel that for this to happen, people need to know themselves in this regard – do they breathe predominantly in and out through the nose when they are awake? What about when they are asleep?

The issues raised here are just the tip of an iceberg. If we regard our research as authentic, then we want ripple effects to search through the community as a whole so that lifestyle changes will occur and result in an improved society.

We broaden this discussion by expanding from wellness and its focus on individuals to well-being, which we associate with ecosystems. Here the focus is on what we consider living and nonliving, and within living – we do not prioritize humanity as having primary importance. Instead, we focus on harmony and equilibria within the chains of an ecosystem, and we recognize that any broken links in a chain can have catastrophic consequences. In a quest for literate citizenry, we have a goal that all members of our society would be able to examine what is happening now in terms of interrelationships within an ecosystem and explore implications for personal lifestyles in efforts to maintain and sustain robust ecosystems. As a starting point, it behooves us to focus on the pandemic and study local contexts to ascertain what is happening, why is it happening, and what more is there to learn about what we know so far? Studies such as this, would necessarily focus on the body and the mind – first knowing ourselves and then zooming out to understand relevant ecosystems.

In studies of the body, we suggest to look beyond the physical body to include energetic body, emotional body, and spiritual body. Also, we should study the mind and we suggest good places to start include mindfulness, meditation, and Samatha practice. Knowing when and how to use Samatha to control spikes in the curve, within the body and the mind seem not only worthy, but also warranted. We regard mindfulness, meditation, and Samatha as part of a toolkit that all citizens must have, growing it from birth through death.

6   Our Research Is Never Static – Always Changing

The bricolage is a good metaphor for our multilogical research. As bricoleurs we are artists who seek answers to what is happening now and why is it happening. Then, we may know better than to assume we have all we need to have completed the study. Always there will be more. We know from experience that what is happening depends on who you ask and how you choose to look at the world. With different lenses you see different views and derive different understandings. It behooves us to continuously change our lenses as well as explore difference through the same lens.

As we learn we remain cognizant of crises of representation. We always know more than we are aware of and we can always know more than we know now. The search is emergent, contingent and without end.

Here we address the issue of whether the bricolage we use over the years is static or dynamic. Like all culture, nothing is produced exactly the same as it previously was produced. Even if we sought to use the same methodologies | methods, the best we could do is to produce what we have previously described as a family resemblance. We represent this as production = reproduction | transformation. Accordingly, similar is the closest we can come to exact. Having said this, it is not common for what we are studying to be experienced in similar ways from study to study. When spikes in the curve occur, we seek to learn more about the spikes and at the same time we use the available tools, artistically, to explore what is happening, why is it happening, and what more is there? Our explorations are expansive, not convergent and we are always looking for new theories and new methods to add to the resources that constitute the bricolage. We acknowledge that in a macro sense, what we do can be captured by the kinds of labels we have used in this volume (e.g., event-oriented inquiry) – however, the micro view will show an ever-changing flux as we employ tools that emerge with every new now, new technologies, including theories and myriad gadgets that expand our horizons of possibility and curiosity.

References

Campbell, D. T., & Stanley, J. L. (1963). *Experimental and quasi-experimental designs for research.* Rand McNally and Company.

Chernin, E. (1975). A worm's-eye view of biomedical journals. *Federation Proceedings, 34*(2), 124–130.

Council of Graduate Schools in the U.S. (1991). *The role and nature of the doctoral dissertation.* Council of Graduate Schools in the U.S. ERIC Document Reproduction Service No. ED 331 422.

Duke, N. K., & Beck, S. W. (1999). Research news and comment: Education should consider alternative formats for the dissertation. *Educational Researcher, 28*(3), 31–36. https://doi.org/10.3102/0013189X028003031

Fraser, B. J., & Tobin, K. (1991). Combining qualitative and quantitative methods in classroom environment research. In B. J. Fraser & H. J. Walberg (Eds.), *Educational environments: Evaluation, antecedents and consequences* (pp. 271–292). Pergamon Press.

Fraser, B. J., & Tobin, K. (1992). Combining qualitative and quantitative methods in the study of learning environments. In H. C. Waxman & C. D. Ellett (Eds.), *The study of learning environments* (Vol. 5, pp. 21–33). University of Houston.

Institute for the Public Life of Arts and Ideas. (2013). *White paper on the future of the PhD in the humanities.* McGill University. https://www.acfas.ca/sites/default/files/fichiers/1536/white_paper_on_the_future_of_the_phd_in_the_humanities_dec_2013_1.pdf

Kessler, G., Rizzo, S., & Kelly, M. (2020, July 13). President Trump has made more than 20,000 false or misleading claims. *Washington Post.* https://www.washingtonpost.com/politics/2020/07/13/president-trump-has-made-more-than-20000-false-or-misleading-claims/

Kincheloe, J. L., & Tobin, K. (2009). The much exaggerated death of positivism. *Cultural Studies of Science Education, 4,* 513–528. doi:10.1007/s11422-009-9178-5

Lévinas, E. (1999). *Alterity & transcendence* (M. B. Smith, Trans.). Columbia University Press.

Maslin, M., & Lewis, S. (2020, June 25). Why the Anthropocene began with European colonisation, mass slavery and the 'great dying' of the 16th century. *The Conversation.* https://theconversation.com/why-the-anthropocene-began-with-european-colonisation-mass-slavery-and-the-great-dying-of-the-16th-century-140661

Paré, A. (2017). Re-thinking the dissertation and doctoral supervision. *Journal for the Study of Education and Development, 40*(3), 407–428. doi:10.1080/02103702.2017.1341102

Reid, W. M. (1978). Will the future generations of biologists write a dissertation? *Bioscience, 28,* 651–654.

Roth, W.-M. (2007). Theorizing passivity. *Cultural Studies of Science Education, 2*, 1–8. https://doi.org/10.1007/s11422-006-9045-6

Rowe, M. B. (1969). Science, silence, and sanctions. *Science and Children, 6*(6), 11–13.

Rowe, M. B. (1974a). Relation of wait-time and rewards to the development of language, logic, and fate control: Part one – Wait time. *Journal of Research in Science Teaching, 11*(2), 81–94.

Rowe, M. B. (1974b). Pausing phenomena: Influence on the quality of instruction. *Journal of Psycholinguistic Research, 3*(3), 203–223.

Rowe, M. B. (1974c). Reflections of wait-time: Some methodological questions. *Journal of Research in Science Teaching, 11*(3), 263–279.

Shadish, W. R., Cook, T. D., & Campbell, D. T. (2001). *Experimental and quasi-experimental designs for generalized causal inference.* Cengage Learning.

Tobin, K. (1987). The role of wait time in higher cognitive level learning. *Review of Educational Research, 57*(1), 69–95.

Tobin, K., & Alexakos, K. (Eds.). (forthcoming-a). *Wellness and well-being: Educating the citizenry from pre-birth through death.* Brill | Sense.

Tobin, K., & Alexakos, K. (Eds.). (forthcoming-b). *Transforming learning and teaching: Heuristics for educative and responsible practices.* Brill | Sense.

Tobin, K., & Fraser, B. J. (1998). Qualitative and quantitative landscapes of classroom learning environments. In B. J. Fraser & K. Tobin (Eds.), *International handbook of science education* (pp. 623–640). Kluwer.

Tobin, K., & Kincheloe, J. L. (Eds.). (2006). *Doing educational research: A handbook.* Sense Publishers.

Tronsgard, D. T. (1963). A common-sense approach to the dissertation. *Journal of Higher Education, 34*, 491–495.

Index

Printed in the United States
By Bookmasters